MARKET EVALUATION AND ANALYSIS FOR SWING TRADING

MARKET EVALUATION AND ANALYSIS FOR SWING TRADING

Timeless Methods and Strategies for an Ever-Changing Market

DAVID S. NASSAR

WILLIAM LUPIEN

McGraw-Hill

New York   Chicago   San Francisco   Lisbon   London
Madrid   Mexico City   Milan   New Delhi   San Juan   Seoul
Singapore   Sydney   Toronto

1 2 3 4 5 6 7 8 9 10 AGM/AGM 0 9 8 7 6 5 4 3

ISBN 0-07-137833-2

McGraw-Hill books are available at special quantity discounts to use as premiums and sales promotions, or for use in corporate training programs. For more information, please write to the Director of Special Sales, Professional Publishing, McGraw-Hill, Two Penn Plaza, New York, NY 10121-2298. Or contact your local bookstore.

 This book is printed on recycled, acid-free paper containing a minimum of 50% recycled, de-inked fiber.

Library of Congress Cataloging-in-Publication Data

Lupien, William.
    Evaluation and analysis for swing trading : methods and strategies
for an ever changing market / by William Lupien and David S. Nassar.
        p. cm.
    ISBN 0-07-137833-2 (hardcover : alk. paper)
    1. Investment analysis.   2. Stocks.   I. Nassar, David S.   II. Title.

HG4529.L87 2003
332.63'2—dc21

                                                                                      2003000688

The work that went into this book could not have been accomplished without the incredible people who supported our efforts. We dedicate our work to our amazing spouses,

Tracy Nassar and Bonnie Lupien

DISCLAIMER

This book is intended for educational purposes only. It is expressly understood that this material is not in any way intended to give investment advice or to act as a recommendation to buy stock or any other security. The trade examples in this book are for illustration purposes only. The authors and the publisher assume no responsibility for the investment results obtained by the reader. Investing is inherently risky, and results obtained by some investors may not be obtained or obtainable by other investors. The reader assumes the entire risk of investing, trading, and buying or selling securities. The authors or publisher shall have no liability for any loss or expense whatsoever relating to investment decisions made by the reader.

CONTENTS

Chapter 13

Systems Trading   249

Chapter 14

Pairs Trading   267

Chapter 15

Seasonal Trading and Tax Loss Selling   287

Chapter 16

Risk Management Strategies   303

ACKNOWLEDGMENTS

Because trading strategies evolve over time and are ever-changing, a great deal of what we know about the markets is an outgrowth of our experiences, input from mentors, and influences from unnamed market participants. We are grateful for the opportunity to work with the many professionals of our fine industry that we have met along the way.

There are many wonderful people who have contributed to this book. Our greatest fear is that we may forget to mention one of them. Therefore, we wish to thank categorically all the great people we work with at MarketWise and TerraNova Trading. It is because of the efforts that our teammates contribute each day that we have the opportunity to bring our ideas to print. For that, we are both very fortunate and very grateful. In particular, we would like to acknowledge the following contributors to the book:

Brian Shannon, who contributed in the area of technical analysis. Brian is our editor for *WiseGuide*, which has enjoyed consistent profitability with very little drawdown. Brian is also our chief market technician at Market-Wise—he is outstanding.

Eric Erickson, who worked extremely hard on research, edits, and organization. Eric is a trader and research analyst at MarketWise.

John Seckinger, who contributed to our E-Mini chapter. John is a research analyst with MarketWise and has experience as a trader on the floor of the Chicago Board of Trade.

Rick Ackerman for his views on stochastic models. Rick is our editor for *Black Box Forecast* and is considered an uncanny stock picker.

John Burbank for his expertise in pairs trading. John manages Passport Capital, a long/short equity fundamental value hedge fund. John and his staff also write *The Pairs Report*, a fundamental pairs research publication for the broader hedge fund community.

Wai Cheong on systems trading. A friend whose experience ranges from holding the posts of deputy chief executive and director of the Singapore International Monetary Exchange to a successful money manager.

Other people who aided us in research include:

Brian Cheap for scans on tax loss selling.

Jim Sloman on Adam Theory.

And all the exceptional authors and systems designers from whom we referenced information.

We would also like to thank our partners, MarrGwen Townsend, Stuart Townsend, Chris Doubek (Foreword), Jerry Putnam, and Jack Whitehouse, for all their support. And we do not want to forget Stephen Isaacs, our editor, for signing us, and thanks should also go to all the wonderful people at McGraw-Hill. Finally, we would like to thank our families for being the excitement in our day.

FOREWORD

When David and Bill asked me to write the Foreword, I was honored, knowing the experience that these two individuals have in the market. As president of the brokerage firm at which they trade, and from knowing them on an individual level, I have personal knowledge of their qualifications and abilities as active traders. If they could pass on to our customers, including institutions, even a small percentage of what they know as professional traders, our customers would take a quantum leap forward in their trading. This is my motivation in writing this Foreword.

With David and Bill's input we have been able to construct dynamic educational tools that we feel greatly contribute to the education and success of traders. I believe that individual analysis (trade analysis) is as important as market evaluation to the success of traders. As traders learn to read patterns in the market, they also must learn from their personal trade patterns while engaging in the market. It is mechanisms like these and the methods taught in this excellent book that contribute greatly to success. The group that insists that success is a matter of luck, or that relies on message board prophecies and other such nonsense, quickly becomes a self-limiting species. Those of you trading successfully today know that successful trading is based on a simple formula: education, preparation, and diligence. It is no different than striving for success in any other endeavor.

Just as in any industry, successful traders begin with a formal education to provide theoretical knowledge and methods. They can then progress to practical application, putting the theory into practice. As most successful businesspeople know, ultimate success is governed by the ability to apply formal education to the real world. As confidence and knowledge grows, successful traders evaluate performance in order to improve. An entrepreneur who is going to succeed appreciates the importance of developing and managing a business plan—and following that plan. Trading is no different, and should be treated accordingly.

And there is another key. Successful athletes and business professionals alike embrace generalized education, but also take it one step further by utilizing the expertise of coaches. The seasoned guidance and constant feedback on performance that an experienced coach can offer steers athletes or business professionals in the right direction and helps them make increasingly better decisions as time progresses. I believe that trading requires at least the same commitment.

With David Nassar and Bill Lupien as your veteran instructors during this exciting read, you're going to learn how to navigate the ups and downs, recognize the signs, understand the psychology, and better manage the risks of this business and incredible icon of capitalism called trading. Both David and Bill have been very successful using the very techniques explained in this book, and they are eminently qualified to be your guides. I know because they trade at our firm. Whether you need education and preparation to get you started or you would like to strengthen your existing trading methods, this book will be your guide.

My office is directly across the street from the Chicago Mercantile Exchange, and I work every day with floor traders. I know from their experiences and mine that education is continuous. Professional traders on the exchange floor constantly hone their skills and expand their opportunities by treating trading like the business it is, as all traders should. Like any business, trading requires continually gaining and applying knowledge while evaluating performance. This book is the culmination of methods and insights from experienced professionals who live every day with that end in mind.

Christopher Doubek
President
Terra Nova Trading, L.L.C.

INTRODUCTION

The authors have spent a combined total of more than 50 years working to understand the stock market and profit consistently from what they have learned. Although each found his own path to success, the road was never easy. Psychologically as well as financially there were deep potholes and challenging hills along the way, and only rarely was there a downhill stretch or smooth straightaway.

Would it surprise you to learn that the authors—and indeed, most successful traders—have discovered that the simplest methods are those that work best? Or that the stock market's simplicity is ultimately what makes it so challenging? For in the end, the force that moves stocks is the interaction of simple emotions, not some inscrutably evil intelligence. It is only when we learn to distance our own emotions from the process of analysis that we begin to understand how fundamentally simple the "secrets" of the stock market really are, and to trust that at any level, the game is neither mysterious nor unbeatable.

A PARABLE OF THE MARKET

A young immigrant, chasing the capitalistic dream somewhere near the ports of New York, saw an opportunity to sell sardines on the street corners of lower Manhattan, where those with an acquired taste enjoyed them with their lunch in Battery Park. He managed to persuade a local distributor of sardines to give him two cases of the product to sell, with the payment to be made later. Thanks to hard work and diligence, he sold them both promptly for a value greater than he owed.

The very next day he returned to pay his debt to the distributor. As he approached the distributor to do so, the distributor stated that he would accept the money but that he would also extend comparable leverage and lend the young man four cases of sardines. The eager young man proceeded to sell the four cases for a profit and discovered the true meaning of capitalism.

The relationship continued to be fruitful, and soon the young immigrant's business was growing on an exponential scale. Within a year, the man acquired enough wealth to purchase a truck and sold the sardines from the back of it. Within a few more years the man was able to acquire a warehouse, and amassed a huge fortune distributing sardines as his mentor had, while also staking a new generation of sardine salespeople.

The years passed and his business achieved international success. The man, now not so young, was grooming his son to take over the successful enterprise. One day his somewhat less entrepreneurial son was strolling in the warehouse and out of boredom decided to open one of the cans. For the first time ever, the son decided to eat a sample of his father's product and determine what the fascination with sardines was all about. The son immediately spit out the canned fish with a gagging sound and rushed into his father's office to complain, "These fish taste horrible!" His father immediately stood up and slapped the boy to the ground. The boy, holding his head, cried out, "Why did you do that?" His father replied, "You idiot, sardines are not for eating, they are for buying and selling!"

Sardines may taste bad to some, but if they can be bought and sold for a profit, who cares! From this parable we derive the simple moral for this book: Stocks are for trading, not owning.

PHILOSOPHY OF THE BOOK

The philosophy of this book is based on basic principles of the market. An interesting fact, and one learned by most who journey down the road called *Wall Street*, is that the simplicity of the market is its greatest disguise.

This book represents what we have learned thus far in our travels. It is by no means a final thesis. The market has no final thesis. It only evolves and iterates on its own dynamic plane. What we can say conclusively is that the market is a living organism, its vital organs composed of individual participants. Each and every market participant, professional or otherwise, contributes to the condition of the market as a whole. This organism, while not physiological like us, functions purely and perfectly around the study of aggregated human behavior known as *crowd psychology*. Whether we look at market movement from an institutional level or a retail perspective, in the final analysis all is driven by psychology, both market psychology and personal psychology. It is from this vantage point that our strategies are employed.

Personal psychology from a market perspective is defined in terms of the individual trader's approach to the market as he or she deals with probabilities, statistical edges measured through analysis, discipline, risk management, and the inevitable losses that are incurred.

While market psychology is measured by looking at prices as a byproduct of this market organism, price dynamics, when measured statistically, speaks about the propensity for the market to repeat its past; it basically assumes that crowd behavior is measurable. Approaching the market with both market and personal psychology in mind, our strategies draw on the interpretation of market data, technical levels, and mathematical systems to measure statistical probabilities.

Some choose to see the market as a game that few can master, while others see it as a war. In reality it is both, since success in each is dependent on mastery of the concepts and skills involved. We do not claim to have mastered the market. We instead seek to master a way of thinking about the market, a way of anticipating it and participating in it. We don't try to control it, for that would be impossible. Instead we try to see it with humility, grace, and optimism. Using the philosophy communicated in this book will help any trader develop an approach that sees the market as the psychological organism it is while respecting it with the humility it requires.

As we present our view of the market, we do not suggest that our viewpoints and methods are completely new or invented by us. We have assembled a unique combination of insights, viewpoints, and strategies that we have discovered along the way into a practical approach of thinking and trading that has proved successful for us.

Our approach to the market is a combination of "feel" (or instinct) and momentum-based trading that is as close as possible to a statistical edge provided by historical market data and technicals. The statistical edge is defined as an advantage gained by the trader by first observing crowd psychology as represented by charts, technicals, and historical data, and then recognizing the statistical probabilities of human behavior repeating itself. The cyclical nature of the market is driven by the repetitive human actions and reactions that can be collected and objectively measured through analysis, reducing the need for excessive subjective interpretation.

Market analysis encompasses many approaches that can collectively produce what can seem like a sea of information. Through our philosophy of trading and the methods we employ, we feel this sea of information can be navigated by utilizing a few basic principles, ones that are often overlooked. As these strategies are explained, it will become clear that whether you use Japanese candlesticks or western bars, chart formations or technical indicators, or trend-following tools like the MACD as opposed to trend-turning tools like stochastic models, the building blocks and raw materials of the market don't change and are central to all analyses.

Proper market analysis that incorporates a technical approach is where the statistical edge lives. The ability to scientifically, artistically, and successfully evaluate these sometimes competing signals is the individual trader's greatest challenge. The reason most participants fail at trading is not because the market is random or not quantifiable, but because most see the market with subjectivity. It is our goal to help the reader see the market with objectivity through the use of data and, in the process, filter out mixed signals and market noise. Once objectivity is achieved, through statistical analysis (the edge), one must recognize that feel, or instinct, never completely dissipates, nor should it; instead, it is complemented by quantifiable market data.

In this book we will go through a series of methods and systems that work best, based not only on theory but, more importantly, on actual trading and interaction with the market every day. The authors of this book, and the contributors to it, trade the market almost every day, and apply the techniques presented in actual practice. Therefore, we are grounded to the method of trading the statistical edge.

But we must be cautious. We also remind the reader that this edge alone, while invaluable, is not nearly enough to achieve profitability. Your personal psychology and ability to apply a rules-based approach is by far the dominant factor in successful trading. The best representation of personal psychology is the acceptance of the fact that in the end the ultimate teacher is the market itself. As time unfolds and experience is gained, a visceral feel will also develop to complement your objective views, not jade them.

In the absence of experience, a reliance on instinct leaves the individual exposed to the emotional influences which are detrimental to success. Not unlike a batter, golfer, or anyone else who has to have a swing pattern burned into his or her muscle memory, the reader can burn that swing pattern into his or her trading muscle only by active trading. No book can ever do this for the individual and we don't make that claim.

Anyone who leads you to believe that there is a literal interpretation of the market is simply lying to themselves and to you. We suspect that if you are foolish enough to believe such nonsense, you will likely get what is coming to you in the market. These are harsh words, but it is better for you to get your head on straight now than for the market to teach you firsthand the dangers of chasing false hope. Ironically, the market is both a lousy classroom and the only true teacher. For that reason the aim of this book is to communicate proven and enduring methods that we think contribute to gaining a statistical edge (or ability to accomplish objective analysis), but only under the auspices of good discipline and rule management (personal psychology). Even if these methods are followed perfectly, there are no guarantees, no promises. It is a perspective that has worked consistently and profitably for us. In the final analysis each participant must find his or her own recipe for success.

Our market analysis begins with what we call *foundational analysis*, which maintains that there are only a few basic variables that can affect the pricing and direction of the market and stocks. These variables are the most simplistic building blocks of the market: price, volume, time, and velocity. Any analysis that includes the use of indicators beyond these foundational components tends to become biased, less valuable, and prone to subjectivity.

The skills that a trader strives to build will only be improved by focusing on what is real and available in the market, not by focusing on something mystical, subjective, or too far beyond these foundational variables. We will spend time with some quantitative data that mathematically measure these foundational variables, but you should understand that diminishing results are achieved the moment one of them is put on your trading screen. This is simply because your mindset tends to build some level of dependence on the indicator and is susceptible to bias based on the signals the indicator produces. Every indicator is prone to a high degree of false signals, which are not only intrinsically detrimental to traders but will also draw their attention away from foundational variables.

Foundational analysis suggests that traders should spend the vast majority of their time and effort monitoring raw market data, in terms of price, volume, time, and velocity, from a source that is current as well as historical data that represents what is objective and real. We have seen pictograms, heat maps, and formation patterns that produce bullish and bearish signals, but that information is utterly useless in itself. Without sound principles of risk management, supporting data, and historical comparisons, pattern trading is only a few ticks away from reading the stars.

We have spoken with some of the best speculators on the street, and the common method for consistent success is market analysis that is not easily replicated or explained through books, courses, or otherwise. This is because experience is an essential ingredient to our method, and we make no attempt to offer the next new magical indicator to relieve you of the responsibility of learning through active trading. That's a hoax that we refuse to participate in. Experience must be earned over time, and the collection of information we offer is designed to be an aid to trading. Do not rely upon a literal interpretation of the principles found in this book. Although foundational analysis is about recognizing the building blocks in the market and never deviating from them, it is also a mindset, a way of thinking, and a commitment to study only market data that is real, rather than what is contrived through off-topic tools with hopes of applying them to the market.

Perhaps the best example of this would be using Fibonacci principles in a literal fashion. We will speak about Fibonacci in Chapter 4, but those who think that there is a correlation between the arithmetic form in the way rabbits reproduce to the manner in which the stock market trades, miss the point. The value lives in the perception and reaction that market participants act on, not the intrinsic mathematical model or pattern. If you are well grounded in foundational analysis, you can then filter in some of the other tools and techniques that technology has wonderfully offered. But if your objective is to utilize systems to replace your own judgment, you will be making a dire mistake that we believe will lead to your ultimate failure in trading.

Our job is to give you what we believe to be an edge, not an absolute. Keeping that edge includes finding your own way, learning from people who are making money, keeping your mind open, and never believing that any one method or technique will endure over the years. The only method or technique that endures over the years is that of embracing change, because the market is completely dynamic and it will change. How we made money yesterday is not the same way we make money today. Contemporary day traders found this out when the market stopped on a dime with the bear market that began in March 2000. Therefore, many of these traders perished with the arrival of decimalization and the bear market.

Although the market changes, the foundational variables of the market do not change. These methods will be the focus of the rest of the book, just as they have been the focus of our entire trading careers. The authors of this book have come to trading from different backgrounds. (Bill is a product of the floor of the Pacific Stock Exchange, and Dave is a product of electronic quote dissemination.) Yet both of us agree that the core of our success is our ability to react to and anticipate daily price changes based on time, volume, and velocity. Whether you own a seat on an exchange or trade a virtual exchange, markets are markets and people are the common theme. Foundational analysis measures crowd psychology, and psychology (market and personal) is the way to trade successfully.

The stock market is all about the unknown hard right edge of the chart. This translates to the fact that the most recent past will have the greatest influence on the near-term future. The farther you try to project a trend out into the future, the farther back in time you must look. Because time distorts crowd psychology, the farther back you go the less reliable your analysis will be. As you progress, the projection of the market action simply fades into the haze of time and becomes more and more adulterated by the *systematic risk* of unknown variables.

Systematic risk is created by time itself and can be affected by political, economic, or psychological dynamics not under the control of any individual. Therefore, the future is both less reliable and increasingly difficult to project with time.

Since philosophically we don't see the value in gambling, we don't place trades involving uncontrollable future events. Only extreme events, things that are dramatic, are memorable. Most events in the stock market, most price action and volume, are driven by ordinary events, and the ordinary is quickly forgotten. Therefore, looking deep into the past for predictions of what the future will be is the most unreliable thing we can do in active trading. While a different argument can be made for investing, this book is about trading.

COMPOSITION OF THE BOOK

In our first section on psychology and patterns, we discuss how to view the market from a completely new perspective. We delve into the psychology behind market movements (patterns) and the data that we study to uncover market opportunity. We start with personal psychology and then transition to overall market psychology. In exploring personal psychology, we look at market realities that directly and indirectly affect the decision-making process.

In our examination of market psychology, we introduce a unique trading method we call *elasticity*, which focuses on price, time, volume, and velocity (foundational analysis). We then immediately move on to strategy and elasticity trading techniques. These techniques build on structures and forms, which reoccur over and over in the market, called *symmetry*. As you will discover, market symmetry is built on mathematical structures that are identifiable and tradable.

In Chapter 5, the last chapter in the first section, Brian Shannon, chief market technician of MarketWise, gives a practical view of how to use technical analysis in conjunction with foundational analysis. Technical analysis encompasses a large amount of data, but it is an approach that when applied to momentum indicators, can reveal the true statistical edge. By understanding the cycles stocks and markets trade through, traders begin to understand how to anticipate trends and measure their maturity. Chapter 5 brings together personal and market psychology in the form of patterns and structures that can be viewed on charts and then applied to trading on any time frame.

The second section of the book on methods and tactics is where "the rubber meets the road." This section offers our favorite trading methods and the psychology behind them. We describe in detail our preferred indicators, strategies, setups, and vehicles, along with the mathematical basics of each. Through this insight you will not only learn how to apply technique but also gain a trust in each strategy.

We also discuss an essential, but often overlooked, subject "the tape," and give you a fundamental lesson in tape reading that every trader should find interesting and useful.

It is a rare opportunity to step behind the curtain of the NYSE and review techniques specialists use and the rules that the exchange itself binds them to. In Chapter 11 you will discover strategies that the professionals of the floor use every day. This is an exciting chapter that Bill takes particular pride in, as a 16-year veteran specialist.

In the second section, you will also be introduced to esoteric and professional trading tactics that will take you to the next level. We begin with the futures market and the E-Mini contract in particular, and then move to systems trading discussing the pros and cons of back-testing. We also cover institutional-level trading techniques, which include pairs trading and tax-loss selling.

In our last chapters we present perhaps the most critical aspect of trading, risk management. It has been said by many professional traders that those traders who wisely manage risk can literally throw darts at a wall covered with the names of liquid stocks and securities and make a living trading random stocks. While we can't agree to this statement completely, it makes the point that risk management is perhaps the greatest challenge to traders. Traders who are not emotionally attached to any one idea or method possess the prerequisite for risk management. If a disciplined, market-wise approach is applied to the market, using the protective stops and other methods that we discuss, traders will never become so emotionally attached that they can't apply a rules-based approach.

We expose you to a variety of concepts, tools, methods, and philosophies to one end, to make money. We promise no more than that, as the market is the only true teacher. Active trading is the classroom, and those tentative and fearful of trading will get the poorest education. With that, we wish you great success as you embark on the journey. We hope that you find this book as rewarding and gratifying to read as the authors who put it together found it to write.

Trade wise!

SECTION ONE

PSYCHOLOGY AND PATTERNS

1 CHAPTER

THE MINDSET OF MARKETS

Understanding the market, cracking the code of the market, figuring it out completely, and aspiring to a system that always works—these are some of the fallacies that people chase in their quest to master the market. Well, we have a hard truth for you. You may not want to hear it, but deep down you already know it is true. You will never crack the code of the market. It can't be broken, and it can't be mastered or ever completely understood. The best you can hope to achieve is to gain a fine statistical edge over mass-market consensus, also known as *price*. But even if your edge gives you a winning trade less than 50 percent of the time, by applying proper risk management principles you can still be quite profitable.

This book is designed to teach the reader how to find a statistical edge, then enter and manage trades based on risk management principles. That isn't the way most people engage the market. Greed governs most participants' imaginations, and therefore most participants enter on weak foundational analysis and exit on strong emotion. Fear is that emotion. Before we discuss strategy, we must start with developing the reader's "market mindset" so as to recognize and exploit the statistical edge.

RATIONALITY AND IRRATIONALITY

Participants' views of the market and the approach they take to it are generally based on objective and sound reasoning built upon research and analysis, at least regarding most participants. The research done on weekends when the markets are closed or during the quiet periods embodies reasonableness, objectivity, and good intentions, as a rule. Unfortunately, the markets pay few dividends for seemingly rational thought, built solely on research analytics. The market demands emotional control and recognizes behavioral issues with equal if not greater weight than strict objective market analysis. Rationality is often sought after through tangible devices, such as charts, at the expense of emotional considerations, which can open the door to irrationality, which diverges from logic. A market sage would say that emotion is the nemesis of traders, and while true, we have yet to find a way to truly break off emotion from trading. Systems trading, which is discussed in Chapter 13, is perhaps our best chance to do so, but emotions will always exist to some degree and are better anticipated than ignored.

Data does not lie, nor do charts, but people do. They lie to themselves because they encounter emotions, most often greed and fear, which test their conviction as well as their discipline. The way to mitigate and hedge against these subjective influences is to first understand market psychology and then apply it to the data and charts, offensively rather than being a defensive victim of it.

Extremes of irrationality reveal themselves on charts through *price dispersion*, which occurs when the extremes of exuberance or pain present themselves as convergences on and divergences from key moving averages (MAs). It could be said that the convergence of price and moving averages represents the efficiency of markets when they are calm and rational. On the other hand, the divergence of price from moving averages could be said to represent the inefficiency of markets when they are prone to emotions and even irrationality. Such is the case whether dealing with extreme bullishness, when prices are fully divergent above moving averages, or extreme bearishness, when prices are fully divergent below moving averages. Therein lies the psychological backdrop of the moving average convergence/divergence (MACD) oscillator, for example. Therefore, to use the MACD literally without an understanding of the psychology that it measures would be a mistake.

Converting market phenomena into mathematical indicators helps us in understanding market psychology. However, an understanding of what is being mathematically defined is required before you can trust the indicator. Gerald Appel, the MACD's creator, developed a powerful tool, but it should not be used without understanding what it quantifies mathematically (as we will see in Chapter 7). To use a medical analogy, while it is not the job of physicians to create a drug, it is their job to understand how to prescribe the right drug in the right circumstances. We cannot apply the proper mathematically derived indicators with confidence and trust if we don't understand them. Once we understand the indicators, we can interpret and administer them within the proper time horizon and the rules for which they were created.

Without a specific rules-based approach such as the one described extensively by David Nassar in *Rules of the Trade,* you'll have no way of smoothing out the raw, jagged edges of volatility and market indecision on short-term charts. Money management techniques assembled around solid rules that have proved themselves over time are built on the principles of human nature and are measured with data. These form the building blocks of an objective view of the market. It is within the context of these rules and this system of objectivity that we begin to see the market through the eyes of a trader and learn how to trust data. To think and act properly as traders, we must first know what to study, how to study, and what the study measures. Simple data do this best and most objectively while excluding irrationality and emotions.

On a market wide basis, irrational behavior begins with the opening bell. It is at this precise moment that the monster of irrationality is let in. Although most market participants have good intentions to trade in accordance with their market analysis, it rarely happens. Understanding this one fact alone will serve you well in dealing with the demons within all traders. Recognize now that we are all capable of irrationality, and the best way to hedge against irrational behavior is to gain a thorough understanding of market analysis. For those experienced traders, an analogy makes the point. Think of market analysis as your long-term moving average (rational), while emotions are represented by the price divergence from it (irrational). Traders must recognize when a deep divergence occurs between the two and that consensus must return. Market analysis reveals that all pricing, action, rationality, and irrationality are played out in the data and on the charts of the market. When emotions govern markets, tops and bottoms are close at hand.

Some of the theories that you may have read about, such as random walk, efficient market theory, and countless others, conclude that the market is composed of priced-based randomness and also perfect efficiency, with the end result being that price patterns are mere reflections of unpredictable human behavior. While this may be true when measuring a narrow stream of data, the market is certainly *not* narrow based; it is made up of the actions of millions, all representing human opinion. As Isaac Asimov stated, "The reaction of one man can be forecast by no known mathematics; the reaction of a billion is something else again."

The fact is that within seemingly random data, there exists what is known as *lumpiness.* This is the official term that statisticians use to describe a run of events (in this case, trades) that moves in one direction based on no driving information. The concept of lumpy statistics is important to understand. What it really means in terms of the market is that you can get a run of trades that all go in one direction and yet are actually just random. They are not being driven by any information, news, or any other reason other than the fact that there's just a string of 7 or 8 or 20 sell orders or buy orders coming in at the same time (narrow based). It's important to understand lumpiness because it is the reason why many people say the market is a random walk. However, over time, over millions of trades (broad based), the market is not just a random walk. You can in fact observe trends develop, and exploit these trends. But you must learn to recognize the difference between lumpiness in the statistics and a true trend. Something random walkers are blind to.

It is hogwash and utter insanity to believe that all market action is so efficient and zero-sum that its patterns are merely the by-product of fundamentals and rational prices. What is forgotten by academics and theorists is that dominant market action is the result of irrational behavior driven by emotions such as greed and fear. The proof is that *most participants lose money!* Does that mean the markets are random and money cannot be made trading the market? If this were true, how do academics account for the Stan Weinstein's and the Warren Buffett's of the world? The truth is, the markets are both rational and irrational. While true professionals ignore the urge to make an emotional trade, most participants do not follow this path. If the market were composed of only these true professionals, the pricing in the market would be more efficient and based on fundamentals. But in fact another dominant crowd comprises the majority of the trading public, and this second crowd operates on emotion and irrational behavior.

This irrational crowd cannot be ignored. This crowd is your potential profit resource as a logical, rules-based market participant. Academics seem to ignore this irrational market segment. Irrationality is a huge part of the market, and being able to see this side of the market provides an opportunity that traders can profit from.

STUDYING CHARTS

The best way to start seeing the patterns of irrationality in the markets is to review several charts. Start with a series of short-term charts, such as a five-day period with one-minute bars, western or candlestick style. Observe the jagged, hard raw random edge of each minute of each day in that five-day period. You're looking at the market under a microscope, and those sharp, raw jagged random edges of volatility are caused by the lack of consensus of participants. With slightly larger periods of time, like hours, the microfibers of minutes become somewhat smoothed. That same stock or index viewed on a five-day hourly bar in which each western bar (WB) or candlestick represents an hour, suddenly looks efficient, smooth, and even predictable.

What most participants don't realize is that the raw, jagged random edge of the market under the microscope is what traders deal with every day. The volatility and the emotions that the raw edge represents and elicits are what whipsaw the amateur's conviction and discipline, while the successful trader copes and deals with risk through knowledge and experience. Without this recognition, participants have difficulty distinguishing conviction from discipline. The unforgiving nature of the market and the raw edge of volatility will test your conviction since it is here that irrational behavior is born. Without a proper time horizon and rules on which to base trading decisions, participants can find themselves cut up, victims of the hard right edge through the loss of conviction. Perhaps conviction is the opposite end of discipline. The conviction to stay with a trade by stepping back from the market in terms of time acts as a hedge to discipline when seeing the market too "close against the glass." Whipsaw is the result of losing perspective. Therefore, seeing the market from different vantage points of time will help balance conviction and discipline.

Irrationality comes in many forms. We have briefly discussed market irrationality. Personal irrationality comes in many varieties. Perhaps the most common example we see is new traders trying to scale the steep learning curves of both methods and mindset at the same time. To build strong methods, you must become a strong analyst. To manage emotion, you must become a strong trader. They are truly different skills and best approached separately.

THE DIFFERENT SKILLS OF TRADERS AND ANALYSTS

A trader's skill in terms of interpreting market data correctly is not always reflected in the way he or she trades. Many participants fall victim to the market because they do not have the ability to be both a strong analyst and a good trader. I've met many great analysts in the market, and I've met some great traders. There are not many that can do both. Outstanding analysts who are also able to trade their analysis well are by far in the minority.

Some analysts have the ability to see the market correctly and objectively only when they are not engaged in it financially. They are able to apply a very strong understanding of market psychology to the data, they can find excellent setups and opportunities, and they have finely honed analytical skills. But often they can do this only when they are not financially engaged. The ability of these analysts to make money is often negated by emotions that are elicited on the trading side of the equation.

Conversely, I've met many excellent traders who are masters of managing the extremes of their emotions, but don't see the market analytically.

Sometimes they're too busy reading the tape like floor traders do. Because they are able to make money that way, they don't feel the need to engage the analytical side of the market. (Bill himself would tell you that as a specialist and market maker, he didn't apply a technical approach to the market because the floor didn't necessitate it to make money.)

Analytical skills are absolutely essential for success in modern electronic trading. However, the joint skills of market analysis and trading are difficult to cultivate in one person. This is not a bad thing after all: We have found that the best profit generation emerges when the two skills come together through two separate individuals. Many hedge funds have technical analysts who don't trade; since they are not financially engaged, they can see the market objectively. Traders who do not analyze, implement the analyst's findings without being emotionally attached to the decision-making process.

Regardless of how you engage the market, mastering both market analysis and trading will mean acquiring separate skills that must converge. How you achieve this will be an individual process, but realizing that they are very different skills is a good first step. I've seen this dynamic within our own firm. I've seen analysts who are able to see the market with incredible accuracy struggle when trying to implement the ideas. And I've seen traders crowd around these same analysts in order to glean objective analysis. Through this unique combination of talent, I've seen phenomenal profits and returns. Remember, a great analyst can make a lousy trader and lose money, but a great trader can be a lousy analyst and still make money if he or she can find the right combination of analyses on which to depend.

However you approach these required skill sets, whether you seek them alone or with a partner who possesses complementary talents, we would advise you to seek regular and uninvolved counsel. Many rewards come from having a person who can review your trading performance and track record with objectivity. We will speak more on this in Chapter 2, where we show a trade evaluation, compliments of Terra Nova Online.

SUCCESS REQUIRES MORE THAN SKILL

People who make consistent money in the markets have mastered personal psychology and the ability to apply rigid rules to their own behavior. They do not credit their success to any literal interpretation of a market indicator or even to solid objective analysis. They credit success to self-discipline and hard work.

The process of finding a method of trading is difficult and time consuming, and it requires a lot of energy. It also requires a passionate attention to the work of trading. Many amateurs seeking quick gains in the market are not motivated by passion, but by greed and an unhealthy obsession with money. These would-be traders are the first to replace effort with systems under the mistaken impression that the systems will uncover one profitable trade after the next. These strategies are complete nonsense. The true, best system is diligence and the willingness to engage the market through disciplined effort.

We have a friend who believes in the value of the data and hard work so much, that to this day he still does much of his charting by hand. He does this to gain a better feel for the data and trends. Perhaps the old-fashioned pencil and graph paper provide a better feel than the computer. The more than $40 million he has made over the years makes it hard to argue with his approach.

The first step in mastering personal psychology and discipline is accepting responsibility. Over time and through exploration, trial and error, and a willingness to work and keep learning, you alone are responsible for developing methods of trading that will work for you. It has been said that people support the things they help to create. Trading based on a system you did not have a part in creating will lead to difficulty and a lack of discipline. We believe that while most participants have good intentions, the lack of responsibility in doing the work is the seed of bad money management. If you will do the work, the rewards will follow. Therefore, you must become the system, and not let the system become you.

2

CHAPTER

DEFINE YOURSELF IN THE MARKET

The market behaves as if it were a fellow named Mr. Market, a man with incurable emotional problems. At times he feels euphoric and can see only favorable factors, while at other times he is depressed and can see nothing but trouble ahead for both the business and the world.

—*Warren Buffett*

TRADING VERSUS INVESTING

So what attributes and skills do traders possess that are lacking in the casual investor mentality? The difference between what one does in terms of market engagement over the other is dramatic. The investor tends to have little interest or time to devote to the market, evidenced by the fact that they divorce themselves from the process by hiring a professional to manage their money. They pay others to make financial decisions for them. Be it through fund expenses or direct payment such as commissions, the investor may believe they are engaged intellectually, but in reality they are only engaged emotionally. The emotions are elicited as a direct result of the performance of the market. The extent of engagement is for the most part limited to the hiring and firing process of fund managers. The traders' engagement, on the other hand, is far more demanding, yet also far more rewarding; intellectually, financially, and emotionally.

Perhaps the greatest attribute of an active trader is the ability to subjugate both methods and mindset (psychology). While the investors' greatest attribute is to recognize that they lack the time or interest to effectively self-manage their investing decisions. But it is a new participant who emerges that is most self-injurious. This party, who we will call the reckless investor, develops an audacious approach driven by greed and perceived easy money. They live in an abyss between trading and investing. As online trading exploded in 1996 with the emergence of technology and the growing dot-com revolution, these players began to emerge in the market more dominantly than ever before. They exist in the online virtual universe, and that is precisely where some fast money is made but most is lost. In a bull market, conviction, in the form of holding onto losing positions, often gets rewarded; because stocks often do come back, providing positive reinforcement of profitability on poor methods, and rewarding conviction in a bull market, but this is a poor practice in any market.

Bear markets are far less forgiving. False conviction is ultimately punished because these reckless investors have been trained to hold losers the longest, expecting stocks to come back. Conversely, good traders rarely wake to 10-point gap ups that reckless investors gamble on, in that they control risk. Although disciplined traders are sometimes perceived to be working too hard in bull markets, bear markets remind us that discipline has greater enduring rewards. While huge profitability per trade is sometimes diminished, trade consistency and steady growth are the compensation.

The end result is that bull markets may temporarily reward the reckless investors' conviction, but bear markets will later punish it, and to a much larger degree. Conversely, disciplined traders in bull markets may limit profits per trade, but discipline always proves to be the enduring strategy in all markets.

Peter Lynch is correct in saying that "investing is not about timing the market—it is time in the market." The casual investor will do well following his advice. But trading the market is not time in the market; it's timing the market. It is the abyss in between where online investors (reckless) seem to fall. It is this participant who has the conviction of a casual investor, but lacks the discipline of a trader, who gets punished the most.

Which approach is more risk averse? Most retail brokerage firms would have you believe that investing is safe over time, while trading is very risky business. But common sense suggests that systematic market risk becomes increasingly elevated over time because of political, economic, and even catastrophic uncertainty. Therefore, perhaps it's time to think differently. While we agree that the long-term investor fares better than the online investor, traders have been mislabeled as reckless gamblers for far too long. In fact, we are the most risk averse and disciplined segment of all.

Active swing trading and long term investing both have inherent risks. Trading requires large sums of money being committed to the market at any given moment, but only for relatively short periods of time with controllable discipline as the central theme. Timing, stop losses, trailing stops, and other devices are within the control of traders. What we trade, how much we trade, how long we're in the trade, where we're wrong, how long we let the profits run, and so on are all controllable. Investors, conversely, have very little control in those areas, as they principally rely on fund managers. Therefore, their risk is defined by the abilities of fund managers and the tides of the market. Given the natural bullish nature of most funds, not only are they limited in profitability during market downturns, but they also historically suffer. Perhaps mutual fund managers could learn from traders who, as a rule, stay liquid (in cash) more than in any other state of capital. Traders not only avoid drawdowns during bearish trends but also profit from them.

One of the dire realities of mutual funds today is that they are subject to redemptions, which can amount to a genuine run on money. Under pressure to meet or beat the benchmark S&P 500 Index, most funds are ill-prepared for bear markets because they are heavily invested and have little liquid capital on hand to handle redemptions. In order to generate enough capital to satisfy investors, mutual funds have to rapidly sell stocks in the marketplace, driving the market down even further. Having liquid redemption capital available as opposed to fully indexed capital would mitigate much of the harsh sell-offs. Given the fact that "runs on money" tend to occur at or near market downturns, the worst time for funds to sell, the carnage is exacerbated and felt financially and emotionally by the casual investor.

Funds should always have liquid capital on hand, redeemable capital, available for those periods in time when downturns occur and there is a need for cash.

This would seem to suggest that traders should be otherwise invested. This is not the case. Traders do not want to be in a position where money is continually going in and out of their trading accounts. We have adopted the strategy of funding our trading accounts with a fixed amount of capital and maintaining that capital base through the year. Each quarter the account is either refunded, if losses have occurred, or stripped back to its base level if we have seen profits, so that the psychological and literal accounting of trade performance can be better monitored.

For example, we start the year with $1 million in trading capital. After the first quarter, any profits realized are taken from the account and put aside and invested accordingly, based on personal investment objectives, whether they be real estate, T-bills, or other vehicles outside the stock market. So, in that example, if $200,000 were made in the first quarter, that $200,000 would be taken out and reinvested somewhere outside of the trading account, putting the account back to $1 million. This process would continue until the end of the year, at which time decisions as to how much trading capital will be traded for the next year will be made. This not only keeps the accounting simple and clean, but psychologically each quarter the mindset is somewhat cleansed and you start anew. The value of this can't be overstated.

The differences between the mentality of traders and investors should be clear. The investor adopts the mentality of the fund through association. Or is it the other way around? Is the fund nothing more than one giant investor? We think so. Regardless, this mentality has no place in the traders' world. Funds possess a fatal bullish bias as a rule, with an added incentive to always be invested in order to compete with the S&P 500. This twin-headed monster is destined to dramatic swings, while the trader is again on the opposite side of the spectrum. Traders maintain a neutral market bias, with cash on hand, giving them the striking capability for short-term bullish or bearish trends. We call this neutral bias *directional indifference.*

As part of the process of defining ourselves in the market, we must learn to see the market with indifference. We have seen that most funds are categorically rigged to the bullish side of the market. In the same way, most investors' opinions of the market have the same bias. Ask the question of most people, "What is your view of the market?" You will get answers such as "I think we are near the bottom," "It's going to come back," "The third quarter looks strong." When we hear these opinions we immediately know that the individuals expressing them are in trouble. The best view of the market is not one of bullishness or bearishness; it is one of indifference. Indifference allows you to see the market with no emotional attachment, with no hopes or desires that will manifest themselves in holding positions or being invested in the market. Investors and their fund managers are most prone to a bullish bias, one that is miserably punished in bear markets. Good traders don't own stocks; they rent them! Traders play the market from either side, long or short, with equal interest, only influenced by what the trends, statistics, and data tell them. Once invested in a position, it is hard to maintain indifference.

CYCLICAL MARKETS VERSUS MOMENTUM TRENDS

As part of seeing the market with indifference, traders must also try to recognize market action and the market's response to news. While trading news directly can be risky business, we feel it is imperative to recognize the market's reaction to news as a gauge to measure market sentiment and the propensity for markets to follow through with prevailing trends. Once a feel for market action is sensed, the techniques that follow influence a trader's conviction and discipline.

Cyclical markets are larger recognizable patterns that the trader wants to follow. *Momentum trends* are short-term sentiment-driven movements that tend to reflect indecision and transition in the market. For example, a market that shrugs off bad news such as poor earnings reports, political strife, and economic slowdowns is generally a cyclical market that wants to trend higher, regardless of the news. The market in this case has put in at least a temporary bottom and traders simply want to participate with the emerging trend. Conversely, a market that shrugs off good news and can't seem to rally even in the face of positive economic reports, earnings forecasts, and the like is also in a downward trend and warrants a defensive strategy. In either case, cyclical markets tend to follow through regardless of news. Therefore, the market action and data, which measure the cyclical market, overshadows the breaking news. As traders, we observe the market's reaction to news as opposed to anticipating or trading the news. For example, the market action following a Federal Reserve rate cut will tend to elicit a momentum trend, but does little to turn the cyclical market. Multiple rate cuts will be necessary to accomplish this. (See Figure 2.1.)

F I G U R E   2.1

Notice the trend of the market and where the rate cuts occur.

The momentum trend is one that moves sharply in a given direction and then exhausts its move quickly and reverses. Sharp rallies quickly find resistance, and momentum traders will want to fade strength by getting short. If momentum is sharply negative, the same logic applies and momentum players will want to fade the move by buying weakness, anticipating a reversal. Momentum trends are therefore associated with indecision. If a market is cyclical, news will not be its master, overall market sentiment will be. Momentum traders who sell strength on rallies in upward cyclical markets get crushed as markets follow through. Conversely, momentum traders who buy weakness in downward cyclical markets also get crushed as markets follow through to new lows. This example represents a known market trait that bad news tends to come out at the bottom and good news at the top. Recognizing market action tells us more about how to trade the market than market opinion and the media do. Most participants want to think in directional terms; traders want to think in terms of market action. For now, you should try to understand the importance of seeing and interacting with the market from this broader perspective.

PROFITABILITY INDIFFERENCE

A trader has to be indifferent to the outcome of trading. A fixation on being on the winning side of the trade is an expensive attitude. Getting attached to a "streak," whether it be a winning streak or the breaking of a losing streak, is an emotional device that hinders objectivity and therefore performance. Each trade must be its own individual event. Whatever approach you take to the market, whether technical, tape reading, momentum, quantitative, fundamental, or otherwise, every trade must stand on its own. Traders who can learn to flow from one trade to the next without any regard for the outcome of the prior trade will ultimately develop indifference in terms of performance, a quality that is crucial to successful trading psychology. Traders need to let go of performance and focus on trading method and managing risk. The performance will take care of itself.

Given the low frictional cost of trading today in terms of transaction costs, technological access, narrow market impact cost of low spreads, and high liquidity, it makes no sense to develop an emotional attachment to any given trade. When feel is lost in a trade, or there is simply no data to support continuing with it, we need to blow it out (exit positions) and take a new look.

Seeing the market from the sideline can be invaluable in terms of objectivity. Stepping out of an uncertain trade to get an objective look at the market usually brings a dramatic improvement in the trade to follow. This will either take you out of a loser quickly or confirm with greater conviction that you want back in the trade you just exited. This simple technique will go a long way toward avoiding a fixation on profitability and allow you to instead focus on the levels of the market and its propensity to follow through or reverse.

It is important to understand that prices either follow through or reverse; these are the only real things the market can do. Certainly stocks can become sleepy and stand idle, but in that case, there is no reason to be in the market at all, as no trade warrants the time risk of being in a directionless market. Obviously, during periods of consolidation and stabilization, traders should stand aside.

Each trade has to be thought of individually, and the decisions made must be based on the data, technicals, and the visceral feel that you gain by trading. Those who trade too little get the least experience and hang on the longest due to emotional attachment. Those who trade actively acquire a cold logic that allows for an easy disconnect when trades take too long to develop or move with you.

In any given trade if one adheres to sound methods, but results are not yet realized, one must not use profitability as the literal barometer. In time, positive results will come to far outweigh negative returns.

INVISIBLE HAND THEORY

As we engage the market wisely, we learn to trust objective data. But you must also trust the action of the market. That action, when properly understood, is as objective a source of information as raw numbers. The key to successful trading is to learn what this combination of data and market action is saying and then learn how to rely on it. When we learn to trust what the market is telling us, we can free ourselves from emotional constraints and let the market determine our approach. We believe that following the action of the market will actually push us to results as though it were an invisible hand.

The *invisible hand theory* as applied to the market simply states that methods must be consistently followed if results are to be achieved. Methods are defined in terms of tactical strategies for finding trades as well as managing risk. This must be understood before we explore our strategies.

The invisible hand theory originates with Adam Smith. In his book *A Wealth of Nations*, he relates this premise to a macroeconomic view of the economy, but it can be applied to trading as well. After all, stocks are microeconomies of capitalism. Smith stated, "Every individual necessarily labors to render the annual revenue of the society as great as he can. He generally neither intends to promote the public interest, nor knows how much he is promoting it. . . . He intends only his own gain, and he is in this, as in many other cases, led by an invisible hand to promote an end which was no part of his intention. Nor is it always the worse for society that it was no part of his intention. By pursuing his own interest, he frequently promotes that of the society more effectually than when he really intends to promote it. I have never known much good done by those who affected to trade for the public good."

In order to act in their own best interest, traders must prepare their minds to follow the right beacons. To develop indifference toward market direction and profitability, traders are then guided by an invisible hand that hedges emotion and adheres to objectivity. When this is achieved, profitability will soon follow.

Consider this scenario: At the precise moment we enter a trade, our emotions rear their ugly little heads and we begin to look at the market on a tick-by-tick basis, far too closely. Each uptick and downtick affects our conviction. We begin to make decisions based on our fear of losing money and our greed for the best possible profit. This is the wrong activity to follow in the market and leads to whipsaws and negative results. Following every tick on the tape is the wrong action and whipsaws many traders out of the market. The tape is our strongest tool, but it is much like the engine of your car. While it can produce tremendous power, without the wheels and axles you are not going anywhere.

Let's start the trade again. We enter the market at the same point, but we look to indicators, charts, historical data, and risk management techniques, to temper our emotions. By allowing the data to speak through technicals, we allow ourselves to ignore emotional inputs, like the ones caused by watching on a tick by tick basis, and let the market show us the way. Using the data as the beacon, the trader employs the invisible hand theory by managing the right activities (methods) as a means to a desired result. The focus is on the data, not the result.

If the data suggests that the trade is not working, any anxiety would be felt early on and dealt with quickly to keep the losses small. In this way our result is dictated by the market, not by our emotions.

The invisible hand theory simply keeps us focused on the activity at hand and lets the market run its course. We don't fight anything; we only participate with the market while employing sound principles of risk management. Certainly technique plays into why a trade is made, but once in the trade, proper risk management principles should drive most decisions.

If you develop strong trading habits, which you can do quickly through active trading, a statistical analysis of your own trading will reveal the strength of your discipline. The accompanying trade analysis, compliments of Terra Nova Trading L.L.C., is one example of a statistical analysis that can be done. Notice the stats. Day trading was the strongest approach. Losses were smaller than winners, and activity was strong with a high number of trades made. Indifference is clear. More money was made on the short side of the market, but this trader also exhibited strength in both stocks and options. Also note that during the same period the NASDAQ composite index moved lower by over 9%.

Trade Analysis (between 06/1/2002 and 06/30/2002)

Long vs. Short	Matches	Trades	Gains	Losses	P/L	Best	Worst	% Gainers	Average Trade
Long	873	440	294	146	9,137.25	144,199.65	−75,461.09	66.8%	20.77
Short	203	122	96	26	57,265.16	9,277.50	−1,398.90	78.7%	469.39
Long vs. Short Net	1,076								

Shares Traded	Matches	Trades	Gains	Losses	P/L	Best	Worst	% Gainers	Average Trade
Less than 200	2	2	2	0	59.20	41.21	18.00	100.0%	29.60
201–500	15	8	7	1	622.61	324.04	−270.95	87.5%	41.51
501–750	0	0	0	0	0.00	0.00	0.00	0.0%	0.00
751–1000	562	381	261	120	−127,041.64	3,469.57	−75,461.09	68.5%	−226.05
Greater than 1000	550	171	120	51	238,315.76	144,199.65	−20,600.00	70.2%	433.30

Share Price	Matches	Trades	Gains	Losses	P/L	Best	Worst	% Gainers	Average Trade
Less than $10	211	109	63	46	108,218.02	144,199.65	−13,772.38	57.8%	512.88
$10.01–$25	268	141	100	41	6,300.65	3,469.57	−16,887.87	70.9%	23.51
$25.01–$50	364	176	125	51	62,183.24	8,076.12	−6,815.57	71.0%	170.83
$50.01–$100	169	93	70	23	19,038.87	2,694.38	−3,173.09	75.3%	112.66
Greater than $100	58	43	32	11	−83,784.84	18,555.00	−75,461.09	74.4%	−1,444.57

Term of Trade	Matches	Trades	Gains	Losses	P/L	Best	Worst	% Gainers	Average Trade
Day Trade	655	352	293	59	186,312.73	8,076.12	−3,155.54	83.2%	529.30
Non-Day Trade	390	210	97	113	−119,910.33	144,199.65	−75,461.09	46.2%	−571.00

Minutes-in-Day Trade	Matches	Trades	Gains	Losses	P/L	Best	Worst	% Gainers	Average Trade
0–5 minutes	27	20	18	2	1,331.76	309.19	−24.75	90.0%	66.59
6–15 minutes	114	55	51	4	22,500.81	2,340.03	−457.86	92.7%	409.11
16–30 minutes	80	51	40	11	11,154.97	2,381.16	−270.95	78.4%	218.72
31–60 minutes	106	62	53	9	47,380.90	4,220.47	−290.81	85.5%	764.21
61–120 minutes	145	82	67	15	40,849.95	8,076.12	−1,410.93	81.7%	498.17
More than 120 minutes	148	85	66	19	63,468.74	7,238.31	−3,155.54	77.6%	746.69

Time-Sector-of-Day Trades	Matches	Trades	Gains	Losses	P/L	Best	Worst	% Gainers	Average Trade
Premarket	34	21	17	4	12,124.28	3,089.13	−501.36	81.0%	577.35
9:30–9:59	96	52	41	11	33,840.89	4,431.67	−370.21	78.8%	650.79
10:00–10:29	84	43	38	5	46,437.27	7,238.31	−721.10	88.4%	1,079.94
10:30–10:59	36	21	14	7	6,293.27	6,535.94	−3,155.54	66.7%	299.68
11:00–11:59	66	37	34	3	15,307.58	2,158.34	−968.66	91.9%	413.72
12:00–12:59	87	40	37	3	34,165.97	8,076.12	−98.18	92.5%	854.15
1:00–1:59	48	33	21	12	2,083.95	1,636.93	−415.39	63.6%	63.15
2:00–2:59	147	71	59	12	30,081.10	2,381.16	−1,410.93	83.1%	423.68
3:00–3:29	32	23	21	2	5,977.23	1,929.05	−70.56	91.3%	259.88
3:30–4:00	33	17	15	2	1,686.85	549.13	−202.60	88.2%	99.23
Postmarket	19	8	6	2	−2,549.34	134.94	−2,900.45	75.0%	−318.67

Trades by Symbol		Matches	Trades	Gains	Losses	P/L	Best	Worst	% Gainers	Average Trade
AETH										
	Long:	2	1	1	0	39.91	34.92	4.99	100.0%	39.91
	Short:	0	0	0	0	0.00	0.00	0.00	0.0%	0.00
AMD										
	Long:	2	1	1	0	479.42	479.42	479.42	100.0%	479.42
	Short:	74	27	24	3	87,441.04	14,812.00	−200.58	88.9%	3,238.56

continues

Trades by Symbol		Matches	Trades	Gains	Losses	P/L	Best	Worst	% Gainers	Average Trade
+AMD										
	Long:	2	1	1	0	479.42	479.42	479.42	100.0%	479.42
	Short:	74	27	24	3	87,441.04	14,812.00	−200.58	88.9%	3,238.56
AOC										
	Long:	1	1	1	0	329.08	329.08	329.08	100.0%	329.08
	Short:	0	0	0	0	0.00	0.00	0.00	0.0%	0.00
AOL										
	Long:	24	8	6	2	1,970.85	1,597.97	−852.03	75.0%	246.36
	Short:	0	0	0	0	0.00	0.00	0.00	0.0%	0.00
ASA										
	Long:	12	2	2	0	8,315.16	1,997.40	77.71	100.0%	4,157.58
	Short:	0	0	0	0	0.00	0.00	0.00	0.0%	0.00
AWE										
	Long:	5	4	4	0	1,656.36	798.41	29.78	100.0%	414.09
	Short:	0	0	0	0	0.00	0.00	0.00	0.0%	0.00
BGO										
	Long:	6	1	1	0	1,249.06	499.63	−98.37	100.0%	1,249.06
	Short:	0	0	0	0	0.00	0.00	0.00	0.0%	0.00
C										
	Long:	18	10	8	2	1,827.12	778.81	−1,402.78	80.0%	182.71
	Short:	0	0	0	0	0.00	0.00	0.00	0.0%	0.00
CCU										
	Long:	6	3	2	1	2,294.36	3,858.10	−2,821.86	66.7%	764.79
	Short:	0	0	0	0	0.00	0.00	0.00	0.0%	0.00
+CCU										
	Long:	6	3	2	1	2,294.36	3,858.10	−2,821.86	66.7%	764.79
	Short:	0	0	0	0	0.00	0.00	0.00	0.0%	0.00
CNXT										
	Long:	9	3	3	0	4,540.64	2,229.23	9.96	100.0%	1,513.55
	Short:	0	0	0	0	0.00	0.00	0.00	0.0%	0.00
CSCO										
	Long:	2	1	1	0	239.58	189.67	49.91	100.0%	239.58
	Short:	1	1	1	0	49.57	49.57	49.57	100.0%	49.57
CVC										
	Long:	5	5	2	3	78.31	1,579.72	−1,140.56	40.0%	15.66
	Short:	0	0	0	0	0.00	0.00	0.00	0.0%	0.00
CY										
	Long:	1	1	1	0	19.47	19.47	19.47	100.0%	19.47
	Short:	0	0	0	0	0.00	0.00	0.00	0.0%	0.00
DELL										
	Long:	43	28	19	9	4,146.34	759.27	−1,050.72	67.9%	148.08
	Short:	0	0	0	0	0.00	0.00	0.00	0.0%	0.00
DIA										
	Long:	62	33	25	8	6,554.16	2,118.16	−3,173.09	75.8%	198.61
	Short:	70	35	25	10	3,463.06	737.06	−1,398.90	71.4%	98.94
+DJXRJ										
	Long:	2	2	0	2	−26,850.00	−6,250.00	−20,600.00	0.0%	−13,425.00
	Short:	0	0	0	0	0.00	0.00	0.00	0.0%	0.00
EP										
	Long:	22	14	11	3	9,178.35	2,129.33	−1,020.65	78.6%	655.60
	Short:	0	0	0	0	0.00	0.00	0.00	0.0%	0.00
FLEX										
	Long:	14	8	5	3	−1,418.30	409.44	−930.45	62.5%	−177.29
	Short:	0	0	0	0	0.00	0.00	0.00	0.0%	0.00
GLG										
	Long:	24	7	4	3	892.24	1,079.52	−1,640.46	57.1%	127.46
	Short:	0	0	0	0	0.00	0.00	0.00	0.0%	0.00

continues

Trades by Symbol		Matches	Trades	Gains	Losses	P/L	Best	Worst	% Gainers	Average Trade
+GLG										
	Long:	24	7	4	3	892.24	1,079.52	−1,640.46	57.1%	127.46
	Short:	0	0	0	0	0.00	0.00	0.00	0.0%	0.00
GLW										
	Long:	17	9	6	3	1,298.50	649.37	−260.14	66.7%	144.28
	Short:	0	0	0	0	0.00	0.00	0.00	0.0%	0.00
GM										
	Long:	32	22	18	4	9,006.67	2,476.69	−381.57	81.8%	409.39
	Short:	5	3	2	1	14.98	148.29	−202.60	66.7%	4.99
GNSS										
	Long:	9	4	1	3	−198.05	79.78	−93.17	25.0%	−49.51
	Short:	0	0	0	0	0.00	0.00	0.00	0.0%	0.00
HGMCY										
	Long:	5	4	4	0	347.75	209.61	−6.53	100.0%	86.94
	Short:	0	0	0	0	0.00	0.00	0.00	0.0%	0.00
INTC										
	Long:	98	56	33	23	−37,140.87	639.35	−2,060.58	58.9%	−663.23
	Short:	4	2	1	1	−6.44	33.21	−70.56	50.0%	−3.22
JDSU										
	Long:	1	1	1	0	9.93	9.93	9.93	100.0%	9.93
	Short:	0	0	0	0	0.00	0.00	0.00	0.0%	0.00
JNPR										
	Long:	2	2	2	0	429.67	349.83	79.84	100.0%	214.84
	Short:	0	0	0	0	0.00	0.00	0.00	0.0%	0.00
L										
	Long:	3	2	1	1	18.72	859.49	−783.74	50.0%	9.36
	Short:	0	0	0	0	0.00	0.00	0.00	0.0%	0.00
MEE										
	Long:	1	1	1	0	79.62	79.62	79.62	100.0%	79.62
	Short:	0	0	0	0	0.00	0.00	0.00	0.0%	0.00
MET										
	Long:	2	2	2	0	538.28	269.14	269.14	100.0%	269.14
	Short:	0	0	0	0	0.00	0.00	0.00	0.0%	0.00
MLNM										
	Long:	1	1	1	0	29.66	29.66	29.66	100.0%	29.66
	Short:	0	0	0	0	0.00	0.00	0.00	0.0%	0.00
NEM										
	Long:	7	5	3	2	−687.74	189.15	−1,150.84	60.0%	−137.55
	Short:	0	0	0	0	0.00	0.00	0.00	0.0%	0.00
NITE										
	Long:	2	1	1	0	117.85	87.88	29.97	100.0%	117.85
	Short:	0	0	0	0	0.00	0.00	0.00	0.0%	0.00
NT										
	Long:	6	6	2	4	−66.95	825.72	−340.10	33.3%	−11.16
	Short:	0	0	0	0	0.00	0.00	0.00	0.0%	0.00
NVR										
	Long:	6	1	1	0	2,370.29	746.05	48.04	100.0%	2,370.29
	Short:	0	0	0	0	0.00	0.00	0.00	0.0%	0.00
NXTL										
	Long:	19	13	8	5	4,727.01	2,879.22	−270.10	61.5%	363.62
	Short:	0	0	0	0	0.00	0.00	0.00	0.0%	0.00
Q										
	Long:	8	6	3	3	−967.84	5,639.60	−7,358.10	50.0%	−161.31
	Short:	0	0	0	0	0.00	0.00	0.00	0.0%	0.00
QQQ										
	Long:	265	106	73	33	63,152.94	5,425.78	−4,492.95	68.9%	595.78
	Short:	85	53	42	11	10,014.27	909.30	−170.85	79.2%	188.95

continues

Trades by Symbol		Matches	Trades	Gains	Losses	P/L	Best	Worst	% Gainers	Average Trade
RAD										
	Long:	52	9	0	9	−52,714.87	−36.02	−6,500.96	0.0%	−5,857.21
	Short:	0	0	0	0	0.00	0.00	0.00	0.0%	0.00
RNR										
	Long:	8	4	1	3	−6,763.63	107,966.74	−74,951.09	25.0%	−1,690.91
	Short:	0	0	0	0	0.00	0.00	0.00	0.0%	0.00
SLR										
	Long:	7	7	5	2	408.83	349.83	−170.16	71.4%	58.40
	Short:	0	0	0	0	0.00	0.00	0.00	0.0%	0.00
SYNM										
	Long:	5	2	2	0	113.87	43.31	11.13	100.0%	56.94
	Short:	0	0	0	0	0.00	0.00	0.00	0.0%	0.00
SZ										
	Long:	3	1	1	0	454.63	252.82	97.93	100.0%	454.63
	Short:	0	0	0	0	0.00	0.00	0.00	0.0%	0.00
TXN										
	Long:	0	0	0	0	0.00	0.00	0.00	0.0%	0.00
	Short:	1	1	1	0	9.20	9.20	9.20	100.0%	9.20
TYC										
	Long:	35	17	15	2	16,982.42	3,429.60	−50.33	88.2%	998.97
	Short:	0	0	0	0	0.00	0.00	0.00	0.0%	0.00
VSV										
	Long:	5	2	2	0	424.35	199.67	14.95	100.0%	212.18
	Short:	0	0	0	0	0.00	0.00	0.00	0.0%	0.00
WCOM										
	Long:	7	4	2	2	−3,490.67	18.40	−2,470.36	50.0%	−872.67
	Short:	0	0	0	0	0.00	0.00	0.00	0.0%	0.00
WMB										
	Long:	23	19	8	11	−3,052.22	1,859.51	−1,090.20	42.1%	−160.64
	Short:	0	0	0	0	0.00	0.00	0.00	0.0%	0.00

Trades by Type	Matches	Trades	Gains	Losses	P/L	Best	Worst	% Gainers	Average Trade
Equity	1,074	522	359	163	47,698.88	208,993.47	−135,475.94	68.8%	91.38
Option	55	40	31	9	64,257.06	17,946.17	−25,262.90	77.5%	1,606.43

Industry Description	Matches	Trades	Gains	Losses	P/L	Best	Worst	% Gainers	Average Trade
**Index Derivatives	482	227	165	62	83,184.43	7,238.31	−6,815.57	72.7%	366.45
Bituminous coal underground	1	1	1	0	79.62	79.62	79.62	100.0%	79.62
Cable and other pay TV services	5	5	2	3	78.31	1,579.72	−1,140.56	40.0%	15.66
Cathode ray television picture tubes	21	15	10	5	−1,009.47	441.68	−1,559.34	66.7%	−67.30
Communications equipment	1	1	1	0	9.93	9.93	9.93	100.0%	9.93
Computer integrated systems design	2	1	1	0	39.91	39.91	39.91	100.0%	39.91
Diagnostic substances	1	1	1	0	29.66	29.66	29.66	100.0%	29.66
Drug stores and proprietary stores	52	9	0	9	−52,714.87	−1,070.89	−13,772.38	0.0%	−5,857.21
Eating places	3	1	1	0	454.63	454.63	454.63	100.0%	454.63
Electronic computers	43	28	19	9	4,146.34	759.27	−1,195.72	67.9%	148.08
Fire, marine, and casualty insurance	8	4	1	3	−6,763.63	144,199.65	−75,461.09	25.0%	−1,690.91
Gold ores	42	17	12	5	1,801.31	1,783.07	−1,640.46	70.6%	105.96
Information retrieval services	24	8	6	2	1,970.85	2,154.16	−1,398.71	75.0%	246.36
Insurance agents, brokers, and service	4	3	2	1	347.80	859.49	−840.77	66.7%	115.93
Investors	12	2	2	0	8,315.16	8,076.12	239.04	100.0%	4,157.58

continues

Industry Description	Matches	Trades	Gains	Losses	P/L	Best	Worst	% Gainers	Average Trade
Life insurance	2	2	2	0	538.28	269.14	269.14	100.0%	269.14
Motor vehicles and car bodies	37	25	20	5	9,021.65	2,476.69	−381.57	80.0%	360.87
National banks, commercial	18	10	8	2	1,827.12	1,544.43	−3,155.54	80.0%	182.71
Natural gas transmission	45	33	19	14	6,126.13	2,129.33	−1,501.32	57.6%	185.64
Nonferrous wire drawing and insulating	17	9	6	3	1,298.50	649.37	−260.14	66.7%	144.28
Petroleum and coal products	5	2	2	0	113.87	83.96	29.91	100.0%	56.94
Radio broadcasting	6	3	2	1	2,294.36	3,858.10	−2,821.86	66.7%	764.79
Radiotelephone communications	24	17	12	5	6,383.37	3,089.13	−270.10	70.6%	375.49
Residential construction	6	1	1	0	2,370.29	2,370.29	2,370.29	100.0%	2,370.29
Security brokers and dealers	2	1	1	0	117.85	117.85	117.85	100.0%	117.85
Security systems services	35	17	15	2	16,982.42	7,559.17	−50.33	88.2%	998.97
Semiconductors and related devices	198	95	65	30	55,144.41	18,555.00	−16,887.87	68.4%	580.47
Surgical and medical instruments	5	2	2	0	424.35	314.44	109.91	100.0%	212.18
Telephone and telegraph apparatus	11	10	6	4	651.87	825.72	−340.10	60.0%	65.19
Telephone communications, exc. radio	15	10	5	5	−4,458.51	8,463.27	−7,358.10	50.0%	−445.85
Unclassified	2	2	0	2	−26,850.00	−6,250.00	−20,600.00	0.0%	−13,425.00

Performance Summary

Total Net Profit	$66,402.41
Winning Trades	390
Largest Winning trade	$144,199.65
Losing Trades	172
Largest Losing Trade	−$75,461.09

Term of Trade	More profitable trades were made using a day trade strategy.
Minutes in Day Trade	More profitable trades were made with a round-trip trade time greater than 120 minutes.
Time Sector	More profitable trades were made between 10:00 and 10:29.
Long vs. Short	More profitable trades were made going short.
Shares Traded	More profitable trades were made when trading greater than 1000 shares.
Share Price	More profitable trades were made on stocks with prices less than $10.
Trades by Type	More profitable trades were made trading options.
Industry Description	More profitable trades were made trading **Index Derivatives.

We begin our journey into trading with a strong and healthy approach to the market based on psychological aspects. Much more could be said, and we could dig deeper into the very intriguing topic of what causes human beings to act or react in certain ways. In fact, additional training is probably not just a good idea but necessary to gaining maturity as a trader. We recommend taking the time to meet with a professional, either a sports psychologist or someone who specializes in trader coaching. The money paid for that training would be well spent. This is a very deep pond, and one that gets too little attention from most traders. The correct mindset is the greatest single attribute you can have as an active trader and many great resources such as *www.innerworth.com* exist for this type of education. We now move to strategy and technique by applying methods of trading centered on the foundation we built in Chapters 1 and 2.

3
C H A P T E R

THE ELASTICITY OF PRICE

Are the markets random? To explain the way markets trade, we must first take a brief walk down Wall Street to address the random walkers and hopefully bring light to perhaps the most neglected, yet valuable, theory on understanding the markets—elasticity theory. For now, understand that elasticity is defined as the range of human emotions as applied to the market on any time frame. It encompasses the laws of supply and demand, the underlying force of all price action in the market.

RANDOM WALK THEORY

The random walk theory is ridiculous at heart, though it is a profitable one for authors. Many books have been written on random walk. Notably, in 1973 Burton Malkiel published the first of several editions of *A Random Walk Down Wall Street*, which is based on a paper written in 1900 by Louis Bachelier, titled "Theory of Speculation." This paper became the basis for the random walk theory that many academics have accepted and embraced ever since. Random walk is truly a direct attack against traders and the market. It discredits all forms of analysis, whether fundamental or technical, under the assumption that the market itself is random, haphazard, without order and, therefore, unpredictable by any method. Random walkers, the vast majority of whom are academics and not traders, make us think of the old cliché: "Those who can, do, and those who can't, teach." While we are not necessarily believers in that statement, we think that it is applicable in the case of the random walkers.

Random walk subscribers believe that the stock market has no memory in terms of its price actions and behavioral characteristics over time. They also believe that the analysis of market activity cannot be interpreted in any meaningful way in order to provide a tradable edge. They think that those who attempt to use any methods of analysis to achieve better-than-"average" (Dow or S&P) results will fail. While we agree that most participants will fail at trading, their doom comes at their own hands, not at the hands of impossible market analysis. Market analysis, as we explain throughout the book, provides a statistical edge. This edge can be achieved only if individuals can embrace the art and science of trading while controlling personal psychology through risk management.

Random walkers have forgotten about individual traders. Individual traders have the significant advantage of managing small amounts of capital compared to institutional funds, and they can use technicals and risk management principles that clearly offer an edge. While we would agree that as the equity in the portfolio grows, the job becomes more and more difficult and the random walk theory gains more weight, but it never gains enough weight to prove that the market is haphazard, arbitrary, and unbeatable.

Malkiel's theory cannot explain the Warren Buffetts of the world (fundamental and value orientated), nor the Stan Weinsteins (technically oriented), nor the many other individual speculators that have not only beaten the averages but shattered them. Success or failure depends on how serious individual money managers can be in managing their funds. While we agree that on a market-wide basis most individuals will fail to beat the averages, this is a function of individual psychology and not randomness in the market.

The recommended application of the random walk theory is that investors are far better off buying and holding index funds (known as indexing), than trying to buy and sell individual securities. We believe the random walk theory is hogwash because academics who subscribe to the buy-and-hold approach seem to ignore the high risks associated with this strategy and the disastrous results it has produced during documentable time frames. Even during bull markets, the results that index funds produce on average are still subpar compared to the results traders seek to achieve. This is principally due to the inefficiency of managing massive sums of money.

Most of the investment community buys and holds index funds over several years. We hear fund managers report, "The fund is doing great; we beat the S&P 500." If the S&P 500 loses 30 percent in a given period, should losing only 21 percent be considered a success? This is a ridiculous notion. In

Figure 3.1, we see one of many historic examples that holding an index over a two-year period of time, in this case from September 2000 to September 2002, would have yielded dismal results. While one could argue that a bull market example would show otherwise, we counter with the fact that investors and even institutional fund managers have a poor record of knowing when to sell, hence they give back much of what is gained during a bull market. Traders, on the other hand, are conditioned to turn over shares and therefore control systematic market risk.

F I G U R E   3.1

Notice how the buy and hold strategy would have worked on the S&P 500 from 2000–2002.

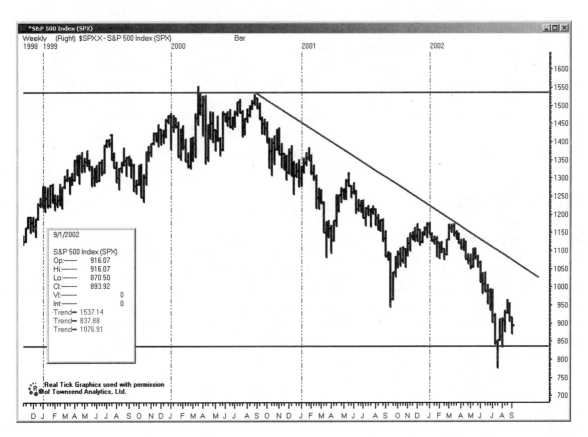

We agree that the idea of random walk is supported by the behavior of large institutional funds, namely mutual funds. However, given that most fund managers can't beat the S&P 500, the funds' success or failure is not a function of market impossibility, randomness, or haphazard pricing of the market. It is a function of the fact that institutional mutual funds are simply too large, too expensive, and too inefficient to manage their investors' capital effectively and consistently. Individual traders can mitigate many of the inefficiencies of mutual funds, such as large management fees, portfolio turnovers, bad decision making, bull market biases, and so on. Traders have been proving Louis Bachelier wrong for more than 100 years. Traders can trade with low frictional costs and an indifferent bias to the market, thereby profiting from both directions, bullish or bearish, not to mention more advanced option strategies of trading volatility and a market-neutral scenario. Individuals can handsomely beat the S&P 500 by applying rules based on letting profits run and cutting losses short. This sounds a bit simple, but if individuals can adhere to these principles consistently and with discipline, the ludicrous nature of random walk theory will be apparent. With that, let's begin our discussion on where order and symmetry exist in the market, and how patterns can give astute observers an edge.

Patterns in the market represent forms and structures built on market (crowd) psychology. Therefore, the topic of time must be explored in order to define the value of a given pattern. Because patterns present themselves over and over in the market, traders must recognize the time frames in which patterns are built. As we explore the relationship of time and market symmetry, we must begin with simple facts regarding how market history is made.

MARKET MEMORY

Market patterns and structure are simply reflections of human nature and the market's memory of it on a mass scale. The market remembers events essentially two dimensionally, not unlike individual memory. These dimensions include the reactive short-term memory (emotional) and the predictable long-term memory (structural). For example, the statement "time heals everything" is based on a belief that events are forgotten, or at least that their impact is diminished by time. This speaks to both the long-term nature of "market structure," as well as the short-term "reactionary view" that the most recent past will serve as a more accurate prediction of the near-term future (emotional and reactive). As traders learn to keep these two dimensions in perspective, they build the foundation needed to see the time relationships to trend. Certainly, cataclysmic events have a propensity to be remembered with greater accuracy, but most market events are of the ordinary variety and their impact tends to dissipate as time goes on. With this understanding, traders can trade both dimensions of time with an edge. Essentially, the short-term dimension is traded as a contrarian and the long term is traded on trend. Our services at Market-Wise offer research and analysis on both through our Simple Swing Trader (SST) for a contrarian view and through our WiseGuide for a trend view.

As traders, we recognize and exploit past market events while the investment community is often controlled by them. Why is that? Traders are rarely in the market long enough to let extreme market events have a lasting impact. For example, on October 19, 1987, while Bill had traded during the period, since he wasn't invested in the market and didn't come into the day with positions, the damage of this infamous day had minimal impact. In fact, it was an opportunity for very strong trading over the few weeks after. The investment community, on the other hand, was hit very hard, since they were "long and wrong." Traders like Bill made enormous amounts of money for two reasons. First, they incurred no massive losses. Second, the events gave them the opportunity to buy undervalued, oversold securities. Bill's reasons for buying were based on no knowledge of the market action other than wanting to buy capitulation. His moves were based on pure instinct and experience and nothing more—in this particular example there is no technical theory or technique that can anticipate these events, except that it represented the nature of market psychology to overreact from a short-term perspective.

Most market events are quite insignificant. Most events, such as earnings, economic news, and ratings changes are ordinary, and while they ripple the water temporarily they soon dissipate into the overall tides of the market.

Because of the shorter time frame, the market's impact is always somewhat minimized for traders while the investors' fate is determined by its ebb and flow. Since most market action is ordinary and soon forgotten, the most recent past will have the greatest reactionary impact in the near-term future. So it is most useful to learn to read both short-term formation patterns of elasticity while also understanding how these patterns form the larger trend. These patterns, both short term and long term, are not random; they are natural reflections of psychology as represented through market action. Based on this understanding, we introduce two methods of trading on different time frames.

1. Elasticity Swing Approach
2. Opening Price Intraday Approach

ELASTICITY SWING APPROACH

Over 10 years ago, we discovered, or we would even say stumbled across, a theory that is so simple and obvious that many would dismiss it. Simply put, *elasticity trading* is a method of making trades based on recent pre-established price levels. In layman's terms, what has happened recently is likely to be mirrored in the near future. Which market you trade—futures, equities, options, or foreign markets—is irrelevant. Elasticity is simply a concept of trading based on one core principle: Do what the market tells you to do based on volume and price and manage your risk along the way. For those of you who can appreciate the simplistic genius of trading market psychology while managing personal psychology (emotions and risk), this approach will either introduce you to a common sense approach to active trading or confirm an existing approach. What we stated earlier bears repeating: The most simplistic approach to the market is often the best, yet most overlooked.

We have heard many times, "The market is always right." This is another way of saying that the price action in the market is the consensus of the beliefs and opinions of all participants. (We recommend you read the book *The Market Is Always Right* by Thomas McCafferty.) As traders, we can only profit by anticipating the market's perception of value. This is accomplished when traders follow clues left by the market's price/volume (PV) patterns and elasticity (range). The trader's job is to do nothing more than receive the signals sent out by the market. Because of this, fundamentals and other market events that "should" impact the market are really irrelevant, since PV action is all that matters. Fundamentally, how or why a given security is priced has nothing to do with how it should be traded. Traders need not divert themselves from market dynamics by trying to discover why things are as they are.

Given the "Market is Always Right," the question really is, are you listening to what it has to say? The tape and the charts present visual images of human psychology, action, and reaction. Through the process of evaluating formations, patterns, moving averages, oscillators, and other indicators presented through mechanical systems, you gain a statistical advantage or edge. The edge is defined as the propensity for a security to move in a particular direction a certain percentage of the time. At the end of your analysis, whether made complicated or kept simple, you will be left with the decision of choosing how to deal with the outcome of your analysis. This is where market psychology (analysis) meets personal psychology (emotions and risk management). Did you gain the statistical advantage and trade the propensity of the market or did you overcomplicate it, misinterpret it, or just not listen?

Elastic levels are created in the market by emotions. Participants do not maintain a cool head, so levels tend to overshoot and undershoot the "true level of value." It is in these extremes that traders find opportunity in the short term as contrarians. From a trend perspective, opportunity is found at the "true level of value." As we will discover, once the elastic range can be defined on any given chart, opportunities will emerge. Look at Figure 3.2.

Notice the narrow range compression of the market on day 1 (D1). We think of this as a spring, ready to uncoil. The bulls' maximum strength is shown at EH and the bears' at EL. As day 2 unfolds, the bulls' maximum

Elasticity theory states that the EH and EL are fadable levels for the contrarian. Contrarians will tend to take profits intraday from these levels, while trend traders will react to these levels being broken.

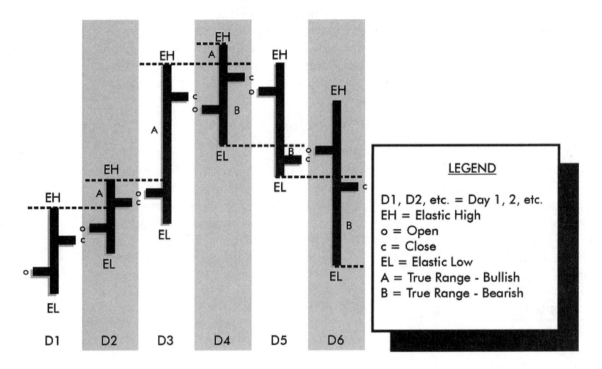

LEGEND

D1, D2, etc. = Day 1, 2, etc.
EH = Elastic High
o = Open
c = Close
EL = Elastic Low
A = True Range - Bullish
B = True Range - Bearish

A Bullish True Range occurs when the current bar's EH is higher than the previous bar's EH.

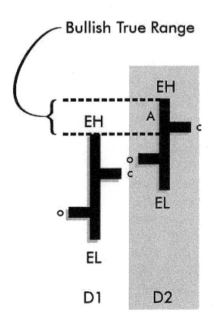

Bullish True Range

strength grows as day 2's (D2) EH becomes greater than D1's EH, and the bears maximum strength shrinks as D2's EL is less than D1's EL (higher low). This is our first clue or signal as to which way the spring wants to uncoil. In this case, the bulls are gaining control. We look at the range between D1's EH and D2's EH as our true range (TR) and dominant market event, since the elasticity has grown or stretched with the bulls and contracted with the bears.

   True range is defined as follows:

   Bullish True Range = A a new EH (see Figure 3.3)
   Bearish True Range = B a new EL (see Figure 3.4)

   This gives us a buy signal on D2 at D1's EH or better. D2's EH is greater than D1's EH, illustrating a higher high, while D2's EL is greater than D1's EL, illustrating a higher low. The application of elasticity trading defines the extension of true range as the dominant event, not the extension of c (closing price) as most systems and methods do. This is critical, as c will often extend above or below the prior day, while true range sends a different signal. No-

F I G U R E   3.4

A Bearish True Range occurs when the current bar's EL is lower than the previous bar's EL.

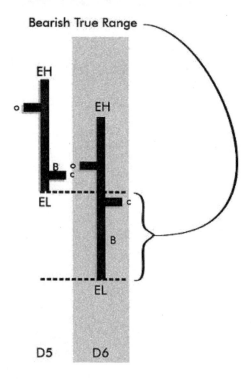

tice that D4's c is greater than D3's c, yet D4's A range is less than D3's A range, illustrating the bulls are getting tired. This signal shows the bears gaining strength but still not yet in control, as D4's A has failed to extend D3's A. Traders in this scenario should be poised to trade the short side the following day (D5) as long as price is less than D4's EH. In this example, on the morning of D5, shorts would have been entered with a stop placed just above D4's EH. Since this did not occur, the D5 short remained open, with a target of D4's EL. The method of trading elasticity as explained begins to build a foundation of trade entry, protective stop, trailing stop, and exit. While no setup is perfect and there will always be a degree of uncertainty, we begin to see an edge based on the clues the market gives us. As we apply the strategy of elasticity, we must first understand that regardless of the value of the setup, traders always act on uncertainty, meaning risk is ever present.

MANAGING UNCERTAINTY WHILE TRADING STRATEGY

We will spend some time defining mathematical models and systems to trade to gain an edge when trading, but you should not expect any degree of certainty from these signals. A slight statistical edge is all that is offered. There are many mathematically driven models that promise financial gain, but real speculators thrive on the very concept of trading on uncertainty or risk. Traders must adapt to this fundamental reality of the markets. Elasticity theory brings this dynamic into light, and once accepted and understood, produces an incredible relief, absolving individuals of the unrealistic expectation of finding certainty through any system or complicated model. In fact, most believe that the more complicated the model is, the more certainty is gained. This tends to translate into a great fascination for complex systems. Our experience is that most complex systems only mask the simplicity of the market, as expressed through elasticity theory.

The concept of elasticity trading occurred to David 10 years ago while reading J. Welles Wilder, Jr.'s book *The Adam Theory of Markets*. Wilder is perhaps best known for creating the relative strength index (RSI) and the directional movement indicator (DMI), both of which are covered in Chapter 6. Jim Sloman, the creator of Adam Theory, the basis of Wilder's book, is a highly spiritual individual who believes that getting in tune with your environment is the first step to finding success in trading. Interestingly, Jim does not define success in monetary terms, but instead by how successfully you can follow market activity (the environment) of price action. You may recognize this as being very similar to what we covered in our discussion of the invisible hand theory in Chapter 2. The environment we seek to get in tune with is obviously the market, and the barometer of success is defined in terms of how well we listen to what the market is saying. We define it in terms of our ability to act in a certain way to produce desired results. You can't get results by searching for results. You must act in a certain manner and have the discipline to do certain things (such as cutting losses) that ultimately lead to the results desired.

We did not invent this philosophy, but we have adapted it as a method of actively trading the markets that works. Once the concept is broken down, this simplistic view of the market and the rules we apply can easily be made use of. But it is not until we believe in these rules that we can accept them. As we describe what these rules are, you must realize that the rules have no value if you simply apply them literally. You must first understand what market psychology they seek to measure and then apply an amount of visceral feel as well as chart recognition.

The fact that markets move based on price, time, volume, and velocity is a very simple one. It may be exactly this simplicity that leads people to reject the fact; they want a complicated theory that represents new and secret knowledge and they discard the knowledge they already have. Almost all speculators, whether card players or traders, can, with incredible accuracy, remember the losers—and especially the large losers. But most have little or no recognition of the winners. In the same way, what one wins in trading tends to be quickly forgotten. Keeping that paradox in mind may help you stay grounded to basic principles that work. In fact, many new participants have done very well in the market by taking something of a passive, simplistic role and making trading decisions based on subtle, simple evaluations of the market that tend to be correct. It's when participants try to take market assumptions to a much more serious level that the problems seem to emerge. Many find some immediate success in the market, but the pressure of needing to make money as skills develop creates baggage and stress, which hinders results. This has caused the demise of many traders. We believe the reason for this scenario is that the passive participant with a day job is more inclined to accept trading simple ideas on uncertainty than those who newly transition to trading full-time and look for increasingly complex systems.

We can now move to specific strategies of elasticity trading while understanding that uncertainty must be accepted and the rules of risk management applied. The reality is that the techniques used by most traders are not the problem. Risk management skills and emotional attachment to ideas are.

ELASTICITY—RULES AND TACTICS APPLIED

When applying the term elasticity to the market, we mean it has the propensity to stretch in a given direction, whether to new highs, new lows, or new levels within a certain time frame. The elasticity of the market can be measured, and that result will tell you whether prices can be expected to retest set ranges. Elasticity increases when given levels are broken the first time, meaning that the next time a price tests the level there is an even greater likelihood of a breakout. If the bulls have the ability to push markets to a new level and the markets then retrace from that level, we know the buying strength can achieve that level again. That increased elasticity creates an expectation that the level, or a range around that level, will be tested again. We also call these "tests" of levels S1, S2, R1, R2, meaning support was tested once at S1 and a second time at S2 (same concept for resistance, i.e., R1 and R2).

Because charts and time horizons can be arbitrary, it is important to understand what time range defines the level of elasticity of the security. Do we look at yesterday's high? Last week's low? The 10-period moving average?

The answer supports our prior point that it is the most recent past that best predicts with greatest accuracy the near future. A short (between two and five days) time frame tends to show enough of the past to predict the next day's future, but is not long enough for the details to be forgotten by the collective mind of the market.

Looking at it as a western bar or candle, whichever you'd prefer, you can clearly see an intraday high, low, opening, and closing price. These define the daily bar. Suppose, for example, that we look at two one-day bars. On the first day, the market finds a new low, elastically stretching to a place it hadn't been before within the time frame being measured. Before the end of the first day, the security closes above its intraday low. On the second day, now the present day, the market opens higher than the prior close, perhaps a dollar above its closing price. We'd like to think that there is now support at the prior close or near it, but elastically, true support will not be defined in this two-day analysis unless it challenges the prior day's low. That low defines the very point at which the bears could not push the price any lower and the bulls regained control. The high/low price set the prior day defines the bulls' and bears' range.

In the example in Figure 3.5, when the market opens on day 2 the trader has a tradable range defined by the Inside range between the close and the low or the range between the open and the high. This is not to be confused with the *True range* which was defined in the previous section. The *Inside range* is defined as the range between the open and close.

On 9/03/02 the S&P 500 made an elastic low at level 3, an elastic high and open at level 1, and closed off its lows at level 2. On 9/04/02 it opened near its 9/03/02 close at level 5. The True range of elasticity to trade would have been to short on 9/04/02 under the 9/03/02 close at level 2 and expect the elastic low at level 3 to be tested and penetrated for a breakdown. Again keep in mind this is the tradable true range. True range is defined in this example as the difference between level 6 and level 3. Tradable True range is

F I G U R E   3.5

This is an example of elastic levels of the S&P 500 Index.

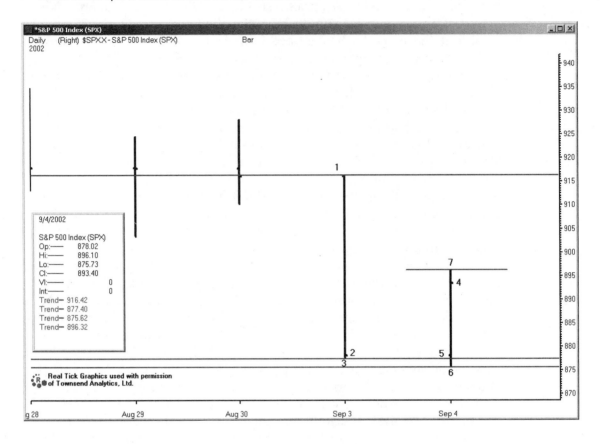

defined as the difference between levels 2 and 3. This is exactly what the market is telling us to do. The S&P 500 clearly broke new elastic lows on 9/03/02
and left clues that the bears controlled the elasticity. It is telling us that the
bears took the market to level 3 and tested the bulls' strength at that level,
where support was put in for that day. As the S&P opened (5) at the prior
close (2) on 9/04/02, looking at the true range told us to short the S&P for at
least a downside test of the elastic low (3) on 9/03/02. As the short worked,
a trailing stop at level 3 was initiated to allow for the S&P to follow through
and break down. If level 3 had been broken (it was not), traders could have
expected an increase in velocity to the downside (new elastic lows). The reality of the trade was that we were stopped out almost immediately and
scratched the trade since the market rallied from level 6. As the market
rallied off the elastic low at level 6, we were stopped out for no gain but

without loss. This is an example of a trade that didn't yield profit but did represent the statistically correct trade. We referenced this realistic scenario using these techniques, since the rules of the strategy and the risk management associated with this method are far more important than whether or not the trade yielded a profit.

The second trade was to buy the S&Ps after they broke above the prior day's close (2) and set a protective stop at the elastic low (3). The market never looked back and we were in the money as the market traded inside the consensus range (traditional open/close). We then set a trailing stop with two points' discretion and let the profits run. As the market rallied, we targeted the prior day's opening price at level 1. We tightened our trailing stop to 1 S&P point as velocity improved and were stopped out 1 point under level 7, which turned out to be the day's EH. The trade resulted in a 17-point winner. If the second trade (long) had failed at the entry level (above number 2 in the prior day's elastic close), our protective stop would have stopped us out 2 points under the opening position at the prior day's elastic low (3) and current day's elastic low (6).

Knowing the prior day's elasticity creates a range of reward potential that intraday traders should recognize as a clue. If the market gains enough strength and causes the market to open strong the next day (9/04/02), and continues to follow through to test the prior day's highs at level 1, then all short-side plays are off, and the prior day's high will act as your protective stop for trades (long) made above level 1.

If the prior day's high on 9/03/02 is penetrated, your protective stop on the long is not adjustable. This stop is ridged and should signal a follow-through of bullish strength. As we reviewed, we flipped our position on the second trade from short to long, buying back more shares than we were short and allowed the market to elastically test new levels. The trailing stop allowed us to participate in the rally as the market strived to make new highs. While the market did not test the elastic high on 9/03/02, we gave ourselves the chance to participate if it had. If the issue actually had elastically stretched to new highs above level 1, traders could have gone back in time on the charts to the prior five days, looking for higher elastic levels such as those reached on 8/30/02. As Bill likes to say, "I'd rather be a participant in the market rather than an observer, since you learn more about what is happening." Participating in the first trade was perhaps a bit aggressive, but its risk was mitigated with good rules, and this allowed for the highly profitable second trade. Without the first trade, we would have likely missed the second.

While a simple intraday trade technique such as the elastic play is only one of several powerful trading strategies we employ, keep in mind the concept that the market's most recent past will be the most accurate indication of its near-term future. The deeper you probe into the past, the more arbitrary the market becomes. In fact, the market becomes arbitrary on an exponential scale, not on a linear one, the deeper you probe. To reinforce this fact, we take a brief sidebar to explain the exponential moving average (EMA).

The EMA is a mechanism that gives more weight to recent data and less weight to older data. This formula follows the logic stated in elasticity trading. Here is how an EMA is calculated:

$$EMA = CP\,(w) + P_{EMA}\,(1 - w)$$

where

CP = current period price

$w = 2\,/\,(x + 1)$, where x = number of periods

P_{EMA} = prior period EMA

By modifying the value of w we can place more or less weight on recent data. To demonstrate this, let's look at some EMAs calculated from the closing prices of the S&P 500 index from 11/13/02 to 11/15/02 in Figure 3.6.

F I G U R E   3.6

Period	Price	SMA	Short-Term EMA	Midterm EMA	Longer-Term EMA
1	882.53	882.53			
2	904.27	893.4	901.86	897.1	894.12
3	909.83	898.88	906.76	903.47	900.7
4	900.36	899.25	903.75	902.23	900.58
5	896.74	898.75	901.01	900.42	899.44
6	914.15	901.31	905.21	904.35	903.23

In Figure 3.6, the MA's are calculated progressively starting with period 1 and recalculated for each new period that is added to the data. The simple moving average (SMA) gives equal weight to all the data, so we can use the SMA to show how much weight the different EMAs give to more recent data. If we view the market from a short-term perspective, we want most of the weight given to recent data. To change the weighting of the short-term, midterm, and longer-term EMAs, we alter our formula for calculating w:

For our short-term, we use $w = 2\,/\,(x + 0.25)$

For our midterm, we use $w = 2\,/\,(x + 1)$

For our longer-term, we use $w = 2\,/\,(x + 1.75)$

Looking again at Figure 3.6, notice how the short-term EMA is highly affected by the current period price, while the midterm EMA is less affected by the current period price and the longer-term EMA is most similar to the SMA, which gives equal weight to all data.

In our view of the market, we need to look at levels and data like the EMA does, not like the SMA does. We need to look at past data and realize that more recent data, which is still fresh in market participants' memories, should have more importance. This is valuable knowledge to have since we weight much of our decisions around elastic highs and lows as anticipation of velocity. As markets either approach or penetrate these levels, we can expect more intensive price action (velocity). To keep it simple, velocity is defined as the change in price divided by time. If price change increases (rally or retracement) over shorter periods of time, we have increased velocity. Because recent highs and low are remembered by participants, once these levels are tested, participants will react. Their reaction can take many forms. For example, these levels represent where electronic stops exist, institutional buy/sell programs activate, automated quantitative Black Box Systems produce signals, or just simple emotional reactions happen. Regardless, when recent new highs and lows are approached, and especially when penetrated, markets react, which is why velocity increases. As you learn this reality, you begin to understand how to read markets, be it on an exchange floor, or electronic tape, or otherwise. This understanding is fundamental to the elastic play, and explains why professionals tend to be contrarians at these levels for short-term opportunities and also recognize the penetrations of these levels as the earliest signs of new trend for longer-term swing trades. The EMA/SMA comparison serves as a more tangible reference to the same philosophy of seeing and measuring market action. Because this insight is less tangible and more feeling, hopefully you can recognize the logic through the math of the EMA.

ELASTICITY AND STOPS

Before we discuss stops, you should understand that a stop order should be placed at the same time, and with the same consideration, as the trade itself. So before we make a trade, we also need to know where our stops belong in order to manage risk. Most participants carefully consider trade entry and exit, but often pay too little attention to risk which can be managed with stops.

Stops are best utilized with an electronic execution system such as the RealTick platform. They should not be mentally executed nor should they be committed to paper; they should be committed to a system that can objectively act on them without arbitrary inputs like emotions. Think of the technology that initiates your stop as imposed discipline, or an "emotional hedge."

The primary stops we use are protective and trailing stops. *Protective stops* are simple stops that should never be changed or moved if the trader is to remain true to the original trade. (Trailing stops are discussed a little later in this chapter.) Once a protective stop is moved, the trade is not the same. Trust this basic rule: Protective stops should never be moved. Once a protective stop is changed, so is the risk in the trade. As more risk is "let in," more opportunity is "let out," which changes the risk/reward relationship of the original trade. For example, if you were willing to risk $1 to make $3 (1:3), but then allowed for more risk by moving the protective stop, the trade could change to something like a 1:1 risk/reward ratio, which is not the trade initiated.

A quick sidebar is necessary here to clarify our next point. Many amateurs, observers, and media sources regard shorting stocks as a damaging element to the market. This is utter nonsense. Shorting stocks is no different than selling. When shorting, you are simply selling shares that someone else already owns through hypothecation agreements. Short sellers can't sell shares that don't exist; they can only short (sell) existing outstanding shares that were purchased on margin. If anything, short sellers are providing a valuable service to the market by providing liquidity to meet demand by the buyers, thereby providing more orderly price dynamics by keeping supply (sellers) and demand (buyers) more balanced. Futures are a financial commodity and trade on a zero-sum game. One party wins at the expense of the loser. It is a zero-sum game, therefore, shorting futures is healthy for the market since it provides liquidity. When shorting futures, you are betting against other traders who are long the contract.

We raise this point to address our next trade, made September 12, 2002. We decided not to short stock on the 9/11 anniversary out of respect, but as stated, shorting is a fact healthy for the market. On 9/12 we traded the futures market through the Chicago Mercantile Exchanges (CME) E-mini S&P 500 futures contract. This contract is a downsized version of the full S&P 500 futures contract that is traded on the floor. The symbol for this contract is ES. Referencing Figure 3.5, Level 1 indicated the market's strength as the high. Level 2 indicated the market's open. Level 3 marked the close of the market and indicated weakness. Level 4 marked the extent of the weakness during the day. Level 5 represented where we took our profits, as we will shortly explain, and level 6 indicated the elastic low that supported the market and initiated the ultimate trailing stop in the trade.

The trade was made shortly after the open on 9/12/02 (see Figure 3.7), since we had a bearish true range between levels 3 and 4. While the range was small, we were still able to use it to set stops to manage risk. Our open-

F I G U R E   3.7

This is an example of elastic levels applied to the S&P 500 Index.

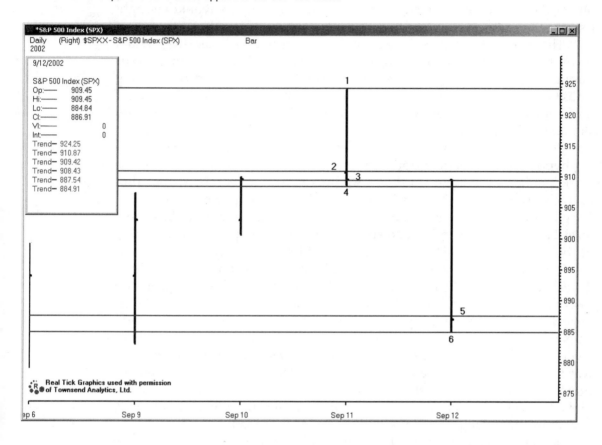

ing trade was a short at the 909 level. The protective stop was set at level 2, two S&P points above the prior day's open of 910.63. The opening point was the high of the day, and our initial three-point trailing stop allowed us to participate in most of the breakdown. We widened to a 5-point trailing stop as velocity subsided, and as we approached the end of day we tightened our trailing stop to 2 points and were stopped out for a large winner at level 5. As the levels indicate, the market told us what to do; it left clues. Because on 9/11/02 the market made a new elastic high at level 1, we were prepared to trade the bullish true range had the market traded above level 2. Obviously this failed, and once we penetrated below level 3, we traded the tight bearish true range between levels 3 and 4, expecting the dominant elasticity to change by breaking level 4. Once it did, the velocity increased dramatically and the sell-off was fierce. We kept our trailing stop tight at 3 points during the sell-off. As velocity subsided we widened it to 5 points, because we were deep in the money and were prepared to risk some profit for a deeper sell-off. As the day came to the close, we tightened our stop to avoid overnight risk.

The market showed us the way and the rules told us to use the marked pivots for our entry, protective stops, and exit. This information is given to us through objective data (elastic levels). Subjectively, we moved our trailing stops based on feel and velocity, but we only did so once we had the peace of mind of assured profitability. This is the only time the door of subjectivity should be opened.

To explain why protective stops cannot be moved, let's view the following hypothetical scenario: Suppose the trade works out differently and the market rallies against our short and we broke our rule by moving our protective stop from level 2 to the hypothetical level 7, as shown in Figure 3.8. Imagine the very different trade we would create. If the market broke the level 2 protective stop and traded above the prior day's open, the elastic high of the prior day on 9/11/02 at level 1 would be the likely next level and would indicate that the bulls were in control. Remember, once we cross level 2 we step into the bullish range. Moving the stop to level 7 would abandon discipline and break rules, which can only lead to one result: great losses. Level 8 represents the new hypothetical reward target if the rules were broken and the protective stop was moved to level 7. Since level 8 is equal to level 4 (the elastic low of the day prior), this illustrates how much the risk/reward scenario changes whenever a protective stop is moved. Never move a protective stop! The shorts should be covered at level 2 and never allowed to move to level 7. Instead of moving a protective stop from level 2 to level 7, deeper into loss, long positions should instead be opened.

In trading, your responsibility is to make money in the trade zone—the middle to middle third of the range. Don't expect to sell the tops and buy the bottoms. Using proper stops and elasticity levels will bring you as close to that scenario as is possible. As Rollie Massimino once said, "The harder I work the luckier I get." Markets trade to and from elastic levels. If stops are set properly, trading at these elastic levels is more likely to keep losses small and profits strong.

Trailing stops are the second genre of stops. The *trailing stop* is a statement that you are willing to risk some of your profits. It is used to measure when profits are to be taken (as opposed to a protective stop, which measures when a loss is to be taken). Trailing stops are to be entered soon after the trade is opened and as soon as you are in the money. The amount of discretion in the trailing stop determines the amount of profit in the trade you are willing to give back. In the Figure 3.8 example, suppose the market immediately starts to come in and the trade is in the money 4 points. If the trader is

FIGURE   3.8

Elastic levels, the protective stop, and the target are highlighted in this figure.

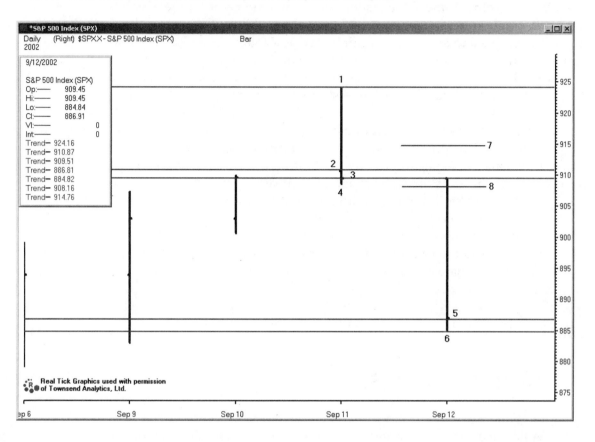

willing to set a 5-point discretionary trailing stop, the risk in the trade is now reduced to only 1 point. If the market rallies against the short position the trader can only lose 1 point. In this case, the trader is willing to forego 4 points' profitability for the opportunity to let profits run. This is the decision of the trader, but this strategy ensures a maximum of 1-point risk from the original position. The trailing stop is simply a mechanism that practices discipline to let profits run, while the protective stop is a mechanism to cut losses short. For example, with the 4-point trailing stop, if the market rallies 3 points and then subsequently retraces 8 more points, the stop would not be initiated on the rally and the trader would be "in the money" 9 total points from the original entry level. If the market then finds support and rallies 5 points from its lowest level, the trader is giving back 5 points of profitability but still netting a 4-point profit; hence the trader is trading somewhere in the middle to middle third of the range. This is where traders will do the most business.

Played another way, if the trader felt the market came in the 9 points hard with high velocity, he or she might tighten the trailing stop from 5 points to 2 points and book more profit by taking 7 total points. This is an example of where feel for velocity plays into the trade, and this can't be taught in a book. The point is, the trailing stop is used based on elastic levels and subjectivity (feel), while the protective stop is strictly placed around elastic levels and objectivity.

A protective stop should never be moved, and a trailing stop should always be moved. This practice allows profits to run and cuts losses short. In this case, we are not expecting to buy the bottom to cover the short. Forget trying to trade the ends of elastic ranges; it is nearly impossible. No one is that good consistently. Trade the middle third of the trade zone using stops placed when the opening trade is made in the case of protective stops, and as soon as you are in the money in the case of trailing stops. A protective stop that is rigid will automatically guarantee *small losses.* A trailing stop that is not rigid will automatically *let profits run.* Using a trailing stop means you won't sell the perfect top or buy the perfect bottom, but that's okay. The risk/reward scenario is good enough without it. If you practice this, you automatically practice discipline; the most critical thing you can do.

MENTAL TRADE EXERCISES

Discipline can be practiced (and should be), therefore do an exercise in your head, without a chart. It's easy and fun. In the case of getting short, if you get short at $45.95 and the trade does not break down to the next elastic target at the $45 level but instead rallies back to a protective stop of $46.25, assuming you gave it that kind of room, you've lost $0.30. Remember, the protective stop cannot be adjusted; it absolutely cannot be moved. It is not flexible. If you change it, your discipline is eroding. You're not in the same trade you started with!

What would we change if the market goes our way? If the trade is working, breaks down below $45.65, and looks like it has the propensity to target the $45 elastic level, we would then enter a $0.25 trailing stop. If it now breaks down to $45.50, our new stop is $45.75. It breaks down to $45.25, and our trailing stop moves to $45.50. It breaks down to $45, our stop moves to $45.25, and so on. The only question is how much discretion we put in our trailing stop. Do we leave $0.25, $0.30, or $0.50? It's a function of risk/reward and is a combination of visceral feel and what profits you are willing to risk in the trade. As a practice, we like to widen trailing stops *once the price goes through an elastic level* and tighten them as we approach an elastic level, since we expect support at the target or elastic level (in this example). Support is expected at elastic lows and resistance is expected at elastic highs, so tightening at these levels is often a good idea, but again this is up to the trader.

Overly tight stops can be a problem and invites whipsaw risk. To avoid whipsaw risk, you first need a good risk/reward scenario. Don't take a trade that requires an overly tight protective stop, because $0.05 stops don't work. When good trade setups exist, you can afford to take a little bit more heat by setting protective stops at reasonable levels.

As you can see, the placement of stops is as important as the entry of the trades themselves. The two processes are inseparable. Keeping rigid protective stops and flexible trailing stops puts you in a good risk/reward scenario and imposes discipline. You can't be partially disciplined. If you cancel your protective stop and move it either higher on shorts or lower on longs, you might get lucky on some trades, but as a consistent practice you will lose. Discipline is everything.

OPENING PRICE INTRADAY APPROACH

As explained throughout this chapter, the elastic levels (intraday highs and lows) represent the extent of bullish and bearish sentiment within any given time period. Therefore, we could also say these levels represent the crescendo of emotion. The elastic high is Mr. Market's (as Warren Buffett referred to it during a Berkshire Hathaway annual meeting) moment of mania, while the elastic low is his moment of depression. Like most emotional extremes, these moments don't tend to last long, yet they are nonetheless intense. The psychology of markets simply mark these extremes as price points where Mr. Market expresses his range of emotions. Like individual psychology, we tend to exist on an even keel during most times, but on occasion find ourselves brought to emotional extremes (mania or even depression, or joy or sorrow, etc.). Mr. Market is no different except that he tends to be more schizophrenic than most individuals. Mr. Market is capable of explosive moves each day and is impacted by many potential influences. Because of this fact we must understand how to deal with Mr. Market's personality. Professional market makers, specialists, floor traders, and the like understand not only how to deal with it but also how the amateur is likely to react. As a result, the professional sees to it, to give the public something to react to every morning through the "opening price." The opening price represents Mr. Market's initial view of the day based on the many influences it must digest, such as news, analysts' viewpoints, ratings changes, fundamentals, economic out-looks, earnings, etc. The professionals use these events to stretch price levels (elasticity) to extremes under the guise that amateurs will spend much of the day reacting. Hence, "the Opening Price Play." For intraday trading, as each market opens, the opening price will tend to represent the extent of elasticity for the day in terms of tops and bottoms. These opening prices can be retested many times within a trading day, but are first seen as suspect at the open when at extreme levels (gaps).

While these extreme levels can mark where the market could go in the future, these opening prices very often must first fight a few battles. We see these opening price levels as markable inflection points and expect the market to retest these points, and therefore we pay close attention to them throughout the day. We assume that the opening price will be the level of resistance or support for that day's trading range unless penetrated. For an example, see Figure 3.9.

F I G U R E   3.9

The opening prices for the last two bars are highlighted in this figure.

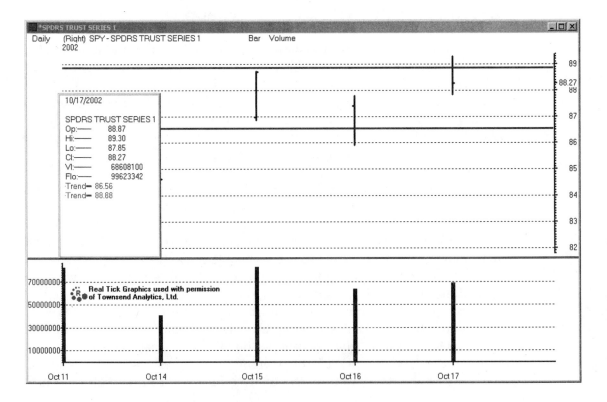

On 10/16/02, the SPY's closed at $86.56. It opened on 10/17/02 at $88.88 for a strong gap higher. The gap indicated the sentiment of the market at the open and, statistically speaking, the participants on the opposite side of the gap (those attempting shorts) were squeezed. Participants on the long side of the market will tend to take profits in such a situation since these participants include the market makers and specialists who gapped it there. The process of longs selling to take profits and shorts buying to cover creates the battle of supply and demand, which tends to create price stability until a dominant trend can take control. Hence the higher open is a signal that a trend is going to develop once the battles between longs and shorts have been fought.

Usually a higher open means stronger trends ahead, but trends will not develop until these battles are fought. For that reason, swing traders should stand aside until the opening price is penetrated (breakdown in this example), while day traders may see the opening price as resistance. When prices open high, the propensity will be for this level to fall as profit taking ensues. Therefore, shorting the higher open for an early intraday trade makes sense, but the trade methodology for the day trader is much different than that of the swing trader.

Once sellers (profit takers) are gone, the squeezed shorts and the reentering longs will create a stronger overall upward trend that you don't want to short into. Shorting the high open is for a fast play, not a longer-term swing trade. It is important to remember that yesterday's closing price is irrelevant in this strategy. The fact that the market is gapping higher or lower is not important except to predict that those participants that took overnight positions will buy or sell accordingly, and profit takers usually act faster than losers. Other than this psychological notation, the prior day's closing level is not relevant.

The greatest elastic range tends to exist above low opening prices (support) and below high opening prices (resistance). Given the symmetry of the market, it is not hard to understand why. Market makers and specialists tend to open the markets at the perceived elastic levels, where buying and selling reaction will be greatest. See Figure 3.10 for examples of both day trade and swing trade plays.

As seen on Figure 3.10, Citigroup's price trades greater volume above low opens and below high opens. The horizontal lines represent the opening price on each day. Notice that on 10/11 the price activity lives above the low open and on 10/14 the same is true. On 10/15 the stock opens high and the price action lives below; the same is true on 10/16. On 10/17 a potential breakout pattern is setting up, as given by the fact that while the market opens high, the price action is still above the opening price. This indicates that the bulls are now truly strong and the stock should trend higher; therefore, 10/17 would represent a breakout day that swing traders would want to trade.

F I G U R E   3.10

Notice the intraday range compared to the opening price on this Citigroup chart.

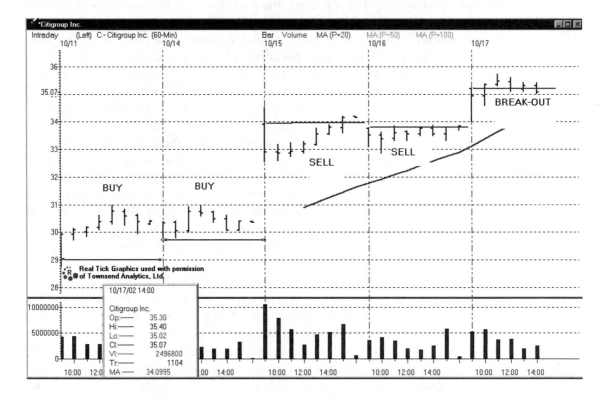

Because we cannot look at opening prices and short high opens and buy low opens without confirmation, we must use other indicators to confirm the bias, and most importantly we must use stops to protect us from the inevitable losing trades.

The elastic range between the high and low of the prior day sets the range upon which we calculate our relative protective stop. In this case, the prior day had a high of $27.72 and a low of $25.52 for an elastic range of $2.21. The protective stop was set at 20 percent of the range, or $0.44 ($2.21 × 20% = $0.44), below the low opening price (roughly $25.82). The target is the prior day's high of $27.72. Our trailing stops were tightened as we traded toward the prior day's elastic high.

The important thing to remember is that this is an intraday method only. When stocks are trending we want to follow the elastic swing approach. Swing traders will see opening prices as support for high opens and resistance for low opens as long as the levels are penetrated. See Figure 3.10 for the breakout on 10/17 where we switch from the opening price intraday method to the elastic swing method. As you can see, both approaches are effective, yet very different. Traders should pay close attention to the elasticity method for swing trades and opening price for intraday trades. They are never to be combined since one is a contrarian view (opening price play) and the other a trend view (elasticity play).

4

CHAPTER

MARKET SYMMETRY

Adam Theory is getting in tune with the universe, not insisting that it get in tune with me. To insist that it get in tune with me would be arrogant, and it would be my own arrogance that would destroy me. To get in tune with it is to be humble, willing to follow wherever it goes.

If I fight against the river by trying to go upstream, it seems like a relentless implacable enemy constantly pushing against me, constantly trying to thwart me. But the river is not against me, it's just flowing the way it's flowing. If I can get in tune with it, mirror it, go the way it's going, then life—or trading—becomes an effortless, serene, beautiful float down the stream.

—*Jim Sloman*

Now that we have taken a look at price dynamics as seen through the eyes of a contrarian (intraday approach), and through the perspective of a trend trader (swing approach), we can introduce market structure, which will define when to use each approach. Traders will find themselves trading on a variety of time frames, therefore, one must first learn how to see the market and then flow with it. Before traders can begin to understand patterns on charts, they must first understand market structure. *Patterns* are subsets of market structure that illustrate crowd behavior, while market structure is a collection of patterns. Patterns can be as subjective as reading the stars or as accurate as locating Polaris in the northern sky. It depends on their application. While many mathematical attempts have been made to quantify patterns, relying solely on "canned" systems should be viewed with a fair dose of pessimism. Patterns are best applied when they are used as a confirmation of other indications and ideas, not as stand-alone forecasts of directional bias. *Symmetry* is defined as a series of patterns that develop over time in a harmonious arrangement. As we've explained, the market's components of patterns are based on price, time, volume, and velocity. Symmetry measures the relationship of all four, while recognizing market psychology as the driving force of each. In other words, *price* is the current consensus of value. *Time* measures how long it takes for that consensus of value to evolve. *Volume* measures the extent to which the market agrees. *Velocity* measures the intensity of the market's belief in whatever value price defines. Symmetry represents the historical patterns of the four principles above and the harmony in which those patterns will repeat in the future. These principles of the market provide plenty of perspective, analysis, and interpretation (both subjective and objective). Symmetry becomes a focal point of market analysis because it draws on historical events to predict future events which, as we have emphasized, is the only accurate way to create a picture of what is to come.

A SPECIAL NOTE ON VELOCITY

You must realize velocity is a derivative of changing price divided by time; therefore, the greater the velocity, the more likely it is that there will be symmetry: To put it in literal trading terms, the faster the price gets to a given level, the greater the propensity for a reactionary correction. Velocity increases when price changes more quickly with time and it decreases when price changes more slowly with time.

By measuring velocity we can also make some statements about the market's symmetry. When breakouts or breakdowns occur, we expect high velocity and trade with less conviction and more discipline (we reduce our size in the trade to allow for increased risk). When velocity decreases, the market is more likely to settle in channels, and we allow for more conviction and time for trades to develop.

PATTERNS AND SYMMETRY

The theory that the markets have order (as opposed to being a random walk) is based on the psychology of market participants, including the general public and institutions. This order and its repeating characteristics manifest themselves as market symmetry. These structures are simply the market's ability to repeat what it has done in the past by doing it again. Let's take a look at two basic types of market symmetry: rotational symmetry and reflectional symmetry.

ROTATIONAL SYMMETRY

Like an automobile wheel with five lugs, rotational symmetry exists because each lug has a symmetrical relationship to the next. Rotational symmetry is based on the principle that after each partial revolution the wheel will look as it did before the rotation (harmonious). When lug number two comes to the top, the wheel is indistinguishable from when lug number one was there. The basis number of the rotational pattern depends on how many identical positions are possible within a complete revolution. So in this case, an automobile hub with five lugs would have a five basis (72 degree) rotational pattern. The market is not this symmetrical, but it has its own symmetrical patterns, and many market technicians have written about the power of these repeating patterns. In order to understand these rotational patterns, we must explore what drives them outside the scope of a purely physical example such as the wheel. The axle drives the wheel, just as psychology drives the market. In both cases, the result is rotational symmetry. While the physical example is completely symmetrical, we need only to know that the cyclical nature of the market is ever present, just not quite as symmetrical.

A trade has a cyclical life cycle, just as our economy does. Economists, politicians, and others have been puzzled by business cycles since at least the early nineteenth century. One of the more unusual explanations was proposed by English economist William Stanley Jevons in the nineteenth century. He believed the ups and downs of an economy were caused by sunspot cycles, which affected agriculture and caused cycles of good and bad harvests. Another novel solution was proposed by Russian economist Kondratieff. He came up with a 50-year-cycle theory that resembled the Jovian 60-year cycle used by astronomers and astrologers in India to make economic forecasts.

As we all know, business cycles are subjective, as are trading cycles, but we have attempted to define the stages of a trading cycle, just as most economists have agreed on the stages of the business cycle. In the case of trading, the business and trading cycles mimic each other as follows:

Stage 1: Expansion/Accumulation
Stage 2: Peak/Markup
Stage 3: Contraction/Distribution
Stage 4: Trough/Decline

See Figure 4.1 for an example of the business cycle, then take a look at Figure 4.2 which is an example of a trading (market) cycle. Regardless of which label you attach to this known cycle of both the economy and stocks, these patterns are rotational.

The psychology that drives this market cycle seen in Figure 4.2 is driven by greed (Stage 1), fear (Stage 4), and indecision (Stages 1 and 3). The trust one has in the cyclical nature of the markets is based on one's belief that these emotions will not only drive the cycle but also the extent to which one believes the past determines the future.

Simple business cycle that most economists agree drives capitalistic society.

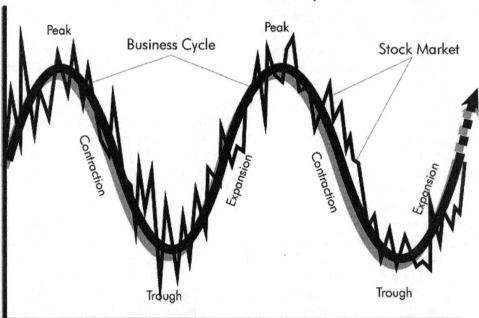

The Business Cycle

Microcosm of the business cycle on an individual stock (or security) basis.

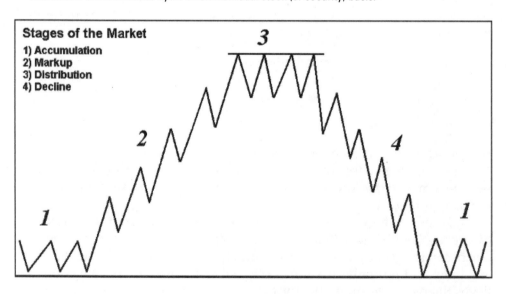

Stages of the Market
1) Accumulation
2) Markup
3) Distribution
4) Decline

Obviously, shorter time periods will distort these symmetrical patterns and cause them to look asymmetrical and random, but the market does have symmetry and there is a statistical likelihood that these patterns will be tested and repeated. While in Stages 2 and 4, the markets can also have rotational symmetry within each stage as well. See Figures 4.3 and 4.4 for examples.

In a range bound, sideways market (Stages 1 and 3), there can be signs of rotational symmetry as well. We call this rotational stabilization and consolidation. See Figure 4.5.

Again, think about the psychology of the cycle; once bulls can't run any more (end of Stage 2), bears begin to gain control as Stage 3 develops. Once decline (Stage 4) sets in, fear is in control until we have our first signs of Stage 1 accumulation where the bulls slowly regain their footing. This pattern will continue and repeat, creating a channel, until something breaks the pattern and the market accelerates in the direction of the trend.

If the bulls take the market to a pattern high where resistance stops the rally (seemingly Stage 3), it does not mean Stage 4 is inevitable. This

F I G U R E   4.3

Rotational uptrend (Stage 2).

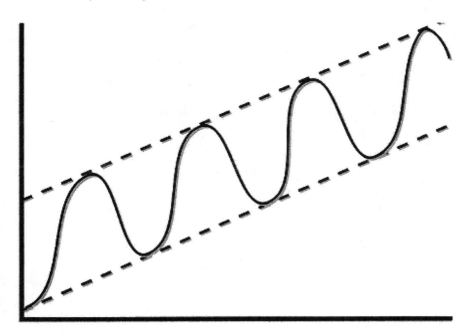

Rotational downtrend (Stage 4).

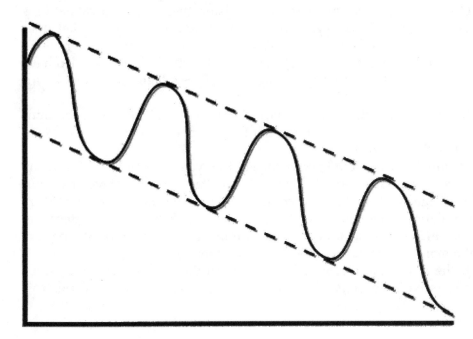

Rotational stabilization (Stage 1) and consolidation (Stage 3).

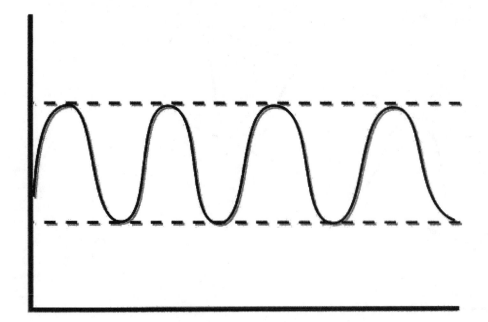

F I G U R E   4.6

Notice that what looks like a Stage 3 is merely a pause in a Stage 2 uptrend.

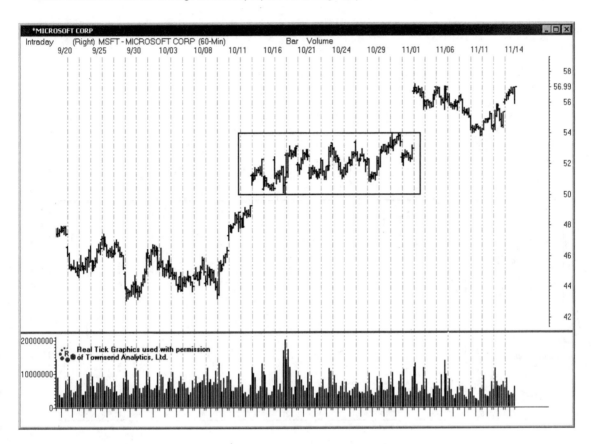

"headfake" often invites eager short sellers who fall victim to accelerated breakouts as seen in Figure 4.6 starting on 11/01. The opposite is true of sell-offs and breakdowns. While these patterns are statistically likely, good traders trade the high percentage zones of these overlapping patterns, but always see them as a confirmation of other indicators.

Referring to Figure 4.7, trading the short side in area 3 (not Stage 3) represents a statistically better trade than area 2. Because the right leg of area 2 is broken once price breaks support (as shown by the top horizontal line), the left leg of area 3 is forming and looks symmetrically similar to the left leg of area 1. While this is far from a tradable pattern based solely on these merits, it does represent rotational symmetry in the market.

F I G U R E   4.7

This chart demonstrates the Rotational Symmetry of the S&P 500 Index.

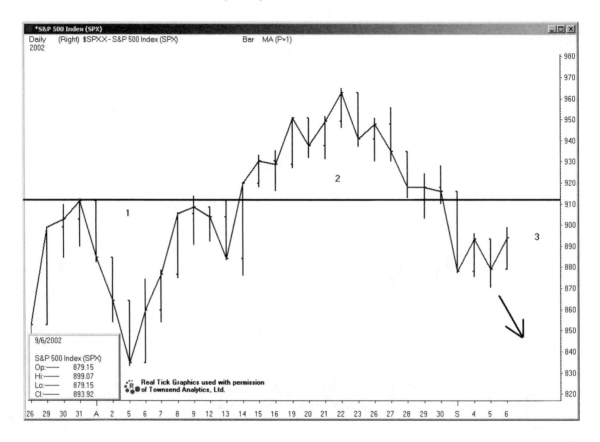

REFLECTIONAL SYMMETRY

You have performed reflectional symmetry exercises before. Take a piece of paper, fold it in half vertically, and cut one half of a heart out of the folded side. Then open the paper back up and look at the full heart. This is a very simple example of reflectional symmetry. While the market is not this abiding, reflectional symmetry can offer a physical measure of market symmetry. If the elasticity of the market to the downside is measured by the distance of its move from its beginning point to its ending point and, for example, the time in which it took to move that elastic range is three days, the market has extended the limits of its elasticity over that three-day period. For example, if the S&P 500 comes in 50 points, the likely rally once support is achieved will reflect a percentage of the retracement range that preceded it. If the market does not rally at this support level and continues to break down, we can expect an even greater retracement.

To see market reflection, we once again draw on history as our teacher. The best example of reflectional symmetry as applied to the market would come in the form of Fibonacci levels. Let's take a brief step back in time to explain. Pre-Renaissance, most historians would agree that risk was not quantified or measured in intrinsic terms since there was little mathematical structure to do so. The Roman numerical system simply did not have the sophistication to allow for expanded calculations. This limitation hindered architecture, decision-making regarding risk, and even religion. Because of mathematical limitations, "fate" and pure religious faith commanded most decisions of man. Even games of chance, the earliest forms of gambling which date back to the beginning of recorded history, were dictated by fate and chance. Strategies in war, architectural design (rounded and spherical), and religious beliefs were all influenced greatly by this mathematical limitation. An early form of dice played with sheep's angle bones known as astragalus was played with little recognition of odds. All because math as we know it was yet to be discovered. In craps we now know that when throwing a pair of dice the number 7 has the greatest odds (6 possible combinations), hence the casinos own this number and are able to build pyramids in the desert using it and other statistical advantages. The point is that pre-Renaissance chance and fate would all change at the hands of many great mathematicians in history, but it all began with Leonardo Pisano, now known as Fibonacci. Fibonacci came from a derivative name of his father, Bonacio. Fibonacci means son of Bonacio. Fibonacci learned of an Arab-Hindu numbering system that Arabs introduced to the Western World during the Crusades. This numbering system allowed for an infinite number of calculations, far beyond what was capable using the Roman numeral system, and Fibonacci helped to develop its usefulness. While much more can be said about Fibonacci in history, today we apply his original principles to many applications including market symmetry. His best known work appeared in his original book *Liber Abaci* whereby he determined the multiplication of rabbits beginning with a single pair if given a year to reproduce. He discovered a symmetry of numbers which would be produced as follows:

1, 2, 3, 5, 8, 13, 21, 34, 55, 89, 144. . .

The symmetry within these seemingly random numbers is found by adding the two preceding numbers to find the next number. For example, $8+13=21$, $13+21=34$, etc. These sequences form a proportion, or harmony, that is now not only well regarded in history but still used extensively today in architecture, the markets, and even religion. By dividing any Fibonacci number by the next higher number, after 3 the number is always 0.625. After 89 it is

0.618. If you divide any Fibonacci number by the preceding Fibonacci number, after 2 the number is always 1.6, after 144 it is always 1.618. We call these proportions the "golden mean." This golden mean can be seen throughout history, such as in the cross. The horizontal member of the Christian cross crosses the vertical member at the 61.8 percent ratio, meaning the horizontal member is placed 61.8 percent from the bottom of the vertical member. At this point this may sound mystical or unrelated to stock valuations or charts, but now we can start to explain. Since the golden mean is so recognized and utilized in history, architecture, etc., it is familiar, consciously or unconsciously. Because of this familiarity, participants perceive these levels on charts and react. Statistically speaking, the reaction to these levels is undeniable as pivot points, and therefore represent reflectional symmetry of the markets we trade. This isn't literally perfect, but the correlation is undeniable on daily bars.

There is also a psychological explanation. Once a market moves within a given range, it attracts participants both on the long and short side of the market. These participants will represent weak holders of stock at resistance levels, since many of these participants own the stock at these resistance-level prices. When markets go against these people, a large majority of the crowd will ride the retracement down, through a combination of poor discipline and hope. If this majority is fortunate enough to get an exit hatch on the next rally and break even on the trade (or close to break even), they will be the first to sell. The more sellers there are at this resistance level (i.e., the greater the volume), the stronger the resistance level becomes. Symmetry shows the market as run by human nature. Generally, with reflection, the closer the time series to the most recent period of time (what we would call the current market), the more accurate the prediction will be. Sir Isaac Newton explained it best: for every amount of action there is an equal amount of reaction in the opposite direction. While the markets are not as law-abiding, they do possess similar guidelines.

The markets are simply broken into past, current, and future periods of time. What occurs in the near future will be most influenced by the current moment and the recent past. We have applied this logic to established Fibonacci patterns and found that when reflection occurs within the dominant trend, whether it be bullish or bearish, the patterns of the future move in channels with tighter elastic ranges and low Fibonacci numbers such as 1, 2, 3 meaning little volatility. When the markets break a trend of the recent past, on the other hand, they break prior elastic channels with greater velocity and create new elastic levels. The range between these levels tends to reflect larger Fibonacci numbers such as 5, 8, and 13, meaning greater price change. This in turn forms the reflection of the new "future" moment. Once these newly formed elastic channels form, markets tend to reflect them until they change, and so the patterns continue to form symmetrically.

While the approach is simple, it is amazingly effective and therefore we feel no need to complicate it. Effectiveness is what matters. When a rubber band stretches to a new level, the intensity with which it snaps back from that level is much greater than if it had extended the range several times before. The rubber band that continually stretches from highs to lows within a designated time frame is a channel. A breakout is when that channel is penetrated. The intensity of the break, both through the channel and back, will be high. While this physical example sounds quite simple, it explains the similar physical properties associated with market psychology and elasticity. Once price levels are perceived and digested by the market (reported into the news), people will believe that new levels can go lower or higher much more easily than they had before. This is why elasticity theory and market symmetry work; perceptions of prices become more recognizable and perceivable, and therefore, repeatable.

TRADING FIBONACCI LEVELS

As stated earlier, Fibonacci was best recognized for defining a relatively simple way of adding numerical values in order to find definable patterns within a group of seemingly random numbers. Fibonacci's work is the foundation of chaos theory, which is a twentieth century system of mathematics drawn upon the fact that patterns exist in seemingly random samples of data. The patterns that Fibonacci found also apply to music in what is called the harmonic mean, a mathematical principle that takes its name from the application of its generated ratios to musical compositions. What Fibonacci found was that patterns in seemingly random numbers begin to form after eight successive iterations. Fibonacci noted these number patterns echoed in the proportions of the Egyptian pyramids. Subsequent followers of Fibonacci and, later, chaos theorists, brought this mathematical logic of pattern recognition to many applications, including the market. The patterns that the market reveals are measured by price action, filtered through the psychology of the participants and how they react to the price dynamic. Here is an example of Fibonacci at work.

When two random numbers are added together and that result is added to the former addends in a particular pattern, after eight reverberations we can divide the former number into the latter number and find a definable pattern. Let's start with two random numbers 63 and 17.

Reverberation 1: 63 + 17 = 80
Reverberation 2: 80 + 17 = 97
Reverberation 3: 97 + 80 = 177
Reverberation 4: 177 + 97 = 274

Reverberation 5: 274 + 177 = 451
Reverberation 6: 451 + 274 = 725
Reverberation 7: 725 + 451 = 1176
Reverberation 8: 1176 + 725 = 1901

Now divide the seventh reverberation by the eighth. The result is 0.618:

$$1176 \div 1901 = 0.618$$

Where the Fibonacci sequence becomes fascinating is when you try different random numbers for the first two addends. No matter what two numbers are chosen, the result after eight reverberations will be the same 0.618 ratio. Here again appears the golden mean.

This discovery by Fibonacci is just one example of how patterns exist within what seems to be chaos. Remember, this in relation to the market; most participants consider the movement of the market to be chaotic and completely random, but when we apply mathematical function to seemingly random data such as prices, patterns form. Wise traders can use these patterns.

As markets and stocks approach certain price levels, traders of the quantitative variety initiate statistical trades based on back-tested empirical studies that illustrate the statistical success or failure of such patterns. These patterns are often hard coded to systems, together with ridged risk management principles. As these patterns are successively traded, they tend to deteriorate over time as they become known to the market and the market begins to react to the pattern rather than being described by the pattern. Before that time, however, systems that draw on such statistical analysis can be very profitable, assuming that accompanying risk management parameters are also hard coded into the system or applied by traders. Perhaps you recall one of the world's largest hedge funds, founded in March 1994 by John Meriwether, a former bond trading star at Salomon brothers. This is perhaps one of the best examples of a system that proved highly profitable but in which there was too little risk management. Coupled with overleveraged positions based on its confidence in the system, Long Term Capital was nearly obliterated and only survived due to the Federal Reserve's rescue in September 1998. Even with talent like economist Robert Merton and Nobel prize winner in economics (1997) Myron Scholes (Black and Scholes Options pricing model), complete objective analysis without some subjective input is destined to fail. The point being, before we dive into tools like Fibonacci, one must remember that no system is foolproof.

RealTick offers outstanding systems tools that can help you apply the Fibonacci sequence and set up strong plays. Figure 4.8 shows the process.

The Fibonacci sequence has been adapted to use in the charting process. Here we set up Fibonacci studies on an exchange traded fund (ETF) of the

FIGURE   4.8

Fibonacci levels applied to the QQQs.

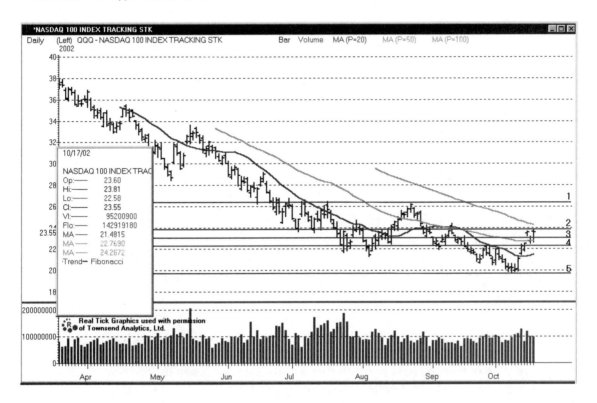

Nasdaq 100, or NDX, called the QQQ. We see on this daily chart of 150 days that the QQQ has rallied into a potential Fibonacci resistance level as shown in Figure 4.8

That is, the 61.8 percent level on the chart in Figure 4.8 represents the constant ratio between a number in the Fibonacci sequence divided by the larger number that follows it, and is closely related to the golden mean. Most active traders choose to draw Fibonacci levels that view a shorter term trend. Position traders might use these broad levels, but active traders do not as a rule. As stated earlier, these Fibonacci numbers simply represent levels on charts that are familiar to participants unrelated to markets. These proportions are seen in everyday life such as spirals commonly seen in nature.

Take a look at Figure 4.9; notice each successive square is determined by the Fibonacci sequence whereby it begins with two small squares of equal

FIGURE   4.9

A spiral is made from the Fibonacci sequence.

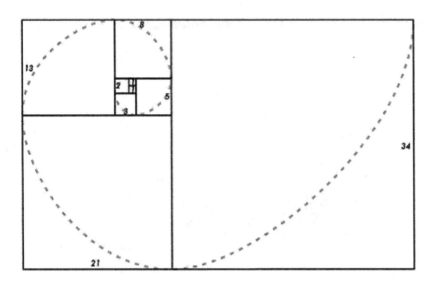

size and then grows in proportion to the Fibonacci sequence. The area of the first two squares equals the third, which is twice the first two squares. The third square plus one of the first two squares equals the fourth square and so on (1, 2, 3, 5, 8, 13, . . .). These Fibonacci sequences produce proportions of the golden mean, which are also seen in common shapes such as sea shells, ocean waves (coils), and even a ram's horn. The value that these proportions have to the market is that many participants pay deep attention to them and trade at these pivots. Furthermore, these proportions reflect order in seemingly random numbers that also attract traders. As markets make higher highs, higher lows, lower lows, or lower highs, these proportions have statistically proven relevant, hence reinforcing their importance. While Fibonacci levels do not account for all criteria used to make trading decisions, they do contribute to them. With this stated, lets go through a few charts to explain the application of Fibonacci analysis to markets.

We draw the Fibonacci levels based on the high/low range we want to measure. In this case, level 1 is the high and level 5 the low. Level 3 represents a 50 percent rally from the low at level 5, and level 4 represents a 38.2 percent rally. As we can see, the QQQs are approaching a 61.8 percent rally from lows at level 5 relative to the highs at level 1. Many traders see this golden mean as a potential correction level, suggesting a needed breather for the market. This level would represent a very shortable level, as Figure 4.8 indicates. Also keep in mind that the dominant trend is still very bearish (defined by the last 150 days). Additionally, notice how the rally from level 5 reflects the rally in early August. As these patterns are perceived, it is apparent that we are not using Fibonacci levels exclusively. We are also applying moving average (MA) studies as well as support and resistance. But these MA levels also indicate potential resistance levels. Specifically, the 100-period MA and the 61.8 percent Fibonacci level live at the same price point at level 2. Because these also agree, we see confirmation of a greater level of resistance at this point.

The level at point 2 is called an inflection point, a level where the market has the propensity to explode in either direction. While at this point we are inclined to trade from the short side, we also must protect ourselves against a break above this level.

We now take the 150-day chart down to 50 days (see Figure 4.10) for the setup on the QQQs, which closed below the level 2 Fibonacci line (see right side tick on the vertical bar). The market hits the Fibonacci level 2 on an intraday elastic high and retraces from the level 2 Fibonacci line, further

F I G U R E   4.10

Fibonacci levels set up on a 150-day chart of the QQQs.

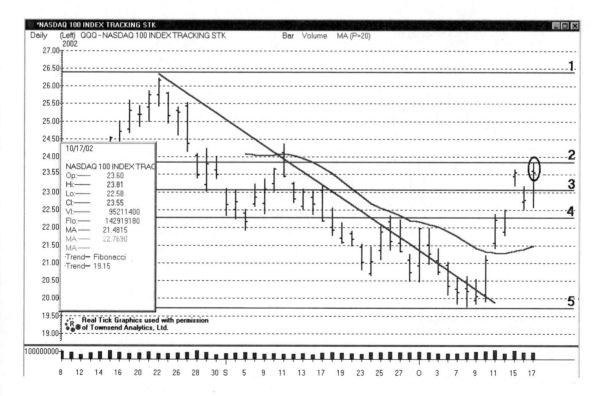

indicating the resistance level. If the market retests this level, we open shorts into the Fibonacci level as well as the 100-period (daily) moving average (another great confirmation of bearishness). If the market rallies through the Fibonacci level 2, we cover shorts and expect a breakout rally. Our target on the short will be the 50 percent Fibonacci retracement at level 3. We will tighten our trailing stops at level 3 expecting a rally, but if we are not stopped out, we can expect an increase in velocity and a retracement to Fibonacci level 4, reflecting the 38.2 percent Fibonacci level relative to level 5.

Because we trade at a key inflection point in the market, it is imperative that we remember our protective stop. It is not hard to imagine where it belongs. It will naturally be just above the prior elastic high set intraday at the $23.87 level. This price level is reflected in Figure 4.10 as level 2. It is a 61.8 percent Fibonacci level as well as the location of the 100-period moving average and the intraday elastic high. The market simply does not give you any better protective stop levels than that! If the QQQs can break this level, we must flip and go long, since this is what the market is telling us to do!

FIGURE   4.11

Redrawn Fibonacci levels on the QQQs.

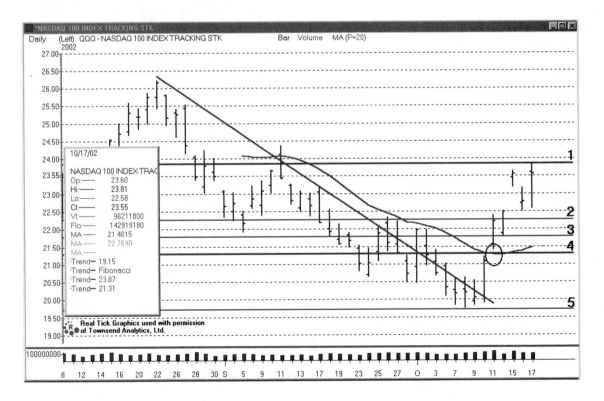

As you can see, we redrew the Fibonacci levels on Figure 4.11 to the new perceived high set from the old Fibonacci level 2 as shown on Figure 4.10. The new Fibonacci levels on Figure 4.12 indicate the potential reward targets at the new Fibonacci level 2 for a near-term target, Fibonacci level 3 for a midterm reward target, and Fibonacci level 4 in the case of a severe sell-off of the QQQ (the $21.31 price level). The Fibonacci level at 4 also represents the 20-period moving average, which is showing strong support by turning positive; therefore, trailing stops should be tight if this level is achieved.

To create a visual image of the trade, we indicate in Figure 4.12 our short entry (SE), our protective stop, and our target (T). For this trade we take 20 percent of the target as our protective stop, thus giving it a bit more room than our Fibonacci level 1 from Figure 4.11. Once the QQQs retrace 20 percent of the target range, we set a trailing stop to ensure a no-loss situation and eliminate risk. If the setup is real, the probability (not certainty) for further retracement to the 61.8 percent Fibonacci level (shown as T on Figure 4.12) is greatly enhanced, creating an excellent risk/reward setup of two to one.

F I G U R E   4.12

Fibonacci levels highlighted along with Short Entry Point (SE), Protective Stop (PS), and Target (T).

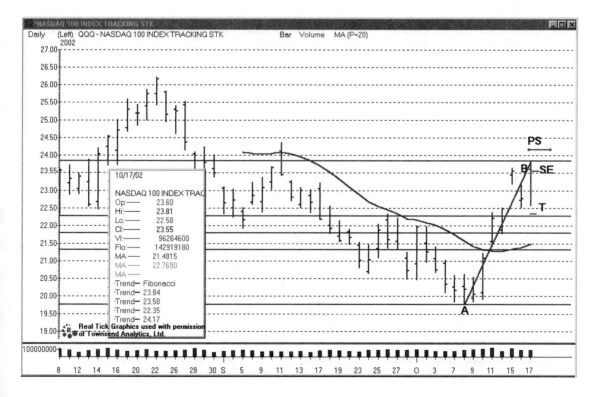

Let's explain the math. Referencing Figure 4.12, look at levels A and B. From Fibonacci level A we have a 100 percent rally to Fibonacci level B. We are now expecting a pullback of this bullish trend to a higher low to the 61.8 percent Fibonacci level relative to Fibonacci level A (38.2 percent pullback from Fibonacci level B). Our protective stop is set at $24.17, our short entry is at or close to $23.58, and the target is $22.35. The risk/reward is $0.59/$1.23, slightly better than a one to two risk/reward ratio. All that we require is that the market meets our criteria for the trade. If the market gaps far below our SE, we must consider whether we still want the trade. It is important to not want it so badly that you chase the market. If the opening price gaps too low, we must consider passing on the trade and looking for the next setup.

Our next logical step is to set up the same trade on an intraday chart. This puts the setup under the microscope and allows us to see micro inflection points or price levels that could create minor support within our shortable range. Good traders see these inflection points as levels to scale (size) deeper into the shorts, not levels to be shaken out (whipsaw risk). Figure 4.13 reflects

FIGURE 4.13

Intraday chart of the QQQs displaying Fibonacci levels, Short Entry (SE), Protective Stop (PS), and Target (T).

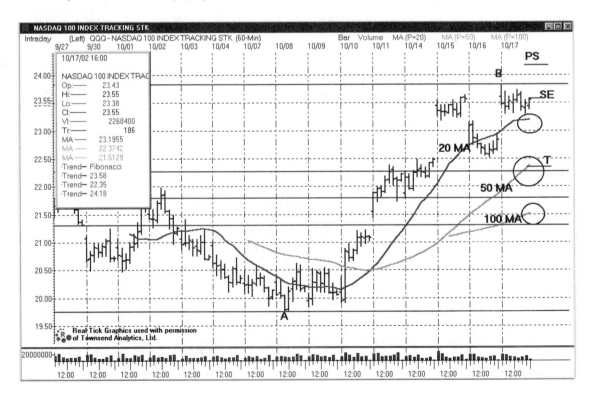

the same Fibonacci levels on a 15-day, 60-minute chart. Notice that in this case the inflection points exist at key moving averages levels; defined as the 20-, 50-, and 100-period MA, respectively. Keep in mind, moving averages on hourly bars are not the same as daily moving averages. In Chapter 5 we will explain how to see parity in moving averages on different time frames.

The SE, protective stop (PS), and T are the same as shown on Figure 4.13, but we now see that we can expect minor strength along the retracement at the 20-period MA and stronger support at the 50-period MA. We would obviously be more inclined to add to our position at any rallies at the 20-period MA, but more inclined to tighten our trailing stop at the 50-period MA. If we are fortunate enough to get a breakdown through the 50-period MA to the 100-period MA, our TS will be tightened even further, given the strength of this level (the 61.8 percent retracement relative to B). The hourly (60-minute) MAs reflect the inflection points since they are near the Fibonacci levels.

Our final view of the market can be seen intraday on the 10-minute chart as shown in Figure 4.14. This is the day trader's last stop in terms of

F I G U R E   4.14

Intraday chart of the QQQs showing the MA cluster which is an area of possible support.

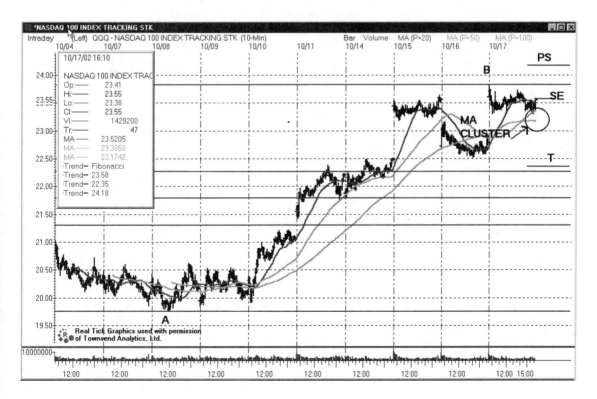

seeing the market from a technical point of view. Anything inside 10 minutes is considered too microscopic from a technical viewpoint. If looking for price levels on less than a 10 minute time frame, use the time and sales (TAS) and the Level II (LII).

In Figure 4.14, we can see on the 10-minute chart that the 20-, 50-, and 100-period MAs cluster to form short-term support for any declining market in the QQQs. Traders need to anticipate these strength levels and use them to scale into the short but also guard themselves against high-velocity rallies. The tools for precision execution that traders pay great attention to come from reading the tape from TAS and Level II. Only time and feel for the market can teach this skill. The best traders in the world acquire the skill of tape reading early on and pay close attention to it. Too many technicians ignore tape reading because they want everything in the market to be literal and consequently miss this important visceral feel. It is when traders become skilled in both technical analysis and feel for the tape that excellence is found.

Fibonacci levels in conjunction with moving averages provide a strong technical pattern that can be implemented nearly every day while trading liquid instruments such as the QQQs, SPYs, and their close cousins in the futures clan, the Nasdaq 100 E-Mini and the S&P 500 E-Mini. Even more opportunities exist when the universe is opened to the entire marketplace of listed and OTC securities. The important things in all trades are the technical setups, the risk parameters, the risk/reward relationships, and the continual observation of the tape. To end this section, let's see how the trade worked out.

In Figure 4.15 you see that we entered a trade with a 1000 lot of the QQQs and then let the trade work. The market gapped slightly lower and opened at $23.28. We made our first trade at the $23.19 level. Because of this, our target was reduced to $0.84 ($23.19 − $22.35). Our new PS was set at 20 percent of that target, or $23.36 [$23.19 + ($0.84 × 0.20)]. Our PS was not met initially and the QQQs sold off nicely. It is important to remember that this was a day trade. In this case, we set a trailing stop with $0.20 discretion when the QQQs were at $22.98. The QQQs found a low at $22.93 and rallied from there. We were stopped out at $23.14 and made $0.06. Surprise—no big winner, but we controlled risk and recognized the strength of the QQQs since they could not sell off.

Because the TS is entered with $0.20 discretion, we can only make money on the trade, reducing our risk to zero (excluding the low frictional cost of commission). On 10/21/02 we realized how strong the market was for the NDX QQQ. Once the Fibonacci level 2 on Figure 4.10 was broken at $23.81, we flipped and took a long position for a breakout play. What is very

Intraday chart of the QQQs showing the subsequent move after the trade was put on.

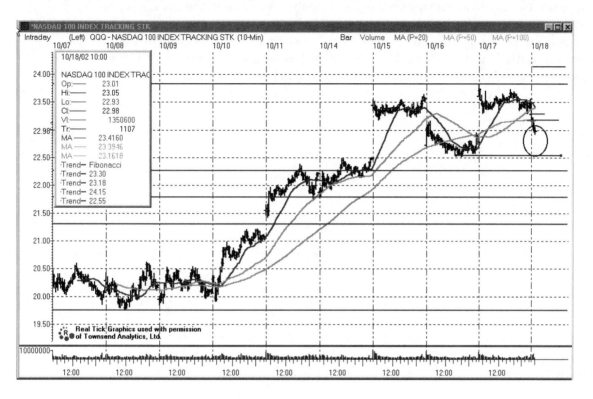

interesting is that the QQQ traded to the Fibonacci level 2 inflection point on 10/18/02 and closed at exactly $23.81! While this may seem quite coincidental, we believe market reflection has a tremendous propensity to repeat itself, especially on a short-term basis. Remember, 10/17/02, the most recent past, started the analysis, and it is no coincidence that the QQQ closed at this level on 10/18/02. The fact that the elastic low on 10/18/02 could not penetrate the elastic low on 10/17/02 told us that if the 10/17/02 and 10/18/02 elastic highs were broken we should go long and expect a high-velocity rally. Once the QQQ broke the $23.81 level, we bought the break with large size and booked over $0.45 profit. While $0.45 may not seem like a huge percentage gain, on large size it adds up quite nicely. Remember, these are short-term strategies using methods of symmetry such as Fibonacci levels. The same approach could just as easily be applied to swing trades. The important lesson is to recognize how symmetry in the market limits losses and lets profits run.

The example may have been specific to time, but the methodology is as timeless as Fibonacci himself in our opinion. Follow these principles of market symmetry and you automatically begin to see the "forest from the trees." Most traders see the market too close (micro) and suffer the inevitable whipsaw risk associated with this shallow perspective. Good trades take a top-down approach of market analysis, and this is defined as seeing the market from the broad perspective of both time and structure, also known as symmetry.

5

C H A P T E R

TECHNICAL ANALYSIS

Now that we have explored market trend, symmetry, and market structure, we can begin to apply both foundational and technical analysis. In this chapter, we apply market theory to practice. We have explored market psychology and the understanding of how it plays itself out symmetrically on the charts, as well as how these principles shape into tradable patterns.

Technical analysis is the process of seeing structure and form in the market as a reflection of crowd behavior, and we have asked our chief market technician at MarketWise, Brian Shannon, to cover this important chapter. Even if you already have a solid knowledge base in technical analysis, we think you will find this information useful.

YOUR OPINION OR YOUR MONEY

There are two traditional ways to analyze stocks. The first is called fundamental analysis, which uses cash flows, price/earnings ratios, and other formulas to try to answer the question of *why* a stock moves. The second is technical analysis, which focuses not on *why* a stock moves, but *how* and *when.* In this chapter we take the technical approach, but it is important to be aware of a third approach that few books have covered, called foundational analysis. The importance of foundational analysis draws its strength from the most neglected yet profitable market segment, the floor trader. Through this unique and original view, foundational analysis draws on raw market data of price, time, velocity, and volume to utilize the best parts of technical analysis without overcomplication. With Bill's extensive floor trading experience as a specialist, he made money by recognizing patterns in the foundational variables. Many of the same patterns are observable through today's electronic trading platforms; it was in this arena that David learned of the importance of foundational analysis. Regarding fundamentals, we want to be aware of when fundamental news may be released in order to make trades based on the market's reaction to that news rather than on our interpretation of the news.

Like it or not, when you commit capital to the stock market, you also commit your emotions to some degree. This is the downfall of most traders. It has been said that 70 percent or more of all traders lose money in the market. Why is that figure so high? What are the winning traders doing to take the money from the majority of participants? The winning traders understand that human nature repeats itself, and the same thing that motivates you to buy and sell also motivates others. Have you ever sold a stock because you just couldn't stand to see it decline further, then it turns around and makes a big move without you? Who bought that stock from you? It was probably someone who understood cycles and human nature and took advantage of your weaknesses.

WHAT IS TECHNICAL ANALYSIS?

Technical analysis (TA) is the study of market action, primarily through the use of charts, for the purpose of forecasting future movement. Technicians attempt to identify trend changes at an early stage and attempt to stay with a trend until it becomes apparent that the trend is dissipating or about to reverse. At its core, technical analysis is a science, but the actual interpretation and implementation becomes more of an art because we are individually interpreting the decisions made by other individuals. Subjectivity enters into the equation whenever human nature is involved. Nonetheless, when studied and applied to any time frame, technical analysis will allow you to form an opinion on exactly what to do (buy, sell, or nothing) in nearly every situation.

By the time you reach the end of this chapter, you should be able to look at a group of charts of companies you know nothing about on a fundamental basis and be able to recognize which stocks are worth further review for a possible trade. More importantly, you will be able to recognize the stocks that aren't worth any further consideration—freeing your time and capital to focus on opportunities that make sense.

FOUNDATIONS OF TECHNICAL ANALYSIS

Price discounts everything. This means that everything known to all participants is reflected in the current price at any given time. Stocks are bought and sold for what they are worth, and the current prices reflect all the supply and demand factors relevant to where stocks trade at any given time, regardless of fundamentals. The second foundation of TA is that *prices move in trends.* A trend once established is more likely to continue than to reverse. As we noted earlier, Sir Isaac Newton's law of motion basically states that an object in motion will continue in that direction until met with an equal or greater opposing force. Stocks, once in a definitive trend, are no exception to this rule. A stock that is moving higher will continue to do so until it moves to a level at which sellers are motivated to offer out enough stock to overwhelm the buyers, thus halting the advance.

The third foundation of TA is *history repeats itself.* As George Santayana said, "Those who forget the past are condemned to repeat it." Historical patterns reflect the collective psychology of market participants.

The final foundation of TA applies more to the art of trading than the science of chart analysis, and states that wise traders *have a backup plan.* Trading is an art, not a science, and the market will not always go along with your analysis. The market does not care what you think a stock should do—your opinion does not count. The market is always right.

THE PSYCHOLOGY OF STAGES

The four stages of the market, as shown in Figures 5.1 and 5.2, are accumulation, price markup, distribution, and decline. For simplicity, they are often referred to as stage 1 (accumulation), stage 2 (markup), stage 3 (distribution), and stage 4 (decline). These four stages are found over and over in all stocks, regardless of the time frame. One of the keys to success in the market is trading with the prevailing trend, which is why we purchase stocks in the stage 2 markup phase, sell short in the stage 4 decline phase, and avoid trendless stocks in either the stage 1 accumulation or stage 3 distribution phases.

STAGE 1: ACCUMULATION

There is a saying, "If they don't scare you out, they'll wear you out." People who ride a stock down while waiting for a rally that never materializes get tired of seeing the stock on their statements as a reminder of how stupid they were not to sell earlier. This is the point at which they sell, known as stock "moving from weak hands into strong hands," and the moment at which accumulation begins.

The volume and moving averages are of little value while a stock is in the actual healing process of back-and-forth action, but they can provide us with some clues as to when the stock may be ready to advance to the markup phase. Volume begins to portend the action to come when there is a period of sustained high volume after the stock has been trading in narrow sideways action for at least three to six months. This pickup in volume is a sign that the buyers are getting more aggressive and depleting the supply available at these levels. They are setting the stock up for the markup phase and higher prices. Moving averages are of little value while a market is not trending, and the price will usually stay below the longer-term MAs during the healing process. If looking at shorter-term MAs, you will notice a lot of back and forth action as the stock price rises above and falls back below these moving averages. This is called whipsaw action, and it can give numerous

FIGURE 5.1

Here is a view of a daily chart with the four stages. This time we have moving averages overlaid on price to aid trend clarification.

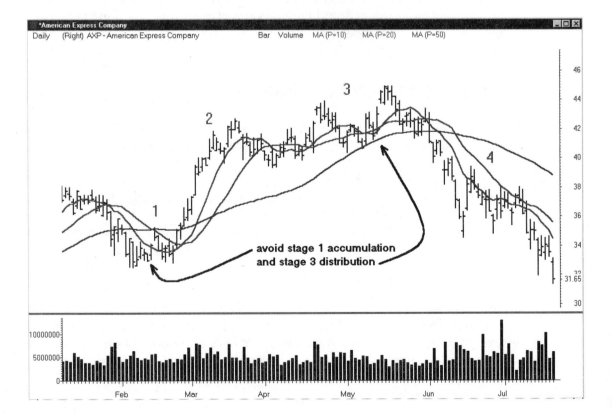

conflicting signals. After the stock has recovered for some time, the longer-term MAs will slowly begin to flatten out, but until they do so, any attempt at a rally by the stock should not be trusted, as it will usually be met by sources of longer-term supply. One sign that many market participants look for to confirm that a bottom has been put in place is a crossover of the 50-day MA up through the 200-day MA. If you are looking to trade this type of setup, it is important to remember not to trade based only on the moving averages. If we are truly to have the odds in our favor, we want to see some confirmation from price, volume, and some of the other indicators we will study as part of our foundational analysis.

STAGE 2: MARKUP

The stage 2 markup phase of a stock's cycle is the most exciting time and, if you are a bull, where the real money is made. The markup phase begins as the accumulation phase ends, and there are many characteristics on a chart to indicate that this phase has begun. First, we need to realize what happens as the stock transitions from the accumulative to the markup phase. Those participants who are bullish on the stock's future have presumably built large positions at lower levels while the risks were higher, and they are now ready to participate in the upside as the stock advances. The methodical buying at lower prices has taken half of the supply/demand equation out of the picture at the lower prices; the demand has reduced supply. These buyers have taken up the supply from the previous large owners while the stock was in the accumulation phase, and anyone still long the stock will now demand higher prices. The perception of what the stock is worth is beginning to change, and in the markets, perception *is* reality.

Stocks sometimes enter this new uptrend on some bullish fundamental development, but usually the fundamental picture isn't very favorable at the beginning of stage 2. This is a good time to point out that the market is a discounting mechanism and assigns value based on future events, not on what may be happening today or what happened yesterday. The market is an anticipator, and those with the greatest knowledge of a situation will buy today based on what they believe a company's fundamental position will be in the future. You will often hear it said that the stock tells its own story first. Following the psychology of the market is what technical analysis is all about, and the flow of money reflects the market psychology. This understanding is what gives you an advantage over those who wait for good news to buy a stock or bad news to sell. A good way to remember this is that news and surprises tend to follow the trend, not initiate it.

Besides the obvious upward movement in price, probably the biggest clue that a stock is ready to make a sustained move higher is the increased volume. As a stock breaks out past resistance, many of the people who missed buying the stock as it was consolidating at lower levels feel that they must own the stock now; amateurs jumping into the stock with market orders. The markup phase is driven in large part by greed, and this increased volume is the first sign of it. The overwhelming demand for the stock causes prices to break out violently on a huge surge in volume. At this point, the move upward has begun. As a trader, you should take notice of high-volume breakouts from a stage 1 base, because they often signal the beginning of a sustainable move higher. By recognizing the beginning of a trend, we can find many opportunities to trade the stock from the long side, since a trend once established is more likely to continue than it is to reverse. After a breakout, prices will be above all relevant moving averages on the weekly and daily charts. Ideally we want to see the faster MAs leading the slower MAs higher. If any significant consolidation in price occurs, the strength of the new trend can easily be measured by which MAs hold as prices continue higher.

There are many patterns that repeat themselves while a stock is trending higher. These are called *continuation patterns.* Continuation patterns allow traders to buy a stock with confidence, because the downside risk is easy to identify and there is objective data about where the stock is likely to move. See Figure 5.2.

STAGE 3: DISTRIBUTION

The third stage of a stock's life is distribution, which is the reverse process of accumulation. It is a period when the stock's advance from the markup phase begins to slow. The stock will usually trade in a sideways action for some time, leaving it vulnerable to an inevitable decline. This phase is created when the previously bullish accumulators of the stock begin to dispose of their large positions and their selling gradually equals buying pressure that leaves the stock trading in a range. Again, it is said to be a period where the stock moves from strong hands to weak hands.

It is often said, "All the good news comes out at the top." Analysts are extremely bullish at this point, practically competing to have the highest price targets and being on record with strong buys. At the same time, the company offering the stock is usually floating more stock to the public through a secondary offering in an attempt to raise additional operating cash while the stock is temporarily overvalued. It is also common to see stock splits at this stage of the cycle.

Some of the best clues that a stock is undergoing distribution come from volume and moving averages. As the stock nears the end of the markup phase, the buyers are not as confident because the stock is extended in price. The stock has already moved up from any significant level of support and the

F I G U R E   5.2

Entering a stage 2 stock at the right time is done by buying as the stock breaks out past resistance levels or as it pulls back to support. We never know when a trend will end, which is why we always need to use stops.

risks on the downside are greater. Although the risk of a stock correcting from these levels is increased, it will often make short-lived moves higher in price; however, these moves will also be lower on volume. The lower volume is due to a lower level of buyer confidence, as well as the fact that those who are long the stock are looking to ride it up as long as possible and therefore are unwilling to offer any meaningful supply. At this point, the stock is ripe for a correction; the fruit is ready to fall from the tree.

One of the best signs that a stock is undergoing distribution is that prices moves back and forth above and below the moving averages, defining the choppy action in this phase. See Figure 5.3. This whipsaw action between the stock price and the various moving averages represents indecision and disagreement as to the value of the stock. This action is the opposite of the accumulation phase, and the stock shows the same characteristics as a stage 1, with the key difference being that a stage 3 top occurs after a sustained

F I G U R E   5.3

It is important to monitor a stock during a stage 3 distribution for signs of weakness. As the stock breaks down, it often leads to nice downside profits for the short seller.

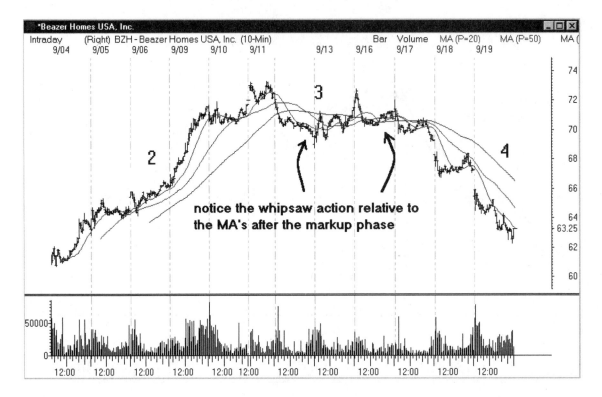

markup phase, while a stage 1 occurs after a stock has been beaten down over the course of a stage 4 decline. If the stock were still in its markup phase at this point, it would still have excited buyers pushing it higher. Instead, the action becomes a fierce battle between the bulls and the bears, with the supply of the sellers gradually overwhelming the demand of the buyers. This action puts a lid on the stock, and its action is described as acting "heavy." There are often wide swings in price on large volume during this phase, but the net result is that the stock is unchanged. Eventually the sellers of the stock who bought it at lower levels become more aggressive and overwhelm the new buyers of the stock, and the stock enters the decline phase.

STAGE 4: DECLINE

Once a top has been put in place, the final phase of the stock's cycle is the inevitable decline in prices. Aggressive sellers bring on a decline as they attempt to get out of their remaining shares before the stock gets too far away from them. The uninformed buyers that were so prevalent in the distribution phase are less anxious to purchase, and supply gradually overcomes demand. While the bulls find the advancing phase to hold the most profitable and exciting prospects for a stock, the declining stage is the environment that bears thrive in. The action of a stock in a downtrend is usually quicker and more severe than the slow and steady upward movement that most stocks follow, simply because the fear in a downtrend is much greater than the greed in an uptrend. These quicker moves lower are also very appealing to short-term traders, because they can make a lot of money in a short period of time.

A stock's decline is marked by brief rallies, usually on light volume, that are soon overwhelmed by waves of fearful selling pressure. Most rallies in this phase are short-lived and usually fall well short of the previous rally high. It is important to know that in a prolonged downtrend there will often be sudden and sharp rallies due to short-covering. When a stock starts moving higher in a downtrend, shorts will attempt to lock in gains by buying back the stock they had previously sold short. Once a short-covering rally has begun, short-term traders who are looking to make a quick profit on the long side will exaggerate the upside in order to lure in the dumb money that gets sucked into believing that the stock has made a bottom. As this sort of rally starts to stall out, it provides the best opportunities to initiate short positions. The brief rallies that give sellers a chance to reassert their strength are repeated as prices continue lower.

Another factor to take into account in a declining stock is the presence of short sellers. Any time a stock starts to show signs of weakness, there will be a new source of supply from those who wish to make a profit from the downside action by selling short. Short sellers have often been likened to vultures circling overhead waiting for their victims to perish, but the truth is that shorts merely observe a downtrend and see an opportunity to make money. Short sellers are taking big risks with their capital and are looking to make money like anyone else who is in the market. Short selling is often viewed as being riskier than trading from the long side, but if you have a forced exit strategy through the use of buy stops that are based on sound money management principles, the risks are only what you let them be.

Once the stock is clearly identified as being in the decline stage, there is no excuse for holding onto any remaining long positions. Investors can be lulled into a false sense of security and will continue holding their long stock positions because the stock is selling off on low volume. Volume can be very misleading in a stock that is declining, so price action should take precedence over trying to interpret volume in a downtrend. Prices can decline sharply on lower volume, and these declines often do severe damage to the stock simply because of a lack of buyers. Stocks are said to fall under their own weight. As the perception of value worsens, there are fewer buyers willing to take the stock from the all-too-eager sellers and losses will mount in long positions even on very light volume.

Moving averages are helpful in measuring the rate of decline in a stock because they provide a good reference for the price action. In a downtrend we typically want to see the faster MAs leading the slower MAs lower, with price action under these MAs. Moving averages also provide us with a quick and easy way to see how strong the trend is and how aggressive we should be in initiating a short sale, or how quick we should be to admit we are wrong and exit the position. It is the combination of long holders selling and the added supply from short sellers, as well as a lack of demand that creates the fast and furious downside moves in a stage 4 decline. See Figure 5.4.

Investors should never try to search for a bottom in a stock that is in a downtrend, no matter what the fundamentals are telling you. If the stock is

FIGURE 5.4

Short sales should be initiated as a stock rallies up toward resistance levels or as it breaks down through levels of support.

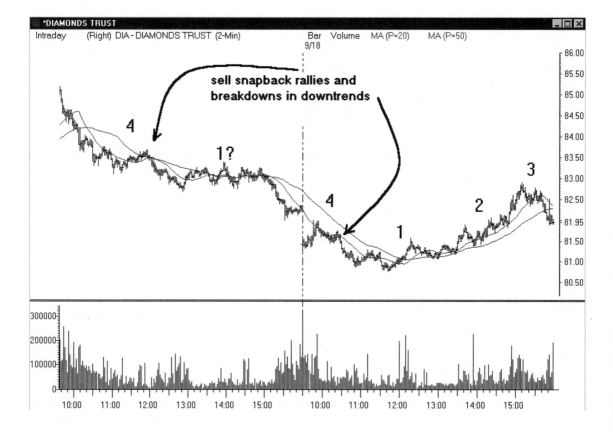

going down, it's going down for a reason and should be avoided like the plague. Interestingly enough, many stocks finally bottom out when the news stories on the stock are at their worst, hence the phrase "All bad news comes out at the bottom."

While our discussion of these four stages has been limited to examples of daily charts, it cannot be emphasized enough that these cycles are repeated over and over again on all time frames.

SUMMARY OF STAGES

Stage 1 and 3 stocks should be avoided by investors and scalped by traders. These stages are easily identified by the crossing back and forth above and below key MAs. A stage 1 or 3 stock is identified not only by current price action, but also by understanding where the stock has come from. That is, if the stock has recently experienced a prolonged upward move, it is likely that sideways action represents a distribution. Sideways action in a stock that has seen a longer-term decline is likely indicative of the accumulation process and will lead to an eventual upside.

Stage 2 stocks should be bought on breakouts past resistance levels and pullbacks to support. These stocks should never be shorted because the risk of loss is too great when fighting the larger trend. Stage 4 stocks should be sold short on breakdowns through support levels and snapback rallies to levels of resistance. Never buy stage 4 stocks!

Although there are times when going against the prevailing trend can be profitable, the odds of failure are considerably high. The only approaches that work are very specialized strategies that require absolute adherence to discipline.

TIME ANALYSIS

As first noted in Chapter 4, all stocks go through four distinct phases: accumulation, markup, distribution, and decline. Each of these phases must be viewed and accurately interpreted on all time frames, from monthly charts all the way down to one-minute charts. To make correct decisions based on phase interpretation and anticipation, it is important to make sure that the trend is the same on each of the time frames: that is, we want the long-, intermediate- and short-term trends to send us the same message. If there is inconsistency between time frames, the probability of a winning trade is diminished. When there is an alignment of trend across various time frames, the odds of a successful trade are greatly increased, provided that the proper entry is made and there is a favorable risk/reward ratio. We will explore three different time frames for each security to ensure that shorter-term trends aren't in conflict with a larger, more powerful trend on a longer-term chart. We believe this method is superior to looking solely at the shorter-term time frames to time day or swing trades. When all trends agree, the stock is a good one with which to anticipate short-term price movements.

DAILY CHARTS

We study first the daily chart (where each bar or candle represents one day of trading data), as shown in Figure 5.5. In this time frame we are looking for overall trend verification as well as important areas of support and resistance.

FIGURE   5.5

This chart shows the four stages in shares of Amazon over the course of nearly one year. Each bar represents the trading activity for one day.

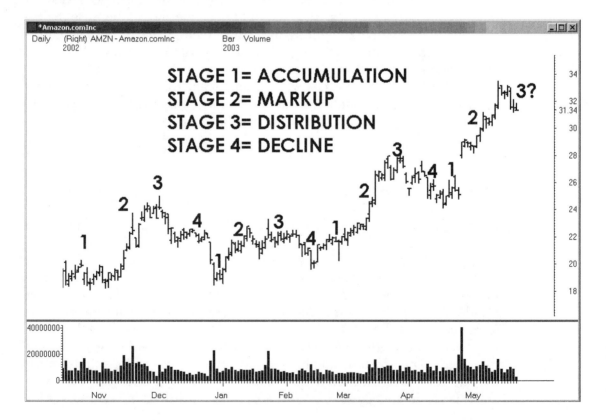

HOURLY CHARTS

The next time frame that we look at in Figure 5.6 is the hourly chart (each bar represents 60 minutes of trading). The hourly time frame is probably the most important period of time to study for swing traders, and it is where we develop our trading plan. A successful trading plan is based on a risk/reward ratio of at least one to three. A one-to-three risk/reward ratio means that for every dollar we risk, there should be a potential to make three dollars. Having a favorable risk/reward ratio allows only for occasional small losers, and by eliminating the large losses we can increase our probability of overall success. While many seasoned traders will trade one-to-one risk/reward scenarios, it is important to remember that they are seasoned pros

F I G U R E   5.6

Shares of Amazon are represented below on the hourly time frame. This time frame shows the four stages of a stock's life in the most valuable time study form for swing traders.

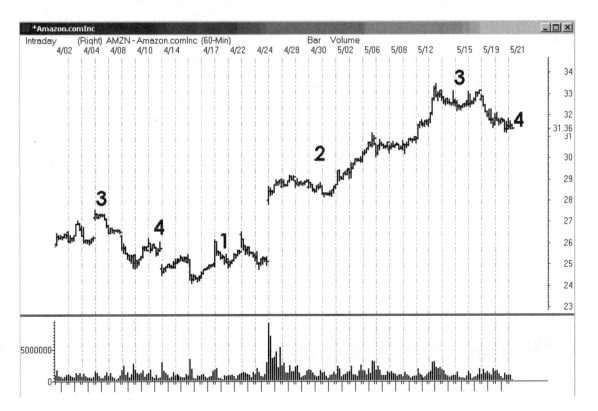

and have great discipline. The one-to-three ratio noted here applies to fledg-
ling participants.

10-MINUTE CHARTS

Taking a closer look at the action in Figure 5.7, we study the 10-minute chart
(each bar represents 10 minutes of trade data). It is in this time frame that we
become more detailed in our analysis and clearly identify short-term levels
of support and resistance.

Using these three time frames together allows for a consistent and disciplined approach to trading, one that takes advantage of shorter-term movements within the larger trends.

F I G U R E   5.7

Drilling down to an even shorter-term time frame allows us to observe how the four stages are repeated on all
securities. Your objectives for time in a trade will dictate which time frames you want to focus your cycle analysis on.

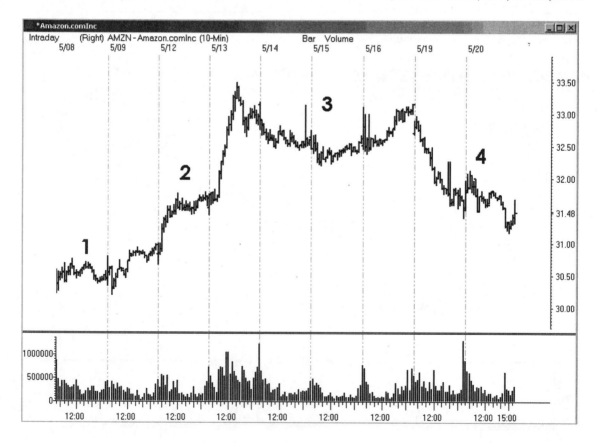

SUPPORT AND RESISTANCE

Good technicians study support and resistance and how a stock reacts to those battles. When a trend reexerts its strength in either direction, these traders are more likely to be on the right side and able to participate in the continued moves that follow. Support and resistance levels are two of the most important forces to recognize in technical analysis, because they are the foundation upon which trends are built.

Support levels are areas or price levels where buying pressure (demand) offsets selling pressure (supply) and provides a temporary halt to a decline. It is important to remember that support on a daily chart is usually a range rather than a precise number. However, on shorter-term time frames support is often a very specific price, and this is one of the biggest benefits to trading on a shorter-term time frame.

Resistance levels are areas or price levels where selling pressure (supply) offsets buying pressure (demand) and halts an advance in the price of the stock. Resistance represents the other half of the supply/demand equation. Resistance is supply. Resistance levels are like a rubber ceiling; the price is driven up to a point where sellers overwhelm buying pressure and the stock retreats. Like support, resistance on a longer-term time frame is also found in a range rather than a precise number, but it can be a specific number on shorter-term time frames. Once again, this is a benefit to traders; we can be more precise in our entries and take smaller risks. See Figure 5.8.

Now we will examine some general rules of support and resistance that will help us not only as we enter trades but also as we manage trades, once we have put our hard-earned capital at risk.

The more often support or resistance is tested, the more likely that level is to fail. After multiple assaults on the sellers of a stock at a particular resistance level, supply will eventually be overwhelmed and the stock will experience an upside breakout. Put simply, when demand exceeds supply, the stock is free to move higher. Similarly, the more times support is tested, the less likely it is to hold. When selling pressure exceeds demand at a support level, the stock will break down, create lower lows, and begin a downtrend. Breakouts and breakdowns are a popular way to trade because they often lead to dramatic short-term movement. One of the better clues that a breakout or breakdown is imminent is an increase in the frequency of the tests of support or resistance. If a stock takes eight days to reach resistance, then four days, then a day, then a few hours, a

FIGURE   5.8

While consolidating in a stage 1 accumulation or stage 3 distribution, stocks trade between levels of support and resistance until the buyers or sellers gain control of the momentum and push the stock higher or lower.

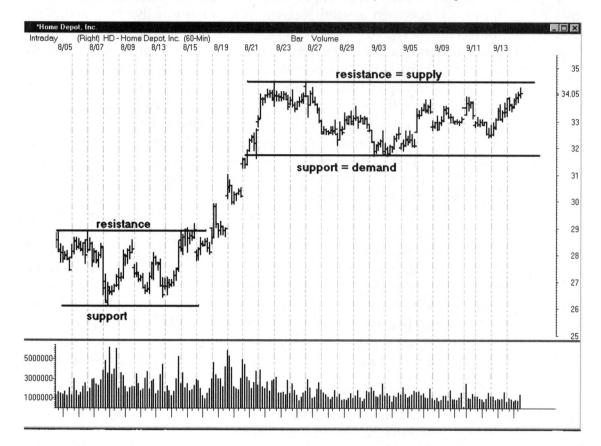

breakout is most likely right around the corner. See Figure 5.9. In this scenario three things happen:

- Buyers become more aggressive as the stock retraces its gains, as shown by successively higher lows. This impatience to purchase the stock is a sign that the buyers are gaining control of the direction.
- This desire to own stock, and the tenacity of the buyers, is evident in time as well as price. The second and subsequent tests of resistance come increasingly closer together.
- The supply available at the resistance level is reduced every time this level is tested. The aggressive supply (those who drive down

price by hitting bids) is being systematically removed; once the passive supply (the offers at the resistance level) is freed up, the stock can move higher. At this point there will typically be a big surge in volume as the last of the stock at the resistance level is bought, and then the stock will experience a breakout that sees the stock move up 5 or 10 points in a few days. Does this action paint the image of any bullish continuation patterns in your head? If you are thinking "ascending triangle," you are absolutely right.

You should interpret tests of resistance not just as easy-to-recognize patterns but also as battles between buyers and sellers. Eventually, one group will win. By understanding the participants' actions and what those actions represent, we glean insight into the psychology of the crowd responsible for

F I G U R E   5.9

Resistance at the 10.50 level was tested numerous times before the demand gradually overwhelmed the supply being offered at that level; the stock then broke out and trended higher.

producing these formations. Consistent with the fact that a trend once established is more likely to continue than reverse, the odds are greater for a price to eventually move up through supply than for it to fall further below resistance.

Once broken, support becomes resistance. See Figure 5.10. If a stock has been trading at a valid support level over a six-month period and then suddenly breaks down through that support and drops 5 points, a predictable event occurs if the stock rises back up to the resistance level. Typically, the people who bought at that prior support level will be looking to get out breaking even. Short selling as a stock returns to prior support is a favorite strategy in a weak stock, because the short sellers realize there will be a

F I G U R E   5.10

Once shares of Amgen broke down through support near $54, the stock found resistance at that level as it bounced higher. Notice how the stock stair-steps lower with support levels becoming resistance as the stock makes lower highs and lower lows.

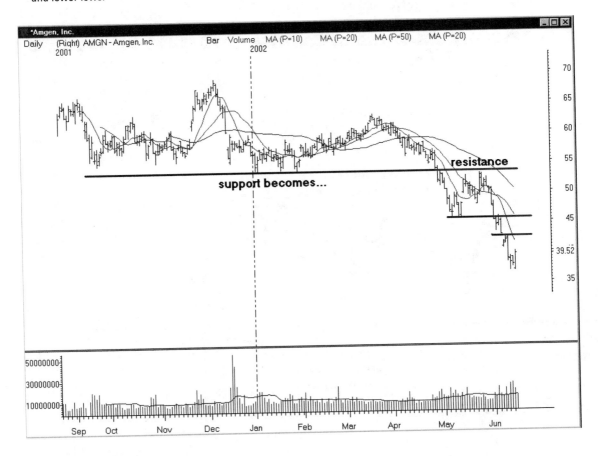

natural source of supply from an emotional crowd. That supply can help to send the stock quickly and sharply lower. The combination of prior demand becoming supply, the added supply from short sellers, and an absence of demand (because savvy market markers and specialists will not be willing to risk their money in a downtrending stock) leaves the stock vulnerable to far more serious declines. The best way to avoid being part of that emotional crowd is to have your selling decisions in place before the stock actually breaks down. Does support once broken always become resistance? Of course not, but that is the most likely outcome. If the stock moves back up past the prior resistance, it is easy to cover your short or even get long again.

Once broken, resistance becomes support. Let's say you purchase a stock at $16 and own it for six months. While you've owned the stock, it has traded within a range of $15 to $18 per share. This cycle may repeat several times, and being the smart person you are, you figure, "Why not sell it the next time it trades up to $18, and buy it back again near $15?" So you sell your stock at $18 on the next rally and then, instead of pulling back down to support at $15, the stock breaks out past resistance at $18 and makes a quick move up to $21! At this point you're probably thinking, "If it comes back down to $18, I'm buying that stock back." This sounds sensible, but remember that you are not alone in that thinking. The stock may have gotten a little bit ahead of itself in the short term by running up to $21 after the breakout, so the tendency is for the stock to start drifting back down toward $18, but it usually won't make it all the way down to that level because there are others looking to participate in what might be the beginnings of a new uptrend, thereby providing demand for the stock as it drifts lower.

What about the shorts? If you are short under $18, you're losing money. The only way to stop the losses from mounting in your account is to repurchase the stock you sold short, thus adding further demand. So as the stock pulls back toward the old level of resistance, the demand for it is building. And not only is there added demand for the stock, but there is also an absence of meaningful supply, as those long the stock recognize the shift in supply and demand and want higher prices for their stock. This is how resistance, once broken, becomes support, and that process is repeated over and over again in an uptrend. See Figure 5.11.

The longer the trend has been neutral (consolidating), the more significant the eventual breakout becomes. See Figure 5.12. It is much more significant if a stock breaks out of a trading range that lasted six months or a year than it is if the stock traded in a range for a couple of days or weeks. Longer consolidations typically lead to bigger, more sustainable moves in either direction. It makes sense that the longer a stock has traded in a stage 1 accumulation pattern, the more powerful the stage 2 uptrend will be. After a long stage 1, an uptrend can last months, or even years! Another way to measure

F I G U R E   5.11

Notice how shares of Royal Gold found support at prior resistance levels as the stock moved higher in this stage 2 uptrend.

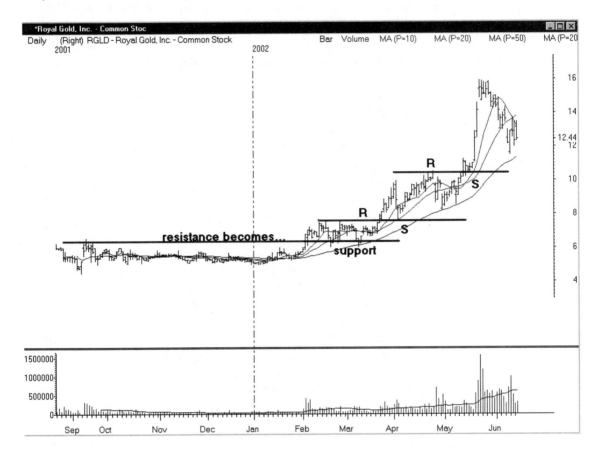

the importance of an area of support or resistance is to monitor the amount of volume that has traded in the range. Typically, the heavier the volume, the more important that area becomes. As we'll learn in the section on volume later in this chapter, large volume in a trading range can be viewed as pent-up supply or demand as a stock either breaks down through support or breaks out up through resistance.

In an uptrend, resistance levels represent a period of consolidation as buyers become less aggressive and sellers become more aggressive. Resistance levels are often areas where the stock has previously traded on a prior level of support, and old buyers are looking to get out. Typical old buyers might have acquired a stock in a trading range of $35 to $40 and then not sold

FIGURE   5.12

When shares of Hovnanian Enterprises broke out past multiyear resistance near $10, the stock began an uptrend that saw the stock advance more than 300 percent over the following two years.

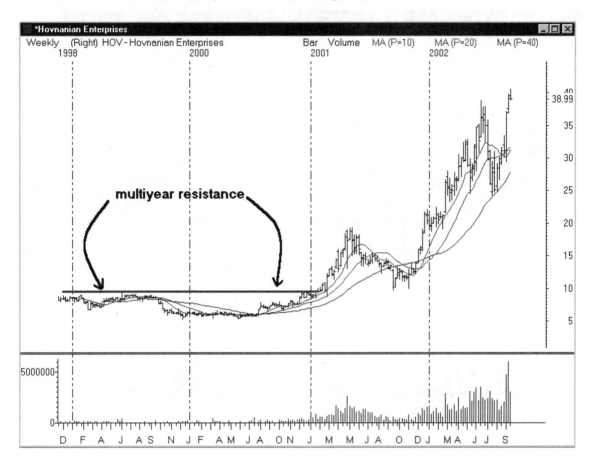

as the stock broke down through support because they thought it was a good company and would probably come back. If the stock falls even more, they become reluctant to sell until they get their money back, which might take years. If, 18 months after purchase, the stock finally makes it back to $37, most people who made the mistake of holding as the stock declined will be desperate to get their money back. Therefore, those who bought in that $35 to $40 range will sell their stock, creating a temporary resistance in an uptrend. See Figure 5.13.

Prior levels of support are good potential price targets as a stock rallies up to that anticipated source of supply. But it is very important not to assume

FIGURE   5.13

The advance in shares of Kroll Inc. slowed as the stock met a source of supply from previous buyers near the $15 level.

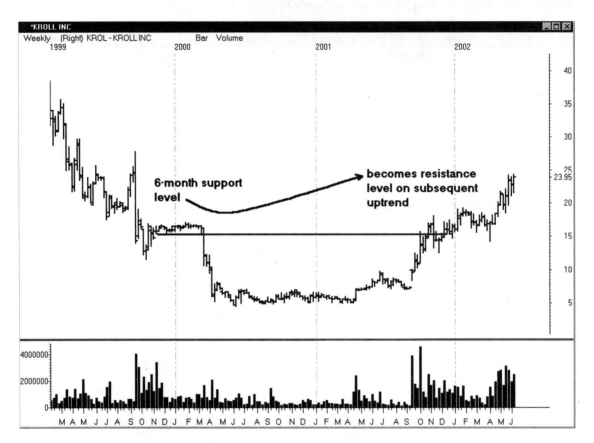

that just because a level has acted as support in the past it will become resistance now. Resistance exists only once a stock shows an inability to push past a price level. The market may not do what we expect it to do, and by holding on to a stock that is able to push past resistance levels we are in a better position to maximize our profits.

In a downtrend, support levels represent a period of stabilization in which sellers lose strength and buyers temporarily take control. These support levels often occur at a level of resistance that existed when the stock was moving higher. See Figure 5.14. Many times this brief leveling off is due to short-covering. Again, just because a stock may find temporary support does not make the stock a buy. Stocks in downtrends should be avoided from the long side completely. A better ploy is to look for an opportunity for a short

FIGURE   5.14

The sharp pullback in Proctor & Gamble was halted at a prior level of resistance near $75.

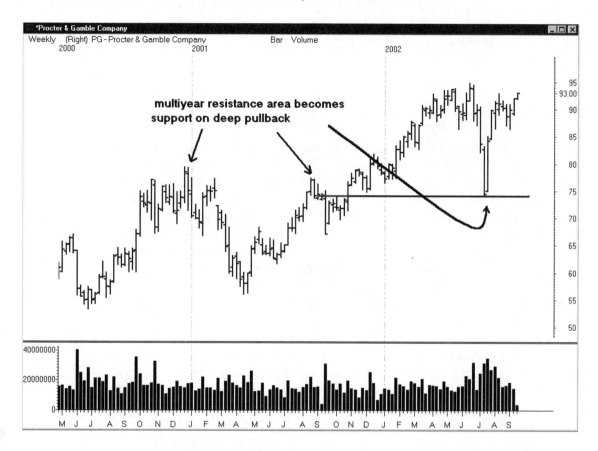

sale by monitoring how a downtrending stock acts on a rally and then looking for the short-term countertrend rally to fail.

Support and resistance levels are useful for determining if a stock is acting as expected. In an uptrend, as long as support levels are held, the stock
will usually move higher. If resistance levels contain rallies of downtrending
stocks, the stocks will usually continue lower along their path of least resistance. As you'll learn in the next section on trends, stocks do not go straight
up or down. They move in a stair-step pattern of higher highs and higher
lows in an uptrend and lower lows and lower highs in a downtrend.

There are a few more things to remember about support and resistance.
For an uptrend to continue, each successive low (support area or trough)
must be higher than the one preceding it. Each rally high (resistance) must
also be higher than the one before it.

For a downtrend to continue, each successive high (resistance area or peak) must be lower than the one preceding it. Each sell-off low must take the stock lower than the previous sell-off lows. Finally, consolidations often occur at or near round numbers (such as 10, 20, 30, 40, etc.). This is due to options strike prices and psychological motivation; people want clean numbers for their stock.

TRENDS

Our goal as traders is to take money from the market on a consistent basis, and the most important thing we can do to stack the odds in our favor is to trade with the trend. Trends are one of the foundations that technical analysis is built upon, and they should be considered the backbone of a trader's directional bias. Because trend identification is so important in making money in stock trading, we will explore how trends are created; the interrelationship of trends on different time frames, how their strength can be measured, and how we can use trends for important money management decisions. If the market is entered at the proper time, trending stocks offer the greatest probability of making larger profits and formulating intelligent levels for stop placement.

As we learned earlier, one of the foundational assumptions of technical analysis is that once a trend has been established it is more likely to continue in its original direction than to reverse. An additional assumption is that the strongest stocks will not go straight up; they tend to move in a stair-step pattern that is defined by a series of peaks and troughs. It is the direction of these highs and lows that determines the overall trend.

An uptrend, which is found in the stage 2 markup phase of a stock's cycle, is defined by a series of higher highs and higher lows. Each time a stock in an uptrend pulls back after getting ahead of itself, it finds support at a level higher than the last time it experienced profit taking. See Figure 5.15.

Think of what causes an uptrend to develop. A stock that had been trading in a longer-term accumulation pattern suddenly breaks out past resistance with a surge in volume before continuing higher for a few days and then consolidating on lighter volume or pulling back to a moving average like the 10-day MA. If those gains have consolidated for a few days, the low volume is a good clue that sellers weren't really aggressive about getting out of their positions; owners of the stock can now demand higher prices before selling. Since there wasn't a lot of supply released on the pullback, when demand picks up the stock continues higher again.

This is a good time to point out that not all corrections will occur with a pullback in price. Stocks can correct in two ways, either through price or over

F I G U R E   5.15

The diagram below shows how a stock is supposed to look in an uptrend. The uptrending stock is formed as the stock makes higher highs and higher lows; the pullbacks are what allow traders a low-risk opportunity to get long on a stock whose path of least resistance is higher.

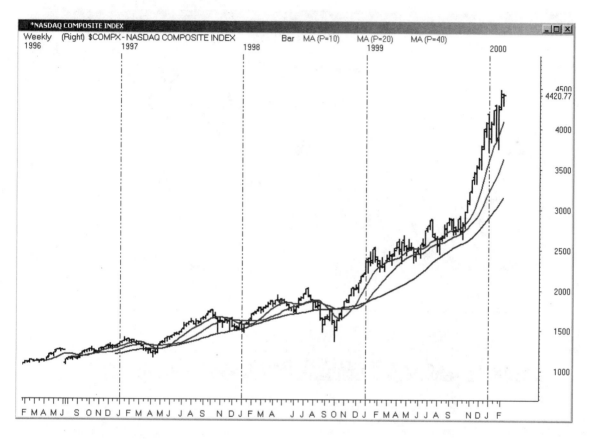

time. A correction over time is actually indicative of a stronger stock, because the stock trades sideways as buyers temporarily go on strike, hoping for a pullback to develop. Once it becomes obvious that no meaningful source of supply is being offered, buyers often become more aggressive and push the stock higher again. See Figure 5.16.

What causes a stock to violently break out of a longer-term accumulation pattern? Many times it is a fundamental development that changes people's perception as to a company's prospects. This could be a new product announcement, an earnings report, an FDA announcement, or numerous other fundamental reasons. What is most important to the technician is not the *cause*, but the *effect*. The cause is irrelevant. There is a phrase that goes,

F I G U R E   5.16

After breaking out on heavy volume, shares of Amgen traded sideways as the stock corrected over time. After the move from $42 to $47, the stock corrected by price. Notice how the resistance at $42 became support on the pullback.

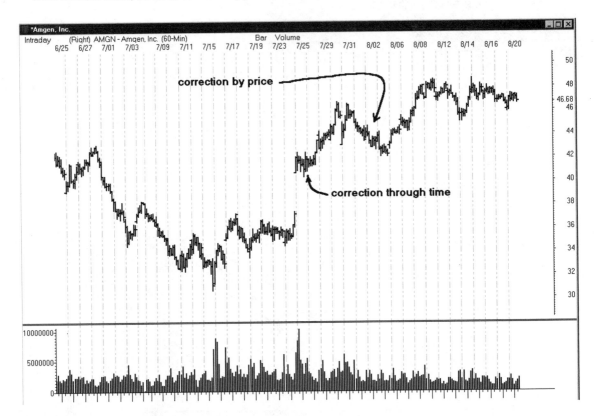

"Suspend what you believe and trade what you observe." The reason we mention this now is that many times a stock will break out without any fundamental development, even when a company's fundamentals look poor. Remember, the stock market is a discounting mechanism. Stock prices trade based on future expectations, not just on today's news. Stocks often move higher and continue in that direction long before any good news is released about a company. So why even mention fundamental analysis in a study about technical analysis? Because TA is about studying human behavior as represented on a price chart, and if we can understand the motivations of others to either buy or sell, we can use that information to our advantage in developing our trading plan. As we'll see later, how stocks act on pullbacks, most particularly their volume trends and where stocks find support in relation to moving averages and prior support and resistance levels, can help us determine the likelihood of a continuation of their trends. The key thing to remember about an uptrend is that stocks will be making a series of higher highs and higher lows.

It is important to recognize that there are trends within trends, and a longer-term trend is nothing more than the sum of shorter-term trends. For our purposes, we will be looking at stocks that are trending on a longer-term basis and then time our entry into those longer-term trends by recognizing opportunities on a shorter-term time frame. What we want to do is make sure that the short-term and longer-term trends are in alignment, allowing us to gain a statistical advantage in our trading decisions.

How many times have you purchased a stock in a healthy stage 2 up-trend on a daily chart only to have that stock decline for a few days before turning higher again? This retracement weakness can be avoided by making your buying decisions on shorter-term time frames, such as a 10-minute chart that shows 15 days of trading history. See Figure 5.17. Buying a stock that is

F I G U R E   5.17

As shares of Amazon.com move past stage 1 resistance, the stock should be purchased. In order to enter a stock at the correct time, we want to wait for the momentum to accelerate to the upside rather than buying as the stock undergoes a short-term correction.

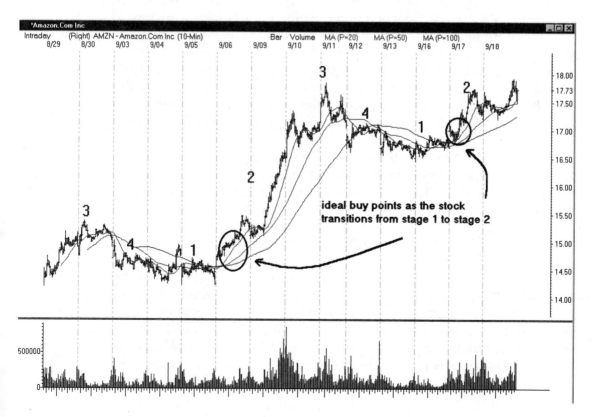

in a stage 2 uptrend is the first important step to finding a good candidate for trend continuation, but is absolutely essential to make sure that trend is confirmed on a shorter time frame. After a stock has corrected for two to five days (meaning it is now in stage 4), it will typically consolidate those gains for a day or two (a new stage 1) and then enter a new uptrend (stage 2) on the 10-minute chart. As the stock is entering stage 2 on the shortened time frame, the stock is in alignment with the longer-term, more powerful uptrend. Purchases at this point offer the greatest upside potential and they afford us an excellent point at which to enter our initial protective stop. We'll address this more fully when we deal with stops.

A downtrend is the reverse of an uptrend, and it is found in the stage 4 decline of a stock's cycle. A downtrend is defined by series of lower highs and lower lows. When a stock breaks down to new lows, the subsequent rally will take the stock up to a level that does not exceed the previous rally high. Each time sellers reassert themselves, the stock price makes a lower low. See Figure 5.18.

Now that we have a definition of a downtrend, let's understand what causes downtrends to develop and continue. Stocks in a downtrend tend to trade on emotion more than stocks in an uptrend. People become complacent when things are going well and fearful when there is uncertainty. Fortunately, with a trained eye and good instincts, a stock in a downtrend can be a very profitable time to trade from the short side. We will focus on trading the short side of the market in a downtrending stock since there is *never* a good time to be long a stock that is in a clear downtrend. After a stock has had a good run up in price, the stock will undergo distribution as holders from lower levels sell to the latecomers. The supply will eventually overwhelm the demand for the stock, leading to a breakdown in prices.

Many times a stock will break down from a stage 3 distribution to a stage 4 decline on a negative news item, but that's not always the case. It is actually very common to have an absence of negative news associated with the stock until much later. Remember that institutions with large positions are trying to stay ahead of the market, and as a result expend tremendous amounts of capital on research to out-game conventional thinking on Wall Street.

One interesting characteristic of downtrends is that stocks will often break down on light volume. This situation leaves investors with a false sense of security, because after a stock breaks important support (at $50 for this example) and drops down to maybe $45, analysts will come out and reiterate their opinion to buy the stock. The stock will then rally up toward $50, which was support but has now become resistance. Astute traders will use this rally to get out of their long stock and perhaps contribute additional supply by

FIGURE 5.18

The downtrending stock shows a series of sell-offs followed by rallies that fall short of the prior high. It is these rallies that give short sellers the opportunity to profit in a declining stock.

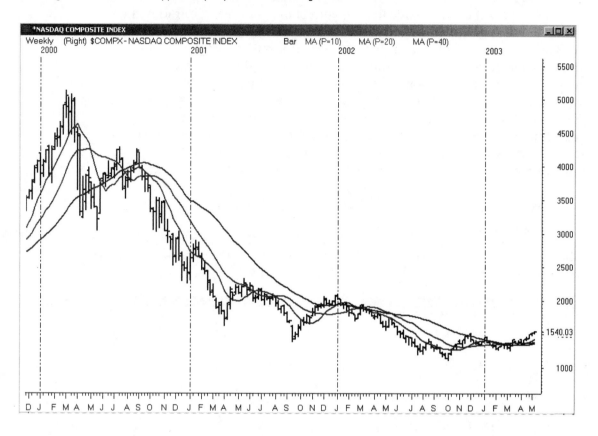

getting short. As supply once again overwhelms demand, the stock drops, often very quickly because the previous buyers of the stock are starting to lose conviction. This creates an absence of demand with an increase in supply—look out below! The subsequent drop might take the stock down below the previous low of $45 to $42 or $43 before shorts cover their positions, traders come in looking for a bounce, or there is another analyst upgrade. Whatever the cause, the buying will temporarily overtake selling pressure and the stock will rally again on low volume. This time, however, it may only make it up to the prior low at $45 (once again, support has become resistance). Once the stock is trending lower, the MAs should be following the stock down. As we'll see in the section on MAs later in this chapter, they will often act as resistance levels for the stock. The process of lower lows and lower highs is continually repeated in a downtrend, and traders should be on the lookout for opportunities to sell these stocks short on low volume rallies with protective stops just above resistance levels. The keys to spotting a stock in a downtrend are *lower lows* and *lower highs*. See Figure 5.19.

Once again, it is imperative to time your short sales using intraday time frames to ensure that you are selling at the optimal point for maximum profit and minimum risk. Just as we saw with uptrending stocks, stocks in a downtrend will not typically drop all at once (though sometimes you get lucky with a short and it happens). Instead, the series of lower highs and lower lows, when magnified on an intraday 10-minute, 15-day chart, shows all four stages of a stock's life cycle within the shortened time frames. The ideal time to enter a stock that is in a stage 4 decline on the daily chart is when the stock is transitioning from stage 3 to stage 4 on the intraday time frame as well. An entry into a short position at this point allows us to limit

FIGURE   5.19

Shares of Mercury Interactive were in a steady downtrend, showing lower highs and lower lows as the stock trended below the declining moving averages.

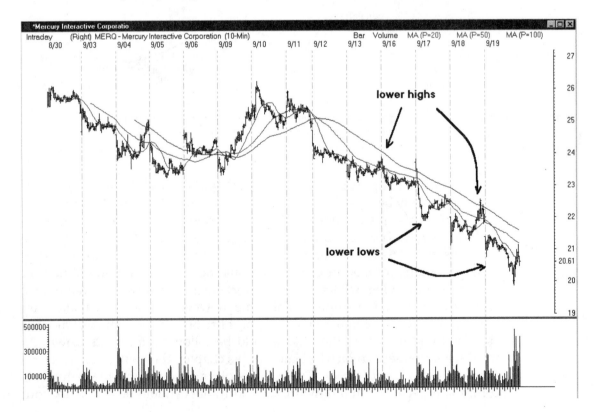

our risk while able to retain the potential to participate in multipoint drops. There's nothing more satisfying in trading than to enter a short at the beginning of a new downtrend and then watch the stock collapse as fear builds among the public.

VOLUME

At the bottom of the chart below, volume is added horizontally with a separate vertical scale. This measures the amount of shares traded on the time frame represented by the price bar directly above. This vertical scale is usually measured in thousands, except on stocks that aren't as actively traded (thin stocks) or intraday charts, where not as much volume trades as we look at shorter increments of time.

Volume is a measurement of how powerful a trend either is or could potentially become. It reveals the conviction level of buyers or how hurriedly sellers want out of their positions. Essentially, volume measures emotional levels and extremes in buying and selling. By monitoring the level of volume traded in addition to price action, we can measure the forces of supply and demand at work in the market and gain valuable insight into what is likely to happen in the future. As we have shown with many of the other indicators, volume is most valuable as a measurement of human emotions and as a means of understanding the collective thought process of the market. Volume allows us a reasonable opportunity to anticipate a stock's next move based upon the emotion of the market. As we will see, volume can be used to confirm whether a trend should be trusted and even help in money management decisions such as how many shares to invest in any given situation. If a stock is less liquid, meaning it trades fewer shares, you generally want to trade fewer shares yourself to compensate for the difficulty you may encounter in closing out your position. By adjusting share size to the liquidity of a stock, you are also lowering your overall risk exposure.

Volume is relative. Big volume for one stock may be considered light volume for another. It is important to know the number of shares available for trading publicly, also called *the float*. The float for a stock may be as little as a few hundred thousand shares or as many as a billion shares. The float represents half of the equation that forms the law of supply and demand; it is the total supply available for trading. The smaller the supply of something is (that is, shares outstanding), the less demand it will take to create an imbalance that moves prices higher or lower. There are many sources that give the figures for average daily volume. On RealTick®, you can actually overlay a moving average on the volume for a quick reference as to how large the volume may be in a stock for whatever your chosen time frame. See Figure 5.20.

F I G U R E   5.20

The moving average over volume shows the relationship between the daily volume and the average of the past 20 days.

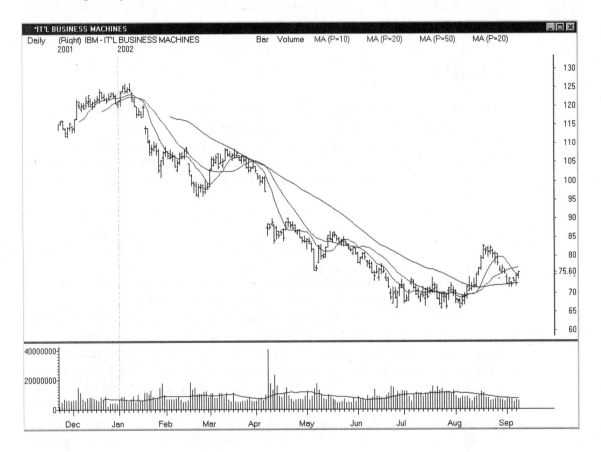

You will often hear traders identify a stock as being "thin" or "thick." This simply refers to the average amount of volume a stock would normally trade on a daily basis, and the price swings associated with the trading activity. Although there is no real formula to determine whether a stock is traded thickly or thinly, a general rule is that thick stocks trade more than one million shares per day and thinly traded stocks less than one million shares per day. See Figures 5.21 and 5.22.

There is a trade-off in the decision to trade thick or thin stocks. Generally speaking, thick stocks are slower-moving and trade more shares at each price level before the stock makes any price movement, but thick stocks also offer plenty of liquidity in case you need to get out of a position in a hurry. These stocks make great day trading candidates, especially for newer traders

F I G U R E   5.21

Microsoft is what is known as a thick stock: Its average daily volume is approximately 45 million shares.

whose execution skills may not be fully developed yet. Thin stocks will have sharp gyrations in price on shorter time frames with fewer shares trading. If your entry is wrong in a thin stock, you run the risk that there won't be sufficient liquidity to exit the position until the damage has already been done. Thin stocks are typically much more difficult to trade because of the lack of liquidity, and are best left to those with greater trading experience. If you decide to trade thin stocks, share volume should be adjusted lower to compensate for the increased risks. By monitoring how much a stock trades in relation to its average daily volume, we can often detect accumulation or distribution of a stock before the price actually starts moving, and then gauge by its volume pattern whether the stock is trading within a healthy trend.

F I G U R E   5.22

Only about 50,000 shares of Charles River Assoc. change hands each day, making it a thinly traded stock.

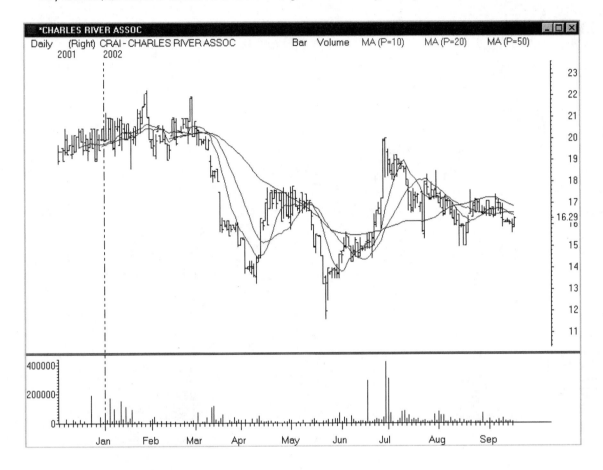

GENERAL RULES ON INTERPRETING VOLUME

1. Volume Is Often the Catalyst for Larger Movements in Price

For instance, suppose a stock trading in a longer-term stage 1 accumulation pattern suddenly breaks out past resistance on heavy volume, meaning heavy *relative* to how much volume is traded on average during the accumulation process. Typically, heavy volume means that a stock trades a minimum of two times its average daily volume. This heavy volume breakout reflects a change in perception as to what the stock is worth. While the stock was be-

F I G U R E   5.23

After shares of Intermune Inc. broke out past a stage 1 accumulation pattern on extremely heavy volume, the stock moved nearly 45 percent higher in just a couple of weeks.

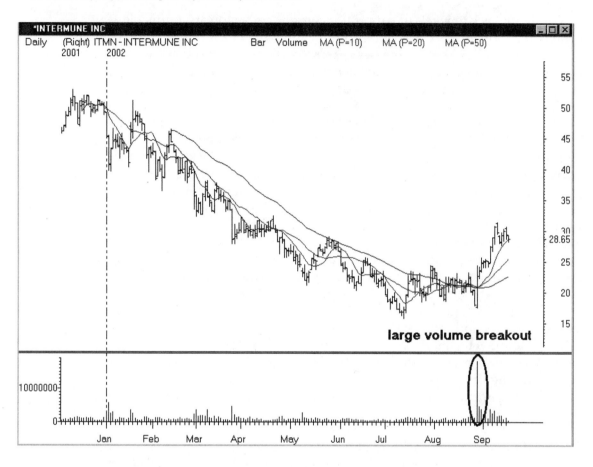

ing accumulated, there was very little interest in owning it, as shown by its sideways action. After the stock breaks out, it attracts the attention of many other participants interested in capitalizing on what is looking like a fresh uptrend. A point to note here is that the larger the volume of a breakout, the greater the likelihood that there will be a continuation in that direction and the greater the chance for a larger subsequent move. Heavy volume breakouts often provide the fuel for new uptrends. See Figure 5.23. Volume on the downside move is also important to monitor, but as we'll see, the beginning of a downtrend is often deceptive to those who are studying volume.

2. Volume Should Expand in the Direction of Existing Price Trend and Diminish on Retracements

An uptrending stock, if behaving properly, should rise on heavy volume days and pull back to levels of support or consolidate on lower-volume days relative to its advance. An early breakout may initially be viewed with skepticism, but the volume soon increases as more participants start to believe the move is one that may last. Those late to the developing trend often encounter heavy resistance on the third to fifth day of an advance as the stock is met with a larger source of institutional supply.

It is a common mistake for newer traders to buy late; they get aboard a trend as it is near the end of its short-term move. Have you heard the phrase "Confidence moves in direct proportion to the price of the stock"? All too often, newer traders wait for too many confirming indicators before entering a trend, even though these indicators are notoriously late in confirming the trend. Trading stocks is risky, and by the time it looks like the perfect buy it is usually too late. It is more accurate to say that the amateur traders are the ones whose confidence moves in direct proportion to price movement. Professionals are more paranoid in nature, and are usually looking for signs of a weakening trend so they can lock in a good portion of gains, even if it means selling early and leaving some money on the table. This stark contrast in outlook between amateur and professional traders is often the difference between success and failure. Professionals anticipate, while amateurs react to the price movements of the professionals and are thus too late for any decent chance of a successful outcome. Professionals truly develop their edge in trading through anticipating future behavior and having a superior money management philosophy that allows for very little tolerance of losing positions.

Strong stocks are marked up in bursts of activity, and we can gain valuable insight into the sustainability of a rally by closely watching the level of selling that comes in after such a move. If a stock encounters heavy resistance and turns lower on increased volume, the chances of a renewed upturn are lessened until the selling pressure subsides. If, however, a stock is not met with much selling pressure and prices contract on fewer shares being traded, it shows that there is a decreased amount of supply available and that people are generally bullish for the stock's future. A low-volume pullback to a level of support (prior resistance) or a rising moving average is often an excellent low-risk place to enter a stock that is in an uptrend. See Figure 5.24. When a stock retreats from highs on lighter volume than it experienced while advancing, it indicates that the sellers aren't being aggressive about exiting their position and are still bullish about the stock's prospects. A low-volume pullback also indicates that short sellers aren't offering a lot of supply because there is not a good reason for the stock to go lower.

F I G U R E   5.24

Shares of InVision Technologies, Inc. show the classic volume pattern of breaking out of a stage 1 accumulation on very heavy volume and then continuing their advance on heavy volume relative to the low-volume pullbacks.

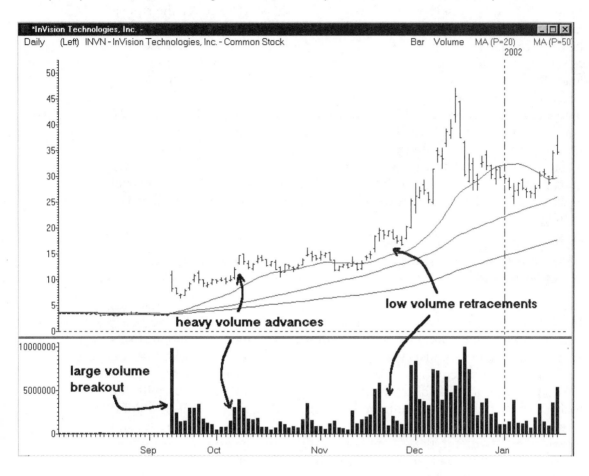

In the case of a stock in a downtrend, an initial breakdown from stage 3 to stage 4 often occurs on light volume. The low-volume breakdown occurs because of the participants who have made the mistake of confusing what might be a good company with a good stock and are reluctant to sell. In other words, they are in denial about the breakdown the stock is experiencing. A low-volume breakdown will eventually find heavier volume as fear builds among long holders of the stock and they sell in a panic. Once the stock has clearly broken support and experiences a breakdown accompanied by increasing volume, subsequent rallies should be monitored closely for signs of failure in order to sell the stock short. After a breakdown that may last three to five days, the stock will find a short-term support level from which to rally higher. This rally will typically occur on volume that is light relative to the volume it sold off on. These low-volume rallies occur after the stock gets ahead of itself on the downside, shorts start to cover their positions, and bargain hunters step in to take advantage of what they believe are cheap prices. Do not be one of these buyers! More often than not, these buyers will desperately be trying sell their positions on the next drive lower. Instead, this is the time to monitor the short-term stage 2 rallies on intraday time frames for signs of a transition to a stage 3 distribution and then to a stage 4 decline. As the stock finds renewed selling pressure on the intraday time frame, the short-term trend becomes aligned with the longer-term trend, resulting in a higher probability of continued selling pressure. The advantage to using short-term charts in conjunction with longer-term trends is that we can capture a move just as it is beginning, and always have a low risk level to place stops in the event that we are wrong and the stock rallies instead of declining.

3. Volume in an Uptrend Is Easier to Interpret Than Volume in a Downtrend

Once stocks start to decline they will usually do so without a really identifiable volume pattern, making interpreting the volume subjective. This is not to say that we cannot gain insight by monitoring volume levels when stocks are trending lower; it's just not always as nice and neat as stocks that are moving higher, particularly at the beginning of downtrends. Often stocks will be in clearly identifiable downtrends but participants will stay with the stocks because they are declining on low volume. See Figure 5.25. That kind of reasoning is a mistake that has cost traders and investors fortunes. If a stock is in a downtrend, there's only one thing to do—get out! Or, of course, you could short the stock and participate in the downside profitability. The reason that stocks will often decline on lower volume than they rose on is an absence of demand for the stocks at each level on the way down. If there are no buyers for a security that is being offered, sellers will become more aggressive and sell bids, driving the stock lower. Again, the most basic rules of supply and demand rule the market. When stocks are trending lower, most rational people will sense that these stocks are headed down and stand aside in hopes of making purchases at lower prices. Fortunately, there are some participants who will still believe a company is good, even though the stock may not be. Why fortunately? Because without these uninformed buyers, stocks would come down even faster than they already do, and without their upticks we might not be able to initiate short positions in order to participate in the downside profits.

F I G U R E   5.25

The decline in Tyco International Ltd. began on light volume, but as the fear built, volume picked up dramatically. You can clearly see the high volume on the drives lower followed by lighter-volume rallies.

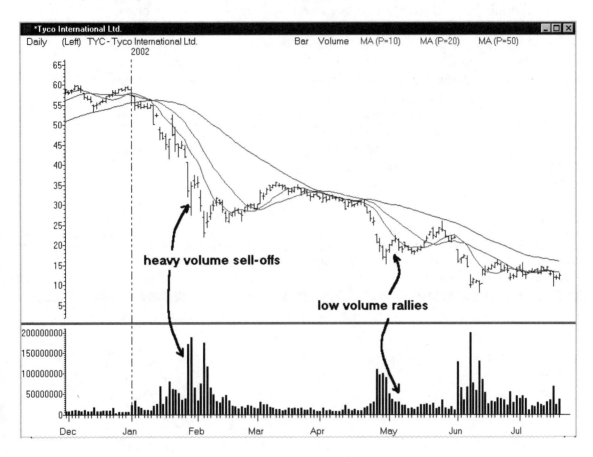

4. Volume Often Precedes Price

Understanding institutional trading decisions helps explain this concept. Think of a large mutual fund that does research on a stock and decides to initiate a meaningful position in the stock. To a fund, a meaningful position may be 1 million shares or even 10 million shares. Obviously, you as an individual trader can't just go and buy that much stock all at once, and even if you could, you would have to wonder what the seller knows. In order to accumulate such a large position, an institutional broker will first contact various large holders of the stock before buying large blocks of stock, perhaps 100,000 to 500,000 shares at a time until the fund has bought up a large portion (70 to 80 pecent) of the order.

Buying the stock in negotiated large-block transactions allows the institution to buy up a large portion of its anticipated position without moving the price higher. This type of volume shows up on a chart as being unusually heavy and should be paid attention to, because what happens next can be exciting. In order to complete the position, the fund will enter the market and buy up whatever stock is being offered, thus driving prices higher. This is to the advantage of the institution: Since they want to attract attention to the stock by showing upside action with volume, their position reaps an immediate profit. They are dealing from a position of strength at this point, so others who see the action in the stock will come in and help move the price higher. Many times, a significant move is likely to follow, as the buying institution has taken a sizable amount of supply out of the equation. Therefore, volume often precedes a price increase.

FIGURE   5.26

Big volume without further upside progress equals distribution. Traders should be alert for unusual volume after a stock has experienced a short-term move, a situation that suggests a potential reversal.

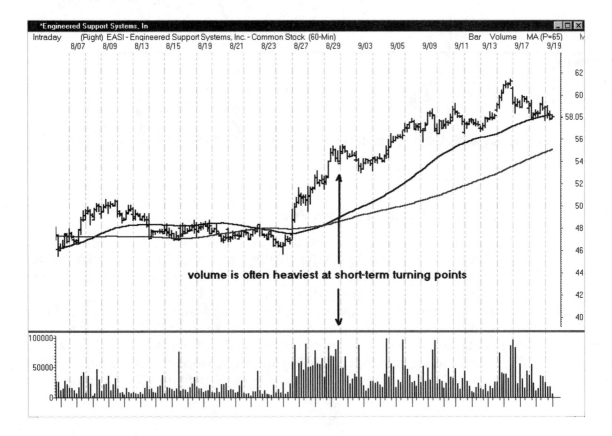

5. Volume Peaks at Turning Points

For a stock that is in an uptrend, there is often initial skepticism that the rally will last, and many participants stand aside waiting for more volume or some other indicator to confirm the strength. When the larger volume occurs, it creates a mini buying frenzy that lasts a couple of days until a larger holder decides to take advantage of the strength in the stock and offers out a larger number of shares. This supply acts as a braking mechanism to the upward momentum and creates a distribution area on intraday time frames, leaving the stock vulnerable to a pullback. Simply stated, large volume without further upside appreciation equals distribution. See Figure 5.26.

As we learned, volume tends to get heavier as fear sets in during stage 4 declines. Volume finally peaks when large buyers come in and buy up the

F I G U R E   5.27

Heavy volume without further downside equals accumulation. It is common for short-term reversals of downtrends to come just after stocks experience a fearful sell-off, as the sources of supply become exhausted.

supply being offered, thereby halting the decline. This heavy volume accumulation paves the way for short-term movements higher. An interesting observation is that heavy volume will often occur when companies report bad news. This should not come as a surprise, because we know that news follows the trend and those who sell short in anticipation of bad news then attempt to lock in profits as the news comes out. Remember the phrase for shorts, "Buy when you can, not when you have to." This simply means that when the news is known to all participants, who is left to sell? Therefore, absorbing supply by covering shorts makes sense. Large volume without further downside progress indicates accumulation, and it leaves stocks in a position from which to rally in the short term. See Figure 5.27.

MOVING AVERAGES

Moving averages are one of the most versatile and widely used of all technical indicators. Because of their ease of construction and the fact that moving averages can be so readily tested, they are the backbone for most mechanical trend-following systems. Moving averages are also the basis for many other popular oscillators and indicators. *The moving average* is a trend-following device that smoothes out price data, which makes the underlying trend easier to recognize and its strength easier to determine. It is known as a *lagging indicator* because it uses data that has already occurred. Moving averages give us a good reference point from which to easily determine the strength of a stock relative to the trend.

Construction of a simple moving average (the variety that is most commonly used and that we will refer to in this material) is calculated by adding the closing prices of the period being studied and dividing the total by the number of periods being studied. On each successive day, the data for the new day is added to the total after the first day is dropped off (thus giving it its moving property) and again divided by the number of days for which the study is being calculated. Because moving averages represent the smoothed trends of the markets or securities they are following, it makes sense that rising MAs represent rising trends and declining MAs represent downtrends.

If a security tracks along a faster moving average (one that is calculated using fewer and more recent price data points), it can be concluded that there is a more powerful trend than if it were following a slower-moving average calculated with more price points and including older data. The tracking of shorter-term MAs tells us there is a greater sense of urgency to own certain stocks and that there is a more powerful trend present than if the stocks were following longer-term MAs.

The *exponential moving average* is another popular type of moving average that some traders prefer to use, because it assigns a greater weighting to

the most recent data in its calculation, but we have seen no advantage to using it over the simple MA (see Chapter 6).

USING THE MOVING AVERAGES

As with any indicator, moving averages should not be used on a stand-alone
basis for making decisions as to when to buy or sell a stock. It is when moving averages, volume, price patterns, and other indicators are viewed together as pieces of a puzzle that we can identify the trends that other traders
and investors are creating. This helps us predict the future action of those
participants based on the behavioral patterns represented on the chart. We always strive to find low-risk ideas with decent profit potential offering
higher-than-average odds of a favorable outcome, because finding these situations puts us at a statistical advantage in attaining success in trading.
Viewing these pieces as a whole puts us closer to achieving that goal on a
consistent basis. Since moving averages are a trend-following device, they
are often criticized as having no predictive value. This criticism is actually
one of the best reasons to use moving averages—they clearly identify trends
as they occur.

How many times have you heard "The trend is your friend"? One of the
most common ways investors and traders use the moving average is to place
trailing stop orders just under the moving average as stocks progress in an
uptrend. The reason for placing a stop under a rising moving average is that
it is thought that as long as the price remains above its significant moving averages, it is bullish; no change has taken place in the basic trend. Placing
stops in this way allows us to stay long in the stock while it trends strongly.
More simply put, it lets profits run and cuts losses short—the most basic
trading goal. While placing trailing stops under a rising moving average will
not ever get us out of a position at a top (because of the moving average's lagging nature), placing stops under a rising moving average does help us capture larger portions of trends and gets us into cash when positions start to
lose their upward momentum. See Figure 5.28.

In the case of a short sale, trailing buy stop orders are placed just above
a declining moving average. A declining moving average confirms the downtrend, and as long as the stock remains below the MA, that trend is considered to be intact. See Figure 5.29.

Using a moving average is one way that traders and investors can
clearly identify a place to take action and exit their long and short positions.
By having a plan of action in place, these traders are way ahead of most
participants in the market. This advantage comes from knowing, in advance, how they will respond to changing prices, freeing them from relying
on an emotional decision when it is time to exit the trade. Once again,
emotions are every trader's biggest enemy, and anything that can be done to

F I G U R E   5.28

Shares of Agnico-Eagle Mines Ltd. held nicely above the rising 20-day moving average, which allowed intermediate-term traders to capture most of the upward movement.

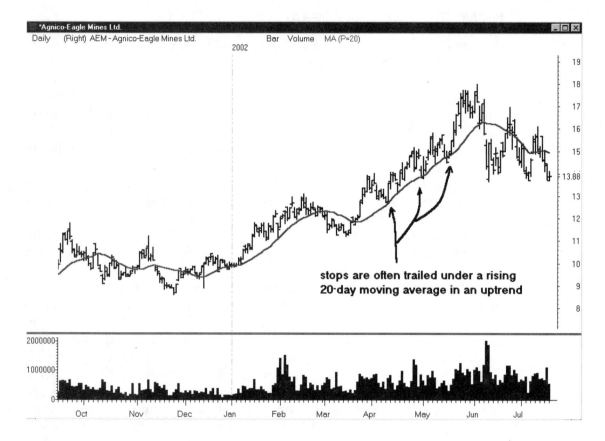

remove emotion from the trading or investing equation increases the likelihood of a profitable outcome.

Another common moving average strategy is to watch for crossovers of a shorter-term and longer-term moving average. *A crossover* is a method that uses two or more moving averages: a short-term (10-day) MA and one that represents a longer-term trend (often a 20-day). The 10-day moving average is considered faster, because it takes less data into its calculation and it follows price action closer than the slower MA, which considers more data in its calculation. A crossover system buys when the faster 10-day moving average crosses up through the slower 20-day moving average and sells as the 10-day MA crosses down through the slower 20-day MA. See Figure 5.30.

F I G U R E   5.29

For almost the whole decline from $35 to $10, shares of Siebel Systems stayed below the declining 20-day moving average.

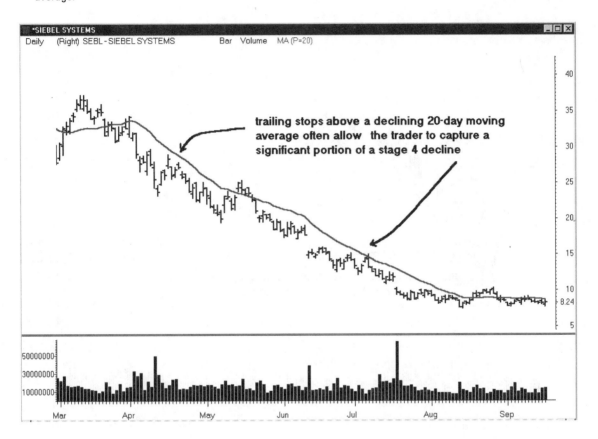

A bullish crossover will typically be found after the stock has experienced a sell-off and the stock begins to move higher again (a stock that is entering a stage 2 uptrend, regardless of the time frame being studied). In this case, once the shorter-term trend has exceeded the longer-term trend, prices can continue higher because the trends confirm each other. When we add a third moving average, like a 50-day MA, a bullish crossover will occur when the 10-day MA pierces a 20-day MA and the 20-day MA is above the 50-day MA. What this really represents is agreement among market participants about the trend of the stock. Agreement among the trends of the short-term (10-day MA), intermediate-term (20-day MA), and longer-term (50-day MA) trends shows that the path of least resistance is consistent among various participants, whose decisions to buy and sell are keyed off of these MAs. A

F I G U R E   5.30

Shares of the Nasdaq 100 Trust showed some nice reversals of trend, confirmed by the faster 10-day moving average through the longer-term 20-day moving average.

bearish crossover will usually be found as the stock is heading from a distributional stage 3 top into a stage 4 decline, regardless of the time frame being studied.

VARIOUS MARKET FORCES USE MAs DIFFERENTLY

There are three major groups of participants in the market, each helping to create trends that are important to their objectives.

The first group consists of the shortest-term participants (day traders and swing traders, as well as market makers and specialists). To this group of short-term traders the trends of interest on the daily chart are best represented by the 10-day MA (short-term trend), the 20-day MA (intermediate-term trend), and the 50-day MA (long-term trend). Day traders will want to make decisions on shorter-term time frames but at the same time be mindful not to fight a longer-term trend on the daily chart. While the swing traders' overall directional bias is usually established on the daily chart by comparing the price actions of the 10- and 20-day MAs, it is on 10-minute charts that the decisions to enter a longer-term trend are made. On a chart that shows 15 days' worth of trading utilizing 10-minute bars, the trends are best represented by the 20-period (short-term), 50-period (intermediate-term), and 100-period (long-term) moving averages.

The second group of influential participants in the market are the hedge funds. Because hedge funds have large asset bases, they do not have the same ability as day and swing traders to move in and out of stocks, so they are forced to take a longer-term look at the market. The trends that hedge funds are most interested in are represented by the 20-day (short-term), 50-day (intermediate-term), and 100-day (long-term) moving averages.

The third group of participants represents the longer-term big money that is run by mutual funds, pension funds, and large endowments. When breaking the market into short-term, intermediate-term, and longer-term trends, this group of players looks to the 50-day MA as the short-term trend, the 100-day MA as the intermediate-term trend, and the 200-day MA as an indication of the longer-term trend. The accompanying table summarizes what the various market participants consider to offer the best representation of the short-, intermediate-, and long-term trends in different time frames.

	Long-Term Mutual Funds, Pensions	Intermediate-Term Hedge Funds	Short-Term Swing Traders	Micro Day Traders
Short	50-day	20-day	10-day	20-period/10 minute
Intermediate	100-day	50-day	20-day	50-period/10 minute
Long	200-day	100-day	50-day	100-period/10 minute

Why is it important for day traders and swing traders to know this? Because if we can understand the reasons behind the major forces in the market, we can gain better insight into not only *how* stocks trade but also *why* stocks trade the way they do. Consider the example of a stock that bounces off a 50-day MA. In an uptrend, a pullback to a rising 50-day MA is often a good, low-risk place to enter a trending stock. This is because there may be swing traders buying a pullback to what they view as the long-term trend, hedge funds buying at what they believe represents the intermediate-term trend, and mutual funds adding to longer-term positions as the stock experiences a pullback to what they view as the short-term trend of the stock. Three different groups of speculators come to the same conclusion (to buy at the

F I G U R E   5.31

Various market participants make decisions using a 50-day moving average, which makes it an important level of support or resistance. Notice the severe drop in shares of General Dynamics when the 50-day moving average is violated.

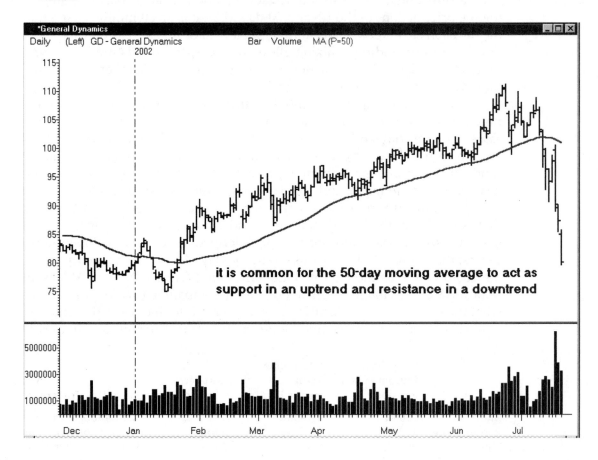

rising 50-day MA) for different reasons. Whenever there is a confluence of technical events that leads to the same conclusion, it indicates a higher probability of a successful outcome. See Figure 5.31.

GENERAL RULES FOR INTERPRETING MOVING AVERAGES

During a bullish phase (stage 2 uptrend), a stock's decline will tend to halt at or near important moving averages before regaining momentum and heading back up. While we will study the action of the daily chart here, remember that the relationship between price and the moving averages is the same on different time frames. The difference is only that we look at dissimilar moving averages on these various time frames.

After a stock has completed a stage 1 accumulation pattern and is early in an uptrend, the 10-day MA acts as support for prices on low-volume pullbacks. Remember that the stock will not automatically halt its decline there, but a halt is very common and something traders should be alert to. As the uptrend becomes more established, the 20-day MA will often be tested and then act as support on pullbacks. While it is important to recognize that pullbacks to a rising MA are often a good place for new purchases, traders need to be looking for other confirmations that it is a low-risk area to buy.

One of the best clues to the quality of a pullback is the corresponding volume. As we learned in our discussion of volume, one sign of a normal pullback (one that makes for lower-risk purchases) is low volume relative to the volume on an advance as the stock comes back to a level of support. As an uptrend matures, the pullbacks will typically become deeper and the stock may find support at the 50- or 100-day MA. It is important to recognize which MA offers support for the stock, because from this knowledge we can gain valuable insight as to the likelihood of a further trend extension. As an uptrend gets more mature it tends to experience successively deeper pullbacks in price. These pullbacks find support at different moving averages as various participants (day traders, swing traders, hedge funds, and mutual funds) decide to support a stock on weakness. It can be inferred that a stock that is early in an uptrend will find support at shorter-term moving averages because the demand is greater early on; as the trend matures and buyers are less motivated in their purchases, the stock will find support near longer-term MAs. This rule is helpful in determining how far along a stock is in its trend and where the risks of a reversal might be greater. See Figure 5.32.

You are probably wondering why a moving average would act as support. The most logical explanation is that history repeats itself. By that we mean that traders have been conditioned to look at MAs as support levels, so that when a stock reaches a support level a sort of self-fulfilling prophesy ensues. Enough people are buying so that their demand is what actually provides support for prices. As we have learned, buying by various groups of participants and the maturity of a trend are what determine which MAs will provide support for an uptrending stock.

During a bearish phase, stocks will often rally up to or near an important moving average before heading back down. Just as rising moving averages offer support in an uptrend, declining MAs often act as resistance levels in a downtrend. Consider a stock in the distribution phase, which is marked by the stock moving above and below the MAs. The stock breaks down and enters the decline phase. While the stock declines it will typically be below

F I G U R E   5.32

Shares of Cisco Systems, Inc. found support along the rising moving averages as the stock was in an uptrend and resistance along the declining moving averages in the downtrend. Notice how the longer-term moving averages are tested as the trend becomes mature; this is often a good warning sign that the trend is near its end.

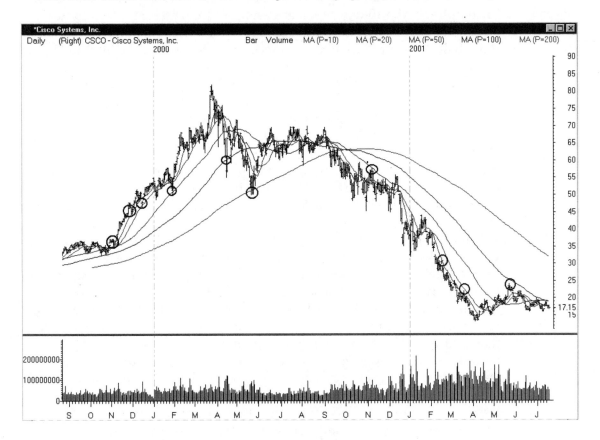

all of the important moving averages. As we know, stocks don't usually drop straight down; they trend lower with a series of lower highs and lower lows. The short-lived rallies in a downtrend often come up to one of the declining MAs. The reasons MAs might offer resistance are analogous to why they act as support in an uptrend. Because traders think that MAs act as resistance, they will offer out stock or defer the decision to make a new purchase. This action repeated by many participants serves to offer supply that acts as resistance for the stock. See Figure 5.33.

F I G U R E   5.33

As Microsoft Corp trended lower, it was turned lower first by the declining 10-day moving average, next by further resistance at the 20-day moving average, and then finally by the 50-day moving average, which acted as resistance for the stock on two separate declines.

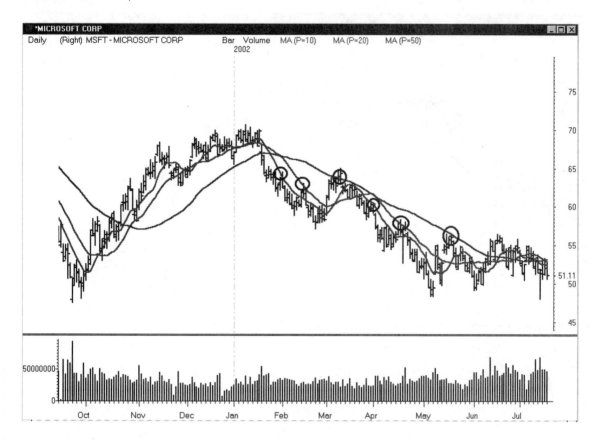

Because they follow trends, moving averages perform poorly in sideways markets. While a stock is in the stage 1 or stage 3, MAs tend to be of little value to traders for determining when to enter the stock. Ironically, that lack of information is actually the value of MAs during sideways periods. When we see a stock crossing above and below the moving averages, it represents indecision as to what the trend should be among different participants and that sends us a very clear signal: Stay away from this stock until there is evidence of a developing or established trend! See Figure 5.34. It bears repeating that traders should avoid stocks in either of these phases, because moves are not typically sustained and the stock will cross back and

F I G U R E   5.34

Notice the way Best Buy Company, Inc. crossed above and below the moving averages during the stage 3 distribution. Once this whipsaw is recognized, traders can quickly move on to a stock that is trending.

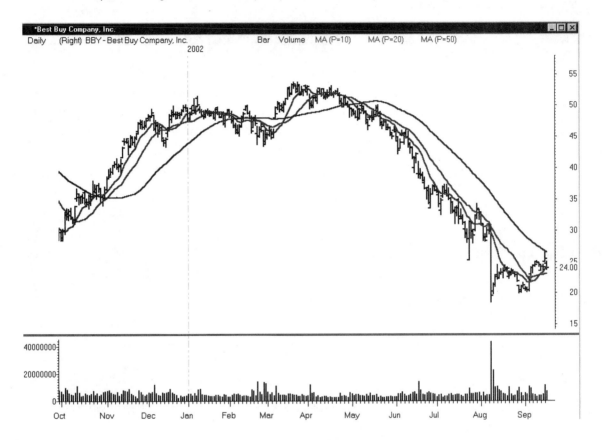

forth above and below the MAs until the volatility is wrung out of the stock. It is important to monitor these stocks for signs of a breakout or breakdown, because this action is typically followed by a large trending move. Moving averages can give us clues as to when stocks might be ready to break out of an accumulation phase. Before a stock enters a new uptrend, we want to see the MAs all flatten out, meaning they should have stopped declining and gradually turn higher, starting with the shortest-term MAs and followed by the longer-term MAs. The MAs, along with volume and certain patterns, can combine to help us enter a trend when it is brand-new and has the biggest profit potential.

It is considered bullish when all significant moving averages are moving higher, with the faster MAs above the slower ones. As we know, the moving averages considered relevant to various participants on a daily chart are the 10-, 20-, 50-, 100-, and 200-day MAs. When all of these MAs are heading higher and the 10-day MA is above the 20-day MA, the 20-day MA is above the 50-day MA, the 50-day MA is above the 100-day MA and so on, the short-, intermediate-, and longer-term trends all confirm strength in the market. It would be less bullish if the 10- and 20-day MAs were moving higher while the 50-, 100-, and 200-day MAs were still trending lower. In situations where the 10- and 20-day MAs are rising and the longer-term MAs declining, good opportunities for shorter-term traders may exist; however, because the longer-term MAs are still trending lower, we know that the primary trend remains lower and that it probably is not a good time to be buying stocks for longer holding periods. This is why as short-term traders we focus on the shorter-term (10-, 20-, and 50-period) moving averages on a daily chart.

It is considered bearish when all significant MAs are trending lower, with the faster MAs below the slower ones. In reverse of the previous example, when the 10-day MA is below the 20-day MA, which is in turn below the declining 50-, 100-, and 200-day MAs, it is easy to see that this is a stock that is in a sustained downtrend. If, however, the stock is below the declining 10- and 20-day MAs but still above the 50-, 100-, and 200-day MAs, it is possible that the stock is just correcting from a short-term overbought situation and can now reassert its strength.

Stocks and market averages will usually deviate only so far above or below a moving average before a turn in the opposite direction is imminent. For example, the Dow Jones Industrial is considered overextended if the average is trading 10 percent above its 200-day moving average. This is a way of saying that the market has gotten ahead of itself and a pullback should not be unexpected to relieve the overbought situation.

What does this mean for us? Simply put, the risk level of new purchases is greater when the market has experienced a significant move. Does that mean we shouldn't make new purchases because the market is a certain percent above a key MA? No, it just means that there is a risk that the stock will move against us, and we should compensate for that risk by taking smaller positions or by being particularly diligent about using stop orders.

We generally want to trade in the direction of the moving averages, with the 10-, 20-, 50-, and 100-periods being most helpful. The trend is your friend, and there is no easier way to see the direction of the trend than by monitoring how a stock behaves in relation to these key MAs. Because we want to buy strong stocks on pullbacks and sell short weak stocks on rallies, we need to be sure we are trading in the direction of the trend, and on a daily chart the 10-, 20-, and 50-day MAs represent the trend. You might be wondering, "What if the MAs are sending mixed signals and not giving an obvious confirmation of the trend?" If it isn't obvious, stay away. There are more than

5,000 stocks trading on U.S. exchanges. Find the trends that are obvious and you will save yourself a lot of frustration and probably a lot of money! One of the most important concepts to understand is that there are many traders who focus on the key MAs we have identified, and that is why those MAs tend to act as support and resistance. Much of technical analysis has merit because there are so many market participants who are technically oriented, making these indicators a self-fulfilling prophecy.

MAKING MONEY

Many traders and investors find it difficult to clearly identify trends and determine when it makes sense to enter trades at low-risk and high-probability areas. Now that we have a solid understanding of the most important concepts of technical analysis, we will explore one of our favorite setups for identifying high-profit, low-risk opportunities that have a strong likelihood for further trend continuation in the anticipated direction. This is where the rubber meets the road. This strategy uses the tools of cycles, support and resistance, trends, volume, and moving averages to formulate exactly when to enter a trend just as the momentum begins to develop after a retracement. We will look at examples from the long and short side of the market.

The goal of a swing trade is to look for a low-risk opportunity with a high reward potential, to initiate a trade in the direction of the primary trend, and then hold that stock until the stock tells us that the short-term move has exhausted itself. These kinds of trades typically last from one to five days. You might be wondering, "How is the stock going to 'tell me' when the short-term trend has exhausted itself?" The answer is quite simple, and it goes back to our previous definition of a trend. By understanding how stocks trade, we can ascertain what the likely course of action is for the stock and then use that knowledge to listen to the message of the stock. Simply put, we want to enter a longer-term trend by finding trend alignment on the shorter-term trend. Our decisions to cover the trade can become just as mechanical as our buys if we set our stops under the successively higher lows in a short-term uptrend and just above the successively lower highs in a short-term downtrend. Of course, as with any method of closing out our trades, we will not get out at the exact turning point when the trend ends, but that is not our goal. Our objective is to remain in the stock until there is a discontinuation of the short-term momentum. It is counterproductive to remain longer; once a trend has exhausted itself it will lead to either a period of sideways action or, worse, a reversal, and that does not help us in our quest for consistent profitability.

The primary trends of stocks are found by looking at the daily charts to see major levels of support and resistance, whether stocks are making higher highs and higher lows or vice versa, and volume clues of accumulation and distribution left by large institutions. As we know, the easiest way to determine trends is to look at the moving averages. On the daily time frame, the pertinent MAs are the 10-, 20-, and 50-day MAs, because they best represent the short-, intermediate-, and long-term trends of the stock. Ideally these MAs should all be heading in the same direction for trend clarification. When all of the MAs are headed in the same direction, there is agreement between the short-, intermediate-, and longer-term participants that a stock is good or should be avoided, a good short-side opportunity. By initiating trades that are in alignment with the direction of these three trends, we are putting ourselves at an advantage based on the premise of trend continuation, one of the foundations of TA. So the first step in initiating a swing trade is to make sure that we enter the trade in the direction of the primary trend. Observing where the stock is trading in relation to the key moving averages allows us to do that.

Now that we understand the MAs on the longer-term time frame, we are going to temporarily skip over the intermediate-term time frame, which uses hourly bars, and focus on the short-term time frame, which utilizes 10-minute periods of data, to understand the timing of entering a swing trade. Assuming that we are entering a trade to the long side of the market, we want to watch for a stock in a stage 2 uptrend on the daily chart and then enter that trend after the stock experiences a low-volume pullback. Such a pullback often halts at or near an up-sloping moving average. The trick to making a low-risk entry is to purchase the stock as the pullback finishes its course and the buyers gain control of the stock again, not to blindly buy the stock in the middle of the short-term correction. In other words, assuming that we magnify the daily chart by looking at 15 days' worth of data with 10-minute bars, we want to wait for the stage 4 downtrend (the pullback within the uptrend on the daily time frame) to complete, then let the stock enter a stage 1 accumulation as buyers start to regain control of the stock on this shortened time frame. Once we have determined that the stock is in a stage 1 on the 10-minute chart, we want to monitor the stock minutely to ensure that we will enter just as the stock is entering a new stage 2 uptrend in the short term.

Ideally, for longs we want to enter a stage 2 stock on the daily chart just as the intraday time frame starts to confirm a new stage 2 uptrend. Even prior to purchasing the stock we want to make note of support levels on the 10-minute time frame and then place our protective stops just under that support level as soon as we enter the trade. By knowing exactly where we will take a loss on the trade, we are freeing ourselves from making emotional decisions or continuing to hold a losing position.

The concept of entering just as the stock enters a stage 2 uptrend on the 10-minute time frame is easy enough to understand; the actual confirmation of that trend is the difficult part. This is where the moving averages can help us in timing our swing trading entries. For the 10-minute time frame, the moving averages that best represent the trends are the 20-period (short-term), the 50-period (intermediate-term), and the 100-period (long-term). These moving averages should be interpreted just as we do the 10-, 20-, and 50-period MAs on the daily chart. In other words, during a stage 1 accumulation the price of the stock will vacillate above and below the MAs, telling us that the stock is trending less at that time. A stage 2 stock is identified as the stock moves above the key MAs and the shorter-term MAs go above the intermediate- and longer-term MAs. See Figure 5.35.

When we have confirmation of an uptrend on the 10-minute chart, it is time to enter our trade. At our entry point the actual slope of all the MAs may not be high, but they should all be lined, with the 20-period above the 50-

FIGURE   5.35

The ideal point to buy a stock is depicted below. When the stock trades above the stage 1 high, the short-term trend is believed to be higher, which puts it in alignment with the larger trend on the daily time frame.

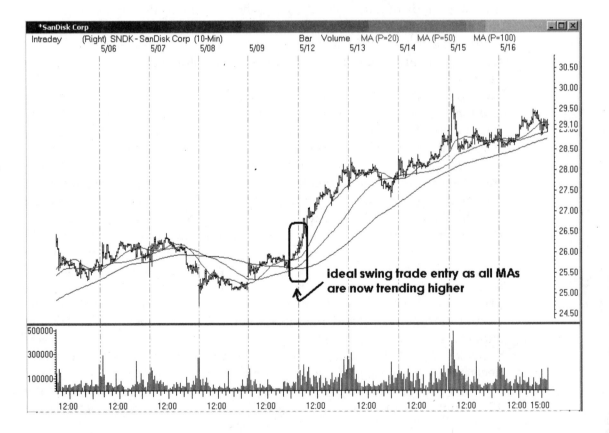

F I G U R E   5.36

These moving averages best represent the trends that swing traders are interested in. Using several time frames together creates an easy way to confirm trend alignment across different time frames.

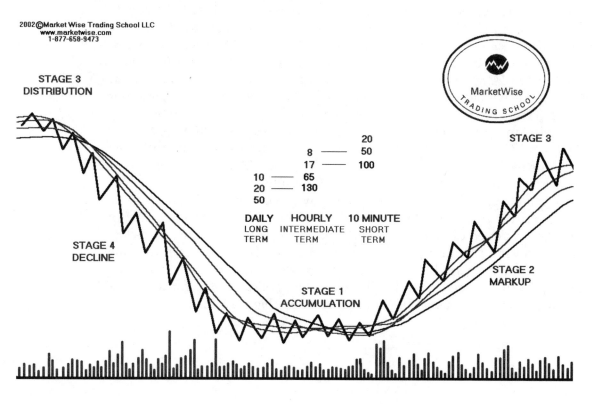

2002©Market Wise Trading School LLC
www.marketwise.com
1-877-658-9473

period and the 50-period above the 100-period. As the stock continues to make higher highs and higher lows, the less sensitive 100-period MA will get dragged higher to confirm the action of the shorter-term trends. Realistically, for this strategy to work all we really need are the daily and the 10-minute time frames, but using an hourly chart allows us to see important larger levels of support and resistance more clearly than the daily time frame can. These support and resistance levels are helpful in determining potential profit objectives for our trade and allow us to determine whether there is a risk/reward ratio that justifies entering the trade. The key MAs become important once more as we reference the intermediate-term chart, which uses 60-minute bars in its study. By the way, the ideal number of days for this time frame is 45.

When comparing price to moving averages, it is important to compare price to a constant, which is why we borrow the two most important MAs from the daily chart (the short-term 10-day and the intermediate-term 20-day MAs) and two MAs from the 10-minute time frame (the intermediate-term 50-period and the long-term 100-period). This allows us to get a blend of trends from different time frames in one concise view. In order to be able to view the 10- and 20-day MAs on an hourly chart, we need to do some simple math. The stock market is open from 9:30 a.m. to 4 p.m. EST each day, which means that each bar on a daily chart represents price action over 6.5 hours. The 10-day MA represents the average closing price for 10 of those 6.5-hour days, or the average closing price over the past 65 hours. Therefore, in order to compare price action on an hourly chart to the 10-day MA we use a 65-hour MA, and in order to see the 20-day MA we use the 130-hour MA (20 days × 6.5 hours). The two MAs that we borrow from the 10-minute time frame are the 50- and 100-period MAs. The 50-period MA actually represents the average closing price over the past 500 minutes on the 10-minute chart (50 10-minute periods). In order to come up with a corresponding MA for the hourly chart, we divide the 500 minutes by 60-minute periods and come up with 8.33, rounded off to 8. The 100-period MA represents the average closing price over 1000 minutes on the 10-minute time frame; in order to come up with a similar period for the hourly chart, we divide 1000 by 60 to come up with 16.66, rounded off to 17. These are the important MAs for our strategy, and we have discussed how to use them. See Figure 5.36.

SECTION TWO

METHODS AND TACTICS

As somewhat of a natural transition to the second section of this book, we have collected here those strategies, time horizons, techniques, and indicators that we use most. These tactics represent our most enduring strategies and are on our radar screens every day. Nonetheless, they are not pat and perfect and ready for direct integration. They represent a way to receive signals about the market. These signals are a collection of technical principles, symmetrical patterns, gut feelings, and strong philosophical opinions. All are based on raw experience. Nothing we present represents theory, only our methods of practice. It is here in this section that any "secrets" to trading we possess are offered. These are the very techniques we teach each day to our friends, customers, and families. They are the heart of the matter.

6
C H A P T E R

FAVORITE INDICATORS

The technical indicators we believe most worthy of discussion are the result of years of trading. These indicators represent both the mathematics and the principles of the tools we believe in the most. The gentleman who has captured our interest most is J. Welles Wilder, Jr. His views of the market and the systems that measure them have provided by far the best results. For a quick guide and review to evaluate historical results on your own, we suggest reading *The Encyclopedia of Technical Market Indicators* by Robert W. Colby.

RELATIVE STRENGTH INDEX

The relative strength index (RSI) was created and developed by J. Welles Wilder, Jr., and can be studied in detail in his 1978 book, *New Concepts in Technical Trading Systems.* This indicator is one of many supported on the RealTick Platform. The *RSI* is an exceptional price/momentum indicator that works by comparing exponentially smoothed price moving averages to momentum. The system relies solely on the changes in closing prices over a given time interval. Do not confuse this indicator with William O'Neal's Relative Strength Index in *Investor's Business Daily* or the traditional relative strength indicator, which is defined as the price of a given stock divided by a broad market index, such as the S&P 500, to arrive at a stock's performance relative to the general market. The RSI discussed here is strictly a technical tool.

This tool is designed to measure the velocity of trend for whatever security is being traded. The velocity of a given trend is an important measure since we believe the greater the velocity, the higher the propensity for a trend to reverse. Therefore, RSI is considered a sentiment indicator that allows traders to fade mature trends. The RSI measures velocity by dividing the exponentially smoothed moving average gains within a given time frame by the exponentially smoothed moving average losses in the same given time frame. By looking at this relational perspective, the velocity of price change can be measured. As with any moving average, the shorter the time horizon being measured is, the more sensitive the indicator will be. The common result of this is that the indicator is prone to false signals when used on short-term charts and can cause overtrading. The short-term trader should focus on RSI as a broad market tracking tool, using it on daily and hourly time frames for directional bias. We believe that 10 minute bars (and no closer) should be used for precision execution, and that time frames inside of 10 minutes are not useful.

Like other oscillators, the RSI indicates overbought conditions when readings extend above 70, and oversold below 30. The 70 and 30 levels are not literal numbers, and the relational change from these extreme levels is of greater value than the absolute number. Once again, literal trading on those extreme breaks, over 70 or below 30, would be a mistake.

We have experimented with RSI using many parameters, finding it works best using a 14-period moving average. If you look at Figure 6.1, you will see a direct correlation between price and RSI, which indicates potentially overbought or oversold conditions.

We start with a broad view by looking at the daily chart of Electronic Arts (ERTS). The RSI of ERTS dipped near 30 several times in the 100 days shown. The first oversold indication we get is in July, followed by a rally. We see another oversold indication in mid-September. The stock rallied again after the RSI put in a low near 30. At the present time, it appears that the RSI has put in a local low near 30. We have already seen the stock find support at the $62 level twice before, and the oversold indication the RSI gives us confirms our bullish sentiment. Our next step is to look a bit closer at the situation by examining an hourly chart in Figure 6.2.

On the hourly chart we can clearly see a support level at $62. The RSI has rallied off a low below 30 put in the previous day. The stock rallied above its 10-period MA, and the move below 30 on the RSI appears to be a local low. Notice how many more buy and sell signals the RSI gives on the hourly chart compared to the daily. We have verified that the stock looks good on an hourly chart as well as the daily. To zoom in even more, look at the 10-minute chart in Figure 6.3.

FIGURE 6.1

Daily chart of ERTS with RSI overlaid on it.

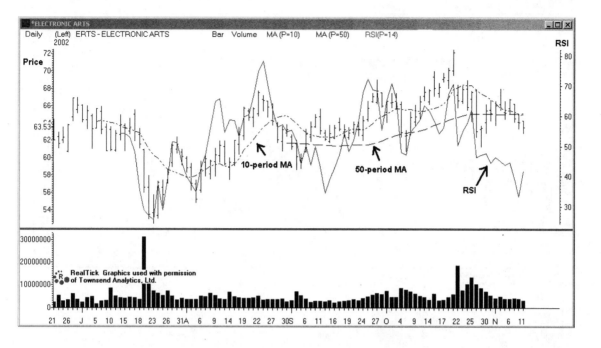

FIGURE 6.2

Hourly chart of ERTS with RSI & MAs overlaid.

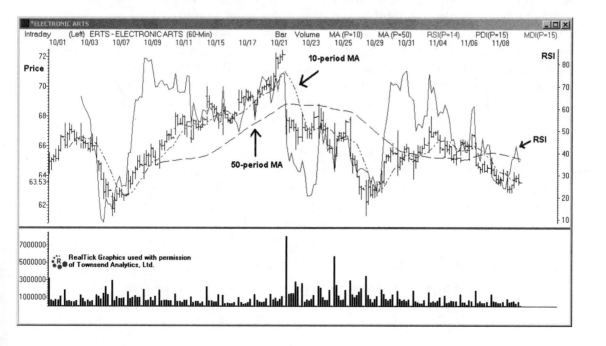

F I G U R E   6.3

A 10-minute intraday chart of ERTS.

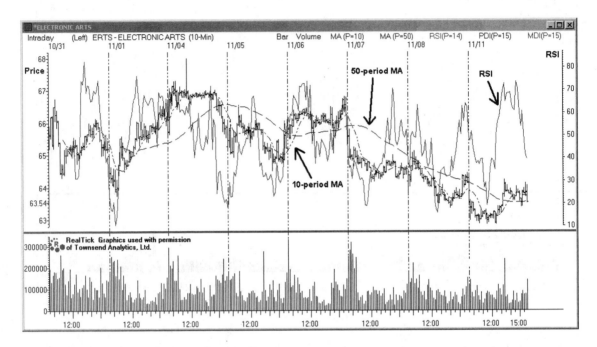

In Figure 6.3, notice that the RSI gives out numerous overbought and oversold indications. Because of this, we would not want to trade based on this chart alone. We are using this tighter view of the market to give us confirmation of the long sentiment we have from examining first the daily and then the hourly charts. The 10-minute chart shows the RSI holding above its recent low near 30 and the price is above the 50-period moving average. These three charts collectively give confirmation of our long bias. They all indicate that this is a good spot to get long. Figure 6.4 illustrates what happened the next day.

The next day, November 12th, 2002, ERTS rallied from $63.50 to the $66.50 level. The RSI is one of the strongest signals we get. While all indicators lag somewhat, we believe that RSI, when viewed on daily charts, gives you an early signal as long as the daily, hourly, and 10-minute charts confirm. In this case they did, and we traded the signal aggressively.

The formula for RSI is important to understand and is as follows:

$$RSI = 100 - 100 / (1 + RS)$$

$$\text{where } RS = \frac{\text{average of up day spreads over ``X'' number of periods}}{\text{average of down day spreads over ``X'' number of periods}}$$

FIGURE 6.4

The resultant rally in ERTS after oversold indications were given by RSI.

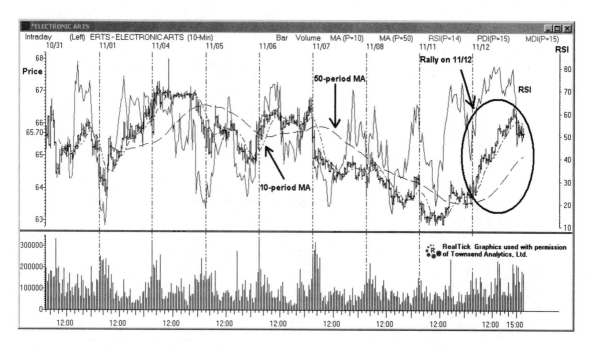

RS is calculated by first determining the number of periods you want to average (X). Let's use 14 days as the number of periods. In this case we define the numerator by the aggregated spreads of up days divided by 14, where *up days* are present-day closing prices that are greater than prior-day closing prices. The denominator is defined by the aggregated spreads of down days divided by 14, where *down days* are present-day closing prices that are less than prior-day closing prices.

Using the data in Figure 6.5, we calculated the RSI using the S&P 500 E-Mini futures contract with a 14-period (day) parameter. For November 26th, 2002 (based on the prior 14 days) we have an RSI as follows:

$$RSI = 100 - 100 / (1 + RS)$$
$$RSI = 100 - 100 / [1 + (4.98 / 5.90)]$$
$$RSI = 100 - 100 / (1 + 0.84)$$
$$RSI = 45.66$$

This RSI number can be found by following the routine shown in Figure 6.6 and continuing the calculations. Simply factor in the change from the close on 11/19 from 11/18 (2 points down).

F I G U R E   6.5

Market data for the E-Mini S&P 500 over a 14-day time frame.

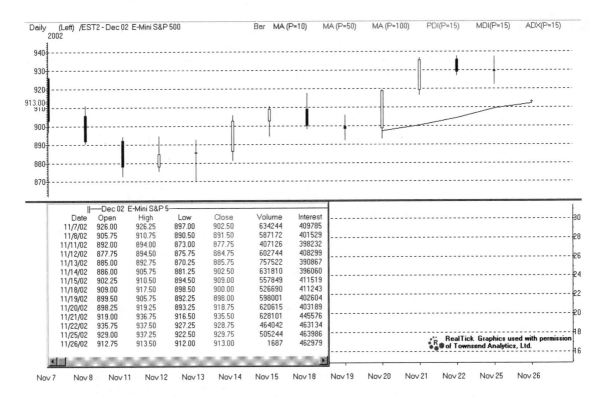

Date	Open	High	Low	Close	Volume	Interest
11/7/02	926.00	926.25	897.00	902.50	634244	409785
11/8/02	905.75	910.75	890.50	891.50	587172	401529
11/11/02	892.00	894.00	873.00	877.75	407126	398232
11/12/02	877.75	894.50	875.75	884.75	602744	408299
11/13/02	885.00	892.75	870.25	885.75	757522	390867
11/14/02	886.00	905.75	881.25	902.50	631810	396060
11/15/02	902.25	910.50	894.50	909.00	557849	411519
11/18/02	909.00	917.50	898.50	900.00	526690	411243
11/19/02	899.50	905.75	892.25	898.00	598001	402604
11/20/02	898.25	919.25	893.25	918.75	620615	403189
11/21/02	919.00	936.75	916.50	935.50	628101	445576
11/22/02	935.75	937.50	927.25	928.75	464042	463134
11/25/02	929.00	937.25	922.50	929.75	505244	463986
11/26/02	912.75	913.50	912.00	913.00	1687	462979

You may ask, why go through this math if RealTick does it for you? The answer once again is that, when you understand the math and what it measures, you understand the value of the measure. You gain trust in the indicator when you know how it works! The RSI is simply measuring the day-to-day momentum based on which market crowd won the daily battle (bulls or bears). By computing the RSI each day, you are able to see a relative change in RSI, and begin to sense the build in momentum as the RSI climbs as well as when it grows tired (which is, of course, your sell signal). This subjective feel can only be derived properly from objective data. When stocks or indices make parabolic moves in either direction, many traders see these moves with a narrow focus and expect the moves to reverse. With RSI, the math tends to smooth a dramatic price move into relative terms and better defines the impact of the move rather than just observing price. Price gaps are the best example. What may seem like a single-day parabolic move may in fact be smoothed when the periods within the study also trend with the spike or gap. For example, if the RSI is moving higher due to seven consecutive up days, and we have an explosive eighth day (GAP), the RSI will be less impacted than if the prior seven days were mixed with up and down days (stabilization or consolidation). Reviewing this calculation is invaluable. Therefore, we suggest building a spreadsheet to do just that, updating at least the major indices each day. You can build formulas into the spreadsheet quite easily, so all that needs to be done is the data input. RealTick allows this data to be cut and pasted directly into Microsoft Excel, simplifying the process. Figure 6.6 is an example of our spreadsheet, and we believe RSI is worth the effort.

FIGURE 6.6

The RSI spreadsheet for the E-Mini S&P 500.

Date	Close	Up Spreads	Down Spreads	RS + 1	100 / RS +1	RSI	
10/30/2002	889.75						
10/31/2002	885.50		4.25				
11/1/2002	898.50	13.00					
11/4/2002	907.50	9.00					
11/5/2002	914.00	6.50					
11/6/2002	925.75	11.75					
11/7/2002	902.50		23.25				
11/8/2002	891.50		11.00				
11/11/2002	877.75		13.75				
11/12/2002	884.75	7.00					
11/13/2002	885.75	1.00					
11/14/2002	902.50	16.75					
11/15/2002	909.00	6.50					
11/18/2002	900.00		9.00				
11/19/2002	898.00		2.00				
11/20/2002	918.75	20.75					
11/21/2002	935.50	16.75					
11/22/2002	928.75		6.75				
11/25/2002	929.75	1.00					
11/26/2002	913.00		16.75				
		14 avg./up	14 avg./down				
11/19/2002	898.00	5.11	4.52	2.13	46.94	53.06	
11/20/2002	918.75	6.59	4.21	2.56	39.01	60.99	
11/21/2002	935.50	6.86	4.21	2.63	38.06	61.94	Notice the climax RSI here. This is a good sign of weakness
11/22/2002	928.75	6.21	4.70	2.32	43.04	56.96	to come. As RSI consolidated between 60.99 and 61.94, we
11/25/2002	929.75	5.82	4.70	2.24	44.65	55.35	recognized the sign and shorted the contract. The next session
11/26/2002	913.00	4.98	5.89	1.85	54.19	45.81	the E-Mini sold off 16.75 index points.

ARMS INDEX

We often hear the market cliché, "Good news comes out at the top, and bad news comes out at the bottom." Perhaps no indicator measures this market fact better than the Arms Index, sometimes called the Short-Term Trading Index. The *Arms Index,* which was introduced by Richard W. Arms, Jr., measures excessive market behavior as defined by volume. When bulls are too bullish we want to short the market, and vice versa for excessive bearishness (which of course indicates a buy). Most market participants also refer to this index as the *TRIN,* meaning Trading Index. The TRIN is calculated by the following formula:

$$\text{TRIN} = \frac{\textbf{Advancing Issues / Declining Issues}}{\textbf{Advancing Volume / Declining Volume}}$$

Mathematically, the TRIN is measuring when volume, in association with advance/decline issues is in or out of step with the trend. We have stated that stocks and markets move the most on the least volume, and this is true during the momentous high-velocity stage (early in the cycle). But as volume grows we must realize that the market crowd knows the obvious. Good traders want to fade the obvious as a rule. When greed runs rampant, prices and volume reflect it by indicating the ratio of advancing to declining stocks as well as the volume associated with advancing and declining stocks. For example, if the number of advancing stocks is twice the number of declining stocks (two to one) while the volume associated with advancing stocks is also twice the volume of declining stocks (two to one), we have a par reading of 1.0, and things are as they should be during a sustainable rally.

TRIN = (2 / 1) / (2 / 1) = 1.0 par

But if the market gets ahead of itself and pushes the ratio of advancing stocks over declining stocks to the point of four to one while volume remains at two to one, we will have a volatile rally on relatively lower proportionate volume. This represents the classic bear market rally (overbought).

TRIN = (4 /1) / (2 / 1) = 2.0

In this case we have a TRIN of 2.0, but this number can mean more than one thing. For example, if we are in a bear market and decliners are leading advancers with high volume, we have another high TRIN, but a much different signal than the previous example. Let's take a look:

TRIN = (1/2) / (1/4) = 2.0

In this example, bears are firmly in control, with a high consensus of weakness as represented with high volume (1:4). In this case, TRIN acts like the classic sentiment indicator and interprets this as oversold and hence a buy signal. So the question must be raised, do we short the first bear market rally example or buy the second oversold sell-off example? The answer is that volume is part of our foundational analysis; therefore, as volume gets too far out of balance to advance/decline, we would trust the second example over the first. This exercise demonstrates why rising TRIN is bearish and ultimately reaches a state of oversold. So as both examples show, low volume rallies and oversold retracements both move TRIN higher.

When markets turn, they often exhibit a rapid rally on light volume (for example: four to one ratio divided by two to one). If the advance has strength, and the volume has yet to catch up, the market should follow through. As volume improves, TRIN will naturally retrace (4/1) / (3/1), confirming a lower risk long position. In this example, TRIN settles down to 1.33, which would indicate a volume-backed rally.

Referencing Figure 6.7, notice where the QQQs (Nasdaq 100 index tracking stock) exploded and the TRIN rallied. As long as the TRIN remained high, we still bought the QQQs. Many traders feel the move is over after rapid low volume; but these are good buying opportunities as long as more buyers subscribe to the rally (reducing TRIN).

It is a good idea to play with these ratios and ask yourself what the data is saying. Once you understand, the strategy becomes clear. Here is one more example in terms of reversal: the market rallies with a two to one ratio (advancers/decliners). Volume is four to one (advancing volume/declining volume).

$$TRIN = (2 / 1) / (4 / 1) = 0.5$$

Here we have a high-volume rally, but the rally is led by sectors and not broad-based. Additionally, the volume is too high, representing that the masses may have already responded. We often see a high-volume rally where the advancing issues are weighted and triggered by a few sectors and ultimately attract huge volume. In this case, traders want to be net short on the broader market, because the rally lacks subscription from other sectors and volume is oversubscribed. Low TRIN (not falling) should be sold for this reason. One strategy here is to simultaneously be long and short on similar or identical securities. This is akin to spreads and pairs trading, which we discuss in detail in Chapter 14. This is a lower-risk strategy that takes advantage of intermarket disparities, as in the case of semiconductors, for example, appearing strong while the broader market appears weak. In this

F I G U R E   6.7

A daily QQQ chart with TRIN overlaid. Note that some traders prefer to invert the TRIN to give more intuitive indications, but we prefer to read the raw data because it forces you to think about the indication.

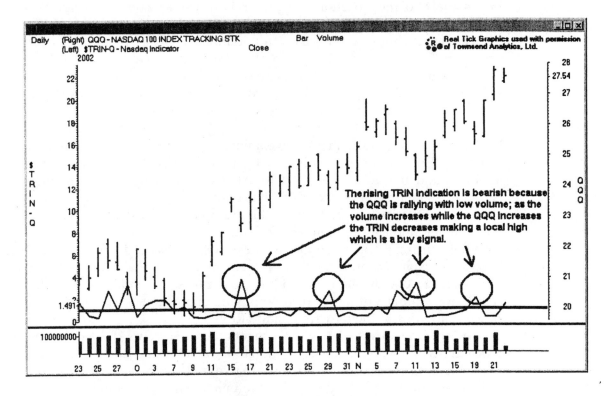

case, the TRIN is a great tool to signal the timing of such events. A spread may look like this:

- You feel the QQQ is relatively weak and the semiconductor sector is making them look more positive than the index really is.
- Because the semis are strong, you feel they need a breather. If they stall, you feel the NDX will fall harder than the semis, since the semis are relatively strong to the index.
- You want to hedge off some risk, so you play the semis long using shares of the Semiconductor Holder Trust (SMH), an AMEX product which is a trust that holds an undivided beneficial ownership in the common stock of a group of semiconductor companies. But you weight more size to the shorts on the NDX through the QQQs. You feel that if the semis follow through, what you make on your longs

will hedge off some risk on the losing shorts (assuming the NDX rallies with the semis).

The setup:

Long 800 shares of SMH @ $28.00 value = $22,400

Short 1 NQ E-Mini contract @ 1096 value = $21,920

- The trader wants to be dollar neutral on the trade, so we calculated how many shares of SMH would be needed to have nearby the same cash value as 1 NQ E-Mini contract.
- Outcome: One week later the semis leveled off and the NDX retraced because the semis were holding the index up, and as they consolidated the NDX fell. Here is the picture:

SMH current market value (CMV) = $27.50 (down $-0.50)

NQ E-Mini (CMV) = 1019 (down -77 points)

P/L Long 800 SMHs = -$400 (800 shares × -$0.50)

P/L Short 1 NQ E-Mini = $1540 (see Chapter 12 to calculate E-Mini value)

P/L Spread Net = +$1140

The spread is a good trade for those who want to trade disparity within the market. When traders recognize disparity by utilizing tools like TRIN, they can employ many methods to trade the bias. The spread is one such method. This trade was based on the belief that the Nasdaq E-Mini would fall more than the SMH (the difference between these two is called the spread). If the entire market rallied, the trader was hedged. While a loss would be incurred on the E-Mini short, an anticipated gain on the SMH long would have alpha, meaning the long position would make more than the losing short due to the relative strength relationship of the SMH over the NQ E-Mini. For example, assume the semis rallied and took the NDX with them.

SMH current market value = $29.75

NQ E-Mini (CMV) = 1175

P/L SMH = +$1400 ($1.75 × 800 shares)

NQ E-Mini = -$1080 (-54 points × $20 per point)

P/L Spread Net =+$320

The TRIN is calculated for you on the RealTick platform and is best used to measure directional strength through volume when following short-term trends and for reversals as trends run their course. The TRIN develops a broader picture for trends that extend longer than just a few minutes. It is an excellent tool because it measures the market relative to where volume intensifies. For example, if more volume is associated with advancing stocks than declining stocks, the TRIN will retrace to a level below its par value of 1.0. This would indicate a bullish scenario market condition, but also a maturing bullish trend. Therefore, traders would be best served to interpret this as potentially overbought, waiting for confirmation (retracements from resistance). Alternatively, if the volume is more intense for declining stocks, the TRIN will rise and indicate a maturing bearish condition more prone to reversal and recovery (oversold). The message here is to evaluate TRIN relative to the maturity of the existing trend. Late stage 2 (mark-up), for example, would indicate a low TRIN (high volume favoring advancing issues), and signs of an overbought market. After recognizing this situation, traders would wait for confirmation of stage 3 (distribution) before opening shorts. Conversely, late stage 4 (decline) would indicate a high TRIN (high volume favoring declining issues), and signs of an oversold market; therefore, traders would wait for confirmation during stage 1 (accumulation) before going long.

Let's take a look back at the bullish scenario in Figure 6.7, which is a daily chart of the QQQs with a Nasdaq TRIN overlay. The solid horizontal line near the bottom of the chart is TRIN 1.00, parity. Notice that, in October, TRIN began trending lower, indicating the market was strengthening. As each TRIN spike appeared we could see the signal as a sell, but as TRIN retraced, we realized the volume was catching up. We could interpret this as a maturing bullish trend and only look for shorting opportunities when TRIN tops out. While we do not have confirmation to short yet (see right edge), if price breaks support and TRIN does not retrace, shorts will be initiated.

For an example of a bearish scenario, look at Figure 6.8. This is a chart of the SPYs, with the NYSE TRIN overlaid. On this figure we see several examples where TRIN signaled overbought conditions by putting in local lows below the parity line at 1.00. These lows indicate a turn is not far away as TRIN made higher lows. When the TRIN ultimately turned positive from its lows, we looked to sell the market.

The TRIN draws its greatest value relationally, so attention should be paid to the direction it is coming from. For example, a low TRIN that begins to rally and show upside bias indicates a weakening market. (See Figure 6.9.)

As it approaches its par value of 1.0, greater indifference is setting into the market. This indicates, from a short-term perspective, that the market is reaching a potential stage 3 distribution. If our systems and pattern analysis also confirm that we are approaching stage 3 or late stage 2, we want to anticipate the short and start scaling in. If TRIN continues to rally, stage 3 is imminent and long players should be out, while short sellers should consider entering the market. This confirmation is invaluable and is best interpreted by measuring TRIN in relation to where it has been. Simply stated, a rising TRIN denotes bears gaining control while a falling TRIN denotes bulls gaining control. Therefore, TRIN is a contrarian indicator and has an inverse relationship to the market.

FIGURE   6.8

A daily chart of the SPYs with TRIN overlaid. Note the TRIN shown in our examples is raw data; when you begin using TRIN, try using a moving average of TRIN so as to reduce the number of indications.

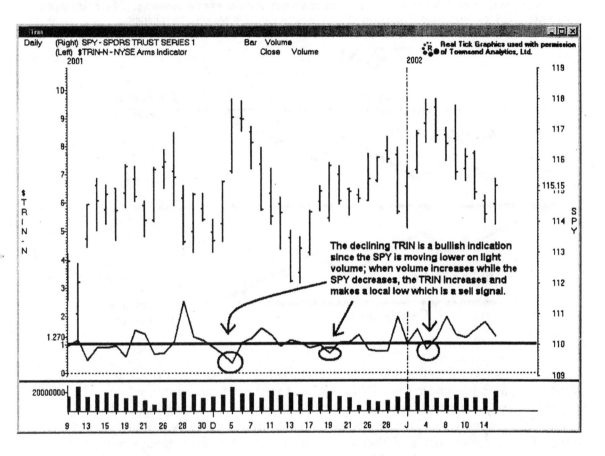

The TRIN provides a broader picture, allowing traders to see the bigger picture and avoid getting too microscopic. If the TRIN continues to rally from its lows, we will expect the markets to accelerate their losses and follow through. As the TRIN starts to top out, we can then expect levels of support to build. This would be a good time to tighten stops or even or buy back shares to cover shorts. When the TRIN is hovering at or near its par value of 1.0, its usefulness is limited. The relational change from par value is where its greatest value will be for short-term trends while reversal signals exist at extreme TRIN levels. If TRIN begins to show signs of retracement and resistance at par, the bulls are gaining strength. Conversely, if TRIN starts to rally, the bears are gaining strength relative to the prior par reading. It is not enough to say that a declining TRIN is strong or that a rising TRIN is weak or that a peak TRIN

FIGURE   6.9

TRIN is best used in relation to where it has been. TRIN that rallies from par (1.0) is gaining weakness and confirms the bearish trend. As volume grows with decliners, TRIN reaches a point of "oversold" and reversal signals to buy become apparent. Conversely, as TRIN retraces from par, it gains strength and confirms the bullish trend. As volume grows with advancers, TRIN reaches a point of "overbought" and reversal signals to sell become apparent.

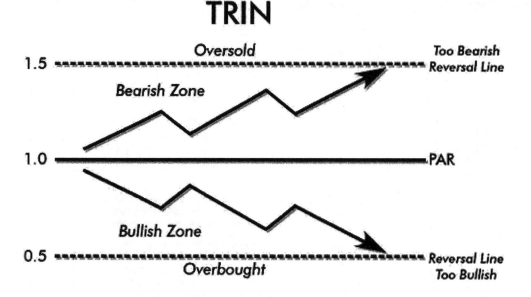

shows bears in control to the point that the market is oversold and ready to rally. It is more important to read TRIN relative to where it came from, while also looking deeper to consider what the ratio is measuring. In summary, don't read the TRIN literally. Read it relationally. And remember, the TRIN measures volume first and foremost, and therefore momentum. Therefore, always remember that as a timing tool the TRIN is excellent, but any tool can trick you.

THE DIRECTIONAL INDICATOR

The directional indicator (DI) is our favorite tool. We like it because most traders don't understand it and therefore avoid it. This fact alone preserves its value. The *directional indicator,* which was also created by J. Welles Wilder, Jr., is considered to be a trend-following tool for uncovering short-term to intermediate-term trends. We have also found it extremely useful as a short-term reversal signal. We feel that the DI is one of the strongest indicators available today because, with proper interpretation, it measures strength of trend as well as direction.

Directional movement is a way of measuring the trading range of an issue by comparing it to the trading range of the same instrument for the prior day. As the days unfold, the data can either be looked at from a simple moving average perspective or continually rolled with time into the exponential moving average, which is a weighted, nonlinear scale. Wilder's formula concentrates on the latter, using the EMA, therefore allowing the natural ebb and flow of the market to be continually updated with proper weighting. We like this approach because it allows traders to use the indicator regularly without the need to continually search and reprogram new indications into their systems.

The *directional movement indicator* (DMI) is a tool we use to highlight trends by comparing one day's trading range against the prior day's range. This system was originally developed as a longer-term trend-trading tool. As market volatility has increased, however, this system has come to work well for traders, who use it to see a broader picture of securities with the intention of finding short-term patterns within each day. With current high market volatility (in comparison to what was considered normal market volatility when this system was proposed by Wilder in *New Concepts in Technical Trading Systems* in the mid-1970s), we feel that, unlike many indicators, its value has actually grown. The mathematics of the indicator measures any extension of range above or below the previous day's range and then averages the data to highlight the rate at which any trend is moving. What is quite interesting about the DI is that it measures high to low range, not open to close as most systems do. Although it lags the market, like any averaging formula, it is particularly valuable because it measures the change day to day (period to period), helping to define whether the trend has the propensity to follow through or fade. If the averages show a continuation pattern, traders have the opportunity to take a small, reliable piece of the move. While this tool works well for a variety of time horizons, we use it to take small moves within the trend while trading with large size. We like it for reversal signals as well. Let's begin to break down the DI with the following steps:

STEP 1- DIRECTIONAL MOVEMENT

Because directional movement (which we will call *DM* for the purposes of this discussion) measures the current period's range (intraday high to low price) as compared to the prior period's range, the DM is always a positive number. The "plus" and "minus" reference with regard to DM is simply a function of the movement above or below the prior day's range. For example, if today's high to low range for AMGN is $50 to $48.50, respectively, and the prior day's range for the same security is $48.50 to $48, there is a *positive directional movement* (PDM). This occurs because the $50 high of the current day exceeds the $48.50 high of the prior day, *and* the $48.50 current day's low exceeds the $48 low of the prior day. The reverse is true for the *minus directional movement* (MDM). The real benefit of this information is as an indicator of when an issue may "spread out" and extend its range by making larger moves.

Range Spreads . . .

Rules of the Trade discusses the term "spread out" as it relates to the Level II screen as the "vertical and horizontal point spread." These are terms that we have coined in order to describe prices that "spread out" on the same side of the market (the prices among all buyers or all sellers) in the case of a vertical spread and that spread out between opposite sides of the market in the case of the horizontal spread (the prices when looking at buyers versus sellers). For example, if the spread on a Level II is $49.50 bid to $49.55 ask, the horizontal spread is $0.05. If the next best bid is $49.40, the vertical spread is $0.10; therefore, the indication of when prices or ranges spread out is valuable in both applications. When prices spread out on a Level II, volatility is upon you. When ranges spread out between trading days, volatility is either imminent or not far away. For that reason, DM is considered to be a lagging indicator as a rule, but has the ability to be coincident or even leading when monitored closely in this context. By contrast, the Level II screen in the current market environment is always a lagging indicator, but still provides tremendous value as a precision execution tool for order routing and liquidity. Once we recognize that DM is defined in terms of intraday range, and that it measures the largest portions of the current period's range that are above or below the prior day's range, we can begin to evaluate the trend. See Figures 6.10 and 6.11 for examples of plus directional movement (PDM) and minus directional movement (MDM):

F I G U R E   6.10

Plus directional movement

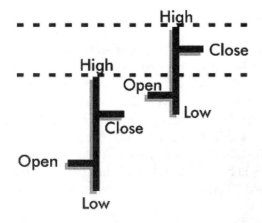

F I G U R E   6.11

Minus directional movement

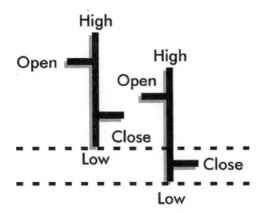

Directional movement can be measured in four ways (where TdR = to-day's range and YR = yesterday's range):

- Positive directional movement (PDM) = (TdR) > (YR)
- Minus directional movement (MDM) = (TdR) < (YR)
- Zero directional movement (ZDM): When the current range is inside the prior range, or if the range above or below the current range is equal to the current range. ZDM has no value because it shows little or no trend, and it is therefore not tradable information. See Figure 6.12 for an example.
- Gap directional movement (GDM): When markets gap, PDM and MDM take on the following definition. PDM is equal to the distance of the current period's close from the prior high. MDM is equal to the distance of the current period's close from the prior low.

F I G U R E   6.12

Zero directional movement

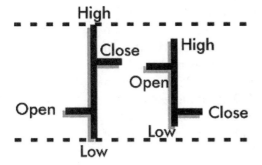

STEP 2 - TRUE RANGE

The next step in using DM is identifying the true range of the issue. In order to create a directional indicator (in step 3), you first need true range (TR). This is a complicated equation. RealTick will do the math for you, but it is still important to understand what the indicator is measuring in order to understand its value. To find TR, take the highest of the following:

- The selected period's high minus today's low
- The selected period's high minus yesterday's close
- The selected period's low minus yesterday's close

Note: TR is always positive.

STEP 3 - DIRECTIONAL INDICATOR

Once the above is known, we can calculate the directional indicator. This is the most important step to understand, since this is the indicator plotted on the chart. DIs are an expression of a given security's directional movement relative to a security's true range. When there is no directional movement (as defined earlier), the indicator is equal to zero. It is only when the formula shows directional movement that the indicator has value. The indication will be either a plus directional indicator or a minus directional indicator and they are defined as:

Plus Directional Indicator (PDI) = PDM/TR

Minus Directional Indicator (MDI) = MDM/TR

STEP 4 - SMOOTHING THE DATA

Now we smooth the data using a moving average parameter. Since the period of time being measured is always critical to indicators, the use of moving averages is of critical importance. The exponential moving average allows you to smooth the data over time by setting the period parameter in the software. By doing so, the relational value of time horizons in the trade can be pegged to the moving average you are measuring against. The default for RealTick is 14 periods, and we suggest you stay with this time horizon when considering intraday-to-swing trade horizons (one to five days). What is of particular value once the indicator is calculated and charted is that the lines have an easy-to-read direct correlation, meaning that when a PDI crosses an MDI, you have a buy signal. When an MDI crosses a PDI, you have a sell signal. Remember, a rising PDI means that we have the current period's range extending above the previous period's range. By smoothing it with a moving average, we take the volatility out of the indicator and it becomes less sensitive. So when the range is consistently stretching higher in comparison to the prior day and we smooth down the indicator with 14 days of data using the moving average, we know that when a PDI breaks above an MDI, the bulls are completely in control and the trend is higher!

The reason why a stock trends higher is not important. It only matters that it is higher and that the trend is revealed early. Once the higher directional bias becomes known, other market participants will tend to buy the issue as they recognize the breakout. This will push the issue higher, and you will have bought the market ahead of the wave. This creates a natural high reward/low risk scenario.

STEP 5 - THE ADX

When a trend is moving with strength, the average directional indicator (ADX) will measure the strength of the trend by measuring the difference between the PDI and MDI. The ADX moves on a scale of 0 to 100; the higher on the scale ADX arcs, the stronger the trend is. As the spread increases, the strength of the trend increases as well, confirming the propensity for the trend to continue. The idea here is to act quickly in order to participate in the follow-through of the trend. Remember, because directional movement tends to be a lagging to coincident indicator, the ability to recognize the trend once in motion is crucial. It is therefore essential to engage the trade early in order to participate in the follow-through. The ADX is an important link to this chain of events and completes the value of this technical approach. We like to pay particular attention to the ADX when it breaks above 30, as this shows a clear indication of the trend (bullish or bearish). The ADX is calculated as follows, after first calculating the directional indicator (DX).

$$DX = \frac{PDI - MDI}{PDI + MDI} \times 100$$

Next, average the DX with an EMA using a desired period such as 14. To calculate ADX, simply do the following:

ADX = Exponential Moving Average (EMA) of DX

I highly recommend you doing the math yourself to understand the indicator. By doing so, you see inside the indicator and understand what it is measuring and over what time horizon. The only way to understand the value of any indicator is to first tear it apart and see how it works. Then will you begin to understand the interplay between the indicator and price action in the market.

THE DIRECTIONAL MOVEMENT INDICATOR IN PRACTICE

The approach is quite simple once the psychology behind the numbers is understood. The market psychology in directional movement indicates when a trading range within a given day penetrates the range of the prior day. When this penetration occurs to the upside, we have a PDM and a bullish indication. When the penetration of the range is to the downside, we have a MDM. At all times the penetration is defined as the high-to-low range of the current period compared to the high-to-low range of the prior period. Therefore, in our earlier example, if AMGN has a range of $50 to $48.50, and the prior day's range in the same security is $48.50 and $48, we have a PDM and therefore a bullish indication. The PDI will therefore move above the MDI on the RealTick chart, indicating that the bulls are winning the battle over the bears. The next question to be answered is whether they continue to win the battle. Figure 6.13 illustrates the biotech sector.

F I G U R E   6.13

Directional movement applied to the AMEX Biotech Index.

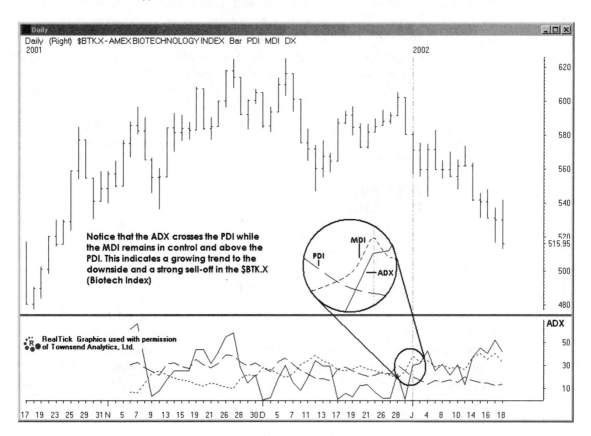

Notice that the ADX crosses the PDI while the MDI remains in control and above the PDI. This indicates a growing trend to the downside and a strong sell-off in the $BTK.X (Biotech Index)

RealTick Graphics used with permission of Townsend Analytics, Ltd.

This is where the ADX comes in. If the bears are significantly in control, the spread between MDI and PDI will widen, as evidenced by the ADX. What also widens is the spread between winners and losers in the market. Active trading is not a zero-sum game, but it is reasonably close to it. As the MDI/PDI spread continues to widen, it will be shown by a steep ascent in the ADX. This is the ideal time to enter the trade. When the ADX is at a steep angle of attack accompanied with an MDI spiking above a PDI, go short (see Figure 6.13). When a steep ADX is accompanied by a PDI spiking above an MDI, go long. If an ADX is peaking or retracing, get out of all trades or sit on your hands if you're not yet in. To keep the application of this system simple, we pay most attention to ADX when it arcs and crosses the lower DI (positive or negative), continuing higher. This signals that the trend is getting stronger and money is flowing in or out (indicating either a bullish PDI or a bearish MDI) of the security or market being monitored. Obviously, when the ADX is calm and not spiking, the trend is weak and the market is in a state of stabilization or consolidation. In this case, the indicator has no real value other than signifying that a stable market may begin to trend again via the ADX.

Remember elasticity trading in Chapter 3. This indicator is an extension of trading new elastic levels. As stated earlier, if the market is to stretch to new highs and lows, the market must have the elasticity to do so. Strength is measured by the ADX in terms of how much the elastic range can run on each span. Like any physical property, markets seek their lowest levels of energy. (This principle is explained in relation to chaos theory in *The Edge of Chaos* by Bernice Cohen.) This simply means that stocks fall under their own weight in the absence of positive energy (buyers) holding them up. The first signal of this is the ADX retracing. Once the ADX retraces, the dominant DI will follow, signaling a reversal. If the ADX holds strong, the dominant DI will follow through. Therefore, the ADX serves both as a trend-following tool and a reversal tool, depending on whether it is rallying (a following trend) or retracing (a reversal trend).

Directional System Indications

- **Bullish**   ADX is breaking 30, crossing MDI, and heading toward PDI; PDI is spiking higher.
- **Bearish**   ADX is breaking 30, crossing PDI, and heading toward MDI; MDI is spiking higher.
- **High volatility**   ADX is above PDI and MDI.
- **Dead calm**   ADX retraces with mixed DI signals. ADX falls below both PDI and MDI. ADX is below 30.

Other signals include the following:

- When a dominant DI begins to retrace, wait for the weak DI to rally. This is the first sign of reversal. The ADX will also tend to show weakness, confirming a change in leadership.
- When a dominant DI loses strength and a weak DI gains strength, trade with new leadership. If MDI is crossing upward through a declining PDI, go short. If PDI is crossing upward through a declining MDI, go long. In both cases the ADX must be at or above 30.

The DMI is a strong tool in association with moving averages. When the moving average trend shows new leadership (the 10-period MA is greater than the 20-period MA, which is greater than the 50-period MA) and the PDI is either crossing the MDI or above it, the signal is to go long. The opposite is true for a case in which the MDI moves up through the PDI and the moving averages confirm new leadership (the 50-period MA is greater than the 20-period MA, which is greater than the 10-period MA). In Chapter 7 we will cover moving average confirmation and stages in great detail. In the next section, we explain stochastic indicators. When trend reversal signals of DMI agree with stochastic signals, the value is undeniable.

THE STOCHASTIC PLAY

Most would credit George Lane for the use of stochastic indicators in the market, but the idea of stochastic indicators is one that is used in various mathematical models of the markets and in other statistical fields. The way we use stochastic indicators will be defined throughout this section, but we will first describe them metaphorically. Imagine a football field. At the 50-yard line there is a big stake in the ground. Attached to the stake is a large rubber band, and attached to it is an athlete wearing a harness. The apparatus is designed so that it is impossible for the athlete to run past the goal post at either end of the field. When moving from the 50-yard line to either of the 40-yard lines, it will be quite easy for the athlete to run. As the athlete approaches the 30-yard line, the increased tension of the rubber band will make moving a little harder. By the 20-yard line, moving will be quite a bit harder. By the 10-yard line it will be very hard to move, and getting to the goal line is the limit of how far the athlete can go. At the goal line, the tension and backward pull of the rubber band are at their height. When the athlete finally stops his or her effort, the rubber band will release its accumulated potential energy and throw him or her back in the other direction with great force. The greater the distance down the field the athlete travels, the more resistance he or she will encounter and the greater distance he or she will move back when the tension releases.

When applying this principle to the stock market, it becomes obvious that stocks also run either up or down toward figurative goal posts (support and resistance). When they get within a technical level of support or resistance, they usually reach the limits of their elasticity, setting up a potential and significant reversal in momentum. The levels that define the figurative goal posts represent the limits that a market can move before there is a contra reaction. These levels of support and resistance are determined by the use of moving averages, and the stochastic is represented by the rubber band. The market or stock one trades is the athlete, and the stake in the ground represents areas of stabilization or consolidation. Therefore, midfield hash marks and the field markers nearby (the 40- and 30-yard lines) represent no real value in terms of stochastic analysis, because in stochastic analysis this is precisely the area that produces the greatest amount of noise. In stochastic analysis, the only valuable signals are produced at extremes. The definition of these levels is best provided when an extreme stochastic reading agrees with longer- and shorter-term moving average support or resistance levels, which we cover in detail in Chapter 7. The DMI, in conjunction with moving averages and stochastic analysis, is among the best signals you will ever get. When these are somewhat in agreement, the market is telling you to act, and you can expect at least a minor reversal and even an extreme reversal from these levels. In our minds, this is the best application of stochastic analysis.

Let's now take a more analytical view of this popular technical tool. The stochastic indicator is quite good at determining when trend reversals are most likely to occur. It is fundamentally an oscillator designed to gauge when trends grow "tired or mature." The theory is based on the idea that in an upwardly trending market price, bars tend to close near their highs, while in a downwardly trending market they tend to close near their lows. Furthermore, as an upward trend matures, prices tend to close further from their highs; as a downward trend matures, they close further from their lows. These ideas are of particular value when using stochastic analysis.

The words *tired* or *mature* in this context are understood by chartists and technicians (there is a difference) to mean either overbought or oversold—the two conditions that stochastic analysis seeks to identify. Thus, if a stock is overbought, price bars will start to cluster around their lows in an uptrending market. When a stock is oversold, prices will tend to cluster around their highs in a downtrending market. These are among the earliest signs that the trend is about to change.

The mathematical derivation of a stochastic is given below, and you should become familiar with the analysis and begin the process of training your eye to recognize telling stochastic patterns on a chart. What is important

to note is that in order to fully understand what the indicator seeks to measure, you must understand the basis of the formula. Once this understanding
is obtained, your ability to see the trend reversals will improve. We'll look at
some charts in a moment, but first we'll go through a refresher on the basics.
You won't need to replicate the following calculations yourself, but it will be
helpful for you to understand the derivation of several variables used in stochastic models. These variables are often supplied as simple plug-ins for
charting software applications commonly used by traders. In the case of
RealTick, the math is done for you.

SOME DEFINITIONS AND CALCULATIONS

The stochastic indicator is plotted as two lines: the %D line and the %K line.
You will notice that the formula is similar in its components to the Welles
Wilder directional indicator that we covered earlier in this chapter. The %K
line is the less important of the two and is represented by the following equation, using a period of 5 for this example:

%K = 100 [(C − L5 close) / (H5 − L5)]

where C = the most recent close

L5 = the lowest low for the last five trading periods

H5 = the highest high for the same five trading periods

The %D line is a smoothed version of the %K line, usually using three
trading periods. The %D equation is as follows:

%D = 100 × (H3 / L3)

where H3 = the three-period sum of (C − L5)

L3 = the three-period sum of (H5 − L5)

The stochastic is plotted on a chart with values ranging from 0 to 100
(like our football field). The value cannot fall below 0 or rise above 100. Readings above 80 indicate that closing prices are clustering near highs in an uptrend, and readings below 20 indicate that closing prices are clustering near
lows in a downtrend. In Figure 6.14, the stochastic indicators are plotted beneath price changes in the S&P 500 futures:

READING THE INDICATOR

Most commonly, the %K line will change direction before the %D line. When
the opposite is true, we should look for a trend reversal. When both %K and
%D lines change direction and the %K line retests the support of the %D line
without breaking it, this implies that the price reversal is likely to have begun

F I G U R E   6.14

Stochastic indications for the S&P 500 index on a daily chart.

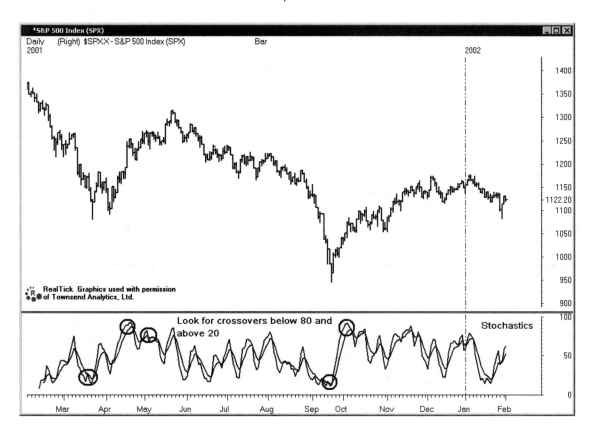

a new trend. Also, when the indicator approaches either 0 or 100, the trend is suspect. If the indicator retests these extremes following a price retracement, it signals an opportune entry point. Quite often when the %K or %D lines begin to flatten, a trend reversal will occur, beginning at the next trading range.

Our use of stochastic indicators emphasizes diverging lines above all. In such instances, prices may be making higher highs while the stochastic oscillator is making lower highs, or prices may be making lower lows while the stochastic oscillator is making higher lows. In either case, the indicator is usually signaling a change in the trend before that change is obvious in the price bars. The ability to interpret such divergences can be very helpful in identifying major turning points in real time. To do so, you must first be able to recognize four different types of divergences, two found at market tops and two at bottoms. See Figures 6.15 and 6.16.

In Figure 6.15, price action in a stock is plotted with a stochastic line beneath. Note that although the stock has made successively higher price

F I G U R E 6.15

Higher price peaks with correspondingly lower stochastic peaks.

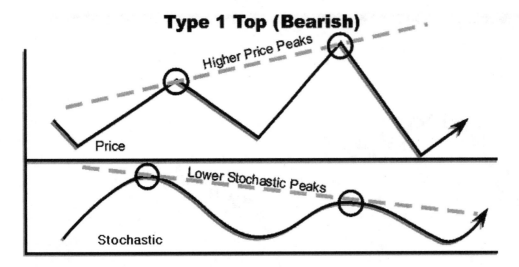

peaks, the stochastic peaks have declined. The most probable real-world interpretation is that as the stock went higher, the eagerness of buyers diminished. Or perhaps the second rally, although producing a higher price peak, failed to get as overbought as the first. This is an intuitively bearish proposition. This is why stochastic divergence associated with rally tops constitutes a flashing yellow signal for bulls.

F I G U R E 6.16

Lower price peaks with correspondingly higher stochastic peaks.

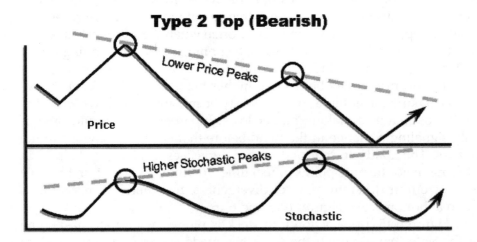

Figure 6.16 illustrates the other type of divergence possible at a rally top, one that is also interpreted as bearish. Here, price peaks have declined while the stochastic peaks that correspond to them have risen. Think of this as implying that the stock becomes even more overbought while failing to make new highs. You could also see it as a distributive pattern, where buyers expend a good deal of enthusiasm and render the stock overbought without being able to push it to new price highs.

Stochastic divergences at the bottom of a chart are typically a bullish harbinger. In Figure 6.17, we see that lower price bottoms have generated correspondingly higher stochastic bottoms. We should infer that even though the stock is moving lower, sellers are less brutal in pounding it down.

Figure 6.18 illustrates the other type of bullish bottom, where higher price lows have generated lower stochastic lows. Based on personal experience, this is a somewhat more bullish pattern than the type 1 bottom. (This observation applies to the examples of diverging tops as well: Type 2s are generally more bearish than type 1s.) We should view type 2 bottoms as implying that sellers have spent their fury: As oversold as the stock gets, the selling cannot push it to a new low. Next we'll discuss a somewhat rarer pattern that can signal a humdinger of a rally or decline: double divergence.

DOUBLE DIVERGENCE

There is another divergent pattern, one that can indicate a powerful trend change at tops and bottoms. We call it a double divergence, and it requires

F I G U R E   6.17

Lower price bottoms with correspondingly higher stochastic bottoms.

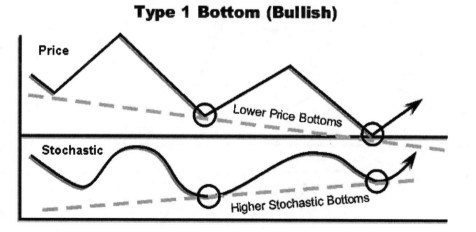

Type 1 Bottom (Bullish)

F I G U R E   6.18

Higher price bottoms with correspondingly lower stochastic bottoms.

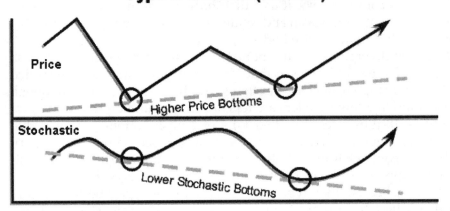

Type 2 Bottom (Bullish)

three discrete peaks or bottoms to manifest itself. See Figure 6.19 for an example of a double-diverging top.

Note that in Figure 6.19 there are three price peaks, labeled A, B, and C, and that they have generated respective stochastic peaks at a, b, and c. What is distinctive about this chart is that *all* of the respective peaks diverge from

F I G U R E   6.19

Notice the double divergence between price and stochastic.

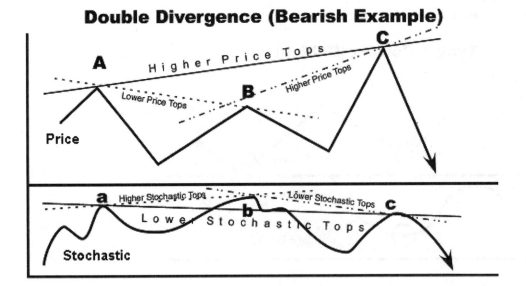

Double Divergence (Bearish Example)

each other—that is, A and B diverge relative to a and b, A and C diverge relative to a and c, and B and C diverge relative to b and c. This pattern is relatively rare, but when you see it taking shape on a chart you should fasten your seatbelt in preparation for a wicked turn. The same pattern can occur at bottoms, producing an inversion of the chart in Figure 6.19.

SUMMARY

Interpreting these stochastic patterns is straightforward and not at all difficult. Remember what we've learned: A divergence of either type 1 or 2 at market tops is bearish, while a divergence of either type at bottoms is bullish. If there is no divergence, it is usually an indication that the trend will continue, possibly following a normal correction.

One more note concerning stochastic indicators: Everything you have learned about them can be applied in any time frame, whether it is a five-minute chart or a monthly chart. Occasionally, double divergences will crop up in the one- or five-minute bars, signaling unusual trading opportunities. By extension, a double-divergent pattern in a monthly chart could signal the beginning of a major bull or bear market.

If the picture is unclear in one time frame, you can step down to a smaller time frame to see whether the one corroborates the other. For instance, stochastic indicators for a daily bar chart might be very bearish, while indicators for the monthly chart are very bullish, and just starting to roll up from extremely oversold lows. If this is the case, you might initiate a long position when the daily chart indicators approach oversold extremes and signal a trend change by way of our test as described above.

Finally, you should be aware that these signals do not often shout "Buy here!" or "Sell there!" In fact, they tend to be both subtle and subjective, and that is why we must study and observe them diligently over time in order to become proficient in their use. In fact, to trade literally on any one indicator is not prudent. All traders must also use confirming indicators to either confirm stochastic signals or refute them. The market alignment of indicators should be the focus. The collection of indicators shared in this chapter represents the instruments we follow every day. Remember, the best signals are when at least two indicators point to the same conclusion. Even when an alignment of indicators occurs, risk management is your greatest tool.

7

C H A P T E R

MOVING AVERAGE PLAYS AND STRATEGY

Markets are reflections of its participants. The collective psychology of the markets are represented through patterns that repeat again and again. These cyclical patterns ultimately form market structure, and this structure is the foundation of technical analysis. We have explored many means of measuring these patterns such as elasticity, Fibonacci, RSI, DMI, and others; however, as earlier stated, these ideas are all simply the derivative of our foundational components, which are price, time, volume, and velocity. Perhaps no mechanism to measure market behavior has been as successful for traders as the moving average.

Moving averages lag the market by nature because they are based on historical price data. Since they lag the market, we use them to detect longer-term trends by measuring the relationship of shorter-term averages to longer-term averages. By doing so, we expect to do two things. First, as discussed in Chapters 4 and 5, we will try to determine what stage the measured security is in. Secondly, we will use the crossing signals of the moving averages to pinpoint entry, exit, and setup levels within a given stage (namely stages 2 and 4). The time frame in which you trade will dictate the strategy. To this end, recognizing that the market knows and has digested these prior price and time patterns within the moving averages, traders are best served in viewing these moving average levels as inflection points. *Inflection points* are simply price levels that elicit greater than average market reaction. The volume and velocity relationship at these inflection points creates tradable ranges as prices converge on and diverge from these moving averages. Therefore, the greatest value we can take from the moving average is the fact that it is both a trend-following tool and a short-term trading tool. Swing traders should use moving averages to follow trend. Wise day traders should use them to time inflection points.

THE SIMPLE MOVING AVERAGE

The simple moving average (SMA) is by far the most widely viewed moving average. Because of this, the SMA is still one of the best indicators, period. A good source in which to research indicators is *The Encyclopedia of Technical Market Indicators* by Robert W. Colby, which we feel is one of the better tools available to help traders digest a myriad of market indicators. This book has helped to define, through back-testing, which systems have done well empirically, and it helps to hone in on the indicators that are worth paying attention to. We can personally tell you that we believe it will take months, if not years, off your learning curve if you pay close attention to Colby's interpretation of many of the indicators.

To this day, no indicator has defined market action better than the simple moving average. We believe it works better than the exponential moving average, weighted moving average, the MACD indicator, and the many other complicated formulas that are derivatives of the simple moving average. Mathematically speaking, the simple moving average is somewhat flawed. This is because past price action has the same impact on the average as current price action, since as each piece of new data is added, old data drops off. If a five-minute MA is being measured, the sixth minute would be added and the first minute removed, with no more weighting being given to the sixth minute price than the first minute price. Therefore the SMA is prone to volatility. This does not agree with the Adam Theory, which states the most recent past should have a greater impact on the most near-term future. So why is the SMA so effective? First we must explore the math, and then we will explain why. The SMA is calculated as follows:

SMA = aggregated prices of "X" number of periods /periods measured

For example, if measuring the 5 periods below:

5 SMA = ($61+$55+$53+$50+$56) / 5 = $55

Once the $61 price is dropped from the average, the average will drop if the next current period maintains its $55 average, therefore indicating weakness in the price average even though prices have seemed to stabilize.

$$5 \, SMA = (\$55 + \$53 + \$50 + \$56 + \$55) \, / \, 5 = \$53.80$$

PSYCHOLOGY OF THE SIMPLE MOVING AVERAGE

As we have mentioned, the SMA seems flawed as a tool to measure current consensus of value, since old data impacts the current SMA just as much as the new data. So how can this be an effective tool? Why use the SMA? The answer is that what gives the SMA value is the market's perception and acceptance of it. Ultimately, the so-called KISS method (Keep it simple, stupid!) proves to be relevant. By keeping it simple, we can prove empirically that the simple moving average has had more success in predicting the market than any other technical indicator. Principally this is because the SMA is the most widely followed and recognized moving average, and we must take into account that technical analysis draws on the fact that as market data becomes known, followed, and anticipated by other participants, both a positive and negative result will be achieved. On the positive side, most participants will react in a specific and predictable way to certain market indications and patterns such as moving average levels. This is positive because those reactions create a small yet definable statistical edge that can be traded in the short term. On the negative side, those same price levels, as they become widely known, become digested by the market, thus leading to their self-destruction. This is why we choose to take a short-term intraday trading approach to viewing moving averages.

While the edge is mitigated quite quickly in the market, active traders can trade this edge if they don't rely on it for long. As markets trade against perceived support and resistance levels based on the SMA, short-term reactions often occur. Therefore, the value of the SMA lies in its perception, not in its mathematical correctness.

The exponential moving average mathematically gives more weight to the current pricing of the market and less weight to the oldest price data in the average. While this seems to make more mathematical sense, the market's perception of and attention to the EMA isn't very strong. Its perceived value is reduced to the point that its mathematical advantage is more than offset. Engineers and other people prone to literal interpretation rarely make good traders because they are too concerned about what the market "should" do by reason of the analytics instead of what the market is doing as a result of the broad market crowd and their collective perception. For this reason alone, you should begin to understand that indicators cannot be measured on only their mathematical merit but should be evaluated for their perceived value and market acceptance. Because the simple moving average is the most followed, it still poses the greatest perceived value, despite its mathematical inefficiencies.

STRATEGY: THE MOVING AVERAGE SIGNAL CROSS

The signal cross is perhaps the best example of where the traders' edge lies in relation to the simple moving average. By studying this approach historically, we have found that its value is undeniable. What we want to look for when using this approach are situations where strong stocks are above their 50- and 100-period moving averages on days the overall market declines. This does not mean the issue itself will not also decline with the market, but it does mean the issue will remain above its 50- and 100-period moving average. If through a scanning process the issue shows these characteristics, this stock should be added to your market minder. As the strategy will show, the signals occur when short-term moving averages rally through longer-term moving averages.

Let's take a look at one moving average signal cross candidate, Dentsply International (XRAY). Figure 7.1 shows the daily chart of XRAY. First note that this was a swing trade. We entered on 7/20/02 once the price moved higher than the 50-period MA and 100-period MA at $38.35. The trade was stopped out on 8/14/02 just below $42.00 as the stock broke down through its 10-period MA.

Because the trade technique requires confirmation of short-term moving averages crossing longer-term averages, it is critical to understand that buying the low will not be achieved. Therefore, getting on board quickly once confirmation is achieved is important. Whether the issue is breaking out of a basing pattern or waking up from a sleepy period, the moving average crossover will represent the inflection point.

When using this method, the important thing to keep in mind is that stocks gain momentum when price levels are broken. In the XRAY chart in Figure 7.1 and in the AMAT chart in Figure 7.2, the indication showed the issues trading above their daily 50- and 100-period moving averages while the rest of the market averages were down during the same period of time. For this reason alone, these issues made our watch list. When utilizing this method, traders must be willing to expect and tolerate pullbacks along the way. These pullbacks are the precise times that most traders are whipsawed out of trades, either because they are stopped out or because they are shaken out. In our ap-

FIGURE 7.1

This chart demonstrates a long trade initiated on a MA, signal cross.

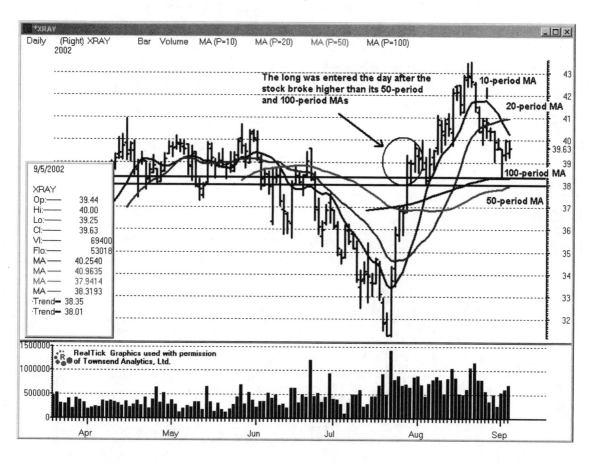

proach, we use moving averages as a way of determining trend and, more importantly, we look for the issue to pull back toward the longer-term moving averages as a sign of consolidation. This allows our conviction to stay intact.

Once the short-term moving averages on the intraday chart cross the longer-term moving averages, we make the trade. In this case we will use a 5-day, 5-minute chart with 10- and 20-period moving averages. Once the 10-period MA breaks the 20-period MA, the trade is on to the long side, as confirmed by two major indications:

- The daily MA indicates a strong stock when above the 50-period MA and the 100-period MA, while it is a weak stock when below.
- On the intraday 5-minute chart, when the short-term 10-period MA breaks the 20-period MA, the market is waking up and ready to

trend. If the 10-period MA rallies through the 20-period MA and
the stock is above its 50- and 100-period MAs, you should get long.
If the stock is below the 50- and 100-day MAs and the 10-period
MA on the 5-minute chart crosses below the 20-period MA, get
short.

Aggressive traders can trade the break on the 10-period moving average
as it moves through the 20-period moving average, or wait for confirmation
as the 20-period moving average breaks though the longer-term moving averages. As intraday traders, we always buy the first break. Short scenarios, as
we have said, are handled in the opposite way.

F I G U R E   7.2

A daily chart of Applied Materials (AMAT) with MAs overlaid.

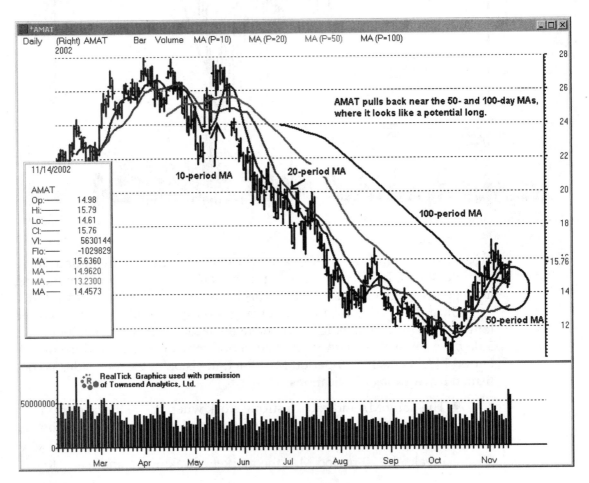

Looking at the 20-period moving average in Figures 7.2 and 7.3 and assuming a larger basis of data (that being 20 5-minute periods, or 100 minutes), the moving average is naturally slower or more smoothed by time than the 10-period MA. This is principally why it acts as confirmation of the "young" trend. While the trend is young and still subject to longer-term follow-through, the consistency of this approach for short-term trading is outstanding. Additionally, by applying proper risk management to the position through the use of protective and trailing stops, traders can mitigate the risk of substantial losses. The important thing to understand is that as prices get above the 20-period moving average due to increasing velocity, a pullback or minor consolidation is both anticipated and likely as the moving

F I G U R E   7.3

This intraday chart of AMAT shows the resultant breakout from the daily chart (Figure 7.2).

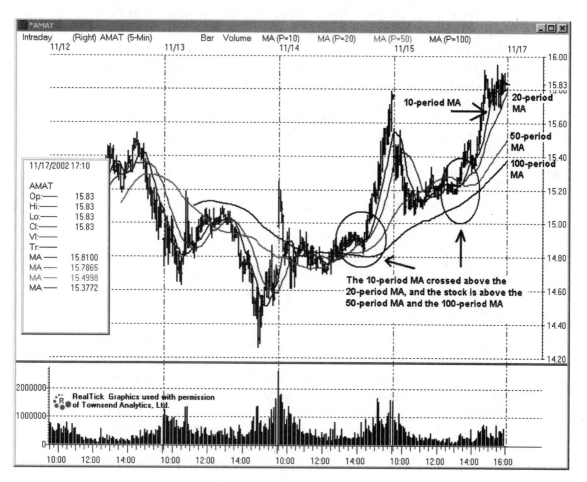

average catches up to prices. The greater the velocity of price and the closer the issue is to the broader daily moving averages, the more likely a pullback will become. Trailing stops will protect you in these scenarios.

When the stock trades higher in the example shown in Figure 7.2, the issue trades above its 20-period moving average and runs to the 50-period moving average because trend and momentum are strong. Since the issue is trading up against stronger moving averages, such as the 50-period and 100-period MAs, pullbacks aren't only likely but expected.

The reason that pullbacks are likely and should be anticipated is that many speculators will have benefited from the initial move and are looking to take profits, thus causing a temporary imbalance opposite to the trend. Early long players are in a position to cause a temporary supply and demand imbalance, which will be reflected as either a consolidation or pullback. Trade management is intensified as trailing stops are tightened or the position is partially scaled out of. Your critical clues are the 20-period moving average (which is the confirming indicator to the 10-period moving average) and the 10-period moving average, which is the wake-up call. The 10-period moving average is the shortest period an intraday trader wants to look at, because shorter period MAs can cause market hypnosis. The 10-period simple moving average on the 5-minute chart (for a total of 50 minutes) is the strongest indication of price action intraday, because this price average represents the most recent past and has the greatest market impact when predicting the near-term future. This is the language the market uses—are you listening?

Many participants impose unnecessary pressure on themselves by trying to buy the bottom, but the low risk entry is found at the 10-period and 20-period moving average cross. Statistically, the signal is not late and the move is not over. If a false signal occurs and the move fails, proper risk management will take care of the losses quickly.

In most cases the fuel for this strategy comes from institutions that have a large amount of capital to put to work. These institutions can't execute large trades very quickly. As they jump on a technical indication of this kind, they trigger a money flow reaction providing strong potential follow-through. Additionally, because these institutions are only trying to beat the S&P, the relative return they find acceptable is much lower than the relative return that traders can achieve by leveraging a concentrated position in the stock. For example, a minor move to a trader with a concentrated position of several thousand shares can mean 3 to 5 percent of total capital. For example, if a $100,000 account were traded with a 5000 share position on Figures 7.2 and 7.3, it would yield over $4900 in profit (5000 × $0.62), or a 4.9% return on capital. The institution's bread and butter is the active trader's seven-course meal. Obviously, similar moves for a larger fund would yield a significantly lower relative return. While these plays seem simple and obvious, because large institutions also focus on moving average crossovers, and because they move huge capital, they are nonetheless statistically valid trades. Essentially, the wake institutions leave behind is very profitable to small capital players by comparison.

In summary, this trading style requires the 10-period moving average to break the 20-period moving average on intraday charts while prices are above the 50- and 100-period moving averages on daily charts. Your entry point should be the first levels above the 20-period MA close, which in this case would be an upward trending close above the prior day's open but still below the prior day's high. This will put you in a position to immediately profit if the trend continues. The profit will come within the range of prices above the prior day's close and below the prior day's high, giving traders the opportunity to price protective stops below the prior day's close and adjust trailing stops along the profitability line.

PLACING STOPS FOR THE MOVING AVERAGE SIGNAL CROSS

The next thing we need to understand is at what levels protective stops should be placed. If entering a long position just above the prior day's close, assuming the prior day was a strong up day, protective stops should be placed either at 50 percent of the range between the prior day's open and close or at the prior day's open, depending on how much risk traders are willing to tolerate. The profit objective is somewhat unlimited with this approach, since trailing stops can allow profits to soar. Statistically the opportunity is greatest when shorter-term moving averages cross longer-term moving averages to accelerate the strength of the move.

Once in profitable territory, trailing stops should be adjusted and widened to allow profits to run. Trailing stops should optimally put you into a break-even situation as soon as possible, thereby giving you the option to widen the stop in order to participate in larger moves at minimal risk. Risk management principles are as simple to understand as the relationships of moving averages. Common sense suggests that if you are long a position and prices are reaching the 100- or 200-period moving averages (on the daily chart), you would expect resistance and dramatically tighten your stops, or scale out part of, if not the entire position.

Like most approaches, the win/loss ratio will change based on a trader's ability to identify the right setups and execute the trades properly. The ratio can vary greatly. The important message here is to stay convicted and look for the right setups before entering trades.

The short side of the market has exactly the same entry procedure, except that we want to see prices below the daily 50- and 100-period MAs, and the rules for entry are reversed. In the short scenario, trades should be entered below the prior day's close but above the prior day's intraday low, putting the trader in a short position between the ranges that we call the *true range low*. Again, protective stops should be placed above the prior day's close (assuming a down day) at a level where there is an acceptable risk relative to the reward target.

MOVING AVERAGE CONVERGENCE/DIVERGENCE AND RISK MANAGEMENT

The MACD is an iteration of the EMA, and in fact uses three EMAs to measure the market's short-term and longer-term trends. The function is quite simple: MACD consists of two line representations on charts. One line represents the short-term market trend, and the other the longer-term market trend. As you should be able to anticipate by now, when the short-term EMA crosses up through the longer-term EMA, momentum builds and the bulls gain control. Conversely, when the fast signal line (short term) crosses down through the slow signal line (long term), bears gain control.

Now let's tear into the indicator to see the psychological condition it presents to us. Essentially, the indicator seeks to do the same thing as the simple moving average signal cross, but does it differently. MACD looks at the market in relational terms, meaning changes in one MA will automatically change the relationship it has to another. Hence its name "moving average convergence/divergence." The components of MACD are the MACD line and the signal line.

1. MACD line: This is considered the fast line, since it is calculated by taking the difference between two different EMAs. Because these differences are plotted to form the MACD line, changes are magnified when either EMA changes with price. For example, using a 10-period EMA and a 20-period EMA, subtracting the 20 EMA from the 10 EMA to find the difference, any change in price magnifies the result, hence why it is the fast line.

2. Signal line: The signal line is slower since it calculates the EMA of the MACD line.

    The signals are as follows:

    ● Bullish – when the fast line moves above the slow line.
    ● Bearish – when the fast line moves below the slow line.

This is not much different than when price moves above or below key SMAs. The psychology is the same, except that the MACD helps to factor in momentum of the market to sharpen timing.

MACD makes good mathematical sense, but we believe traders gain more interpretive value from seeing each of the moving averages (such as the 10-, 50-, 100-, and 200-period SMAs) and the relationships among them. The slope of the short-term MA into a longer-term MA, as well as the spread differential between them, creates a visual representation of the two market styles of short-term and long-term trading. As these MAs get closer or farther from each other, they give traders clues as to the rate at which they will diverge or converge. The MACD is a powerful tool, but if one does not understand what drives it, then its utility is limited. Because most people can

F I G U R E   7.4

In relationship to the fast line (MACD), bulls live above the slow line, and bears below.

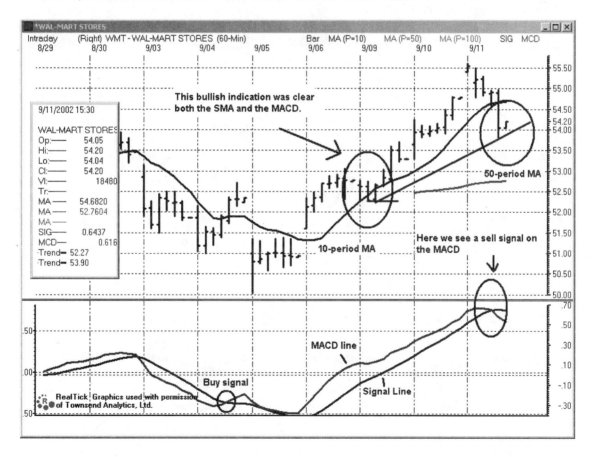

apply logic to the SMA and price, most people can also gain "feel" for the markets' momentum. While MACD mathematically does this well, it is less understood. Let's take a look at Figure 7.4.

Traders who wish to use the MACD lines should use it for longer-term horizons. The value of the tool for short-term trading is somewhat suspect. We bring this point up not to disparage the indicator, but to encourage traders to focus on reading the series of SMAs for short-term trading (within five days). Their relationship, as explained above, makes this a far more accurate and useful tool. If traders wish to apply the MACD for short-term trading, then we suggest using the histogram, as shown in Figure 7.5, because it seeks to measure the strength between bulls and bears by subtracting the signal line (slow) from the MACD line (fast). Because the

FIGURE   7.5

Higher lows on the histogram are bullish, while lower highs are bearish. Notice the MACD histogram is making a higher low and shows early signs of strength.

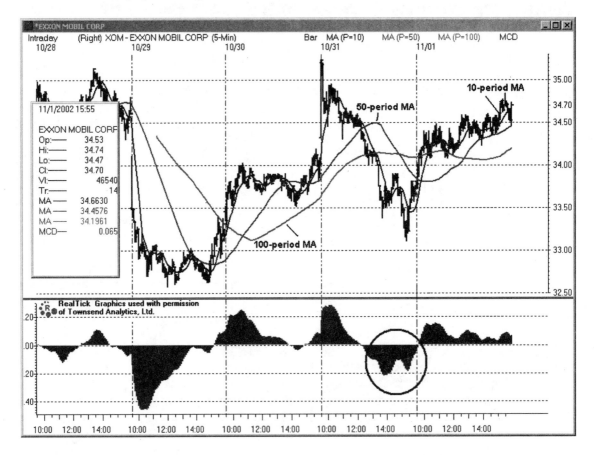

MACD histogram focuses on the shorter-term price action of stocks, we can graphically see momentum building. Essentially we use the MACD histogram as a means of anticipation. When the histogram shows higher lows, we anticipate a rally and expect the histogram to break through the neutral line and move above it. Conversely, when the histogram makes lower highs above the neutral line, we expect the histogram to break down and signal a sell. By subtracting the signal line (the slow line of longer-term market trend) from the MACD line (the faster line of short-term market trend), a bar is created. The indicator measures conditions when the short-term market consensus is greater than the longer-term market consensus, thereby signaling a potential break in either direction. These signals are less effective for longer-term trends but very effective for the short term. If the short-term market opinion is weak, the MACD line will be less than the signal line and show the bears in control. The relational value of the histogram is more important. A histogram rallying from a bottom shows strength for the market, while a retracement from a top signals weakness. See Figure 7.5.

SUMMARY

While the point may be overstated with regard to technical indicators, the moving average in its simplest form best represents the market's historical propensity to repeat itself. Unfortunately, most people focus on historical trend extension as a prediction of price action only for the benefit of profiting. Good risk managers will also use the MAs as a strong indication of future risk. Large financial losses are obviously to be avoided, but consistent small losses have utility and value beyond the fact that they are small. Small losses allow the trader to feel the market—to gauge the ebb and flow. Trading around the moving average signal cross is a great educator.

Moving averages capture some of the most basic and pure elements of the market, such as trend and momentum over a given time series. Simple moving averages tend to signal when velocity, whether bullish or bearish, crescendos. This is visible as the shorter-term moving averages spike sharply through the longer-term moving averages, as shown in the charts of this chapter. When short-term moving averages sharply accelerate, price and velocity are moving with great bullish or bearish force. As they cross their longer-term counterpart moving averages, this indicates a potential for pullbacks toward the major trend. The obvious next question is, Will the market follow through or retreat? As a rule, price velocity begins to dissipate and short-term moving averages converge toward the longer-term moving averages, while prices tend to pull back from rallies and lift from retracements.

Continuing with this simple logic, we also know that once a short-term moving average crosses a longer-term moving average, the support of the market is redefined at the longer-term moving average. Conversely, on the downside, resistance of the market is defined as the long-term MA above the short-term. So in the case of a 10-period moving average crossing upward through a 50-period moving average, the 50-period moving average will act as greater support for the security than the current price of the security or the 10-period moving average. While a divergence is in play in terms of the actual price of the security when trading above the longer-term MA, traders should expect true support at the longer-term MA. As velocity begins to slow and the 10-period moving average line begins to flatten, a retracement is expected to the 50-period moving average or close to it. The 50-period moving average is expected to maintain most of its gains if the bullish trend is real.

On the other hand, if velocity continues to increase, whether because the uptrend is restarted or because the uptrend continues with little or no pullback, the 10-period moving average will pull the 50-period moving average higher and steeper and ultimately create a higher level of support. In that case, a price retracement toward the 50-period moving average is even more likely, as represented by the large divergence. Divergence acts as a precursor to convergence or a potential low-volume pullback along an upward trend line. Many iterations of this could be contemplated, but it is easy to see that a longer-term moving average will provide greater support in rallies, just as a longer-term moving average will provide greater resistance in downtrends. Understanding the psychology of these market dynamics is far more valuable than literally reading the indicator.

The implication here for the short-term trader is that the edge should be used to your advantage, but without being convinced the moving average will always correctly represent the longer term trend of the market. The long-term trend of the market is not what we are seeking with this approach. Instead, we are willing to trade in the high potential profitability of any given major trend for a higher degree of consistency and confidence in short-term momentum trading around moving averages.

8

THE MOMENTUM APPROACH

Momentum trading involves reading the market through a micro approach on shorter time frames. Momentum is generally read in 10 minute periods or less. Effectively, the charts have already been considered and analyzed, leaving the momentum methods to be discussed as the "tip of the sword." Momentum can be used to sharpen execution on swing trades, or applied strictly intraday. Regardless, this approach should be applied to all trading styles and time frames. The reason we focus on momentum is because our job is to make money, and this can be accomplished inside the boundaries of one day, or over several days. Incorporating a momentum approach to "sharpen" your swing trading is different than strictly momentum trading. The two should not be confused or mixed. Therefore, we dedicate this chapter to understanding the momentum approach, practiced according to the time horizon. While technicals are still deeply important, this approach is perhaps more art than science and will complement the technicals.

NEWS DISSEMINATION

Not many events can halt or delay trading on the New York Stock Exchange (NYSE), but news dissemination is one of them. Although we are aware of market news being disseminated throughout the trading session, examples of which include wholesale inventories, consumer credit, consumer confidence, the Federal Reserve Board's *Beige Book,* leading indicators, existing and new home sales, and so on, we do not trade the news as a rule.

The first step to using a momentum style of trading is the research done by examining charts, formations, patterns, and market indications that are displayed from a broad market perspective and successively broken down into minor trends. There is little credence placed on fundamentals or news to make decisions since these events are outside a trader's control. We choose to be out of the market as news is disseminated. When using a momentum approach, what we do pay attention to is the cause-and-effect relationship of reported news and its impact on price. We are not even interested in the cause, but we do care about the effect. Momentum traders trade "effect." We don't care about news in terms of direct indications of market bias. News is only noise that potentially ripples the market, and we do not want to be caught in its wake. Traders must be comfortable with the fact that these events and the reactions to them will become part of the technicals over time. The decision-making process traders go through, and the research done each day focuses solely on levels, and therefore price already digests the effects of disseminated news. While news dissemination is important to be aware of, it is best to get out of the way of news by covering all positions before its release. Any news that can rock the market is not tradable. To hold a position into news when momentum trading is simply reckless gambling.

SPREAD DIFFERENTIAL OF LEVELS

Once technical research is done (both pre- and postmarket), you are in a position to apply real-time price action to your technical setups. The setups should define tradable opportunities with good risk/reward relationships, while real-time price action (momentum) will sharpen your timing. The momentum approach allows us to see the market in the moment as it trades in relation to the patterns we define technically. This is where velocity and minor trends are detected. The technicals are less effective measuring velocity and minor trends on time frames inside of 5 to 10 minutes. As you can see in Figure 8.1, a chart represents price change over time by its angle of attack, but this is best interpreted from the tape inside 10 minute periods. The angle of attack would suggest a severe rate of climb, or what Chairman Greenspan might call "irrational exuberance." The chart may suggest this stock is soon ready for a breather, but this is where charts can lie to the subjective eye. This severe angle of attack is often associated with stock split announcements, earnings, and ratings that "surprise" to the upside.

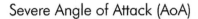

A severe angle of attack where price advances rapidly in a short amount of time (velocity).

Severe Angle of Attack (AoA)

While the opposite angle of attack will be seen on negative news, the momentum associated with either can be radical. Therefore, momentum is the most difficult thing to teach. Perhaps the greatest lesson is to simply be aware that it will develop with time and experience, and also that it cannot be ignored. To lessen the learning curve, let's spend some time explaining what should be studied and monitored to acquire the skill of "reading levels."

To begin this process, we focus on a couple of key tools. First we look at the percentage change for the day for any given security. Next we look at the high, the low, the last price, and the direction of price (uptick or downtick). Figures 8.2 and 8.3 illustrate an example of this data as presented through the RealTick platform.

The value of this information depends on your interpretive skills when reading price levels. Figure 8.2 is a RealTick market minder and is used in conjunction with the Level II and time and sales screens (Figure 8.3). The combination of these tools shows "levels" in the market and, more importantly, the velocity at which the market moves from one level to the next. For example, if the spread differential in terms of the last price and the low price of the day is starting to widen, we know that upside momentum is growing. This occurs because the low price remains static (tape support) until a new low is printed. If the "Last" price column on the illustration in Figure 8.2 represents a widening divergence from the low price, it is important to recognize whether the spread is widening beyond its recent range.

FIGURE 8.2

The "market snapshot" on RealTick allows the trader to interpret real time information, such as net change percent, daily high/low, last price traded, and the change from the prior session's close.

Symbol	Company Name	Net Chg. %	High	Low	Last	Change
$DJI	DOW JONES INDUSTRIAL AVERAGE	+.76	8612.72	8509.22	8581.14	+64.71
$COMPX	NASDAQ COMPOSITE INDEX	+1.09	1509.12	1489.08	1506.08	+16.21
$NDX.X	NASDAQ-100 INDEX	+1.46	1133.02	1112.59	1129.94	+16.26
$SPX.X	S&P 500 INDEX	+.72	932.89	922.54	930.05	+6.63
QQQ	NASDAQ 100 TRUST	+1.48	28.18	27.15	28.10	+.41
SPY	SPDRS TRUST SER 1	+.82	93.92	92.14	93.41	+.76
$SOX.X	Semiconductor Index SOX	+1.44	343.57	335.08	342.42	+4.85
$BTK.X	AMEX BIOTECHNOLOGY INDEX	+2.16	415.43	405.54	414.29	+8.75
$TICK-N	NYSE Tick Indicator	-117.02	1042	-545	-119	-818
$TRIN-N	NYSE Arms Indicator	-25.34	1.746	.421	.551	-.187
$TICK-Q	Nasdaq Tick Indicator	-107.17	339	-359	-18	-269
$TRIN-Q	Nasdaq Indicator	-70.36	.527	.311	.377	-.895
$BIX.X	S&P Banks Chain	+.21	294.03	291.81	293.21	+.62
$OEX.X	S&P 100 INDEX	+.77	470.21	464.88	468.78	+3.58
$XCI.X	AMEX COMPUTER TECHNOLOGY INDEX	+.87	554.96	548.67	553.62	+4.78
$XOI.X	OIL INDEX	-.25	459.20	457.43	457.75	-1.15
$DRG.X	AMEX PHARMACEUTICAL INDEX	+.77	313.1	310.1	312.6	+2.4
$XBD.X	AMEX SECURITIES BROKER/DEALER	-.08	463.86	460.44	461.59	-.36
$UTY.X	PHLX UTILITY SECTOR INDEX	+1.30	276.70	272.46	275.88	+3.53
$XAU.X	GOLD AND SILVER INDEX	-1.69	75.33	74.30	74.30	-1.28
$VIX.X	CBOE MARKET VOLATILITY INDEX	-1.38	23.65	22.30	22.89	-.32
$VXN.X	CBOE NASDAQ VOLATILITY INDEX		32.07	30.65	30.88	

This gets a bit tricky to explain, but its value is tremendous in refining your ability to read oncoming changes in price, range, and most importantly, velocity. For example, let's zoom in on one line of the market minder like the one shown in Figure 8.4. The market in the QQQ has a low of $23.10 and a last price of $23.35. The range between the two has stayed tight: $0.25 ($23.35–$23.10) for the past 10 minutes. The last price has consistently traded near the low of $23.10, but never penetrated it (confirming that $23.10 is tape support). The price trades back up to $23.35, but never penetrates it (confirming tape resistance). The range within this time horizon is defined at $0.25. Suddenly, the last price trades at $23.15, continues to uptick to the $23.35 level, and then trades to $23.36. We immediately recognize that the range or spread differential has grown.

This indication alone is worth taking the trade to the long side if the technicals also confirm that there is strong support. While the indication is microscopic to most, this is a sign of and a precursor to velocity and rapid price succession. This seemingly minor change in range is a technique taken

F I G U R E   8.3

The level II screen and attached ticker show depth of market and the current equation of supply and demand for the security being measured. The ticker helps define where dominant market activity exists in terms of participants "hitting bids" and "lifting offers." This understanding and feel sharpens traders' ability to find liquidity and time entries and exits.

from the New York Stock Exchange that floor traders have used for years to detect minor intraday moves. This recognition will help swing traders make razor sharp entries while also offering day traders quick turn-around profits. It works because many automated BlackBox systems (trading systems that run on pre-coded algorithms) evaluate price–spread differentials of this kind. As soon as these ranges elastically expand, buy programs kick in and accelerate the move. In addition, active professional traders see the same indications and act. It is not unlike a "stop"; once triggered, even if only by $0.01, additional trades soon follow in the prevailing direction.

Figure 8.5 represents two trades made in the SPYs using a similar approach but applied to daily charts. The prior day's elastic range set up the trade and the subsequent breakdown of the spread differential triggered the entry.

F I G U R E   8.4

The QQQ data highlighted from the market snapshot.

Symbol	Chg. Over	Chg. Over %	Company Name	Net Chg. %	High	Low	Last	Change
QQQ	+.15	+.65	NASDAQ 100 TRUST	+1.17	23.67	23.10	23.35	+.27

F I G U R E   8.5

July 31's high ($91.62), low ($89.22), open ($90.49), and close ($91.15) in the SPYs, set the levels of elasticity for the momentum approach.

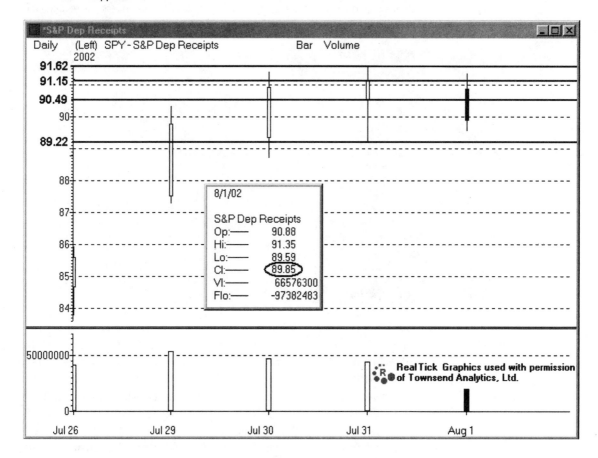

The logic of "spread differentials" can also be applied to charts. On August 1st (Figure 8.5), note that the bulls couldn't take out the prior day's high of $91.62, and only moderately penetrated the prior close of $91.15 (see intraday high of $91.35). As the spread differential widened and retraced off the intraday high of $91.35, the short play was confirmed once we broke the prior day's close of $91.15. The short position was opened and filled at $90.89. The protective stop was immediately set at $91.15. Once the SPYs moved in our favor, a trailing stop was entered with $0.25 discretion. As the SPYs downward move accelerated toward the prior day's intraday low (minor support) of $89.22, our trailing stop was triggered as the SPYs found a bottom at $89.59 and stopped us out at $89.84. We risked $0.26 (based on our protective stop), and had a reward target of $1.67 (based on the difference of our entry level and the prior day's low). We actually took out over 50 percent of the range and made $1.05.

Next we will talk you through the elements of the second trade to explain how the spread differential then signaled strength. The SPY prints the low of the day at $89.59, and we are stopped out of our short at $89.91. As that spread differential starts to accelerate and expand, we get an indication that confirms the technical setup. As we see the SPY trading higher from its $89.59 lows, we also see the spread widen from its low to the current price (last) of $89.85 (circled price in table in Figure 8.5). Because the spread between the low print and the last print is widening, we know buyers are taking the offer, so we use an aggressive leading limit order to take the offer. By doing so, we know that we are getting ahead of liquidity and getting into trades quicker than most other traders, who may be pausing or hesitating due to a lack of recognition of the inflection points or spread differentials. Traders who use technicals, elasticity, and momentum to uncover and execute trades gain the statistical edge. The risk/reward setup is also maintained by sharpening execution timing.

As we have discussed extensively throughout this book, the information necessary for trading the flow of the market and putting the edge in your favor can be found in many places, including spread differentials. These techniques are simply microcosms of the broad market and how it trades in terms of flow. Certainly the flow may be more like ripples within the waves in terms of reading the micromomentum, but this is still momentum. The only difference is how you apply momentum when taking into account your time horizon in the market. As an active trader or participant with a broader time horizon, having these skills can only improve profitability and lower your frictional market impact costs and slippage. As a scalping technique, this recognition is also invaluable to find quick entries and exits.

Getting back to the trade, as we focus on the strength of the SPY, we see confirmation of its strength as it tests the prior day's high on 7/31/02 of $91.62. This becomes incredibly important because we are traveling into what we call the no-trade zone, a high that we have not seen before within the time horizon being measured (three days prior; see 7/29 through 7/31). Many traders in this very scenario are subject to whipsaw risk, since this is precisely where markets fight the most as they seek new highs (or lows). Therefore, trading should be avoided until prices are firmly above the $91.62 level. Traders must then revert to prior highs in order to form a new picture of where the edge is likely to be. We have to see what our elasticity of range, or true range, is (as defined from the prior day), because this is what set up the short on the first trade. Since the market is now reversing and taking us to highs above what we have seen for the past three days, we know that the rally could easily fail.

We have to be careful, because the recent highs we are pioneering into are prone to resistance. Many long players who rode the market down are likely to trade out of their positions as soon as they get a chance to break even. These fearful weak holders contribute to the resistance and must not be forgotten. At the same time they also represent the weak market crowd, not strong enough to keep a strong market down, only strong enough to cause a slight pullback. This is principally why markets tend to pull back at resistance and why many technicians suggest buying only after the first pullback past resistance. If the pullback is slight (low volume) and does not retest the resistance level just broken, the technician has reason to believe the weak sellers are gone and therefore the issue can be bought. Once the market firmly passes through that resistance, it can trade through to higher levels. We must nevertheless treat the prior elastic high as our protective stop if the rally fails.

Traders who revert to the technical view of the market as new highs are printed can then go back in time on charts and look for prior highs as new potential resistance levels. We do not want to step into a no-man's-land where the markets have not been before without recognizing that reversals and pullbacks along the way are likely. The best confirmation that new highs will hold is new spread differentials from higher intraday lows. For example, in the second trade made on August 1 (Figure 8.5), as long as the last price traded as shown on the market minder represents larger spreads from the intraday low, we know the strength is holding. This does not mean that pullbacks will not occur, but if the spread from the lows evaporates, the long position would not be maintained. If the spread differential from the last price and the low price is beginning to show a more narrow range, you should perceive this as bearish compression and a sign of changing momentum. Imagine, for example, that the SPY trades firmly above $91.62 to $91.98. The spread differential is $2.40 ($91.98 high minus the $89.58 low). The SPY next pulls back to $91.78, for a spread of $2.20. The SPY then rallies to $91.90 for a spread of $2.32. Finally the SPY pulls back to $91.60; the spread is $2.02. The bearish compression is defined not only in terms of the declining spread, but also in terms of the lower highs and lower lows relative to the current market at that point in the session. Recognition of *relative change* is imperative yet a subtle nuance many miss.

RELATIVE CHANGE

When measuring price action within the given time horizon, we pay attention to relative as well as actual price change. Seeing the market on a relative basis provides another perspective that can uncover subtle changes in momentum. By using a nonlinear scale, traders see another representation of trend on a relative basis. For example, if Citigroup, symbol C, finds support at $32 and subsequently rallies 10 percent to $35.20, its linear price change is $3.20. If Citigroup then retraces 10 percent from its current $35.20 level, it does not return to its prior level of $32.00, but instead suffers a greater loss relative to the pre-rally price of $32.00. At that point, Citigroup retraces to $31.68, making a lower low relative to its prior support level. Therefore, price action to the downside has increased in nominal terms, but appears the same in relative terms. Traders should remember this fact when stocks reverse direction.

Traders are best served to monitor the rhythm of the market from both perspectives since the market sends a different message when looked at on a relative basis. This movement manifests itself as higher highs and higher lows in uptrends, and lower lows and lower highs in downtrends. The above example represents a situation that traders should recognize when reading the momentum of the market. If Citigroup trades aggressively higher 10 percent in a given period, but subsequently pulls back 10 percent from the new high, traders will know not only that there is zero momentum toward a rally, but that the issue is losing momentum toward the upside and gaining it toward the downside. Certainly prices also show this in linear terms, given the lower low price; but seen in relative terms as well, traders begin to realize how much harder prices can fall on retracements when all things are equal on a relative basis.

It seems overly simple, but we often hear investors state that they saw a 10 percent increase in value and didn't worry if the market gave it back because they believed markets often give back their gains before moving higher. This thinking is ludicrous, since relative moves in opposite directions don't cancel each other out. As traders, we want to monitor what pullbacks look like in relative terms. If a market rallies 10 percent and it pulls back 5 percent before restarting its uptrend, the momentum is strong. The spread differential is important because the greater the spread differential, the greater the momentum (in either direction). Keep in mind that the opposite is also true. If a market retraces 10 percent and subsequently rallies 10 percent, the issue is not relatively strong either. Rallies after retracements must have a greater spread differential if a true support level is to be found. For example, if Citigroup is trading at $32 and retraces 10 percent to $28.80, the $28.80 is not support unless Citigroup can rally higher than 10 percent (to 12 percent, for instance). If Citigroup rallies 11 percent from the $28.80 level, the issue is still considered in a downtrend even though the relative change looks strong. It is simple math, but perceptions are often skewed because of how the data is being viewed. We therefore look at both price levels and percentage changes in order to determine momentum.

Chapter 6 of this book, which deals with the directional movement indicator, does an excellent job of measuring price elasticity and relative range as compared to prior time horizons, whether for the day prior or several days prior. Once again, we choose to measure the most recent past for a greater definition of near-term future prices.

These principles are not new when looking at relative change over time. Scientists, including Einstein, have shown that range of movement expands based on the square root of time. This intriguing view of the market is drawn from scientific principles. While we will not go into the deep mathematics of this approach, its value can be summed up by stating that while mathematics confirm prices, they lose their predictive value the further out in time you go. It can also be said that the effects of wind at the starting point diminish over distance, both in the case of a simple fan in a room or the crest of mountain wind dissipating the farther it moves from its peak. It's simply a law of physics that many brighter minds could explain. To help you along the way, if you find this of interest, you can visit *www.oceantheory.com* for more detail.

TIGHT LEVELS

Many traders attempt to trade levels that should be ignored. We refer to this as trading "tight levels." Suppose the intraday range is $0.45, whereby the levels are $91.25 to $90.80, high to low. Given this information, we already know that the opportunity for strong momentum is limited because the market tells us what its range is at that moment. This range defines the market's current elasticity. If the technicals don't confirm a good risk/reward setup as defined by the prior day's highs and lows, this will not be a tradable range. This is critical to understand.

Momentum, as you can see, is somewhat hard to explain, but once you apply these techniques to a live market you will see and feel the levels. This is part of the art of trading, and it deserves as much of your attention as the science. Too often, because the science is more literal and tangible, traders get an unbalanced perspective. We feel you need both.

9

C H A P T E R

THE TAPE

Tape reading can't be totally taught out of a book, but alerting you to what is important about it can. What we hope to do is convince you that it warrants your time and energy to pay close attention to it. The tape reflects price and volume obviously, but it also reflects the other building blocks that we have discussed, all in one simple tool.

How do you measure 200 days of data on the tape? Well, the tape doesn't measure time historically, but it measures time relative to price levels within the day, which is valuable for timing trades. It measures how long a given price level holds. For example, it might show the E-Mini futures contract holding firm at 945, rallying to 950, and retracing back to 945 or 946. Oscillating back and forth within this tight range over periods of time, perhaps an hour or longer, would indicate that the 945 level is strong. Let's assume that the level is so strong that the next retracement doesn't even allow the market to come back to 945, but instead retraces to a higher low of 947. The spread between 945 and 947 may seem insignificant, but this can strongly indicate that you're not going to get another chance to buy at 945. Traders that understand and see this nuance can improve timing, and realize the 947 level should be taken because the next rally is prone to be a higher high. This is one simple example of reading price and time on the tape.

Using the tape requires a bit of a visceral feel. Once you master this feel, however, you will find that you spend more time trading with the tape than without it, as it contributes a high degree of certainty. With it you will be able to recognize levels, mark and collar those levels, and then look for and anticipate the acceleration or breakdown of levels. These are the skills and methodologies that a good tape reader employs, be it on the floor of the CME, the NYSE, the Nasdaq, or a virtual exchange such as Archipelago (ARCA). Mastering the tape will increase your trading prowess, as you will be able to trade the ranges within intraday trends.

When we speak of the visceral feel that needs to be developed by traders, we simply mean that traders should interpret market data in real time as well as on a chart. Some difficulty in reading the tape stems from the fact that most of the elements that we read through technical analysis and other analytical systems seem to be forgotten when reading the tape. The same components and building blocks we use for technicals are the things that are being measured on the tape. Traders who can successfully read the tape feel the momentum, velocity, and volume of the market for themselves, and this is a valuable skill when trading in real time.

One of the simplest and best ways of reading the tape is also one of the most literal. When looking at the tape in conjunction with high price, low price, and last price as illustrated in Chapter 8 (Figure 8.4), it is important to read spread differentials. Whether you are trading QQQ on the Nasdaq 100 or SPY on the S&P, E-Minis, semiconductors such as the SMH, or biotechs such as the BBH, reading the relative spread differential works. As we interpret these spread differentials, we also feel the liquidity in the market at that given moment. If overhead selling pressure is thinning on Level II along with a widening spread differential with upticks and bidders taking the offer, we know that statistically the spread is going to continue to widen and velocity is going to accelerate, thus lifting the market. This is the simplest form of tape reading and a most reliable indication. There are certainly many dynamics to this method and plenty of variations, but what really needs to happen is for you to spend as much time as possible in front of a live tape acquiring this skill.

READ THE OPEN

When reading the tape, the most important correlations that a trader can look for are tape resistance and tape support levels that are set intraday (also discussed in Chapter 8). Simply mark the levels between the high and low range that the market trades during the first 15 to 20 minutes of the open and recognize the levels when they get tested. The key is to look at the speed of the tape and the length of time the bids and offers survive on each side of the market. To illustrate this interpretation, we have captured an actual live trade and transcribed it to text as follows.

A LIVE READ

We're short 10 E-Mini S&P 500 futures contracts. They are trading between a low of 952.25 and a high of 962.25. We are short at 954.50. The market has continually established the elasticity of this range by testing the upper and lower limits (tape support and resistance). We see that more time and volume are currently on the low side of the range at 952.25 and that support at that level is continually being tested. Each time the market tests that support level, the support level seems to grow weaker. The bears pound on that support level harder and harder as the tape speeds up, with more aggressive sellers hitting bids at 952.25. The tape is speeding up now and we are looking for the ticker to print 952 flat. We print the 952.00 level, and an intraday tape support level has been broken. Now the tape is accelerating dramatically. Sellers are hitting the bids more aggressively because the psychological support barrier of the day has been penetrated. Those bids are being tested aggressively and are now at 951.75. The tape is still speeding up and sellers are hitting the bids more aggressively, finding new lows of the day. The new low indication is being shown to the entire marketplace, exacerbating the selling pressure and demonstrating how strong the bears can be today. The market weakness will continue until new lows are found. The first bullish sign comes when the tape slows down and fewer sellers aggressively hit lower bids.

We are looking for the sellers to continually hit bids more aggressively as those long the market are exiting. As fear sets in, the tape will speed up and result in more pressure to the downside. Once a new low is established and new support is found, we must consider tightening our trailing stop. The support level at 950.00 will seem firm, but will be tested. What we're looking for now is the next break through the 950.00 level to a new, lower intraday high, confirming weakness. The intraday trend is clearly indicating the downside elasticity is stretching and the upside elasticity is contracting; therefore the intraday trend is lower. The strategy here should be to remain short and even add to the position on slight rallies and let the trailing stop determine the exit on larger rallies. If stopped out on these rallies, a long position still would not make sense because we'd be fighting the intraday bearish trend.

The rally failed, and now we're printing 949.50 and the tape is speeding up even more dramatically (high velocity), as a new low has been set. The trend is now being confirmed, and we are able to maximize gains by recognizing what the tape is saying.

The previous exercise of narrating a live trade represents how the tape acts and sends signals. Essentially what we look to do is find levels in the market where we can put ourselves in a position to trade momentum off the tape, since we know that the tape is going to speed up dramatically as new lows are printed for short scenarios or new highs for long scenarios. This example was a short scenario, but the same situation occurs when trading the long side of the market. If we had printed a new high above the $962.25 level and penetrated the high, the bulls would have shown strong elasticity. Ultimately, these are the elements of the breakout and breakdown patterns for momentum as read from the tape, but they are also the same indications we get from the chart. The value of the tape is improved for time frames within 10 minutes where the chart is too microscopic.

Once traders learn how to read levels and read the tape, they are totally in control of their own universe. Tape reading at its very finest involves recognizing the levels, the speed, the velocity, and how long a bid or offer can survive on Level II. If the tape is starting to speed up and sellers are hitting the bid and the bid disappears quickly, you know that the buying crowd is weak. Therefore, any sellers that hit their bids completely destroy that bid level and a new bid at a lower level is shown. Conversely, when markets are strong and buyers are taking the offer and the sellers on the offer dissipate quickly, the selling pressure is light and the market has a propensity to lift. If you can read the tape, you will be the first to recognize breaking levels, both intraday and elastically, over several days. Technicians who ignore the tape are as remiss as day traders who ignore the technicals. Both skills are essential.

Many people ask about the "ax" that David wrote about in his first book, *How to Get Started in Electronic Day Trading*, and why is it more difficult to find the ax today than it was in the past. Before we address this, the ax is a market maker who dominates a stock at a given time. For example, if Goldman Sachs (GSCO) is a huge seller of Intel (INTC), and GSCO's selling action moved INTC more than any other market maker, GSCO is considered an "ax" at that moment in time. Today, the ax is generally no longer a factor since the market changed. Prominent players on the Level II montage when Level II was new often indicated which direction a market maker was biased by their buying and selling patterns. Today, electronic markets (screen-based markets) actually provide safe havens for the ax to hide. With the proliferation of electronic communication networks (ECNs) and electronic exchanges, we now have a wide-open market that provides greater liquidity, making it much easier for the so-called axes to hide. They are not leaving the clues they did when market access was limited. The market makers today are single voices in a stadium of screaming people. The capacity to read the tape and appreciate the information it conveys represents an enduring skill that will provide value as long as real-time quotes are disseminated, but to target any single market maker today is a mistake in terms of decision making.

The cliché "the devil is in the details" certainly holds true in the market, and a fine line exists to define where the market can go at any time. For example, technicians think of the fine line or turning point where markets tend to either break strongly upward or downward as the *apex of a triangle*. The apex is an inflection point where crowd behavior states, "Enough is enough," and the action changes. Distinguishing the apex on an intraday tape, perspective is really no different and is often the determining factor in whether you will win or lose for the day.

While the code of the market will never be cracked, the intuition you develop using the tape as well as the technicals is as close as you'll get. Tape reading, while not a replacement for technicals, is the best companion skill you can acquire. Its origins come from the exchange floors and its value will be ever present because this skill is transferable to virtual markets.

As we apply the momentum approach (which includes tape reading) to the market, we gain a greater understanding of ourselves in terms of the market, especially as we develop the ability to recognize when we are wrong. To be wrong is not the problem, in trading or in life; it is how one deals with being wrong that defines us. Once we gain a greater understanding of ourselves, we have greater insight into how others will act in the market, giving us a keener perspective on market psychology and crowd behavior.

VOLUME/VELOCITY RELATIONSHIPS

Stocks move the most on the least volume per price level when supply and demand imbalances grow. Buyers chase sellers and run prices up, or sellers lean on buyers and push prices lower. Gaps, major moves in price that have almost no volume, are the most extreme example of this phenomenon. Prices change the most when there is the least amount of volume. As prices begin to saturate, velocity drops and volume builds as a consensus of value develops. This results in consolidations on rallies or stabilizations in retracements. Either way, when supply and demand are in balance, buyers and sellers agree, and therefore volume grows through the turnover of shares.

As we saw in Chapters 4 and 5, this action reflects the four primary stages of a trade. Saturation at stabilization and consolidation are really stages 1 and 3 on a microtime horizon. Therefore we should manage the trade as these transitions occur. Short-term traders want to take long positions in a stage 2 markup (as indicated by high velocity) and either tighten the trailing stop in stage 3 or exit. Conversely, during a stage 4 decline (again, on high velocity), trades want to short the market and either tighten the trailing stop or cover in stage 1 (a period of low velocity). It all depends on your time horizon. In day trading, the tape will identify stages 1 through 4 based on volume/velocity relationships, and charts will do the same on longer-term setups. It is all based on perspective and is dependent on your trading method at the time. Either way, day trading or swing trading, the micro- and macrodynamics of the markets and capitalism itself don't change. Therefore, volume/velocity relationships are as simple to see on the tape as they are on the charts.

Another way of looking at it is that volume/velocity relationships are inversely related. As velocity improves, volume tends to diminish, and as velocity subsides, volume tends to increase. So while volume grows at each price level, the turnover of shares grows while volatility fades. When looking at the angle of attack on a chart, the price increase will be steep and fast relative to time. Traders must understand that everything that makes it to the chart must first pass through the tape, so why not master both? Both measure the same dynamics, but they measure them with different mediums.

F I G U R E   9.1

A venturi diagram demonstrates the inverse relationship between volume and velocity.

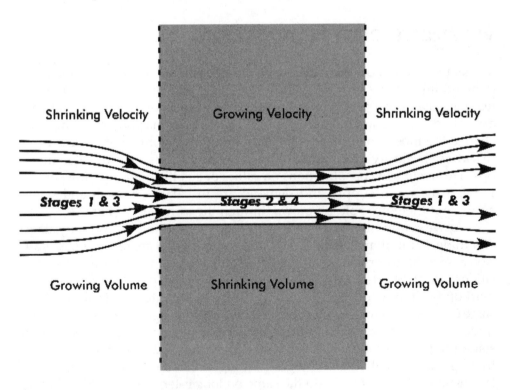

PICTURE THE MOMENT

In concluding tape reading, we will leave you with a few images. We wish we could somehow draw pictures of what we see when we trade, but we can tell you that we are not seeing charts. We are seeing images of growing and releasing pressure, not unlike a dam. Water that builds up at a dam is growing in volume, while decreasing in velocity, since there is a lack of forward movement by the water. When the dam breaks, the volume of water in the reservoir begins to decline because it is flowing out. At the same time velocity is greatly increasing as the water rushes through the relatively small opening. In that sense you have a venturi principle, a common principle of physics. In the same way, we can compare the transition of the market from stage to stage to a mass of water flowing from a larger pipe into a smaller one. The water must gain speed and build pressure as it enters the smaller pipe (see Figure 9.1).

Trading is all about interpreting the present moment to arrive at your best estimate of what the future moment will be. Anyone who leads you to believe that deep study into the past is going to accurately predict that future moment is kidding you. Selling the past is very attractive, easy, and believable. Anybody can look at the past of a chart, to the left of the hard right edge, and say, "Look what happened here, here, and here, and if you had done this, this, and that, you would have achieved your objective." While some participants will be able to manage risk well enough to profit by anticipating future moves, the vast majority will become the liquidity for the few who make money consistently. Reading the tape is not as appealing as a stochastic, a chart pattern, a RSI, or some other indicator that you would love to believe is always correct. It is not sellable. It is not as tempting. It is not as literal. But it is real. Hopefully your own instincts will tell you that the things that are really valuable and enduring are often the most difficult to put your finger on. They are visceral. Learning to read the tape will take time. Make the investment—it's worth it.

10

C H A P T E R

TRADING VOLATILITY

Trading employs many strategies, including using technicals to arrive at decisions; however, not all trades are driven strictly by just technical influences. Because volatility can distort the short-term perspective, traders must also acquire skills of recognizing and trading volatility. Volatility is not a friend to technical analysis, therefore it is important to have a backup plan. The methods we follow are a few favorite techniques we use to complement and round out our technical views of the market. When markets are difficult to read and setups are few, we want to trade the market strictly on a short-term basis (intraday); therefore, we turn to these methods.

PARABOLIC PLAYS

Up until now, we have focused mainly on market symmetry and structure to define methods of trading, but the market is not always so obliging. There are many occasions that short-term charts (inside 10 minute bars) offer a valuable insight into short-term trades regardless of the prevailing trend. In other words, when the markets appear sloppy and highly volatile, we find it best to focus only on trading inefficiencies. Essentially, technical analysis finds its value from market psychology, but when the market becomes somewhat schizophrenic, technical analysis loses some value. As stated in

Chapters 4 and 5, these periods are most associated with Stages 1 and 3. Short-term charts have their greatest value during these times. What we find most interesting about short-term charts is that they send clues regarding the waning consensus of value, which we believe is a better indication of short-term trading opportunities during Stages 1 and 3 than almost anything else. We tend to look at short-term (two- to five-minute) charts with a contrarian viewpoint. We believe they can reveal the exhaustion of short-term trend lines, especially when the bigger picture shows an opposite trend (choppy). One example of a simple pattern would be a rounding bottom or rounding top (see Figure 10.1). Rounding chart formations tend to show market confusion and the turning of events for the preceding trend. As a rule, rounding tops show weakening markets, while rounding bottoms show strengthening markets. Therefore, from a trend perspective, fading rounding formations is a far better bet than trading with the short-term prevailing trend. For example, if a rounding bottom is observed on a five-minute chart over five trading days, traders will be best served to apply a shorter-term approach.

A good confirming indicator to use with this pattern is the relative strength index (RSI), as discussed in Chapter 6. RSI is an excellent velocity gauge, and when trading short term, velocity is something we want to anticipate. Because the reversal of a bearish trend accelerates mania and excitement, just as bull market reversals accelerate fear and panic, velocity tends to increase once a reversal is in play. While rounding bottom or top formations are generally sedate patterns, short-term traders do well to see these patterns as the calm before the storm. Oftentimes these patterns are signals of short-term trend reversals and are precursors to dramatic parabolic moves.

The most interesting fact about parabolic moves is that due to their high velocity, the moves are over in a much shorter time period than the data used to make the discovery in the first place. While a rounding bottom may develop slowly over a five-day period, for example, the reversal can be a "V" bottom pattern that is over quickly. This is where bulls take control, and is also where mania takes over. Excitement is dominant and will present itself as velocity through a steep angle of attack over a short period of time, causing the uninformed trader to miss the reversal. Therefore, traders must learn to anticipate rather than participate. Traders who seek to participate in the reversal rounding pattern are Johnny-come-latelies and are destined to miss trades, while traders who anticipate are willing to get ahead of momentum. Because parabolic moves are essentially situations in which prices get ahead of themselves, in the case of a bullish move, sellers often lag the mania. But once sellers catch up to these rapid moves, stocks tend to run into a large supply of selling pressure from active traders, causing another correction, hence volatility.

What you want to think about in these situations is that while the reversal is powerful, corrections are expected. Many times you will see the rapid parabolic move, then a correction (pullback), and then a more sustainable restart of the uptrend. This is an indication that the issue is strong and the reversal is real, but that the initial move needed to be digested before it could resume.

Obviously, the same is true for the downside. This is something you learn to see and feel; it is not purely mechanical. Therefore, if seeking to trade the initial parabolic move, traders must anticipate by viewing the rounding bottom pattern as a precursor. If traders prefer to participate, wait for the

F I G U R E   10.1

An intraday chart of Amgen Inc. (AMGN) using 10-minute bars shows an obvious rounding bottom.

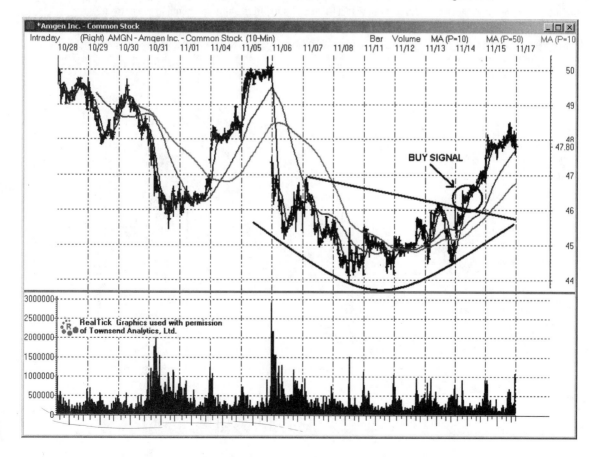

pullback to buy. Certainly stops and predetermined levels of risk must be ad-
hered to with the understanding that fading a rounding pattern may have
only a slightly better than 50 percent chance for success. But that's not the
point. The opportunity for rapid gains that the trade can provide when in
correct relation to the risk is quite significant. Traders who are only right
50 percent of the time when fading a short-term rounding pattern and who
participate in a radical move will see significant net profits over their losing
trades as long as their risk tolerances are tight and the discipline to follow
them is ingrained.

Figures 10.1 and 10.2 are examples of a breakout and a breakdown that
occurred from a rounding bottom and a rounding top, respectively. By fading the downtrend during the rounding bottom in Figure 10.1, there is a

F I G U R E   10.2

An intraday chart of Wellpoint Health Networks (WLP) using hourly bars shows a rounding top pattern.

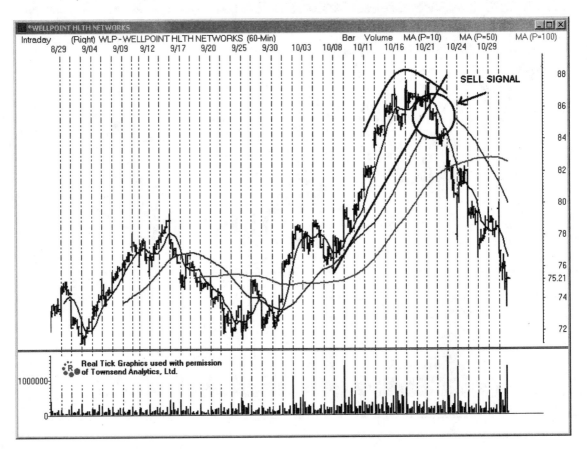

chance to participate in a dramatic rally once the trend line is broken at $46.00. In Figure 10.2, by fading the uptrend the trader could have participated in the sharp decline once the trend line was broken at $86.00.

PARTICIPATING VERSUS ANTICIPATING

In order to properly trade volatility, one must understand when to initiate and anticipate versus when to be more passive (participate). Market analysis is a process of trading on, at best, the small marginal probabilities of the market. Earlier we stated that markets are efficient, and this is true over time, but it is important to always remember that the shorter the time horizons measured, the more inefficient the market. While this inefficiency does not last long, it speaks to the value of the short-term horizon. That's why day trading still has so much appeal. It is the approach that captures the most market inefficiency while at the same time it requires aggressive and prompt action. This approach to the market is referred to as *trading the delta*. A *delta* is simply defined as a small quantitative of anything that is being measured. Many critics would say that day traders attempt to trade an "epsilon" of market inefficiency, which is defined as an indistinguishable margin for profit, but the approach is not to trade just for a small price change. Rather, day traders seek to reveal the signals of an ensuing price explosion and anticipate the move. This is principally because inefficiency is created through emotional factors that cause markets to overreact in a bullish or bearish fashion. It is at saturation points (rounding patterns) that markets show their greatest propensity for ensuing price extremes and reversals. In this situation, anticipation is the better approach for short-term strategies, while participation is more suitable for longer time horizons such as swing trading.

Day traders tend to do better at anticipating reversals on short-term patterns and participating in intraday trends as the day unfolds. Typically, day traders will reverse the first positions of the day, until a true trend can be established and seen as the day develops. Once trends become more perceivable, day traders will then start to trade and participate in a more sustainable trend for overnight positions. One approach anticipates (day trades), and the other participates (swing trades).

Remember that the first few trades of the day are not the most important. Most believe they are, as if they are faced with the challenge of determining the bias of the day at the opening. Too many suffer from the psychology that the opening trades of the day are the acid test of whether or not they called the market correctly that day. Forget this nonsense. Who cares! Traders learn more about markets by engaging them rather than observing them. For example, if you bid a stock and are immediately filled, then chances are the market in that issue is more negative than positive. Conversely, if you try to lift an offer and are not filled, chances are the issue is strong. This type of feedback from the market tells you more as a participant than as an observer. Therefore, trading and anticipating at the open has great value. When you are correct, the profits are significant because you anticipated. If you are wrong and the trade acts weak, you gain more insight into what the developing trend is so that you can eventually participate. So don't put too much emphasis on the opening trades. Test the waters and do what the market tells you to do.

This plays out very simply. For example, suppose that in the morning, within 30 to 45 minutes (but no later) of the open, we buy weakness at or below the bid, anticipating a bullish turn. Then as the trend becomes more known, generally after the first 30 to 45 minutes, we confirm the bullish bias and lift offers. In either case, adding liquidity (bidding) or removing it (lifting), we act according to the situation. Anticipating traders add liquidity by bidding the market or offering the market. Participating traders remove liquidity by lifting offers and hitting bids. Anticipating the opening with good risk management during the first 30 to 45 minutes while participating in the trend as the day unfolds and confidence grows is a key to successful trading.

OPENINGS AND GAP METHODS

Volatility is generally at its greatest level during the opening. During this time we see the most inefficiency in the form of gaps.

The opening is the most emotional time of the session. It is the moment in which most bets are made by the amateur crowd—hence the aphorism, "Amateurs control the open, professionals control the close." The opening is the moment of cause and effect. It is the time of the day in which professionals "feed cause" in order to "eat effect." The amateurs are tested at the open. We must understand that amateurs react to "cause," while traders react to "effect." It is the effect that is relevant. People are constantly paying attention to the causes, whether they are earnings, news, upgrades, downgrades, splits, reverse splits, bankruptcies, corruptions, or what have you. But these do not matter. These causes have already been digested, relegating their value to no more than market waste. Certainly, some events are so radical that the market can't begin to digest the information, and the market, like the human body, has a defense mechanism. It shuts down, backs away from the table, and says, "There's too much to digest here; we need time." Hence the reason for trading halts; but as a rule, market causes need to be ignored and looked at as market waste. The information has already been digested and accounted for through price.

While the opening is where the greatest inefficiencies exist, gap openings are not always head fakes. Many times there is legitimate follow-through. However, professionals know that the amateur crowd's emotions are highest at the open due to news dissemination, and the professionals feed this emotion with gaps. How do we recognize a follow-through gap from a fading gap? Simply stated, when the velocity and time indications show that prices can't follow through and the gap begins to crack or fail, it's better to fade the original gap and relegate the gap to inefficiency. For example, a market that gaps down but can't stay down tends to close its gap and rally. These head fakes are indications of inefficiencies and are most prevalent at the open because professionals influence and cause them. "Amateurs control the open" simply means that professionals expect the amateur market segment to control opening prices based on emotional reactions to events; therefore they gap markets so that they can fade the reaction. While the amateurs may control the open, they don't maintain the open; the professionals do. Amateurs' indications of interest will be evident to market makers and specialists as "market on open orders," leading the professionals to open the market in a direction they can soon fade. Once the saturation point is found, the amateur crowd's participation starts to wane and professionals take a contra position. As a rule, in the absence of immediate follow-through on the opening gap, fade it. When confirming indicators verify the gapped open, markets will tend to follow through. Therefore, gaps will gap and run (follow through), or gap and crack (fail).

When we trade reversal gaps, we bet that the amateur crowd will be panicking to cover its opening longs (assuming a bullish gap), thus exacerbating the downturn. In the case of gap downs, amateurs who own the shares are the first to exit long positions, creating the opportunity to buy weakness. The amateurs' bad news is the professionals' good news. A little Darwinist? Maybe. But remember that we're not in the markets to run for mayor; we're there to make money. So as a rule, think about gap ups this way: If they hold the gap, they tend to run because greed brings follow-through. If gap ups start to penetrate the opening levels (below), fade the gap. In the case of gap downs, once fear has run its course and prices penetrate the opening price (above), fade the gap and go long.

All that glitters isn't gold. At the opening, be skeptical of opening indications. This doesn't mean the indications won't confirm and follow through, but you should be wary of the opening prints. What seems to be apparent, like a gap, is often a head fake, and temporary. Ensuing price activity and volume must confirm the gap; otherwise don't trust it. If new traders are intimidated by the early minutes of the day's activity, then they would do best to stand aside and be patient. It is best to wait for opening inefficiencies to dissipate and look for what we would consider a greater statistical edge in trading the second and more reliable trend of the day. This generally occurs after the first 30 to 45 minutes. This trend tends to be more gradual, but also more reliable. Regardless of whether traders are more aggressive and prefer to anticipate the trend and trade it, or are more conservative and want to wait out the open (participate), they must understand the rules of engagement. Obviously, when trading gaps there are no absolutes, but as a rule the following methods have served us well.

PRICE/VOLUME METHODS FOR TRADING VOLATILITY

Volume is perhaps the most forgotten measure in the market, taking a back seat to price, news, and fundamentals. Yet volume tells us about future price action, since volume represents the purest measure of the market's appetite for shares. Price can move erratically on light volume, but because light volume is not a broad-based consensus of value, the perception of value (price) is called into question. Only volume can confirm price. After all, today we trade more average volume in a single day than was traded in the course of a year in the 1970s (source: *2002 Stock Trader's Almanac*). Volume measures the strength and intensity of any given trend over a defined time horizon, and therefore the consideration of volume is imperative to all traders. The astute trader allows volume to define the fine line between discipline and conviction, often an elusive task. Using volume as a key indication of market trend is not suasion on our part; it is a fact of market dynamics that cannot be ignored. When combined with simple logic, we believe that the best indicator of volume is the TRIN. We covered the TRIN in Chapter 6. Now let's explain some of the logic regarding volume.

To begin, we must understand the price/volume relationships that exist in the market, as well as the psychological explanation for such correlations. Once these are known, traders learn to interpret volume, first consciously and then unconsciously or instinctively.

Perhaps the best explanation of this relationship as applied to the market would be the changing tide of the market during a dramatic downturn. Like a storm, dramatic market events such as Black Monday, October 19, 1987, are high-intensity events that punch hard but move on quickly. These sudden and dramatic events take panic and fear to crescendo levels, thereby exacerbating selling.

Many traders confuse advancing volume with crescendoing volume. Advancing volume confirms trends, while crescendoing volume signals their end. Market psychology dictates that, historically, crowds tend to be wrong during extremes (crescendoing volume). This is the motivation for which traders use sentiment indicators such as put/call ratios. It is expected that at peak levels of consensus (such as high put buying over call buying), the bears are wrong and a rally is imminent. This confirms the maxim we have mentioned several times: "Good news comes out at the top, and bad new comes out at the bottom." The crescendoing volume spike is your signal that tops and bottoms have been put in. When markets top, it is expected that all bullish bias in the markets will be measured through a surge in volume. Traders should sell crescendoing volume regardless of price. This is why volume is as good a barometer of market direction as price.

When markets bottom, selling fear is maximized, margin calls are in play, media sources make sure everyone is scared, and prices are depressed. Welcome bargain hunters of the world! The bottom is in, so buy this capitulation. Day traders recognize these indications on an intraday microlevel. As

F I G U R E   10.3

An example of a stock that moves higher on heavy volume then pulls back on light volume.

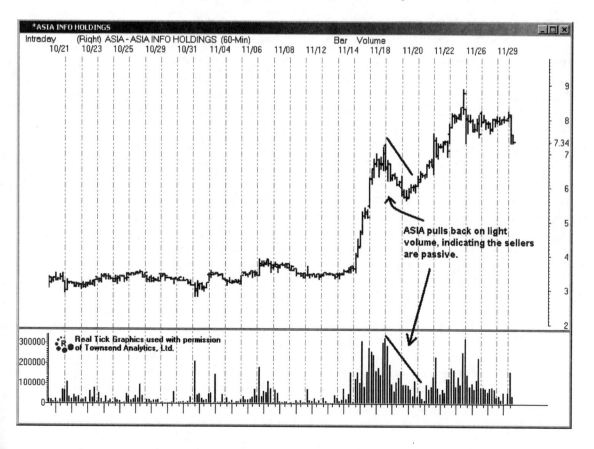

the tape speeds up and prices follow, we want to fade the move as a rule. If after fading the move the issue fails to reverse, we employ a time stop. This means that if, after we enter, the stock trades sideways after a certain period, we recognize this as the wrong trade and exit. For example, if a large mutual fund like Janus is dumping a large position of stock, traders will look for signs that the overhead selling pressure is nearing an end in terms of volume. In fact, it can be said that volume is a better leading indicator of market turns and reversals than price. Volume leaves clues as to where the tail end of trends exist as volume subsides. In the example of the Janus dump, once sellers begin to reach the end of the order, the volume will begin to subside, as will price elasticity. Traders who recognize this will buy the remaining weakness on lower volume, perceiving that the sellers are absorbed and the sell-off is at or near an end. Buying this remaining weakness is far more prudent than trying to pick a perfect bottom. The best tactic is to scale into dissipating weakness as lower volume signals a probable turn. See Figure 10.3 as an example of a low volume pullback.

AVERAGING DOWN OR AVERAGING IN

Many believe and have preached that buying on pullbacks means "averaging down," but this could not be further from the truth. To unilaterally say that averaging down is a mistake is too one-dimensional. We've all heard the phrase, "Don't frown, average down." Averaging down involves buying a sell-off on the way down (assuming a long scenario) for no other reason than to lower a cost basis; this generally puts the victim into the trade at the beginning of the sell-off rather than at the end. The "averaging down" player is late to buy on the uptrend and early to buy on the downtrend, whereas smart traders learn to size up the market by paying close attention to declining volume and the accompanying inelasticity of price (price retraces in smaller increments) as indications that weakness is starting to dissipate. Participants who average down see the market as a vicious enigma that somehow knows their innermost thoughts and fears, and this impression is reinforced by the reality that trades seem to turn positive on them soon after they exit their painful position! These are the very participants who suffer the most, not as a result of the market, but as a result of poor trading.

Scaling into a position within a defined zone of support for long positions or resistance for shorts is good trading. Scaling is defined as adding to position size with several smaller positions—for example, buying five 1000 share trades into an area of support as prices are falling. In this instance, the trader may seemingly be averaging down, while in actuality the trader recognizes support being slowly put in. A rounding bottom as stated earlier in this chapter is a classic example. The trader who anticipates the reversal and scales in with several buys at lower and lower prices is practicing scale trading and acting like a professional. As long as a predetermined protective stop is set that mandates the trade to be covered at some specific point of failure, this practice is recommended. This is an example of the fine line between conviction and discipline. The trader who averages down after issue breaks support has poor discipline. The trader who scales in above support has good conviction. Scaling is a good technique, but only with a rigid protective stop that serves as the threshold for both adding to and holding positions.

If you scale into a position, and by the time you are at your protective stop you are fully scaled in, we venture to say that the odds of being right and making money are very slim.

Traders who lean into a position slowly while some weakness still exists have not adopted a bad strategy, as long as volume confirms that weakness is nearing an end. Volume measures growing and contracting trends. It can be measured in any time frame. Rising volume confirms a given trend, but once volume begins to subside from the prevailing trend, there is a greater indication that the trend has run its course. Remember, prices move the most on the least volume, so this divergence signals turns. Price/volume divergence is a great signal for intraday traders, as well as swing traders.

SUMMARY

Volatility, inefficiency, and the associated trading methods are an almost endless subject. Much more can be said, but if you can understand the relationship between price and volume, as well as the motivations of market makers and specialists to create inefficiencies, you can then self-teach yourself to see countless scenarios that unfold in our markets. Whether reading the charts, the tape, or trading on an exchange floor, the psychology is the same. Therefore, never let the medium in which this psychology plays itself out override your knowledge. The charts can send signals that lie and on the other hand, the charts never lie. Prices and volume are charted based on factual historical data; this doesn't lie. But one's interpretation of the charts formations can lie. Therefore, always stay well grounded to what we call Foundational Analysis as discussed in the introduction. Regardless where one reads the psychology of the market (charts, tape, the floor), the relationship of price and volume endures. Chapter 11 reinforces this fact through the rules and techniques of the specialist.

11
C H A P T E R

LISTED RULES
AND STRATEGIES

In this chapter we highlight the opportunities that exist for electronic traders who wish to engage the listed markets. This understanding begins with knowledge of the specialists' rules and the resulting impact these rules have on their trading patterns.

The complexity of the New York Stock Exchange (NYSE) and the rules that govern specialists, floor brokers, and participants on the exchange not only dictate the proper code of conduct but also have a derivative impact on all regional exchanges because of the Intermarket Trading System (ITS), created in part by Bill Lupien. ITS effectively links the NYSE with national market centers through a communication network, allowing participants (brokers and market makers) to electronically communicate orders and quotes whenever the Consolidated Quote System (CQS) indicates a potentially better price. CQS quotes real-time bids and offers to all market centers trading listed stocks. As we explore these systems and the rules that guide them, we will uncover trading techniques that can be employed by active electronic traders. It should be noted that while the information used by the authors was taken directly from the NYSE floor's official manual of market surveillance, the rules are always subject to change. We recommend frequent reference to the New York Stock Exchange's Web site at *www.nyse.com* to keep abreast of updates and future rule changes.

That said, most of the rules we will discuss have changed very little over time; therefore, we will focus on these more enduring principles of the exchange. Certain rules pertaining to trading halts, circuit breakers, and other computational values have changed, but we don't regard these changes as substantive to trading strategies. The principal methodology of the New York Stock Exchange has changed very little.

WALKING THE BOOK

The term *walking the book* originates from specialists on the NYSE and regional exchanges, describing a process in which floor brokers may execute orders with a specialist on the exchange. The basic premise of walking the book refers to how a floor broker may execute trades for his or her customers (institutional). The two key points per the rules state that the broker can trade with the customer's order while the market in a given stock moves up or down (walking the book of orders). The rules essentially state that if the broker walks the book he or she may not take the other side of the trade when he or she puts up the block. Since we know that the broker can only participate in the block print if he or she hasn't walked the book, we can assume that a block that trades after you see that he or she walked the book has not yet been purchased by the broker. The value of this information is that when the broker fills the customer order (large institutional orders) and prints the block to the tape, traders can interpret this a few ways. First, if the institution is a large seller of shares and the broker crosses the order with a buyer, traders know that it was a natural buyer of the shares. Because the buyer most likely still has more to buy, support is more likely to be found once the sell order is finished. This support is likely to be found since the overhead selling pressure is diminishing, if not gone, once the broker finishes the large block. In the second scenario, if the broker did not walk the book lower, but instead printed the block down without hitting bids, and bought shares from the seller (his or her customer), the broker will want to sell the shares back into the market quickly. From our point of view, we would want to wait until these shares were sold before buying the stock (bid under the market). We would monitor this from the tape as well. While this may seem a bit complicated at first glance, this lesson explains what others are looking for on an exchange level. These are the very traders you compete with when trading each day; therefore, your understanding of the listed markets is equally important.

Walking the book forces the specialist in you, the day trader, to be a spectator of events unfolding around you, so that you can go along with the trend. On the New York Stock Exchange, specialists observe the crowd, participate, and act as auctioneers. Specialists trade around the same data that virtual traders do, but on the floor. Specialists read price action. In this they have an edge, as they have the specialist's book (all of the orders given to the specialist by the various members that are away from the market), even if they essentially read the same raw data we do. Specialists recognize the time horizons over which prices change, the velocity with which prices move, and the volume and size being executed by traders. They are ultimately getting an overall feel for the day or the hour, participating in the market rather than predicting it.

Another type of order commonly seen on the NYSE is the "go-along" order. This order is essentially a type of discretionary order given to the specialist by a broker for the broker's customer. The customer is usually a sophisticated institutional customer; therefore, representing a size player. A go-along order instructs the specialist to fill a given buy or sell order as a percent of the volume that is trading in that stock. A "participate," but don't "initiate" order, means that as orders are filled in the market, the specialist can then "go-along" with the order according to the percent the customer has given him. Therefore, the customer is buying or selling with others (participating) in the market. If you see, for example, a 1500 lot print followed by another 1500 lot (buys), it is likely a 50 percent go-along order. The value of knowing this is that these orders are given by generally size players who may be buying for days. (Note: the same could be true for selling.) When you recognize this type of order, it may not be a sure reason to follow a particular order flow; however, it does show other participants trading in the same direction. This follows the principle that the only way to make money in the market is when after you buy (or sell), others follow to push prices higher (or lower for shorts). Because these types of orders are of the institutional variety, we as traders gain an edge by trading with them, not against.

WIDE VARIATION MARKETS

When markets gain volatility, they widen in price. During wide variation markets and unusual market conditions, specialists rely heavily on floor officials and governors to make determinations regarding the markets in which they are trading. Therefore, before we discuss the rules and responsibilities of the specialist, we must gain some understanding of the authority and responsibilities of the floor official. The scope of floor officials gives them the authority to supervise and regulate active openings and unusual situations, including transactions through the Intermarket Trading System (ITS). This is known as Rule 47. Floor officials are brought in to supervise trading during wide price variation markets, as well as delayed openings, halts, and other periods of market inefficiency. As a general point of knowledge, it should be recognized that floor officials contribute greatly to the maintenance of a fair and orderly market for listed securities, as these officials are disinterested parties with regard to the securities they officiate. Because of this fact, trading listed securities offer many advantages over Nasdaq securities for the tape reader and active electronic trader. Simply put, because listed securities function as an auction market, each new trade represents a new auction at every price level on every stock traded on the New York Stock Exchange.

When one thinks of the auction process, it is usually the image of an auctioneer presenting bids and offers that comes to mind, this being the correct perception of the market as well. The only modification when thinking about stocks is that every auction in the market is automatically restarted with each new trade in a listed stock. Throughout the trading day, participants essentially restart the bidding and offering process as prices rise and fall. This systematic process continues uninterrupted until market inefficiencies—such as wide variations with large supply/demand imbalances—occur at such extremes that the rules call for either halts, circuit breakers, or other intervening mechanisms to restore a fair and orderly market.

It is with this brief understanding of the listed securities market that traders begin to understand the auction procedure. This procedure is essential to a listed securities market, but not to the negotiated market for Nasdaq securities. Negotiated markets are less efficient, allowing for more discretion on the part of the market makers, and can be less orderly in terms of being mandated through rules. *Caveat emptor (venditor),* or "let the buyer (seller) beware," acts as a self-policing mechanism for the negotiated market, while the New York Stock Exchange itself provides floor officials who can intervene when necessary. For this reason and others, there is greater volatility in Nasdaq securities than in listed securities. The greater number of technology companies trading on Nasdaq compared to the listed securities market contributes to this volatility. Often proprietary firms will only allow their traders to trade listed securities because of this fact. So when you think of a listed security, imagine a new auction every time a security trades. Specialists are the auctioneers, and they are closely evaluated by floor officials to ensure order in the auction.

The New York Stock Exchange is a physical environment consisting of four main rooms, and much of the order on the NYSE is provided by its physical aspect. The proximity of the posts calls for a high degree of communication among the participants. A high regard is necessarily placed on dialogue among these participants, especially during wide variation markets caused by market volatility. Traditionally, wide variation markets were more related to the bid/ask spreads, but with the advent of decimalization, this strict definition has become less important with regard to spreads and more important in relation to momentum and volatility. Decimalization has certainly decreased the inherent bid/ask spread, thereby lowering the "frictional cost" of trading. The point is that wide variation situations today are market driven, not spread driven.

Because of this physical auction market, focus is on communication and the rules that govern the exchange participants. Later in this chapter, we discuss the practices of the world's newest fully electronic exchange, Archipelago (ARCA), which we believe brings the benefits of both the NYSE and Nasdaq into one ultimate exchange. While the NYSE has a very functional system, including a complex system for appeals that is made up of floor governors and senior floor officials, its process is based on the rich tradition of the exchange and is based less on transparency and complete accessibility.

THE SPECIALIST

Now that we have briefly discussed the system by which the New York Stock Exchange operates, we can move to the more important subject of trading. By understanding the role of the exchange's most notable (or should we say notorious) participant, the specialist, we begin to understand what motivates trading decisions. As a specialist, members must first be approved and registered by the exchange. Specialists are considered to be professional representatives of the market once assigned a post. As a prerequisite, they must complete adequate training as apprentices under an experienced existing specialist. Additionally, minimum capital in terms of liquid assets of greater than one million dollars, or 25 percent of a specialist's position requirement, is requisite. Therefore, specialists are considered to be both experienced and well capitalized.

One of the most important functions of specialists is to "maintain a fair and orderly market" in the stocks in which they specialize. "Fair and orderly" implies price continuity at each price level, as well as depth of market in terms of supply and demand. Specialists do this by utilizing their capital and liquid assets as dealers in the stocks they specialize in to cushion price movement when insufficient supply and demand exist. Rule 104.10 (1) and (2) states that "any bids or offers made by the specialist on his own account should be such that if the transaction is accepted on his bid or offer, it will bear a proper relationship to the preceding and anticipated succeeding transactions." This simply means that specialists are to act on their own accounts in relation to market direction and provide bids and offers in the market to cushion dramatic price swings by acting in a contra fashion. For example, if the overall trend of the stock is moving higher, specialists are expected to buy on the bid or midpoint, not on the offer; moreover, if the markets are trending lower, specialists are expected to sell on the offer or midpoint, not the bid.

This defines the way in which specialists can participate in the stocks' direction while providing liquidity to the market. This rule allows specialists to act as contributors to the market without exacerbating market moves. Nasdaq market makers don't have this same requirement, which is known as *affirmative obligation*.

Affirmative obligation contributes value-added dealer participation to cushion dramatic price swings. This is not to suggest that specialists can prevent stocks from making these dramatic swings, but it is their responsibility to participate in the direction of the prevailing market by functioning as liquidity providers. Before we start putting any halos over these specialists' heads, as traders we should interpret the specialists' function in light of this fact: nobody puts up a minimum of a million dollars while trading against the minor trend without trading it to his or her advantage.

Because specialists are required to buy on weakness, sell into strength, and act as price-cushioning market participants against the trend, observing their actions is an excellent way to guide your own. Specialists are required to provide price cushioning, and you can expect this cushioning to be greatest as trends near their end, thereby allowing specialists to position themselves ever closer to the reversal pattern of a given trend. Because of this fact, once listed securities begin to show trend change on an intraday basis and actually reverse, these stocks tend to follow-through longer with increased reliability because specialists have had to average into the position or average down as contras to the trend. This translates into a more sustained trend upon reversal in listed stocks. In this regard, trading with specialists and not against them confirms the cliché, "The trend is your friend." This saying can, on balance, be trusted; thus allowing traders greater conviction at turning points than on a Nasdaq issue, with less whipsaw risk.

RAW INTERPRETATION

Let's face it, most substantial activity on the floor occurs as a result of sudden news, and this includes ratings changes and analysts' revisions put out by the very member firms that trade on the NYSE—firms like Goldman Sachs, Spear, Leeds & Kellogg (now owed by Goldman), Susquehanna Partners, Merrill Lynch, and so forth. As riveting market news hits the street, listed securities are going to trade in a wide price range, be subject to delay and halts, and be spread out in terms of liquidity and volatility.

As a result, stock becomes less liquid at each price level, widening the range and resulting in increased volatility. This is where opportunity exists for specialists, who truly have an unfair advantage. When market illiquidity occurs as the result of sudden market moves for whatever reason, specialists will step in to provide liquidity at each price level, done at the end of a given minor trend so as to be with the reversal following a downturn or retrace-ment after sudden rallies. The interpretation is simple: While specialists must be liquidity providers of last resort—buying in the face of sellers and selling in the face of buyers—they will seek, for example, to buy weakness as prices and volume stabilize. Because specialists do not need to step in to provide liquidity during a high-volume sell-off, as it is only necessary to provide liquidity when little or none exists, they are often (though not always) closer to a turning point. In the case of minor but sharp downturns, the market has a tendency to capitulate at bottoms, and this fact is highlighted by high-volume selling pressure that turns to low-volume selling near bottoms or reversals. Specialists want to buy those bottoms. So should you.

STRATEGY

During accelerated sell-offs on higher than average volume, we look for the tape and trend to show signs of a pause in the sell-off. As the tape slows and the price retracement or decline narrows, we begin to scale into the trades like a specialist would—meaning that we will not aggressively open the entire position at any given price level. For example, if prices in IBM retrace aggressively from $80 to $78.50, we look to buy weakness in the issue as volume noticeably slows and prices stabilize. We will begin to open positions by buying weakness at the bid and continue to buy into the sell-off every $0.50 down or so. As the sell-off fades and volume begins to accelerate with stable-to-rising prices, we will add to the position more aggressively in order to complete the trade. Specialists need to entice sellers to the market—if the rally off the retracement is real—by bidding the stock at higher and higher prices. As the bids gain momentum (tape readers should be looking for this), the rally in an issue like IBM can easily run a few dollars or more, providing an exit into strength at prices that are higher than the average price of the scaled position. In the heat of battle, specialists are going to protect profitability for themselves and the firms they represent first. While the rules discourage manipulation, there is no way to completely avoid the specialists' inherent desire to profit from order flow at the expense of the public while trading on the NYSE. This is an inherent human characteristic. You would do the same thing. If you didn't, you would not make it as a specialist!

OTHER RELEVANT RULES AND STRATEGIES

[SEC 11ac1-1; Rule 60] "All specialists must be reasonably certain that all published bids and offers posted to the market are 'firm quotes,' and accurately represent the market on the NYSE."

[Rule 60-20] "The specialist must upon the receipt of an order through SuperDot or any other order entered by the specialist into the display book, 1) immediately (within 30 seconds) publish a bid or offer that would improve the inside market, and 2) display the entire size of an order if it is equal to the inside (unless the order is 10 percent or less of the current bid or offer)."

INTERPRETATION

The markets are firm on the NYSE and reflect reality much more accurately than Nasdaq issues do, as the NYSE can be influenced by all market participants with few or no obligations or rules. Therefore, an individual trader who wishes to improve a market in price or match a market in size will be represented or filled by a specialist with very little potential for manipulation.

If an exchange were unable to publish accurate firm prices through its specialist system, the exchange would become unable to provide a fair market. Hence, adherence to the rules regarding specialists and quoting is strictly enforced by floor officials and governors. Many guidelines have been created by the NYSE to ensure that firm quotes are provided to the public. These guidelines measure the spreads between bids and offers in listed stocks, as well as the depth of the market in these issues, ensuring a vibrant, efficient, and liquid market.

As security prices change, these guidelines essentially provide for less spread when associated with less volatility and higher liquidity. This makes perfect sense from the point of view of capitalism, since, as markets become more competitive, liquidity is increased as volatility decreases. This is why "thick" stocks like IBM move the least on the thickest or heaviest volume, while "thin," low-priced, less liquid stocks move the most (relative to price) on the least volume. But even when $150 stocks start to move, price action covers most of their daily range on the least volume as a rule. While this is not always true, listed stocks tend to trend, but make the biggest advances or declines as volume dries up. The explanation is simple: As passionate sellers get more aggressive, buyers generally dissipate in the face of decline. Therefore, to hit bids (buyers) in the market, you may need to go deeper in terms of liquidity to find additional buyers. This spreads out prices (and volatility) as volume diminishes. Each bid that is hit by sellers removes a bid from the market, forcing traders deeper into liquidity to find support.

So what's the point? The point is simple: If a break in a stock begins, you have to react very quickly and participate in the move if you are trading volatility, or you have to wait for a new trend to begin and trade it on heavier volume. The choice is really yours. If you want fast breaks, trade volatility on light volume but be fast at executing and be prepared to lead the market with limit orders. This strategy is more associated with Nasdaq issues and light-volume, news-recipient listed stocks. A trader could also trade with high-volume trends after reversals like a specialist generally does. As our good friend Matt Nokes, who played catcher for the New York Yankees, said, "If you want to step into the batting cage that fires high power speed balls, be prepared!" The only way to slow down a 100 mph fastball is by seeing a lot of them and gaining comfort. Trading fast-break stocks is like being in that batting cage.

Traders with less experience should stay out of the cage until the requisite experience is gained. Trading listed stocks in the manner described puts you in higher-volume, slower-trending issues that reveal patterns because of the specialist rules, analogous to the slower pitch cage. Which one you drop your quarters into is up to you, but we suggest that you evaluate the risk/reward spectrum of both and work your way up instead of looking to hit pitches you can't even see. Want to do something fun? Go to the batting cages and try to hit in the fast-pitch cage. Unless you are an experienced hitter, you will get a tangible metaphor of what high-volatility, low-volume trading feels like.

HOW SPECIALISTS ACTUALLY GET IN

To ensure that specialists are taking the other side of the trend, rules exist that prescribe how specialists "get in." One such rule is Rule 104.10 (3): "Dealer trades must be effected in a reasonable and orderly manner in relation to the general condition of the market, and the stock. . . ." This means that the following should be avoided by the specialist when building or establishing a position:

1. A purchase at a price above the last sale in a given session (called a plus tick)
2. The purchase of all or substantially all stock offered on the book on a zero-plus tick when it represents a substantial amount of stock for sale in the market, and the purchase on a zero-plus tick of more than 50 percent of all the stock offered at that price
3. The same criteria as (2) when selling stock on a zero-minus tick
4. Failure to reoffer or rebid after effecting a transaction described in (1), (2), and (3) above

"Transactions by a specialist for his own account in liquidating and decreasing positions must also meet the same test of reasonable necessity as acquisitions. . . ." Translation: The same rule applies for liquidating or decreasing a specialist's position. Specialists should avoid selling positions on a minus tick or zero-minus tick, thereby exacerbating a declining stock. Specialists are actually required to be on the other side in order to help cushion or stabilize the issue. The same is true for the purchasing of an issue while liquidating (short cover). Specialists should avoid purchasing on a zero-plus tick (without floor official approval) and trades should only be affected when reentering the market on the opposite side of the market from the liquidating transaction. This process of taking a position against the trend of the market is called *negative obligation.*

INTERPRETATION

Because specialists take the opposite of the trend, they often participate more actively when a sell-off is nearing its end or a rally is beginning to fade. If specialists are selling into a fading rally, they are in a better position to leg into the trade as short sellers, benefiting from a minor retracement by buying weakness (and providing liquidity) into a sell-off at a lower net average price than where they got short. This reaffirms that trading listed stocks like a specialist at or near turning points makes sense for the active trader.

THE LOADED SPRING CONCEPT

Your discipline and methodology of trading must always be correlated to the strategy and time horizon. The focus of this section relates to intraday trend reversals we call the loaded spring.

When microtrading, the trader is more focused on the short-term price patterns of stocks and is most focused on two primary actions:

- *Trend Reversals within a Range.* While it is important to have a strong sense of the overall daily trend, this technique is best utilized after a stock has made its strong moves of the day (establishing the range) and begins to stabilize (loaded spring).
- *Participation in Trends.* When stocks stay true to trends and consolidate gains and support retracements, traders should buy pullbacks in uptrends and sell rallies in downtrends. This trending pattern is not a "loaded spring" technique, and not our focus for this section.

If you monitor listed stocks while they drift lower, specialists often stabilize the bid, indicating a net buying posture in spite of the stock slowly grinding down. Specialists buy weakness at the bid, as sellers hit their bids. If the tape speeds up and the bids hold firm, you can assume specialists are standing on the bid, buying weakness. This is your best indication of a loaded spring, also known as a turning point. As the selling pressure begins to dissipate, the spring is already "loaded" because specialists and other participants bought the weakness into the sell-off. As sellers push the stock lower to a point where buyers continue to be strong, buyer demand creates pressure. Once sellers are no longer willing to hit lower bids, a reversal is likely, and this upside reversal can be very strong as buyers begin to take the offer. Specialists are often the last bids and buy the contra trend into weakness, as in this example. As long as bids are standing at a given price level, traders will want to observe the execution activity at the bids while specialists stand on the bids to buy stock and remain there as high bidders. Once the bids attract fewer sellers, traders will need to take or even lead the offer in order to get filled. Otherwise, these sharp rallies can uncoil the spring and run away quickly.

LONG ENTRY SIGNAL

Once specialists stop lowering the bid and remain at a current bid, continually buying stock, or even uptick to a higher bid, the spring will release and drive the stock to higher prices. This is your long entry signal, whether you are aggressive or passive. The techniques for entering the trade based on these signals include either bidding for the stock at the bid, when sellers are still present to hit your bid, or lifting an offer. In either case, if you wait too long to open a long trade, you increase the risk of missing it as liquidity decreases at the offer. This simply means that less stock will be for sale at the offer and above. In this case, getting into the trade will require a leading limit order bid above the offer. The better trade is getting into a long position by bidding with a specialist while some sellers still exist. This requires more patience, and you can expect a little more heat. Therefore, traders must recognize the level where tape support is broken, defined as a lower level within the time horizon being monitored. But if weakness can be bought as support is "put in," high velocity rallies are very profitable.

RISK ELASTICITY

The loaded long spring tells you that the stock is bullish even if prices are grinding lower once the bids can no longer attract sellers. The following shows the indication that a turn is about to occur:

- Recognition of a support level within the trend as read from the tape (tape support) and intraday charts.
- Fewer trades occurring at the bid relative to the prior time/price range. Generally, this will reflect a support level on the charts as well. If this level is broken, cover the trade if long, or don't make the trade if not yet in it.

- Increased time at the bid by a specialist (NYSE).
- Fewer trades occurring at the bid, indicating that the market cannot attract sellers.
- Upticks indicating higher bids and dissipating offers. In this case, take the offer or go above it.

Once sellers are no longer willing to sell at deflated prices, they will leave the offer and force stock higher as demand will no longer be filled at lower bid prices. When opening your long early by joining the bid, you must expect a bit more heat (loss) in the trade before the stock turns and the spring is released. To avoid whipsaw risk, if the market trades to a lower bid but still

F I G U R E   11.1

On this intraday chart of Alcoa Inc. (AA), notice how each time the price nears $24.10 or $24.40 the spring uncoils and price moves in the opposite direction.

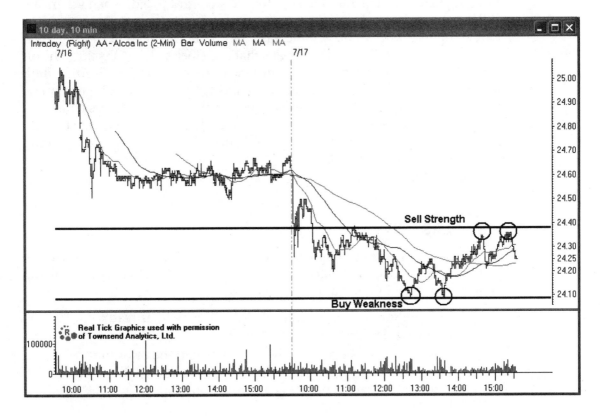

acts strong by remaining at the lower bid with fewer sellers, it pays to be "risk elastic" as you trade near your stop level—even adding to the position. In this case, you are not averaging down; you are buying weakness like a specialist and adding size within the buying zone. If your stop price is ultimately met, then you are wrong and the trade needs to be covered. Buying more weakness as support levels become clear is good trading; averaging down to lower your basis because you are losing money is bad trading. There is a huge difference between the two situations, and that is why it cannot be said that averaging down is a good or bad idea. In the absence of these indications, the odds are very strong that you should not.

The loaded spring concept holds true in the opposite sense for the short side. In that case, you would be selling strength. When stocks are volatile and making big ranges, avoid the loaded spring concept, since this strategy is strictly a tape reading exercise for when stocks are trading honestly within a range, and reversing at support and resistance of the range. This will generally occur after a volatile issue calms down (usually after the first hour or so of trading) and sets into a definable pattern. See Figure 11.1.

ARCHIPELAGO EXCHANGE

ORDER HANDLING

Because of the efficiency of the NYSE, we believe traders cannot ignore listed securities. However, it is more efficient and not to be confused with better order handling. What we mean by "more efficient" is that price levels tend to follow through longer with listed stocks because specialists are mandated to cushion price swings during wide variation situations. This creates a more orderly trend than Nasdaq stocks, with less whipsaw risk.

In terms of order handling, the NYSE falls a bit behind when compared to the Archipelago Exchange (ARCHIP). We believe ARCHIP offers much greater efficiency in this area, since orders can be placed anonymously without a specialist or any other human seeing the order. Therefore, we often use the NYSE tape to monitor a more efficient trend, while using ARCHIP to execute a more efficient order. In fact, benefits such as reserve book, conditional order entry, and electronic stops (protective and trailing) that are available on ARCHIP and RealTick on an anonymous basis, offer huge advantages that are not available on the NYSE. Can you imagine giving a specialist your stop order so that he or she could trade against it? No thanks. That would be like going to a poker game and asking, "Who has kings?" It is of note that the same limitations of the NYSE exist for Nasdaq, in that the market makers see orders like specialists do. In addition, Nasdaq does not have electronic processing like reserve book available for orders (more on reserve book later in the chapter). Therefore, the value of being able to price off the NYSE and Nasdaq while trading through ARCHIP is truly huge.

The Archipelago Exchange is primarily offered through the RealTick platform. The greatest value of this exchange is its order protection through anonymity. All orders through Archipelago receive the same fair treatment, which includes the following:

- *Intelligent Order Routing.* Intelligent order routing provides the fastest and best possible price.
- *Reserve Order Book Availability.* This option allows the trader to show the market only partial size while reserving the larger order within the Archipelago (ARCHIP) Integrated Book. Institutions and larger traders find this feature of particular value. See Figure 11.2 for an example.

FIGURE   11.2

Notice the order entry box. The Show box indicates an order of 100 shares while the Reserve Amt. indicates 10,000 shares. Each time 100 shares trades, another 100 shares replace it until the entire order is complete (assuming the market trades at the limit price entered for the order).

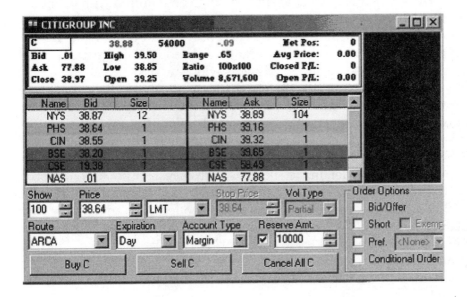

FIGURE   11.3

Various conditions can be loaded into the system, allowing the trader to initiate trades automatically when the conditions are met in the market - all with complete anonymity.

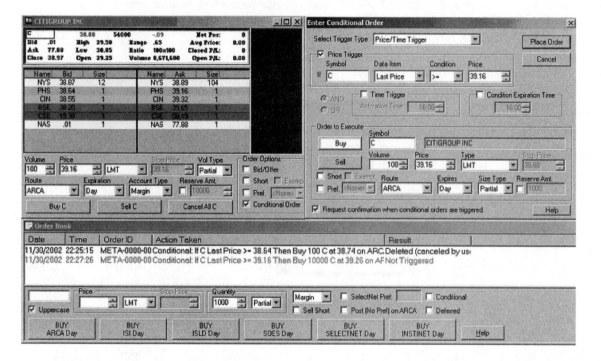

- *Conditional Order Entry (COE)*. Through ARCHIP, this allows the trader to set predetermined conditions of market activity as triggers for execution. See Figure 11.3 for an example.
- *Order Management*. ARCHIP and RealTick allow for a multitude of electronic orders, including stops, limits, best bid or offer, etc. All orders remain on either the trader's PC or the servers at Archipelago. In all cases, no market maker or specialist can see the orders. They are completely protected. See Figure 11.4.

Archipelago by its nature eliminates the inefficiencies discussed, translating into a completely fair marketplace that benefits the average investor and market participant (you) by taking order flow away from specialists. It accomplishes this through its fully anonymous electronic crossing network of buyers and sellers for listed securities, Nasdaq issues, and ETFs, thus providing a level playing field.

F I G U R E   11.4

RealTick and ARCHIP offer a variety of order executions, while exchanges are severely limited due to human intervention (specialists and market makers). Beyond the obvious problems of giving your order to a shark that gets paid to eat you, this limitation in order type creates further inefficiency. Electronic systems such as RealTick and ARCHIP put complete control into the hands that feed you—your hands.

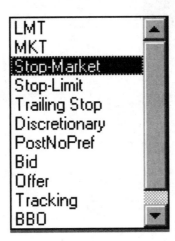

Understanding the NYSE is still invaluable today, since so much order flow passes through it. This can be attributed to its rich history and the iconic value it has in America. But in terms of order handling and efficiency, ARCHIP is hard to compete with. Perhaps the greatest value of centralized Graphical User Interfaces (GUIs), such as RealTick, is that they allow the trader to take advantage of all exchanges on one application, while maximizing total control of orders.

12 CHAPTER

TRADING FINANCIAL FUTURES

Financial futures are still young relative to their time in the investment community. Since their inception on May 16, 1972, under the direction of the Chicago Mercantile Exchange (CME), financial futures have become a dominant investment vehicle. Currency futures started it all, and then on April 21, 1982, the S&P 500 Index futures contract was born. The newest product, the E-Mini S&P 500 contract ("E" standing for Electronic), was introduced in 1997. This product, which trades at one-fifth the size of the full S&P 500 contract, has seen nothing but spectacular growth. It was only in 1999 that the E-Mini Nasdaq 100 contract was introduced. This product has exploded and is growing in popularity with traders, day traders, swing traders, investors, and large individual speculators. Rounding out the "core" E-Mini futures product is the Chicago Board of Trade (CBOT) mini-sized Dow Futures contract, which began trading in April 2002.

In the mid- to late-1990s, the day trading phenomenon was emerging but still relatively unknown. Technology was just beginning to offer direct, real-time quotes, and direct order entry was still not available to most trading platforms. Few people understood the concept of entering and exiting trades within the same day unless they understood exchange trading. In fact, when David started his day trading firm in 1996, it operated with an open outcry trading system, which allowed trades to be entered through an order clerk. This was done through a ring down circuit to a clearing firm. The orders were then processed through Instinet, the first electronic communication network, which was put on the map by Bill Lupien, as its chairman/CEO.

Instinet was so powerful that electronic traders clamored for what was called "I-only" systems. This stood for "institutions only," and a minimum $1,000,000 deposit was required. In 1996, David took a second mortgage out on his home to start his business and gain access to the system because it was such a huge edge. The process of placing trades through it was very exciting. It was the beginning of electronic trading. We used what was then called RealTick III for quotes, and we placed our trades via Instinet, Soes, SelectNet, and Dot for listed securities. Traders on our trading floor barked out requests: "Market on IBM," and Kevin Ward, our current Wise-Ex trader, would ring down to our clearing agent for an Instinet market. Response: "40 1/4 × 5/8 10 × 20." Trader: "Bid 10-40-5 stenths." Kevin: "Bid 10 40 5 stenths." Response: "Clearing . . . filled 1000 IBM at 40 5/16." Kevin: "Your long 1000 IBM at 40 5 stenths." Trader: "Offer 1000 40 9 stenths." And so it went—trading wide variation spreads and markets off the MarketWise trading floor in Broomfield, Colorado, using electronic quotes and our little version of open outcry that only a handful of shops around the country offered at the time. It was an exhilarating time. It was so exciting that we had people waiting in our lobby for a seat to trade. Day trading has since evolved dramatically into a mature business, built on the shoulders of technology pioneers like RealTick as well as sweeping regulatory rule changes.

Once direct access was launched on the Internet, the explosive industry called *day trading* hit Main Street, U.S.A. While E-Trade, Ameritrade, Schwab, and others had online trading during the 1997–1999 Internet boom, they were behind us technologically. Today, we believe we are on the way to new, dramatic advances in trading. While we don't think we will see the explosive proliferation we saw between 1997 and 2000, we are in fact seeing the footprints and clues of the next quantum leap in electronic trading. Today, growth comes in the form of lower capital constraints and greater leverage through futures trading.

The technology for the CME's E-Mini product is the Globex2 system, a fully electronic trading system created and offered solely through the CME. The CBOT, on the other hand, implements ACE, or Alliance of CBOT Eurex. The barriers to electronic trading have been almost completely mitigated for anyone who wants to go head to head with the market. With a relatively small performance bond, the E-Mini products can be traded via these electronic exchanges almost 24 hours a day.

In this chapter we discuss the many advantages of trading the E-Mini futures contract, not just for smaller individual traders, but also for any speculator. The liquidity of the E-Mini as the result of its explosive growth since its inception (e.g., The E-Mini S&P 500 contract went from volume of roughly

11,000 in 1997 to currently closer to 700,000) provides a very simple and afford-able product for the many people who do not have the risk tolerance or capital to trade the full S&P contract. The E-Mini has filled a gaping hole by lowering the risk capital requirement while still offering tremendous opportunity for gain. Certainly, with this opportunity comes risk, but as we explain in this chapter, we feel the rewards of E-Minis offer more than they cost in risk if traders remain disciplined. In other words, these products can provide you with an edge.

E-MINI MECHANICS

Futures traders are perhaps best known for their disciplined approach to the market, because traders are either debited or credited at the end of each day through what is called marked-to-market settlement, as opposed to the transaction plus three days (T+3) settlement on equities. Equities seem to allow holders more room for rationalization, including the concept of unrealized losses. No such myths are allowed to survive in the futures market, a benefit that forces discipline. Stock traders are in a position to let losers linger until a margin call finally wakes up those undisciplined traders who can't cut losses when necessary. The margin between the traders' cash deposit and minimum maintenance on margin can be extreme, allowing undisciplined stock traders to fall deeper into losses. Futures traders are forced to deal with losses almost immediately. This does not mean that a futures trader cannot hold a loser with enough performance bond on account, but at least gains and losses accrue each day, thereby bringing a relatively greater sense of urgency.

Futures accounts must be opened separately from equities under a commodity futures trading account regulated by the Commodity Futures Trading Commission (CFTC). Equity accounts are regulated by the Securities and Exchange Committee (SEC). Consequently, funds cannot be commingled with an equities account. While some see this as a frustration, we think it is also an advantage because trading styles for futures in most cases will be very different from trading styles for equities. The rules and disciplines associated with each account separate the issues very neatly and allow you to apply appropriate discipline per approach. This may seem like mental gymnastics, but we have separate accounts for day trading and overnight positions, and the separation does reinforce discipline per trading style. The idea of account separation is something that is imposed on you regarding futures and equities, but the idea of account separation also has value for equities and options.

The commodities firm that you open your futures account with can explain to you what its performance bond is, but as a rule the Chicago Mercantile Exchange and Chicago Board of Trade sets the minimum performance bond. Certainly, house rules from a brokerage firm can override and increase this minimum, but they can't go below it because the particular exchange must protect its own risk. To date, on average, $3600 is the minimum performance bond for S&P E-Minis, and $2250 is the minimum performance bond for the Nasdaq 100. Given the performance bond requirement, you can quickly see that the leverage one gains with the E-Mini is approximately 10:1 (similar to proprietary equity traders). For example, if you had $100,000 on deposit, a trader's buying power would equate to one million dollars. The Nasdaq 100 E-Mini performance bond is higher due to the greater volatility associated with the Nasdaq. In any case, the more volatile the market is in the given instrument, the greater the performance bond will be. Beyond the mechanical understanding of why performance bonds vary, it is also interesting to know the variation in volatility among various instruments. For example, the Nasdaq has a historical volatility greater than twice that of the S&P 500.

If you have a history of day trading, the differences in settlement between equities and E-Minis don't vary as much as they appear to (see Figure 12.1). Mechanically, stocks settle T+3, which means you have three days to meet a margin call, but day traders are used to end-of-day treatment (not set-

F I G U R E   12.1

Differences between futures and equities

	Stock Index Futures	Equities
Type of Broker	Series 3 Licensed	Series 7 Licensed
Underlying	Cash Index	Ownership in shares
Settlement	Mark-to-Market	Trade date + 3
Margining	Several Fold	Reg. T (2:1 Leverage), or 4:1 during the day
Short Selling	No Uptick rule No borrowing of shares No dividends on futures	Uptick rule Short sellers must borrow shares and pay dividends
Regulation	CFTC	SEC
Financial Safeguards	CME Clearing House	Securities Investor's Protection Corporation (SIPC)

tlement). Certainly other important measures such as contract expiration must also be understood regarding futures before one begins trading, and the CME and CBOT Web site is an excellent source for such information (www. cme.com and www.cbot.com, respectively).

CONTRACT SIZE

The underlying financial assets one controls when trading E-Minis can be a bit intimidating. This section will explain the contract size of each contract for the S&P 500 E-Minis, Nasdaq 100 E-Minis, and the CBOT mini-sized Dow Futures $5 multiplier.

The first step in calculating contract size is to understand ticks. Whenever you trade an equity, option, future, or other commodity, everything trades on what is called a tick. A tick is defined as the minimum price increment in which a security trades. When stocks were traded in fractions, they "ticked" in fractions. For example, a one-eighth tick meant that stocks traded at 12.5 cents, or $0.125. A one-sixth tick was 6.25 cents, or $0.0625. Since the event of decimalization, stocks trade in pennies. What in the past was quoted as "MMM 130 1/8 bid × 130 1/4" offer is now quoted as "MMM 130.12 bid × 130.25" ($0.12 spread). Decimalization has caused spreads to narrow dramatically, creating deeper markets in terms of liquidity. "MMM" today looks like "130.13 × 130.14" ($0.01 spread). With futures, the minimum tick is not as tight and the tick increment is based on an increment relative to an index point. In Figure 12.2, notice the /EST2 representing the December 2002 S&P500 E-Mini contract is indicated at 890.25 × 890.50. This represents a minimum tick increment of 0.25 per S&P point, which is $12.50 per E-Mini tick. Also notice that we did a quick round turn for one full S&P 500 point for a total of $50.00 ($12.50 × 4). The full S&P 500 contract, which trades on the CME, trades at $250 per S&P 500 point (five times the E-Mini).

We wish we could make the subject of trading futures more complicated, but the fact is that they are easier than equities. The Level II shows single source liquidity through the Chicago Mercantile Exchange. There are no market makers to monitor, no dominant ax, only price, size, and depth of the market. The trade illustrated shows a quick three-minute scalp for one S&P 500 point. Generally we trade bigger size, so 10 contracts, for example, would have profited $500. Regardless what size you trade, the E-Minis are a great product for large and small investors alike. This trade would require less than $5000 to open. If a trader only averaged one net winner per day at this level, the return on capital would be more than 100 percent. This is not to say that this is likely or easy, but it does illustrate the tremendous leverage to capital requirement to get started.

F I G U R E   12.2

The round turn scalp took just over 3½ minutes. The E-Minis have become a popular scalping tool.

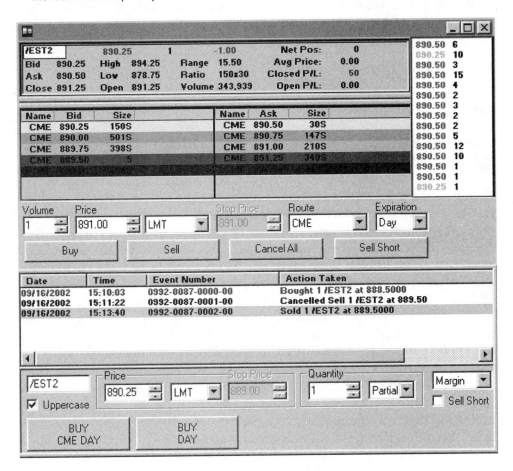

Specifications of the E-Mini S&P 500 Contract

To figure out the contract size of the overall E-Mini contract, you simply multiply $50 per S&P point times the current contract price. For example, if the current contract price of the S&P E-Mini contract is $891.00, you multiply this by $50, which gives you the contract size of the S&P 500 E-Mini: $44,550 (891 × 50). The full contract would have a contract size of approximately $222,750 (five times). The nice feature of the E-Mini contract versus the pit traded contract is that a trader can scale in or out of five contracts, instead of simply buying or selling one full contract. Specifications of the E-Mini S&P contract are explained in Figure 12.3:

F I G U R E   12.3

Contract specifications for the E-Mini S&P 500 (ES).

Ticker Symbol	ES
Contract Size	$50 times E-Mini S&P 500 futures price
Price Limits	5 percent, 10 percent, 15 percent, and 20 percent
Minimum Tick	0.25 index points = $12.50 per contract
Contract Months	Mar, Jun, Sep, Dec
Regular Trading Hours (CST)	Virtually 24 hours per day (from 5:30 p.m. Sunday to 3:15 p.m. Friday)
Last Trading Day	Trading can occur up to 8:30 a.m. (CST) on the third Friday of the contract month
Final Settlement Date	The third Friday of the contract month
Position Limits	Position limits work in conjunction with existing S&P 500 position limits. Please check *www.cme.com*.

Specifications of the E-Mini Nasdaq 100 Contract

As far as the Nasdaq E-Mini contract is concerned, the contract size is calculated by multiplying the contract price by the amount of each Nasdaq E-Mini point. For example, if the Nasdaq 100 E-Mini trades at $915.00, this is multiplied by $20.00 for a contract size of $18,300. So, in the case of the Nasdaq 100, each point for the E-Mini Nasdaq 100 future is $20 (see Figure 12.4). The minimum tick on the Nasdaq 100 E-Mini is a 0.50 E-Mini index point or $10.00 per tick ($20.00 per point).

Specifications for the Mini-sized Dow Futures

Turning to the Dow mini-sized futures contract, the underlying investment value is simply $5 times the current price of the Dow Jones contract. Therefore, if the Dow is trading at 8500, the contract size of the Dow futures contract is $42,500 (8500 × $5). This contract size is more comparable to the ES contract than the NQ; however, average daily volume in the YM contract still significantly lags the ES contract and appears to have not yet attracted an institutional audience. The ES, as previously mentioned, has much greater volume per session due to institutional attention. The NQ currently commands volume of roughly one half the ES contract. Specifications for the mini-sized Dow futures contract are seen below in Figure 12.5.

F I G U R E   12.4

Contract specifications for the E-Mini Nasdaq 100 (NQ).

Ticker Symbol	NQ
Contract Size	$20 times E-Mini Nasdaq-100 futures price, or 1/5th pit-traded contract (ND)
Price Limits	5 percent, 10 percent, 15 percent, and 20 percent
Minimum Tick	0.50 index points = $10 per contract
Contract Months	Mar, Jun, Sep, Dec
Regular Trading Hours (CST)	Virtually 24 hours per day (from 5:30 p.m. Sunday to 3:15 p.m. Friday)
Last Trading Day	Trading can occur up to 8:30 a.m. (CST) on the third Friday of the contract month
Final Settlement Date	The third Friday of the contract month

F I G U R E   12.5

Contract specifications for the Mini-sized Dow Futures $5 multiplier (YM).

Ticker Symbol	YM
Contract Size	Five ($5.00) times the Dow Jones Industrial Average
Minimum Tick	1 index point = $5 per contract
Contract Months	Mar, Jun, Sep, Dec
Regular Trading Hours (CST)	Electronic Trading—8:15 p.m. to 4:00 p.m., Chicago time, Sunday–Friday. Trading in expiring contracts closes at 3:15 p.m. Chicago time on the last trading day.
Last Trading Day	Trading in expiring contracts closes at 4:15 on the last trading session
Final Settlement Date	The third Friday of the contract month
Position Limits	50,000 contracts in all contract months (combined limit for DJIA futures and options and mini-sized DowSM futures ($2)).

These are some of the basic mechanics, and a trader is able to obtain more information at either the CME and CBOT's Web sites or by reading any of the outstanding books that we referenced for the purposes writing this chapter. One of our favorite books is *Exchange Traded Funds and E-Mini Stock Index Futures,* written by David Lerman, and we would highly recommend it for a more detailed understanding.

FINDING A WORTHY BENCHMARK

Perhaps the best place to start is the Standard and Poor's 500 Index. This cash index is a capitalization-weighted index that tracks the performance of the 500 largest capitalized stocks within the marketplace. This is why it tracks the overall market so closely. Because of this close tracking and weighted market capitalization, the S&P 500 E-Mini contract mimics the overall market just like this cash index.

What we like about the S&P 500 is that, because new stocks are constantly added and old stocks removed, a trader is forced to stay current with the market and best tradable issues. While many traders still focus completely on technology, we believe trading securities within the S&P 500, especially those that are added, keeps a trader in issues with good opportunity and liquidity. Many traders like to specialize in only certain sectors and issues, but for those who like to trade around institutional order flow, following the current S&P 500 is a good strategy. Because the S&P 500 constantly updates itself, traders are automatically given a strong list of candidates to trade for individual stocks, in addition to trading the overall E-Mini contract.

Interestingly enough, our publisher, McGraw-Hill, owns Standard & Poor's, and Standards & Poor's has been a financial services company providing independent information on indices, sectors, and research for many, many years. So the marquee value of being part of the S&P 500 is a tremendous attraction to the company, attracting traders and leading to increased activity, volatility, and opportunity for the active trader as well as institutional market segments.

The results show that while this S&P 500 index reflects the market very well, it also leaves margin for disparity. This is where traders really differ from fund managers. Traders don't use the S&P 500 as a benchmark, since they seek much greater returns in all market cycles (bull, bear, volatile, and neutral). If this were not the case, then why would we trade? Why not buy a strong index fund with a good track record? The simplest answer is that index mutual funds have a lot of drag-through expenses (even the no load funds). Why not just buy the SPY? This would be a good strategy if you wanted to peg results directly to the S&P with no benefit for alpha. *Alpha* is another fancy portfolio term that defines the returns a fund manager achieves in excess of the benchmark (S&P 500 for index funds). Alpha's partner is *beta*, which measures the sensitivity of a portfolio (or stock) relative to the benchmark. If the S&P 500 lifts 20 percent and a fund or stock has a par beta of 1.0, it (whether fund or stock) also lifts 20 percent. The same is true for a decline. If the fund has a beta of 1.3, then the fund performs 30 percent better than the benchmark in up markets, but also 30 percent worse in down markets.

The point is traders seek to maximize alpha while minimizing beta. This may seem counterintuitive, in that most contemporary thinking suggests that in order to improve performance you must also increase beta (risk). But this is not necessarily true. Traders seek to accomplish the inverse relationship of improving alpha while reducing beta through strategy, technique, and skill, all of which we will discuss at the end of this chapter.

The Wilshire 5000 Index measures the overall marketplace with 100 percent accuracy because it is an index that measures the entire stock market, whereas the S&P only measures 500 stocks. In order to be registered as an S&P 500 stock, companies must meet strict criteria determined by committees at Standard & Poor's that focus on liquidity, volatility, market capitalization, and other measures that reflect well on the overall market. Because of this, the S&P 500 has close to a 98 percent correlation to the Wilshire Index and the overall market. It is quite amazing that 500 stocks can correlate 98 percent to the entire market. This provides outstanding opportunity and liquidity for the E-Mini, since so many hedgers and fund managers use the full contract for financially engineered positions. This affords individuals a vehicle that is both a strong, broad-based index of the overall market as well as a very tradable index product with good volatility for active trading.

The aforementioned "spiders" are also excellent for the same reasons. However, this contract that trades on the American Stock Exchange (AMEX) requires a great deal more capital when compared to the ES contract. For example, as of December 2002, a trader can trade two E-Mini S&P 500 contracts and control the equivalent of 1000 shares of the SPY. Two E-Mini contracts require less than a $10,000 performance bond, compared to at least $25,000 to trade the SPY, assuming the SPY is trading at $90 per share and the trader qualifies for a four to one margin ($90 \times 1000 = 90,000/4 = \$22,500$). A margin of four to one requires a minimum regulatory requirement of $25,000 margin deposit. Therefore, $25,000 would be the minimum.

But beyond this mechanical fact, here is what is interesting and even ironic: Active traders use the E-Mini product, which reflects 98 percent of the market, in order to out-trade the very benchmark that everyone seeks to meet or beat. Let us explain. Using the example in Figure 12.1, we take a quick scalp of one E-Mini S&P 500 point. We made $50 before commissions, and we assume a $15 round turn cost to net $35 clean (before the 60/40 tax treatment, to be explained). Assuming a $10,000 account, traders who average a 60 percent win rate and keep the 40 percent losers equal to 50 percent of their winners will come out as follows:

Assumptions

Trading Days:	240, but trades 200 days (40 days vacation)
Average Winner:	1 E-Mini S&P 500 point
Average Loser:	0.50 E-Mini S&P 500 point
Commissions:	$15 per round turn
Number of Trades/Day:	10 round turns

Results

Number of Total Trades:	2000
Total Commissions:	$30,000
Gross Winners:	$60,000 (2000 × 0.60 × 50)
Gross Losers:	$20,000 (2000 × 0.40 × $25)
Net before Tax:	$10,000 [60,000 − (30,000 + 20,000)]
Return on Investment:	100%

While this is not a prediction of results, since they vary per trader, it does illustrate that trading the S&P 500 E-Mini product with reasonable expectations for winners and losers does provide the opportunity to crush the benchmark itself (the very instrument you trade). That is irony and opportunity at its finest.

WHAT TO TRADE

Why trade equities or exchange traded funds when futures are so attractive? There really is no hard-and-fast distinction between which products one should trade, but some of the factors to consider are your tolerance for risk in terms of the leverage gained by trading the futures contract as well as the availability of capital. Whether you tend to be undercapitalized, or well capitalized with tax concerns, futures make a lot of sense. In either case, risk should be controlled by your discipline, not the product. The example in Figure 12.2 provides a good glimpse of how even the very small trader can get involved with the market. Equities are not as kind. While many low-priced equities exist, they tend to be associated with poor liquidity and low opportunity, two very strong reasons to not trade them.

The E-Mini contracts give the trader all the ingredients necessary: great liquidity, volatility, favorable tax treatment, and subscription from institutions that are less interested in the minor price fluctuations that active traders love. Add the wider spread variation, and it looks like the trading opportunities from the mid-1990s to early 2000. In addition, the capital requirements are much smaller than for day trading, allowing another quantum leap in active trading. If you're looking for even more action, the Nasdaq 100 E-Mini futures have greater volatility. So, for example, if the NQ E-Mini has an average daily range of 16 index points, a 6-point range will be traveled more swiftly within the day, which means the highs, lows, and midpoints of that range will be seen more often throughout the day. The ES E-Mini and YM mini-sized contract, being less volatile, will have a greater range on average per day, but tend to be more stable in its volatility within the range, so it won't see the highs, lows, and midpoints as many times through the day as a rule. Traders can choose which best fits their appetite. One other great benefit to futures we alluded to is its tax benefit. As most traders understand, a Schedule D must be completed each year, reporting capital gains and losses. Additionally, any income achieved during the year must also be reported and taxed. Therefore, for short-term traders, all gains inside one year and income achieved is reported and taxed as ordinary income. This is a nuisance and a financial burden! When trading futures, the trader uses form 6781 from the IRS, with the amount carried onto Schedule D. All gains enjoy a 60/40 tax treatment, meaning that 60 percent are treated as long-term capital gains and 40 percent are treated as ordinary income. The result of this is very favorable to successful traders who make money. An example is as follows:

Suppose Trader A makes $10,000 trading the Spiders (SPY), while Trader B is able to make $10,000 trading the E-Mini. What would be the tax advantage to Trader B?

Trader A
$10,000 in gains × .396 equals
     $3,960

Trader B
$6,000 × 0.20 = $1,200
$4,000 × .396 = $1,584
$2.784
A savings of $1,176

CASH/FUTURES RELATIONSHIP

As your understanding of futures unfolds, you begin to set the building blocks for understanding what is known as *fair value,* which is really a purely technically driven term, not a function of what is actually the fair value of the cash or the futures. Fair value is a theoretical value that is principally made up of dividends, interest rates, and the date to expiration of futures contracts. As the expiration period of a futures contract draws near, the cash index prices and futures prices converge to nearly the same level. Arbitrageurs and other market participants begin to roll their positions to the next expiration month in the futures contract, thereby transferring the liquidity from an expiring contract to a new forward contract. The spread differential between the cash index and the futures price begins to widen again, a situation called *premium.* Occasionally, cash can trade at a higher value than the futures price, a phenomenon called a discount, but this is more rare and is based generally on market inefficiency caused by severe downswings in the market.

The point here is that fair value is an important measure when looking at the pre-market indications for the equity market. Because futures trade nearly 24/7 on Globex 2 (ES and NQ contract) and ACE (mini-sized Dow, or YM), traders will tend to move the futures market after the close of equities as news is disseminated. As news dissemination moves the futures market, traders can evaluate immediate market reaction because futures are more responsive due to the ease with which they trade compared to the complexities of trading stocks through multiple exchanges.

Futures also reflect the impulse of the market the fastest. This is valuable to traders. For example, if news shakes the market immediately after the close, futures will likely sell off before closing at 4:15 PM, EST (15 minutes after the NYSE). The next morning, the actual cash index will open down, indicating weakness. Whereas futures trade down before the opening, indicating that weakness is already factored into the futures market, equities appear weak by opening lower. Futures deal with the news before the equity market does, thus mitigating much of the impact before the NYSE opens again. This does not mean there will not be amateur reaction to the perception of weakness in the example, but ultimately the weakness is already built in by futures. This is another reason for the saying, "Amateurs control the open, professionals control the close." The point is, don't react to the news—it was already dealt with.

Getting back to fair value, it is important to remember that its impact is minimal. Traders do best by understanding the relationship of the cash index to futures so that they don't react to mixed signals.

As stated, another reason the futures contract can temporarily lead the equity market at the open is because the S&P 500 cash index closes at 4:00 PM,

EST, while the S&P futures contracts trade in the pits (full contract) until 4:15 PM, EST. They then close and reopen at 4:45 PM, EST, trading all night through Globex 2 until 9:15 AM, EST. The Globex 2 session then closes, and 15 minutes later the floor session of the CME takes over. This adds more efficiency to the futures market than the equities market, as any news disseminated in the market or overseas sentiment digested by the market will show up first in the futures market, acting as a temporary lead to the equity market.

As we conclude the argument of trading futures versus stocks, perhaps the most important thing to keep in mind is the risk involved in trading either vehicle. Knowledge of risk is important to have and applies to all disciplines, so risk is really defined by your own individual psychology and application of the proper rules. Perhaps the underlying principle, regardless of which instrument you trade, is that cash is king, and holding your cash most nights is most often the smart play. While trading futures offers the opportunity to trade literally 24 hours a day, discipline is always the prevailing factor regarding success or failure. Success cannot be achieved in either approach without it.

APPLICATION OF E-MINIS

HEDGING

Suppose you are long the market with index funds in your 401K. In this case, you don't have the ability to short, and in many cases you also are restricted in selling your investments in the 401K due to custodial issues. Opening a futures account and taking a contra position in futures relative to your 401K funds when you fear weakness in the market would be a hedging technique. Before doing so, it is important to remember that a proper hedge should have parity in size, compatibility, and correlation to the portfolio you seek to hedge. For example, if you have a $100,000 portfolio in technology, you can't hedge well using an E-Mini S&P 500 contract because the two are not comparable. Perhaps the Nasdaq 100 E-Mini would do better, but there is also a correlation that should be established. If the volatility of your technology portfolio is 2.0 beta to the NQ E-Mini, then the hedge effectiveness is substantially mitigated. For example, if the NQ E-Mini market retraces 10 percent, your tech fund would retrace 20 percent, so any contra position in the E-Mini would only have half the effectiveness. Betas are available on most investment vehicles within 401Ks through MorningStar. You must also take size into account. If your $100,000 account is hedged with one E-Mini, you're out of parity because the contract value of the E-Mini should mirror the contract value of your portfolio. If you are hedging with too large a contract relative to your portfolio, you are overhedged. Don't panic if you can't reach correlation, however; any hedging is good assuming the hedge is correct.

Let's do a simple example to illustrate the concept:

Given:

Portfolio: S&P 500 Index Fund (good correlation)

Size: $100,000 current value

Outlook: Bearish into quarterly earnings season

Strategy: Sell two E-Minis ES short (contract value = $45,000 per contract, or 900 index points × $50)

Total Hedge: $90,000 (900 index price × $50 = $45,000 × 2 contracts)

Portfolio Hedge Ratio: 90% (90,000 / 100,000)

Event: A few weeks later earnings are weak and the S&P 500 falls 10%

Result:

No Hedge

Portfolio: down $10,000

Net: down $10,000

With Hedge

Portfolio down: $10,000

E-Mini short: up $9,000 (90% hedged)

Net: down $1,000.

Event: Market remains steady

Result: Zero impact other than E-Mini commissions and minor price erosion of time.

Event: Market rallied 10%

Result: Gains in portfolio are offset by loss on the hedge; opportunity for gain lost while hedge is on.

SPREADING

Spreading allows traders to trade a variety of strategies. A *spread* is the simultaneous buying and selling of securities such as the E-Mini in order to speculate on price disparities in the market regardless of market bias. By being hedged, risk is greatly reduced in most cases. For example, if you were mixed on market direction (bullish or bearish) but felt the technology sector would have a higher beta than the S&P regardless of which direction the market went, you could spread the price disparity of the two. If you felt that the Nasdaq would rally stronger than the S&P 500, you could get long the NQ E-Minis and short the ES E-Minis. For examples of spreading, refer back to Chapter 6 on TRIN. Much more can be said on E-Minis, futures, and single stock futures, but these basics should help you decide whether they fit your trading style (or complement it).

SPECIFIC TRADING METHODS

For decades, floor traders have used classical pivot analysis for calculating potential areas of support and resistance, as well as a "pivotal" level that can be used as the "proverbial line in the sand" for a particular session, week, or month. Looking at the formula below, the underlying mathematical equation is relatively simple; however, other pivot formulas that incorporate either a session's opening level or "proprietary" variable seem to only add "noise" to this very simple, yet effective equation. Used primarily on *highly liquid instruments that generally trade in a significant daily range,* it should not be surprising that a perfect contract to be used with such a formula would be the E-Mini S&P 500 Index. The NQ and YM contracts seem to work almost equally as well.

THE PIVOT FORMULA

$$\text{Pivot point (P)} = (H + L + C) / 3$$
$$\text{First resistance level (R1)} = (2 * P) - L$$
$$\text{First support level (S1)} = (2 * P) - H$$
$$\text{Second resistance level (R2)} = P + (R1 - S1)$$
$$\text{Second support level (S2)} = P - (R1 - S1)$$

After a trader completes the necessary calculations, the most important level to focus on is the daily pivot, or P, since this is considered to be the equilibrium, or focal point, for market makers, institutions, and retail traders. As a rule of thumb, traders will generally take a bearish approach if the pivot is penetrated from above, while getting bullish if the pivot is taken out from below.

As Figure 12.6 illustrates, traders would buy the E-Mini S&P 500 contract as the daily pivot is taken out from below, placing a stop just below this calculated pivot. The immediate placement of a stop is important, since it adheres to a sound fundamental strategy of discipline via effectively controlling

F I G U R E   12.6

Chart of E-Mini S&P 500 Contract (ES)

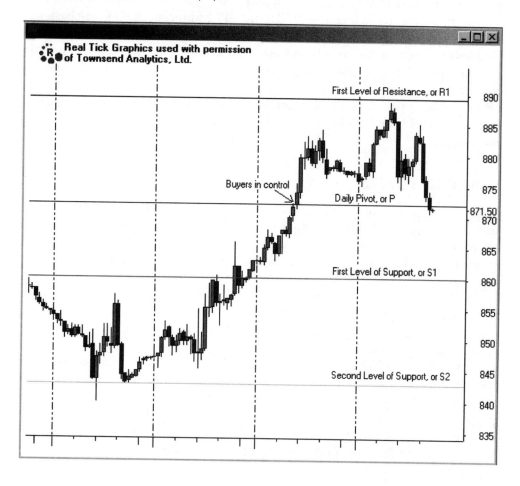

risk. As far as reward is concerned, the first objective would be a test of R1 (shown above). As prices approach Resistance 1, traders could either (a) sell part of their position for a gain just below R1 (half-point below R1, since most traders using pivots will look for an *exact* test of R1), or (b) wait to see if "potential resistance" at R1 is taken out, and if so then place a stop just below the R1 level.

Note: If the position remains open and the contract continues to rally, a trader would then look for a test of the second resistance level, or R2. If a trader is fortunate to see the market rally above Resistance 2, a stop would then be placed underneath R2 while turning to longer-term charts for potential resistance above.

BETWEEN R1 AND S1

In theory, trading throughout a particular session should remain between the first support and resistance levels (R1 and S1), as market makers are better to manage risk during a range bound market. If, however, either one of these first levels is penetrated, it is then time to look for *off-floor traders* coming into the market and taking the contract toward the second levels of support and resistance (S2 and R2). If the velocity of the move is significant and the second level of support and resistance is cleared, intermediate and long-term traders should both become involved and most likely continue the session's momentum.

LINING UP LEVELS

When using pivot analysis on a daily basis, a trader is able to get a solid understanding of market psychology for one particular session. To become an aficionado of pivot analysis, a trader should gather support and resistance levels on *both a monthly and weekly time frame.* The method for gathering the high, low, and close is the same: simply take *the prior* month's and week's high, low, and close; regardless of whether a trading week is abbreviated, only take levels from Monday to Friday.

Before we turn to an illustration, it is important to understand the psychological implications of these different time frames (see Figure 12.7).

As Figure 12.7 explains, there should be more weight placed on either the monthly and weekly pivotal levels than a daily calculation; however, it is most important to look for a confluence of particular levels (e.g. Monthly pivot and Weekly R1 lining up, or the Daily pivot and Weekly S1 level). This confluence will certainly add to a trader's confidence, as well as strengthening a particular "zone of potential support/resistance."

F I G U R E   12.7

Hierarchy of pivot levels.

Time frame	Psychological Importance
Monthly	Very important
Weekly	Very important
Daily	Important for one session
Multiple Confluence	Most important

There is no question that trading is a business that requires the constant pursuit of an edge. Educated traders will basically have the same foundational methodology during this pursuit, however, adding to the probabilities of a successful trade is certainly helpful. This is done via Confluence Zones. Moreover, knowing the "relative extremeness" of a particular contract will give a trader an edge when judging risk on a particular trade. For example, if the ES was trading at 750 and both the Weekly and Monthly S2 levels were at 752, a trader going short might want to consider taking a smaller-than-normal position. For risk purposes, a stop would be placed just above the 752 level, and at the stop level a trader could look to initiate a long position as well.

From a historical perspective, trading outside the weekly and monthly S2/R2 level is not uncommon; however, momentum traders will almost always exit a position as prices gravitate back into this "standard deviation."Put another way, it can be helpful for a trader to monitor what area a contract trades during a particular month. An example would be an ES contract having a Monthly S2 of 750, S1 of 775, Pivot of 800, R1 at 810, and R2 calculated at 843. Then, during the particular month, the ES only trades within the range of 800 to 750 (or 775 to 750). Knowing this information would allow a trader to get a "feel" of market psychology (bearish in the above example).

TRADING A CONFLUENCE ZONE

When trading a "confluence zone," or area that has multiple technical significance, it is critical to first develop an *intermediate term bias,* which can be done with the help of Fibonacci Retracement analysis. Beginning with a weekly chart of the Dow (Figure 12.8), a trader using Fibonacci Retracements will notice that the right side of the chart is just underneath the 38.2 percent level and still within the "aggressive bearish" countertrend move. Does it make sense to simply sell the market? Of course not, since a trader has to wait for confirmation before initiating a short position.

Taking things to another level, it would certainly increase a trader's confidence if he/she knew there was either a daily, weekly, or monthly level(s) near the 8500 level. By recognizing a confluence zone near this psychologically important 8500 level, a trader would then be allowed to construct a "zone of resistance" going forward. On this particular trading session, there was in fact a Monthly R1 and Weekly R2 level at 8525 and 8537, respectively. It also should be noted that the 38.2 percent Fibonacci level is seen at 8515. Therefore, we now have a "confluence" from 8515 to 8537 (see Figure 12.9).

The critical question still exists, "How can a trader use this newly found zone from 8515 to 8537?" With the market currently at 8508, a bullish trader would wait until the entire zone is penetrated, becoming bullish above 8537

F I G U R E   12.8

Weekly chart of the Dow Jones Industrial Average.

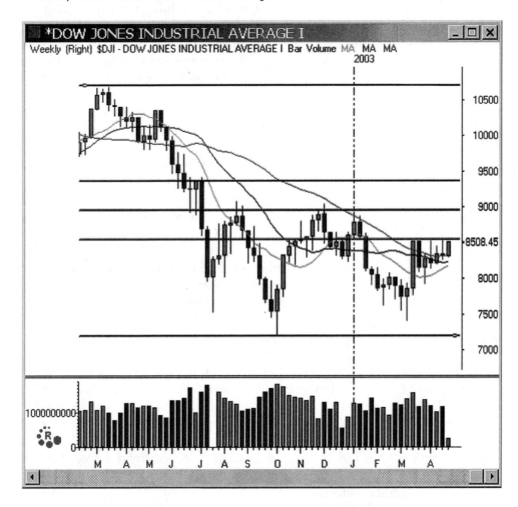

and then only changing short-term sentiment to bearish if 8515 fails to act as support. Therefore, instead of picking one level to focus on, a trader is able to construct a statistically important zone that should increase odds of a profitable trade based on likely demand in the Dow.

SWING TRADING VIA CONFLUENCE AREAS

Turning to the E-Mini S&P 500 contract, a swing trader with a long-term bearish outlook can still trade in a bullish fashion via these aforementioned "confluence zones." Looking at Figure 12.10, the ES contract initially rises

FIGURE 12.9

Construction of a confluence zone.

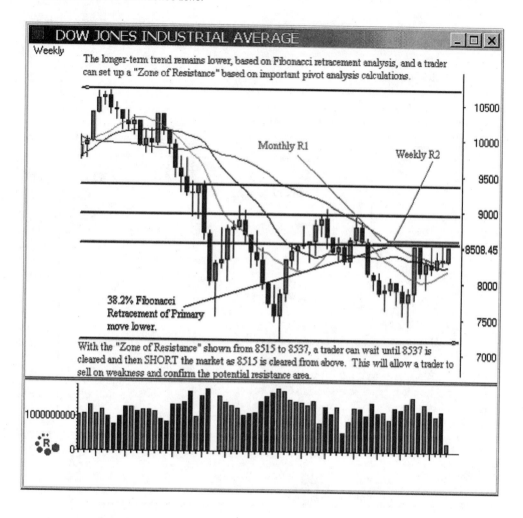

above the Monthly Resistance 1 level, or R1, the calculated Weekly Pivot, and the Daily Pivot as well. This "confluence zone" is then defined between these levels, or from 896.75 to 898.75. The 2-point difference zone would equate to $100 dollars per ES contract. Ideally, the ES contract rises above 898.75 and then falls under 896.75, producing a short signal (sell underneath 896.75 with a stop just above 898.75). However, in this practical example, a trader needs to understand that the aforementioned "confluence zone" can be used by long traders as well. A riskier trade, but one that can potentially be extremely profitable with risk defined. The difference in the long versus the short

FIGURE   12.10

Confluence zone for the E-Mini S&P 500 contract.

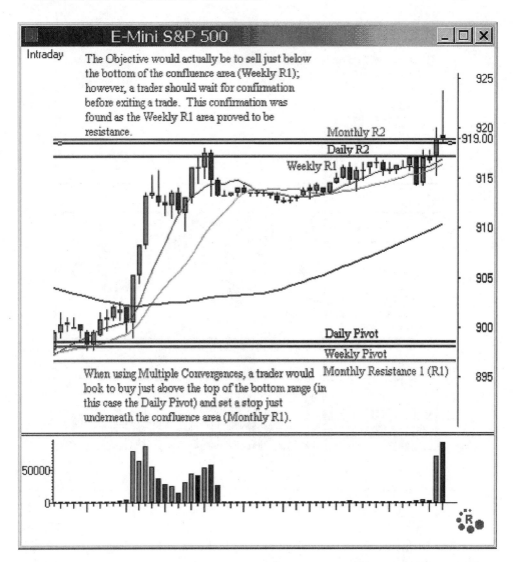

would be that a trader would not trade as many contracts from the long side, since the alignment of trend is not in a trader's favor.

Beginning at the left-hand side of the chart in Figure 12.10, the ES contract initially rises above all three aforementioned "zones," getting traders' attention regarding a potential solid risk/reward trade. As noted, since the ES contract is in a long-term downtrend, a trader would look first to sell the contract underneath the 896.75 level; however, taking a long position just above the 898.75 level on strength while using a stop underneath 896.75 is a viable plan as well. Remember, if stopped out, it would be prudent to take a short position as well, since that is in favor of the primary downtrend.

If day trading, an objective can simply be one of the daily calculated levels (S2 to R2); however, it certainly makes sense to look to see if there is a confluence of indicators between daily, weekly, and monthly charts before exiting. As shown in Figure 12.11 on the previous page, a confluence area did exist above between the 917 and 919 levels, thus allowing a trader to have a solid objective area if a long was taken as the contract bounced near 898.75. Important note: This does not mean a trader should absolutely exit the trade, since this area of "potential resistance" still has to be proven first. As a general rule of thumb, a trader long would look for potential resistance *right below the 917 level (0.50 cents, or ½ point),* since there is likely a large number of institutional traders also looking at this zone from 917 to 919 as well.

As the illustration below shows, the ES contract hit 917 three times before breaking above, and the eventual breakout only registered a high of 918 before reversing. A swing trader would most definitely have exited the profitable trade during this particular sequence, and the exit would have been close to 916.50 after the first failed attempt at resistance. Traders would then be flat heading into the next session.

Of course, when using confluence zones, traders will regularly ask, "Selling the ES at 916.50 was significantly below the 923.75 high set one day afterwards." Remember, these "confluence zones" are high probability areas that *will generally control price action.* We all know how difficult it is to predict highs and lows; therefore, "confluence zones" will allow a trader to look at areas, instead of simply one level, thereby increasing confidence.

Following the price action in the ES contract soon thereafter, notice that the contract did collapse back underneath this "confluence zone" and give short traders a solid entry opportunity as the lower level of support was penetrated. Moreover, it reinforced the fact that the "safe" exit was not a bad exit after all. During the descent, note that two of the three moving averages were taken out as volume increased, most likely signaling that both longs and shorts seemed to favor the sell side (read: long liquidating and shorts initiating). Which moving average should we follow? Looking at the illustration below, it is helpful to a trader to see the longer-term moving average line up with the normal 50 percent retracement area of the recent move. Because of this alignment, 910.50 area would then hold more importance than simply guessing which moving average might contain the recent selling. As always, this small potential support zone still has to be confirmed.

F I G U R E   12.11

Confluence zone for the E-Mini S&P 500, Part II.

F I G U R E   12.12

Marketwise daily E-Mini coverage.

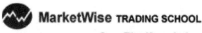

Bias Development

Contract	Long-term	Intermediate	Short-term
S&P 500	Stage 1	Stage 2	Stage 4

Pivot Analysis : Creating a Confluence

Timeframe	Security	S2	S1	Pivot	R1	R2
Daily	SPX	912.07	917.75	920.58	926.26	929.09
Weekly	SPX	923.51	933.90	941.28	951.67	959.05
Monthly	SPX	819.95	868.43	896.34	944.62	972.73
Daily	ES	908.83	915.42	919.83	926.42	930.83
Weekly	ES	919.33	931.92	940.83	953.42	962.33
Monthly	ES	813.50	864.75	894.25	945.50	975.00

**High Probability Trade:
Buy ES at 926.25 with a stop at
923.75. Once 928.25 is hit, move
stop to breakeven. Objective is 933.**

June E-mini S&P 500 Contract (/ESI3)

Taking things to a more practical level, MarketWise Trading School currently offers daily illustrations on the ES, NQ, and YM contract—specifically pointing out daily confluence zones. Moreover, there is a "Bias Development" section that incorporates the philosophy taught at the school (Stages 1–4). With that said, a trader can effectively pinpoint where potential support and resistance zones appear each session, as well as being able to manage risk and define reward at the same time. Figure 12.12 is a screen shot of a publication regarding the ES contract:

13
C H A P T E R

SYSTEMS TRADING

WORDS OF CAUTION

Market data is abundant. This sea of information available to analysts and traders more often drowns them than supports them. Therefore, we introduce this chapter under the caveat that the reader will keep risk management and psychology at the forefront of all decisions. In fact, amateurs who cannot even trade a few stocks successfully are the most prone to seeking systems that are capable of producing thousands of tradable stocks. Conversely, the best traders in the world often focus on trading only a few issues for their entire careers. These participants are floor traders. Floor traders have never had such luxuries as historical price data, back-testing engines, or neural networks with artificial intelligence. They have experience, gut, and instinct.

Trading systems crunch a huge amount of data in order to achieve a minimal amount of predictive value, defined as the statistical edge. The paradox is that systems trading takes a tremendous amount of work, effort, and expense to produce a potentially huge amount of noise which must be sifted through to gain an almost-epsilon of an edge. Perhaps the edge is greater than an epsilon and closer to a delta, but in any case the edge is somewhere between the two. Additionally, the amount of information, depth of research, time in developing, and coding will continue to dominate the energy that participants dedicate to the market. In many cases this work is done at the expense of seeing the market with beautiful simplicity. The dichotomy that we're faced with is whether to even introduce this type of analysis. After careful thought, we decided to break down what systems trading is to us after traveling the relatively long journey of market analysis. We have studied and researched market analysis fundamentally, technically, quantitatively, and through systems, and while we are fans of systems, we are also very cautious of the limitations.

We have worked with floor traders, market makers (Bill has served in both capacities), mathematicians from aerospace and defense—you name it—and we can tell you that no one has cracked the code of the market. The code to crack is within yourself. Therefore, it is with great caution that we write this chapter. This cautionary guidance exists because both of us have spent several millions of dollars on systems technology, and we believe that most analytical systems are destined to fail shortly after their presence becomes known. This is principally because systems that do work can only do so for a short period of time, thanks to market dynamics. Too many traders spend far too much time and money coding these systems at the expense of time that should be dedicated to trading. We have both made this expensive mistake, and it is for these reasons we begin this chapter with these words of caution.

With all that said, we also believe that systems, in the right dosage, are well worth the edge they can provide. But the edge is nonetheless small. The real edge is always with you, the trader. In fact, this point brings to mind the movie *A Beautiful Mind*. John Nash, one of the most brilliant mathematicians of his age, struggled to crack the code of his own mind. He was always faced with imaginary souls that both directly and indirectly attempted to destroy his life. He dealt with these creatures of the mind by first recognizing that they were a problem, and then ignoring them in order to defeat the problem. We must recognize that there will always be imaginary and magical systems out there that promise results that cannot be obtained by literally following a system or model. We must ignore the temptation of subscribing to these devices at the expense of our command over ourselves, our common sense, or our instincts. We must always retain self-control and work on cracking the code of ourselves before ever opening the door to what we call artificial intelligence. Once we gain this emotional "edge," we can pursue other mechanical edges that are available in the market. It is within this context that we can begin to explore systems trading and market analysis. Much of what we will cover in this chapter is a combination of analytical approaches to the market and, more importantly, self-discoveries along the way.

Can a trader automate a system? The answer is yes, yet the best traders in the world don't use fully automated trading systems, just because there are so many aspects of a system that technology can't compensate for. Automated systems can certainly be used to filter out market noise as well as search through a large universe of stocks to find ones that meet certain criteria that help to define potential edges such as elasticity levels; however, to turn on a BlackBox system and feed it money would be irresponsible in our opinion. These systems do exist at institutions involved with complex arbitrage and financial engineering formulas; however, they are extremely expensive to build and maintain, and they can be devastatingly expensive when they fail. John Meriweather proved that with Long Term Capital. Systematic anomalies such as the Asian flu and the Russian ruble crises basically destroyed Long Term Capital because it couldn't account for all the variables in the market.

The only reason that institutions build these monsters is because they index against the averages, and because they have so much capital to manage and maintain the systems. This is burdensome. As an individual, you are programming your mind with algorithms like a system, but you have the added advantage of using your intuition to make decisions that machines struggle with. Essentially, you are the system.

A well-known trader and instructor at MarketWise for whom we have deep respect is Larry McMillen. Larry once said, "A little math goes a long way on Wall Street." This is very true. It is also true that too much math can hinder you. With all that said, we begin our topic with the basic elements of a systems model. Then we'll pass the torch over to a friend and respected market participant, Wai Cheong. Wai Cheong has also spent millions of dollars on systems, and his insights are invaluable and greatly respected.

SYSTEM TRADING AND BACK-TESTING ENGINES

To be successful in trading, you need ideas—brilliant ones if you want to be at the top of the market's food chain. The minimum needed is to at least have sound ideas that can withstand the vagaries of the market. In most fields of human endeavor, there is a marked difference between good and bad ideas—good ideas work and bad ones don't. In trading, there can be a continuum in the value of ideas. After all, how good or bad a trading idea is depends completely on the amount of money it makes, and we can measure that down to pennies. Of course, brilliant ideas make you rich and possibly famous, good ones make you a fabulous living, and bad ones will force you to look for other things dealing with your life. It is a constant challenge to find good ideas. Tape readers, chartists, and event traders have to look for new ideas every single day. They have to work very hard at it, and it is often said that trading is everyone's most intense full-time job.

Then there are those traders who want to work less hard at it, and develop a methodology whereby they will put on the same trades or exit them whenever the same conditions appear in the market. To this style of trading, we attribute the term *system trading*. Instead of looking for good ideas for every trade, this style of trading looks for a good "mechanical" or systems methodology. In this scenario, traders are not looking for a single good idea for a single trade. They are trying to identify the conditions in which a large number of trades can be successful. This means that they are trying to always put on the same trade whenever the same market conditions manifest themselves. In essence, they look to trade market anomalies.

The attraction of this methodology is that once a good system has been found, a whole series of trades can then be put on without the need to evaluate each trade separately. Each trade is just a part of the whole, and it does not matter if a single trade does not do well—or performs marvelously, for that matter. It is the entire series of trades that the strategy activates that is evaluated. It can be considered either a lazy man's game or the science of the disciplined trader who believes that the odds of beating the market are better with this approach.

RULES OF SYSTEM TRADING

System trading requires rules to be established. These rules will determine how trades are put on and exited. Since we need to find those rules that will enable more winners than losers to emerge, or at least enable the total winnings from good trades to exceed the losses accumulated from bad ones, we need to have investigative as well as evaluative procedures. We need to be able to say that some rules are better than others, or that some are great while others are not good at all. That is what the art and science of back-testing is all about.

Let's examine a few of the many rules of back-testing and systems trading that should be considered. To begin this exercise, we need to know what we are looking for. You've got to have an idea of what is considered good or bad. In this regard, the single most important tool is the equity curve. *The equity curve* is really the result of back-testing, or the historical simulations intended to help you understand whether a specific strategy is effective for you.

EQUITY CURVE

What exactly is an equity curve? Actually, it is nothing more than a graph of the cumulative profit/loss of a strategy over the entire time frame of the simulation period.

Why is this important? Wouldn't it be sufficient just to see what the total P/L is? What can the graph tell us that the simple summary numbers cannot? The answer is that in trading, the path through which you travel on the way to acquiring profit is very important. If your strategy goes through a huge loss before it makes a great gain, or is very volatile on its way to success, you must know about it. In the real world, the big loss or the many consecutive losses might not be surmounted. Your account might become irreparably damaged or your psychological attitude toward, and confidence in, the strategy might become so battered that you might not be able to take the upcoming trades to get to the profits. In other words, you need to know how the strategy performs over time. Looking at the equity curve is, in effect, a way to review and monitor the risk of your trading strategy.

In all good back-testing engines, equity curve plotting features are typically available. If not, you should be able to at least download the back-test data into an Excel spreadsheet, and then use the Excel charting functions to avail yourself of different ways of plotting the equity curve.

In general, there are a couple of things you want to check on the equity curve before you can conclude that the strategy you have created has a reasonable risk profile:

- As stated above, there should be no serious drawdowns. The growth path of cumulative profits should be as steady as possible, growing from zero to the total at the end of the test.

- As a corollary to the first point, the strategy should not derive most of its profits from one or two huge winners. If the strategy is dependent on just a few good trades, it is probably a curve fit and you have a perfect way of trading history, not the future.

- The impact of large losses from overnight positions or event risks (such as earnings announcements) is not overwhelming in the sense that such losses (which are inevitable) do not represent huge drawdowns.

- You should also be aware of how the drawdowns come about—whether these are large, one-time events or whether they arise from runs of many consecutive bad trades. Both can be devastating, not just to the bottom line but to your psychological ability to follow the system and take the next trade in actual implementation.

- A good system assumes that the number of trades is reasonably large for big sample effects, but not so large that commissions and slippage eliminate all profits. The average winner should be bigger than the average loser, and the number of winners should ideally be no less than the number of losers (of course, having more winners is better). The Sharpe ratio, which we will discuss later in the chapter, should be high (as close to 1 as possible) and the ratio of profit to maximum drawdown should be greater than 1 (2 would be a very acceptable starting point). None of these are written in stone, so you typically have to compromise.

You can also use any generic back-testing engine and save the strategy results to Excel as an alternative way to plot the equity curve. You can view results in any of the many chart types that Excel carries. All you have to do is to plot the cumulative P/L number in the spreadsheet that has been saved for each stock.

We hope that you will keep in mind the importance of the equity curve in risk management. It's not just the pot of gold at the end of the rainbow that should attract you. If the path going there is full of known risks, you should not embark on that odyssey. The equity curve shows you where a specific strategy has stumbled and fallen in the recent past—learn from it.

BY THE NUMBERS

We explained how to use the equity curves that should come with back-testing engines to evaluate trading strategies. Our aim was to take some simple industry standard indicators to illustrate how to use such engines to create a reasonable trading model. Our focus was not on how great the individual indicators themselves were. After all, these indicators are so common and widely used that there is not a lot more we can say about their effectiveness or ineffectiveness. Suffice it to say that sometimes they work and sometimes they don't. We fully expect you to find other strategies to combine into portfolios, driving toward the type of consistent equity curves that we believe can best be created for multiple strategy, multiple instrument, and multiple time bar combinations.

In addition to the equity curve, back-testing engines always come with full statistical reports on the performance of any strategy tested. These reports have become something of an industry standard in the numbers that are reported. In other words, we will show you how to award Oscars and Emmys in strategy design so that you will know the best ways of deploying your time and capital.

Let's use two industry standard indicators—the 5 × 20 simple moving average and the 12-26-9 MACD as an example. We will not change their trading rules, which are as follows:

- *Double simple moving average* (DSMA). When the 5-period SMA crosses the 20-period SMA from below, buy, and vice versa.
- *Moving average convergence/divergence.* When the MACD line crosses the signal line from below, buy, and vice versa.

Keep in mind, these are simple examples for the purposes of testing the statistical value of any given system. The systems available and those that you can create are unlimited. The statistical results are common to most back-

F I G U R E   13.1

The statistical results are common to most back-testing systems. This illustration is a generic example of what most systems calculate.

Stock:	CEPH
Time frame:	15min
Double Simple MA:	5 period crosses 20 period
Simulation Start:	6/5/2002
Simulation End:	9/16/2002
Share Size:	100
Total Net Profit:	$2,849
Percent Gain/Loss:	68.30%
Max Drawdown:	$958
Sharpe Ratio:	0.55
Total Closed Trades:	143
Total Winning Trades:	61
Average Win:	$143.90
Average Profit/Trade:	$19.78
Average Loss:	$71.43
Largest Win:	$576
Largest Loss:	$214
Average Length of Wins:	30.26 periods
Average Length of Loss:	10.42 periods
Most Consecutive Wins:	6
Most Consecutive Losses:	6

testing systems. This illustration is a generic example of what most systems calculate. Figure 13.1 is an example of strategy summary statistics available on a typical back-test system.

Figure 13.1 illustrates important statistics that you should look at in deciding which system gets an Oscar. Clearly, the total net profit is important, but this must be considered in relation to other things. First of all, it must beat some benchmark, and we should only use systems that beat "buy and hold." If you put money in a mutual fund and it cannot even beat the S&P 500, you should dump that at once. The same thing is true for trading—if you cannot beat buy and hold, don't waste your time.

The size of the maximum drawdown is also very important. Given that in trading some losses are inevitable, we need to know how bad these get. In my book, we do not award Oscars to strategies that produce just great absolute P/L. We want our P to be at least twice that of L. If we risk $1, we want to make at least $2. Some of you may even desire a better risk/return ratio, but trust the battle-scarred market veterans and be a little more realistic about what can be achieved.

SHARPE RATIO

The next thing we examine is the Sharpe ratio. This is expressed as a decimal, usually below 1. You want to get this up as high as possible, and in excess of 1 if you can get it there. There aren't any single strategies popular in the industry that have a Sharpe ratio that exceeds 1. Single indicator strategies with a Sharpe above 1 are called "silver bullets," and they do not exist. With diversification, however, it is easily possible to have strategies with Sharpe ratios above 1 for the portfolio.

The Sharpe ratio is nothing more than an industry standard measurement of the risk/reward ratio. It measures the returns from the strategy as well as the volatility of those returns. If there is a smooth equity curve, the Sharpe ratio will be high, as the volatility is low. High returns, of course, also contribute to a high Sharpe ratio. The relationship of big profits and low volatility will get you a high Sharpe ratio.

Further into our Oscar ceremonies, we are looking to give away prizes to low turnover of trades and a high win/loss ratio. Take a look at the CEPH DSMA strategy:

Total Closed Trades: 143
Total Winning Trades: 61

For a four-month period of trading, 143 trades are not a lot, as they average to just a little more than one trade a day. We would consider that to be relatively low turnover. We would actually look for something that would be somewhere between one trade every two days and two trades a day to be appropriate. Less than that, and the risk management or opportunity capture is not going to be good, as it is very clear that the strategy is sitting out many moves in the market. More than that, and you will have a hard time trying to overcome the transactions costs, particularly the bid/ask spread.

There is no hard-and-fast rule for the win/loss ratio. Don't expect to find strategies that yield 70 percent or more good trades. You should aim for no more than 60 percent winners. On the other hand, if you have less than 40 percent winners, it will be difficult to get enough mileage out of the few winners you do have to cover the losses of the many losers.

In traders' boot camp, we were taught to cut our losses and let our profits run. That is the golden rule for traders. We need to operationalize this rule. Where do we cut losses and how far should we let profits run?

The findings on the DSMA trading CEPH as shown in Figure 13.1 are as follows:

Average Win:	$143.9
Average Profit/Trade:	$19.78
Average Loss:	$71.43
Average Length of Win:	30.26 bars
Average Length of Loss:	10.42 bars

We see that this technique of using the DSMA in fact lets the profits run for longer than it allows the losses to. As such, we have an operating rule to implement our adage. In fact, one of the major benefits of good trend-following trading strategies is that they will allow winners to run far longer than they do the losers. This is true not just in terms of profits, but also in terms of the number of bars the strategy holds in winning positions versus losing ones.

There are other interesting things to be said about the strategy here, including the fact that the largest win looks twice as good as the largest loss looks bad. This is an important confidence booster, and confidence is needed to blindly follow a strategy into the future.

Largest Win:	$576
Largest Loss:	$214

The last criterion we can use to give out Oscars is the number of consecutive winners and losers. In this strategy, the results are shown below:

Most Consecutive Wins:	6
Most Consecutive Losses:	6

Here, we look at the absolute numbers as well as the numbers relative to one another. If you think about it, it is pretty hard to want to doggedly follow a trading method if trade after trade after trade is a loser. You will begin to get the sense that the strategy is doomed and that you should no longer follow it. That is why it is very important to have done your back test over a very long period of time and know that there were a sufficient number of trades processed during the test. You must have the confidence that your tests have seen everything in the pattern of historical prices and have still come out ahead. You want to be able to say to yourself, "Okay, it's a bad run, but we know it has happened before and we can come out ahead."

In Figure 13.2 we show the results of trading CEPH 15m bars on the MACD. Using the principles laid out above, decide for yourself which strategy, the MACD or the DSMA, you would prefer to use.

F I G U R E   13.2

An example of the results from a backtest done on Cephacon Inc. (CEPH) using the MACD on 15-minute bars.

Stock:	CEPH
Time frame:	15min
MACD:	12,26,9
Simulation Start:	6/5/2002
Simulation End:	9/16/2002
Share Size:	100
Total Net Profit:	$3,821
Percent Gain/Loss:	91.60%
Max Drawdown:	$654
Sharpe Ratio:	0.78
Total Closed Trades:	172
Total Winning Trades:	76
Average Win:	$135.20
Average Profit/Trade:	$22.09
Average Loss:	$66.57
Largest Win:	$450
Largest Loss:	$228
Average Length of Wins:	23.6 periods
Average Length of Loss:	9.5 periods
Most Consecutive Wins:	4
Most Consecutive Losses:	6

The answer is not obvious and you have some trade-offs to consider when you hand out that Oscar.

THE PERILS OF CURVE-FITTING

One of the favorite pastimes of system traders is to continuously optimize the parameters in their trading algorithms. For those of you who are new in the game, you will probably want to know what optimization means. To explain this, let's use the example of a moving average. The first thing to determine is what moving average to use. Should we use a 10-period MA? Why not 5, or 28? In the application of moving averages to trading, we cannot say that we have a favorite set of parameters. Unlike other indicators such as the RSI, stochastic models, Bollinger Bands, and other "branded" indicators, for which the creators of the indicators have put on record why a certain parameter should be used, moving averages are so widely used, and in such diverse ways, that there is really no standard, except perhaps for the Donchian 5×20 crossover systems used in daily bar charts and the $4 \times 9 \times 18$ triple moving averages used by futures and FX traders dealing with FOREX (Foreign Exchange) rates.

Therefore, moving averages provide a very fertile field for innovation. One possibility is optimization. This simply means using different parameters to compute the moving averages, possible because the moving average is a simple calculation of a number of data points vis-à-vis prices. The big question is: How many data points should we use? And, a bigger question: How many different combinations of different MAs can we test and trade with?

The standard formulation of a MA is, in nonmathematical parlance, based on the average of prices (usually the closes) over an n-day period. For double and triple crossover systems, the two or three averages are calculated over $n1$, $n2$, and $n3$ periods.

So when we get down to it, what should n be? Unfortunately, when Moses came down from the mountain, he did not bring with him what we moving-average traders would really like to know, and therefore we have to guess at what n should be. Put another way, we all have our favorite n. That is what optimization in moving average crossover trading is all about—choosing the n that we personally like. Since all of us are affected by greed and fear, we ardently desire to find out the magical n that produces the most profits and the smallest drawdowns for a given stock.

The software industry has made it easy for those of us who have a pathological fear that the n that we are using is not the "right" one. Powerful programs have existed for 20 years that allow us to keep changing the n in moving average calculations to back-test them and find the "best." That, my friends, is optimization.

We can make whatever indicator we want fit the chart, and trade history, like a charm. The term *curve-fitting* comes from the process of changing parameters of algorithms until they show a strong historical result. By continuously changing the parameter, we can always find a line that will fit our textbook trading rule. And if we apply back-testing to that line, we will probably find that the P/L will be optimal. However, as of yet we have simply discovered a technique that trades history well. How about the future? Who knows? Therein lies the danger of curve-fitting. We never really know beforehand if what has been optimized to historical data will continue to perform well in the future. Thus, while optimization to some extent is not a bad thing to do, because different markets and time bars have different trading characteristics (such as liquidity, volatility, etc.), being pedantic about finding the absolute best fit to the historical data is a misdirected effort. Through intelligent application of optimization techniques, we can use back-testing techniques to adjust our strategies and rules according to changes in real market conditions and without getting carried away with curve-fitting.

ADVANCED SYSTEMS TRADING

Let us now look at one of the many systems that we have created and continue to tweak and adjust as the market dynamic evolves. This continual maintenance of code, if you will, is required to keep and maintain that very small edge. Therefore, our services at MarketWise appeal to many traders who do not wish to build their own systems.

We first want to determine the stage the given issue is in. In order to determine the stage of a particular issue, we must first calculate three simple moving averages based on closing prices within a given time frame. One moving average represents the very short term, the second the midterm, and the third the long term within the time horizon being measured. For example, if we measure a time frame or period of one day, the three moving averages representing the short term, midterm and long term within a particular day would be the 10-, 20-, and 50-period moving average, respectively.

Our next step is to get rules. In this case we determine the stage of a particular vehicle by means of several rules. Because some rules conflict, we must also test prices against what we call a high or low breakpoint. For the high breakpoint, we take the high closing price of the issue over a given time period of 5 days, 10 days, or longer. The second step in calculating the high breakpoint is to measure the high closing price of the current stage, but only if the current stage is in fact in stage 1, which will be determined once the calculation is complete.

The low breakpoint is defined as the low close of a given time period and the low close of the current stage. If the current stage is stage 3, then we also test price in relation to it. This may initially seem confusing, but the transitions are the most difficult. In this case, we are dealing with measuring the transition of one stage to the next. Because of these transitions, we must use the values of only one stage, which in this case would be the mature stage of the stage prior and will relate to the early stage of the next ensuing stage. This transitional period is critical in measuring the propensity for a vehicle to move from one stage to the next, or even skip a stage altogether.

Once these calculations are processed (based on a study of daily charts), we can then examine the relationship of the three moving averages to each other. Because we are measuring three concurrently running moving averages, 10-, 20- and 50-period MAs in this example, we know that mathematically there are only six possible relationships. They are as follows:

1. The 10-period moving average is greater than or equal to the 20-period moving average, and the 20-period moving average is greater than or equal to the 50-period moving average.

2. The 10-period moving average is greater than or equal to the 50-period moving average, and the 50-period moving average is greater than or equal to the 20-period moving average.

3. The 20-period moving average is greater than or equal to the 10-period moving average, and the 10-period moving average is greater than or equal to the 50-period moving average.

4. The 20-period moving average is greater than or equal to the 50-period moving average, and the 50-period moving average is greater than or equal to the 10-period moving average.

5. The 50-period moving average is greater than or equal to the 10-period moving average, and the 10-period moving average is greater than or equal to the 20-period moving average.

6. The 50-period moving average is greater than or equal to the 20-period moving average, and the 20-period moving average is greater than or equal to the 10-period moving average.

Once we code these six scenarios into our system, we need only feed the system with reliable data. The output of that data will be objective; therefore, the quality of our rules and criteria, which is defined in terms of what moving averages to use, remains suspect, as is the case with any system. Only the market can tell us the strength of our choices.

Determining Price Movement Stages

The four main stages of stock and index price movement can be characterized as accumulation, markup, distribution, and decline. Each of these stages, in turn, can have early, middle, and late substages. For ease of notation, we will use the following numbers to indicate the various stages:

1-1 = Early Accumulation

1-2 = Mid-Accumulation

1-3 = Late Accumulation

2-1 = Early Markup

2-2 = Mid-Markup

2-3 = Late Markup

3-1 = Early Distribution
3-2 = Mid-Distribution
3-3 = Late Distribution

4-1 = Early Decline
4-2 = Mid-Decline
4-3 = Late Decline

To determine what stage a particular stock or index is in, we must first calculate the following:

- Three simple moving averages of the closing price in the given time period: one short term, one midterm, and one longer term. In the current example, the time period is one day; therefore, the three moving averages are the 10-, 20-, and 50-day.
- A high breakpoint, defined as the lesser of
  (a) The high close of the last x time periods, or
  (b) The high close of the current stage if the current stage is stage 1.
- A low breakpoint, defined as the greater of
  (a) The low close of the last x time periods, or
  (b) The low close of the current stage if the current stage is stage 3.

In the current example, the time period is 45 days. Once these values are determined for the specified time period, we then examine the relationship among the three moving averages. For simplicity of notation, the six possible moving average relationships can be noted as follows:

1. 10/20/50: meaning the 10-day average $\geq$ 20-day average and the 20-day $\geq$ 50-day
2. 10/50/20: meaning the 10-day average $\geq$ 50-day average and the 50-day $\geq$ 20-day
3. 20/10/50: meaning the 20-day average $\geq$ 10-day average and the 10-day $\geq$ 50-day
4. 20/50/10: meaning the 20-day average $\geq$ 50-day average and the 50-day $\geq$ 10-day
5. 50/10/20: meaning the 50-day average $\geq$ 10-day average and the 10-day $\geq$ 20-day
6. 50/20/10: meaning the 50-day average $\geq$ 20-day average and the 20-day $\geq$ 10-day

We are now ready to assign the stage for the given time period:

1. If the MA relationship is 50/10/20 then the stage is 1-1, early accumulation.

2. If the MA relationship is 10/50/20 then the stage is 1-2, mid-accumulation.

3. If the MA relationship is 10/20/50, then things are not so simple and this can be a stage 1-3, late accumulation, or any of the three markup stages (2-1, 2-2, and 2-3). This is determined in part by what the previous stage was, and for certain previous stages the closing price's relationship to the high breakpoint and/or the moving averages. See the flow chart in Figure 13.3 for the logic for determining the stage when the MA relationship is 10/20/50.

4. If the MA relationship is 20/10/50 then the stage is 3-1, early distribution.

5. If the MA relationship is 20/50/10 then the stage is 3-2, mid-distribution.

6. If the MA relationship is 50/20/10, then things are again not so simple and this can be a stage 3-3, late distribution, or any of the three decline stages (4-1, 4-2, and 4-3). We must examine the previous stage and the closing price in relation to the low break point and/or the moving averages. See the flow chart on 50/20/10 in Figure 13.4 for the logic for determining the stage when the MA relationship is 50/20/10.

While the value of the given system may be strong for a given period of time, it will not last forever. The market is analogous to an organism made up of millions and millions of living parts. Because of all these living parts (market participants), no trading system can be left unmaintained.

Where the system becomes complicated is in the transitions that have a moving average relationship of 10/20/50 or 50/20/10. These transitions are subjective and more suspect when in the mature state of either stage 1 or 3. In this case, we could just as well be in any of the markup stages (2-1, 2-2, or 2-3). In order to determine exactly where a stock is, the previous stage and previous stage's closing prices in relation to the high breakpoint and the moving average being measured must be known.

The flowcharts in Figures 13.3 and 13.4 help explain this very idea, as well as the logic behind the calculations. Flowchart 13.3 is used to determine the stage that we are in when the moving average relationship is 10/20/50. If the relationship is 20/10/50, then stage 3-1, or early distribution, is in play. If the early average relationship is 20/50/10, then we are in stage 3-2, or mid-distribution. If the moving average relationship is 50/20/10, then things are again not so simple and we could be in stage 3-3, late distribution, or any of the three decline stages (4-1, 4-2, and 4-3). In this case, we are again facing a

F I G U R E   13.3

Flowchart for moving average relationship 10/20/50. The flowchart puts the stage criteria into a logical progression that is easy to follow.

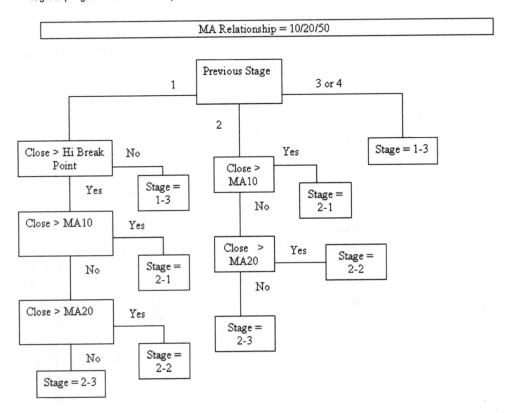

transitional period and we must explain the previous stage as well as the closing price in relation to the low breakpoint and/or the moving average. Again, the flowcharts help to explain the logic for determining what stage we are in and the moving average relationship associated with it.

Welcome to the world of systems programming and systems trading. If you are rubbing your forehead in deep confusion right now, don't feel alone. The process is not simple. So why offer it in this book? Well, the answer is simple. Facilities do exist that offer such programming and coding. What must be realized and understood is that the rules and criteria that you ask to be put into algorithmic form will be subjective in nature, and the quality of the programming in defining those rules and the complexity associated with them can also be subjective if not properly defined. These examples represent only a glimpse of the potential complexity.

F I G U R E   13.4

Flowchart for the moving average relationship 50/20/10.

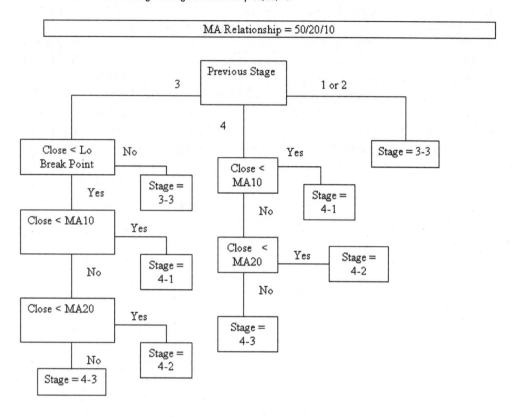

Whether or not our rules are good barometers of market direction can only be determined by the market itself. But to have the ability to program code and develop such systems allows traders to test many scenarios and many possible outputs. This is a tremendous advance, since traders can then apply many scenarios in a brief period of time by utilizing a sound back-testing engine. The predictive value of these rules can only be measured by your ability to apply them to the market.

It is important to note that the value of the signal improves exponentially when multiple systems are running and are cross-referenced against each other concurrently, and all the systems agree. Therefore, using only one set of rules or criteria, even if the output empirically shows strong historical significance, is still very limited in its predictive value. It is only when several sets of algorithms and systems are measured against one another that strong signals, correlations, and coefficients are achieved.

We hope that you've gained at least a basic understanding of systems trading. As you may suspect, the subject is very complex and requires a great deal of study and work. We do not suggest or recommend that you attempt to program your own system. These providers are not interested in trading your ideas; instead, they are compensated for coding and testing your ideas. In doing so, I believe these credible providers maintain the integrity of your system. Therefore, do not shy away from utilizing these services if you feel your view of the market could prove to be an accurate method of trading. For those of you who would like to engage the process further, there are courses and curriculums that you can also take advantage of to learn some of the basic steps. Visit *www.marketwise.com* for more detail.

14

PAIRS TRADING

Pairs trading is a strategy that matches long positions against short positions in order to generate positive returns uncorrelated to the market. These returns are often referred to as alpha. Generally, the underlying companies within the pairs trade come from the same industry or share a set of common variables that cause their prices to move in tandem. The strategy can encompass either stocks, exchange traded funds, or indices, depending on their correlative qualities and the intentions of the trader. This form of trading has grown dramatically in the trading community, along with research reports specific to this particular strategy. In this chapter, we seek not only to explain pairs trading but to show you how to construct and apply pairs strategies.

The objective of this strategy is to create alpha regardless of the direction of potential market moves. Ideally, successful pairs trading identifies a long position that will rise during the trade, while at the same time identifying a short position that will fall. This creates two positive returns (double alpha). However, all that is required for the strategy to succeed is relative positive performance, whether both positions skyrocket or plummet.

Another advantage of pairs trading is that it reduces volatility as alpha is created. Reducing volatility preserves capital, limits risk, and allows for the use of greater leverage if desired. This benefit limits the likelihood that a trade will be stopped out, given strict risk management parameters. In essence, successful pairs trading can improve upon straight stock picking or market timing strategies and deliver higher returns with lower risk over time.

One way pairs trading reduces volatility is by neutralizing both industry and market risk. By removing these risk factors, which are at times unpredictable over the short term, it isolates alpha opportunities that are derived from fundamental or technical factors. While fundamental analysis is not part of our trading strategy as a rule, pairs trading is an exception.

By taking the market out of the equation, traders can focus on what is more knowledgeable and predictable. Moreover, the strategy allows traders to isolate alpha opportunities that do not necessarily exist through a straight long or short position in any particular tradable security.

The types of pairs trading most commonly employed include statistical arbitrage, merger arbitrage, derivative securities arbitrage, and fundamental pairs. *Statistical arbitrage* uses quantitative analysis of historical data to identify high-probability convergence trades where two securities that have diverged in price regress to a historical mean. Divergence trades are also employed where two securities are expected to diverge in price from a historical mean. *Merger arbitrage,* on the other hand, pairs the acquirer and acquired securities between the announcement and closing of proposed merger transactions. *Derivative securities arbitrage* identifies convergence trades where two securities issued by the same company have diverged in price from their fundamental economic relationship.

Pairs trading can be employed on both a technical and fundamental basis. We will cover an example of both. Fundamental pairs trading seeks to identify two companies within the same industry, or that share similar characteristics, that will trade differently in the future depending on fundamental issues such as valuation, operating performance, or investor sentiment. As opposed to other forms of arbitrage, fundamental pairs trading depends on both qualitative and quantitative analysis for its success. Qualitative analysis requires in-depth research, comprehensive understanding, and good judgment to create trades that generate alpha.

IMPLEMENTATION OF FUNDAMENTAL PAIRS TRADING

CORE POSITION

Fundamental pairs trading generally starts with the identification of a core position that a trader can build around. The core position can be either a long or short, but must stand out in some qualitative or quantitative way relative to its matched position. Such factors can comprise of, but are not limited to, the following:

1. Valuation by P/E, P/CF, P/Book, or any other relevant industry metric
2. Growth in sales, earnings, or market share
3. Quality in management, competitive advantages, and balance sheet
4. Technicals via indicators such as relative strength, momentum, etc.
5. Event earnings announcements, product releases, etc.

Traders must determine which of the above issues are not priced into the stock correctly. Subsequently they can initiate the trade by pairing it off with another stock that will effectively isolate the inefficiency (e.g., cheap valuation versus industry norms).

HEDGE POSITION

The ideal hedge is one or more securities that reflect inverse inefficiency (e.g., expensive valuation versus industry or market norms), or relative mispricing across the multiple factors identified above. The more extraordinary the relative mispricing and the more factors identified, the better the chance that pricing anomalies will converge and benefit the pairs trade over time.

If there is no suitable hedge that reflects inverse inefficiency to the core position, control hedges such as industry ETF's or indices can stand in its place to neutralize industry and market risk. The point of the hedge is to remove as much perceived risk as possible in order to maximize the positive performance of the core position.

HEDGE WEIGHTING

According to stock-specific, industry, or market factors, the weighting of the pairs trade should adjust to reflect the bias of the trader and the risks to the core position. The pairs trade can weight the two positions evenly (dollar neutral), or overweight the long or short side to compensate for other concerns. Some of the considerations for appropriate trade construction are as follows:

1. Market capitalization
2. Liquidity and float
3. Beta and momentum
4. Short interest and stock loan availability for the short position
5. Fundamental factors and other relative valuation measures

For example, if traders have a greater degree of confidence in the long position, they may decide to increase the weight of the long relative to the hedge. Alternatively, traders may give greater weight to the long to compensate for a higher beta of the short. However it is done, successful pairs traders attempt to identify the ideal relative weighting of the two positions to achieve the greatest return while taking on the least risk.

CORRELATION

Traders must also determine how closely correlated they want the offsetting hedge to be to the core position. The more closely the two positions are correlated, the more likely the two positions will trade in line with each other and restrain alpha. Having closely correlated pairs is ideal for inefficiently priced events such as earnings announcements, where the correlation might loosen temporarily while the market reprices the affected position. More loosely correlated pairs require more management and understanding as to why the positions will ultimately trade away from each other.

While correlations are easily measured by statistical tools such as R-Squared, which measures historical risk-adjusted returns (return minus the return of risk-free cash), it is important to recognize that such correlations are backward-looking and imperfect when predicting the future. The successful pairs trade anticipates how the correlation will change going forward and plans for its eventual realization.

TIME HORIZON

Traders must understand the time horizon for holding the core position. Is the trade meant to have a long- or short-term holding period? Is there a near-term event to trigger market recognition of the inefficiency, or will time gradually reveal the relative merits of the pair? By definition, having a longer time horizon allows for more volatility because there are more intervals of pricing. The longer the time horizon for the trade, the more management of the volatility and risks is required.

RISKS

Once traders have determined the core position, appropriate hedge and its weighting, correlation, and time horizon, they must finally determine the potential risks to the trade. This will allow a trader to clarify where the core position may trade in the future, as well as establishing the suitability of the offsetting pair in those events. Judging the risks ahead of time also helps traders to understand how large to make the pair as a percentage of their capital and how closely they must monitor and manage the position.

TRADE MANAGEMENT

Prior to initiating a trade, traders should form expectations about potential trade performance, while setting stop losses for any disappointments within the expected time horizon. New fundamental information related to either position or significant changes in correlation should cause traders to adjust the trade. In all cases, traders should treat the paired position with the same trading discipline they would bring to any other long or short position in the portfolio.

FUNDAMENTAL PAIRS MATRIX AND EXAMPLES

Now that we have covered the basic principles of fundamental pairs trading, we can review them in a matrix and go through an example of an actual trade and the logic behind it.

PAIRS MATRIX

Investment time frame and correlation mark the boundaries of the matrix in Figure 14.1. By determining where a pairs trade fits in this matrix, traders can better define their expectations for trade performance and trade management.

For example, a short-term trade with high correlating pairs suggests that both positions will likely move in the same direction and provide a single alpha opportunity (e.g., the long rises more than the short). This type of pairing is ideal for mean regression trades, which predict that two securities will converge and trade once again at their historical relationship. However, if the trade is extended to a longer-term horizon, there is a greater chance that the two securities will trade away (diverge) from each other if factors such as new fundamental information warrant it. The longer the time frame, the greater chance a trader has to actively manage the pair and find increased return. However, trading around the position is not mandatory or even required if the thesis of the trade is powerful enough to produce a sustained return over time.

The pairs trade we present next pertains to the high-correlation, longer-term area of the matrix. This example was an actual trade in our portfolio, and we have attempted to indicate the thesis and reasoning behind it.

EXAMPLE: TK VERSUS OSG

Teekay Shipping (TK) and Overseas Shipholding Group (OSG) operate in the oil tanker industry and are listed on the New York Stock Exchange, along

F I G U R E   14.1

Grid showing alpha and risk versus time frame and correlation.

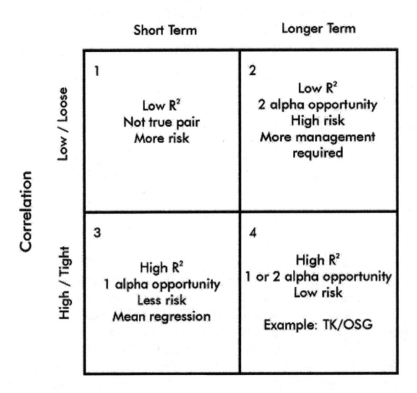

Investment Time Frame

with a handful of other stocks in their industry. Oil tankers pick up crude from the Middle East and other oil-rich regions, delivering their cargo to importing nations around the world.

Although the industry is vital to the worldwide energy infrastructure, we believe few investors understand or appropriately differentiate oil tanker companies, as the industry remains an afterthought in most investors' portfolios. We saw this inefficiency most pronounced in the relative pricing of the industry leader and largest market cap stock, Teekay Shipping, and its smaller rival, Overseas Shipholding Group, in late 2001.

Almost all publicly traded tanker stocks have relatively high correlations to each other due to the industry-wide spot rate pricing structure. Companies receive highly variable spot daily pricing for their services, despite having almost entirely fixed and predictable costs. The high operating lever-

F I G U R E   14.2

Fundamentals of Teekay versus Overseas Shipholding Group.

	Long	Short
	Teekay	Overseas Shipholding Group
	(NYSE: TK)	(NYSE: OSG)
Price (11/16/2001)	$26.79	$23.39
Shares Outstanding	40.0 million	34.8 million
Market Capitalization	$1.071 billion	$814 million
Daily Trading Volume	274,728	111,492
52-Week Range	$54.50–$24.50	$37.5–$19.46
Float	22.8 million	27.7 million
Short Interest	659,000	555,000
Beta	1.01	0.91

Vessels	TK	vs.	OSG
Number	97	186%	52
Dead Weight Tons	9.8	129%	7.6
Class	Aframax		Aframax/VLCC

age of the tanker companies leads to extremely variable quarterly earnings, and the high correlation of the spot rates across tanker classes means that the underlying stock prices generally move in tandem.

Figure 14.2 lists the relevant data and valuation metrics for both companies for November 16, 2001. As we can see, TK was valued 31 percent higher than OSG by market cap (1.1 billion to 814 million), with 29 percent more dead weight tons in its fleet (9.8 to 7.6), yet TK operated 86 percent more vessels (97 to 52). On a tonnage basis the two seem comparable and priced correctly, but this is not at all the case when viewed on a valuation basis.

As shown in Figure 14.3, TK clearly dominated OSG on every valuation metric, from balance sheet to net income. Moreover, we knew TK's management to be the best in the industry; additionally, its tanker fleet size and age

FIGURE   14.3

Fundamentals and relative comparison of TK versus OSG.

Valuation	TK	vs.	OSG
Market Cap*	$1107	136%	$814
Book Value	$1386	173%	$801
Net Debt	$776	128%	$606
EV	$1883	133%	$1420
Ebitda (ttm)**	$595	231%	$257
EPS (ttm)	$10.56	256%	$4.12
Price/Book	0.80	78%	1.02
P/E (ttm)	2.5x	44%	5.7x
EV Ebitda (ttm)	3.2x	58%	5.5x
Dividend Yield	3.2%	123%	2.6%

*Values in million, except per share data
**ttm through Q3 2001

were unique for its scale and young age. We knew of no event risk or technical factor that could account for the relative mispricing of the two companies, save one: September 11, 2001, which had produced a much greater decline for TK than for OSG. We believed that the market simply had not priced tanker companies correctly because TK had suffered much more in the aftermath of the sell-off than OSG. OSG had traded off and then rallied into November, whereas TK had continued to fall (see Figure 14.4).

When reviewing the earnings histories for both companies, we remarked on the fact that TK had annually increased its earnings per share (EPS) relative to OSG and was estimated to outearn OSG five to one in 2001 on a per-share basis. However, we found the companies to be trading only $3.40 apart from each other ($26.79 versus $23.39) despite the superior earnings history for TK. We review our proposed trade of long TK versus short OSG in the following sections.

F I G U R E   14.4

Relative stock price performance of TK versus OSG.

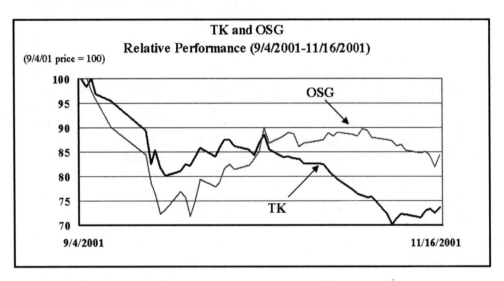

Core Position

We identified TK as the core long position due to these factors:

1. Valuation: It traded at 2.5 × P/E, 80 percent of book with a 3.2 percent yield.
2. Growth: Its sales and fleet growth was among the fastest in the industry.
3. Quality: It was known to be number one in the tanker industry, not just Aframax class.
4. Technicals: N/A.
5. Event: Rectification of post-September 11 oversold condition.

Hedge Position

We identified OSG as the short hedge due to these factors:

1. Valuation: It traded at 5.7 × P/E, 102 percent of book with a 2.6 percent yield
2. Growth: Its sales and fleet growth was among the slowest in the industry.

3. Quality: It had sleepy management and lower-quality ships.
4. Technicals: N/A.
5. Event: N/A.

Hedge Weighting

We decided to weight the trade share-for-share to arbitrage the disparate P/Es between the two companies (2.5 × P/E versus 5.7 × P/E). This left us slightly longer TK (the core position) on a dollar basis, as we believed there was somewhat limited downside risk to TK given its high book value and dividend yield. TK's beta was only about 10 percent higher than OSG (1.01 versus 0.91), so we believed that it was quite comparable and did not need adjusting—in fact, TK's higher beta may have hurt shares in the sell-off, but would help our long position in any recovery scenario.

Correlation

For the previous six months TK and OSG had traded together with an R-Squared of 0.84, which is fairly high but not unexpected given the industry dynamics. We felt confident that the two companies would trade closely together in the short term (good for a pair) but that fundamental factors would enable TK to rise far more than OSG over time.

Time Horizon

We felt strongly that TK would continue to outearn OSG for the foreseeable future, so we set our time horizon to long term, or until we thought TK was valued much higher than OSG to reflect its superior operating business.

Risks

We saw few risks to the trade because of our confidence in TK's business versus OSG's, as well as the relative valuation differential. However, because we did not understand why the market had priced these securities in this way, we continued to research the two companies in order to determine if we were missing something. Since historically TK had outearned OSG by an increasing degree in both good and bad rate environments, we effectively removed the major risk to companies in this industry—the equity price correlation to boom/bust spot rate moves.

FIGURE   14.5

Dollar spread amount of the long TK and short OSG trade.

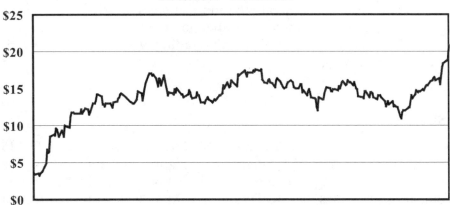

TK vs. OSG
11/15/2001 - 11/20/2002

Trade Management

Fortunately, the trade worked almost right away, as TK finally recovered while OSG eventually fell. See Figure 14.5, which shows dollar amount gained on our TK long and OSG short on a per share basis. We trimmed the position around the $15 level but kept on a smaller weighting until we removed the trade in its entirety one year later on November 20. TK closed that day at $38.35 (+$11.56) while OSG closed at $16.95 (–$6.44) for a total gain on the pair of $18.00 ($21.40 closing price, $3.40 when initiated). Over the term of the trade, the pair returned 67 percent over the long capital employed, while the S&P 500 fell by 17.8 percent.

PAIRS TRADING—A TECHNICAL APPROACH

CONVERGENCE/DIVERGENCE STRATEGIES

The historical relationships between two comparable stocks can be seen technically as well as fundamentally. Profit can be achieved in two ways:

1. Convergence: Recognizing an existing price disparity (mispricing) and profiting as the spread between the two securities converge back toward their historical mean. Keep in mind, the more extraordinary

the divergence, the greater the chance they will converge back to their prior historical relationship. Note: This strategy is event driven and more *fundamental* in nature.

2. Divergence: Anticipating disparity (mispricing) and profiting when the spread between two securities diverge from their historical mean. This approach will generally be more *technically* driven. Therefore, we look for technical indications that point toward one stock outperforming another. Fundamental pairs trading would not be appropriate for this strategy.

THE SET-UP

In this example, we compare Amgen, Inc. (AMGN) and Biogen, Inc. (BGEN) to the Biotechnology sector (BTK.X). Referencing Figures 14.6 and 14.7, we see AMGN is relatively strong compared to both BGEN and the Biotech sector. This comparison indicates that BGEN and BTK.X are well correlated from a technical point of view, since both retraced 5 percent during the period; however, AMGN only retraced 3 percent. While this does not justify the trade in itself, the aforementioned relationship does indicate relative strength/weakness among issues against the common sector they both trade in (biotechnology).

In the example, we are long AMGN and short BGEN. As long as these positions are dollar neutral (equal investment in both companies), overall market direction is not a concern. Our only consideration is that AMGN continues to outperform BGEN, either on the upside or downside. The BTK.X direction is also irrelevant, and only valuable to the extent of measuring the strength/weakness relationship to each stock. Note that although we are separately comparing two stocks to an index, we must look at both stocks and the index as a whole to implement this strategy.

THE TECHNICALS SHARPEN THE SWORD

A trader's world revolves around the process of statistically evaluating good risk/reward trade set-ups while also managing trades to let profits run and cut losses short. We all know this—but how is this achieved?

Step One: DMI/RSI Indications

As covered in Chapter 6, the Directional Movement Indicator and Relative Strength Indicator are excellent companions to the charts. When applied to

FIGURE 14.6

AMGN shows clear relative strength compared to its sector BTK.X. But it is not enough to rely on subjective chart reading. Traders must also "sharpen" decision-making with technical indications before making the trade.

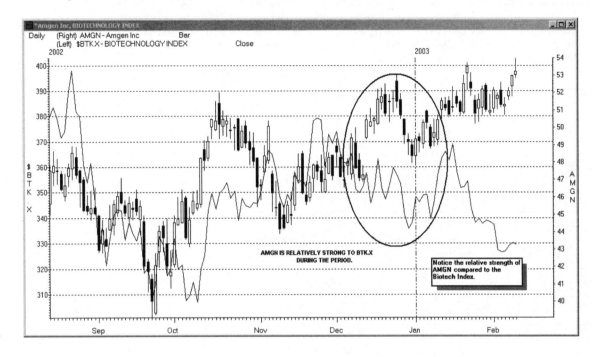

FIGURE 14.7

BGEN and the BTK.X are more closely correlated. This indication helps confirm the relative strength of AMGN versus BGEN. AMGN is not only outperforming BGEN, but the entire biotech sector.

F I G U R E 14.8

On 1/15/03 we show a positive directional bias for AMGN along with a low RSI (strength reading).
Notice we maintained a positive DMI reading until 1/24, while RSI indicated an overbought level the
two days prior (1/22 and 1/23). This indicated we might expect some near-term resistance on
AMGN (see Figure 14.11).

AMGN							
Volatility (Beta) = 1.01							
2000 Shares on 1/15 = $101,440							
Date	Close	Stage	PDI	MDI	DI Bias	ADX	RSI
1/15/03	50.72	2	21.80	16.50	positive	18.84	46.40
1/16/03	51.18	2	24.10	14.03	positive	19.78	52.55
1/17/03	51.32	2	22.08	12.86	positive	20.61	60.09
1/21/03	50.87	2	20.15	16.41	positive	19.31	59.62
1/22/03	52.50	2	29.16	13.10	positive	21.65	71.44
1/23/03	53.50	2	31.43	11.31	positive	24.83	71.50	◄ OVERBOUGHT TERRITORY
1/24/03	52.24	3	26.82	12.70	positive	26.19	64.06
1/27/03	50.78	3	22.32	23.86	negative	23.33	52.27
1/28/03	51.59	4	20.14	20.73	negative	20.60	55.62
1/29/03	52.19	1	21.23	17.91	positive	19.08	64.71
1/30/03	50.98	1	19.58	15.56	positive	18.12	55.54
1/31/03	50.96	1	17.68	15.56	positive	16.65	52.38
2/3/03	52.13	1	18.92	13.69	positive	16.58	52.77
2/4/03	51.83	1	17.14	12.41	positive	16.51	53.35
2/5/03	51.27	1	20.21	10.85	positive	18.21	52.48
2/6/03	51.29	2	18.38	13.94	positive	17.65	50.52	◄ NEVER GETS WEAK PER RSI
2/7/03	52.09	2	22.19	12.63	positive	18.87	53.41
2/10/03	52.98	2	26.39	11.20	positive	21.57	58.99
2/11/03	53.45	2	32.84	10.00	positive	25.54	53.88

pairs trading, these indicators are exceptionally useful for discovering price
disparity among pair's candidates.

To help determine price disparity, notice the relationship between DMI
and RSI as shown in Figures 14.8 and 14.9. Our original technical stops were
set at $41.50 for BGEN and $50.20 AMGN, respectively (see Figure 14.10),
with an important 2 percent financial stop on the core position. While the
trade never experienced much "heat" to initiate either the technical or financial stop, both indicators illustrate strong overbought/sold conditions for
each issue. These indications were sharp, allowing the trade to be almost immediately positive while keeping risk under control.

On 1/15/03 we show a negative bias for BGEN along with a neutral RSI reading. Notice we maintained a negative DMI reading until 2/4/03. RSI clearly indicated an oversold level on 1/23/03 and 1/24/03, leading us to expect strength. Figure 14.12 shows a graphical indication of DMI where PDI starts to rally as MDI retraces. These are more important signals than a literal signal cross of the two. This is where RSI helps "sharpen" the DMI signal days earlier.

BGEN

Volatility (Beta) = 0.99
2469 Shares on 1/15 = $101,451

Date	Close	Stage	PDI	MDI	DI Bias	ADX	RSI	
1/15/03	41.09	3	17.64	23.64	negative	22.95	42.26	
1/16/03	41.73	3	18.34	20.58	negative	20.80	48.05	
1/17/03	37.93	4	12.98	39.65	negative	24.54	39.78	
1/21/03	36.90	4	11.30	43.88	negative	28.85	38.33	
1/22/03	37.02	4	10.23	39.73	negative	32.63	38.52	
1/23/03	36.28	4	8.86	40.94	negative	36.60	28.33	◀ OVERSOLD TERRITORY
1/24/03	35.52	4	8.10	40.96	negative	40.40	27.21	
1/27/03	36.12	1	7.13	38.89	negative	43.97	28.05	
1/28/03	36.75	1	5.60	39.17	negative	47.85	33.31	
1/29/03	37.20	2	11.08	34.12	negative	48.23	37.38	
1/30/03	37.99	2	14.18	30.81	negative	46.83	36.38	
1/31/03	38.25	2	23.11	26.43	negative	41.81	32.48	
2/3/03	39.46	2	20.99	23.25	negative	37.22	37.18	
2/4/03	39.35	2	19.59	21.70	negative	33.21	38.78	
2/5/03	40.00	3	22.48	19.27	positive	30.02	45.38	
2/6/03	40.08	3	21.67	17.58	positive	27.57	42.65	
2/7/03	39.98	4	22.17	14.92	positive	26.56	63.61	◀ OVERBOUGHT TERRITORY
2/10/03	39.47	4	19.60	16.11	positive	24.46	68.33	
2/11/03	38.58	4	17.09	18.26	negative	21.82	58.23	

MAKING THE TRADE

Observing the disparate price structure of AMGN and BGEN as evidenced in Figure 14.10, these issues set up for a divergence spread opportunity. On 1/15/03, a new divergence began to emerge.

Keep in mind: The more these issues correlate to each other, the better we can trust the technical indications as well as the chart formations. For example, since the betas are almost identical (see Figures 14.8 and 14.9), we are not concerned about adjusting the position weighting to compensate. If the betas were not well correlated, share size adjustment could be done to help

FIGURE 14.10

Our stops were nearly executed on both the AMGN long and BGEN short. If they were executed, we would have flipped with a small profit and immediately opened a convergence spread. The reason they were not stopped out is due to the fact that BGEN is relatively weak to AMGN. Notice BGEN at resistance and AMGN at support. The rationale for giving the trade a chance to work is because we expected more weakness at resistance for BGEN than weakness for AMGN at support. This proved to be the right decision, but if the stops were violated, we would have exited both legs immediately!

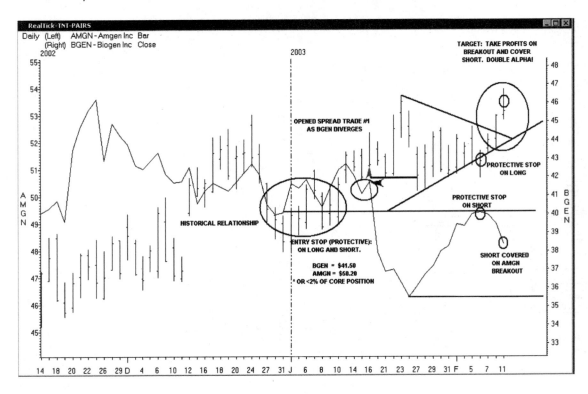

compensate for uneven volatility. Figure 14.10 illustrates both the divergence and convergence trades. This chart should be closely studied with the technical information above on DMI/RSI.

Like all trades, the set-up must first be engineered on factors beyond just the technicals. As we uncovered the opportunity we had, the risk/reward relationship also has to be addressed. To accomplish this, we must consider the inter-market spread between the issues when pairs trading. As we can see on Figure 14.13, on 1/15/03 and 1/16/03 we had little divergence, but as the days went on the divergence was clear, as was the momentum. We could have also traded the convergence, as RSI indicated that BGEN was oversold versus AMGN and poised to rally back toward its prior historical

F I G U R E   14.11

AMGN's graphical indication of both DMI and RSI.

F I G U R E   14.12

BGEN's graphical indication of both DMI and RSI.

FIGURE   14.13

On 1/24/03 we could see, based on the DMI/RSI, that the divergence was losing momentum. This was the first sign that the divergence spread was at or near its peak. Unlike most directional stock positions, spreads tend to take more time to wind up and down. This often gives the trader more opportunity for discovery as well as reduced "whipsaw" risk.

Date	AMGN Close	BGEN Close	AMGN P&L Long 2000 Shares	BGEN P&L Short 2469 Shares	P&L on Trade	% Move from entry date AMGN	% Move from entry date BGEN	Total Spread % between Pairs (Alpha)	
1/15/03	50.72	41.09	$ -	$ (0)	$ (0)	0.00%	0.00%	0.00%	
1/16/03	51.18	41.73	920	(1,580)	(660)	0.90%	-1.53%	-0.63%	
1/17/03	51.32	37.93	1,200	7,801	9,001	1.17%	8.33%	9.50%	
1/21/03	50.87	36.9	300	10,344	10,644	0.29%	11.36%	11.65%	
1/22/03	52.5	37.02	3,560	10,048	13,608	3.39%	10.99%	14.38%	
1/23/03	53.5	36.28	5,560	11,874	17,434	5.20%	13.26%	18.45%	
1/24/03	52.24	35.52	3,040	13,751	16,791	2.91%	15.68%	18.59%	MAXIMUM DIVERGENCE
1/27/03	50.78	36.12	120	12,269	12,389	0.12%	13.76%	13.88%	
1/28/03	51.59	36.75	1,740	10,714	12,454	1.69%	11.81%	13.50%	
1/29/03	52.19	37.2	2,940	9,603	12,543	2.82%	10.46%	13.27%	
1/30/03	50.98	37.99	520	7,653	8,173	0.51%	8.16%	8.67%	
1/31/03	50.96	38.25	480	7,011	7,491	0.47%	7.42%	7.90%	
2/3/03	52.13	39.46	2,820	4,024	6,844	2.70%	4.13%	6.84%	
2/4/03	51.83	39.35	2,220	4,295	6,515	2.14%	4.42%	6.56%	
2/5/03	51.27	40	1,100	2,691	3,791	1.07%	2.73%	3.80%	
2/6/03	51.29	40.08	1,140	2,493	3,633	1.11%	2.52%	3.63%	MAXIMUM CONVERGENCE
2/7/03	52.09	39.98	2,740	2,740	5,480	2.63%	2.78%	5.41%	
2/10/03	52.98	39.47	4,520	3,999	8,519	4.27%	4.10%	8.37%	NEW DIVERGENCE EMERGING
2/11/03	53.45	38.58	5,460	6,196	11,656	5.11%	6.51%	11.61%	

mean. In this scenario, the trader would reverse both positions by going long BGEN and short AMGN. Profit would be maximized at convergence.

TRADE ENTRY STRATEGY RELATIVE TO RISK/REWARD

In order to remain position neutral, the positions are dollar equivalent by constructing a ratio spread of the pair. This way, any price changes in AMGN (long) would be directly offset by the same price change of BGEN (short). To achieve this, we calculate the share ratio as follows:

Marked to Market on 1/15/03 close:

Long 2000 AMGN @ $50.72 = $101,440

Short 2469 BGEN @ $41.09 = $101,451

To help put the position in perspective; the RealTick Trading Platform offers a sorting tool to show the relative net change percentage. This enables us to watch our stocks in percentage terms, allowing for easier management of positions. As we can see from Figure 14.14, the position is achieving double alpha where both the long AMGN leg and short BGEN leg are profitable.

F I G U R E   14.14

RealTick Market Minder with sorting ranked on a relative scale from prior close. Notice the short on BGEN is working as well as the long on AMGN. While this is not required, as long as AMGN is out-performing BGEN, the position is net profitable. The spread is the difference between the "net chg. %" (−2.61+.32).

Symbol	Net Chg. %	High	Low	Last		Change	Volume
BGEN	-2.61	39.82	38.35	38.44	↑	-1.03	3,441,274
/ESC3	-1.02	842.75	827.25	827.50	↑	-8.50	495,751
$DJI	-.92	7985.52	7846.20	7847.57	↓	-72.54	166,931,700
$SPX.X	-.83	843.02	829.00	829.00	↓	-6.97	
$COMPX	-.35	1315.04	1292.13	1292.13	↓	-4.55	
$NDX.X	-.22	989.32	967.86	967.86	↓	-2.10	
BBH	-.06	89.65	88.22	88.35	↓	-.05	869,000
$BTK.X	-.02	336.23	329.46	330.13	↓	-.06	
AMGN	+.32	53.96	52.85	53.15	↓	+.17	10,717,118
/NDC3	+.78	985.00	969.00	969.00 S	↑	+7.50	1,497

CONCLUSION

It is important not to build any sort of false security when pairs trading, expecting the hedged position to cushion any negative market move. Risk management always applies through the use of technical and financial protective stops. The important lesson is to remember to implement a solid technical foundation for each trade, while setting trailing stops along the line of profitability.

15

C H A P T E R

SEASONAL TRADING AND TAX LOSS SELLING

Seasonal trading is often an overlooked and underutilized strategy. In fact, many operators are less active during seasonal shifts, such as year's end, because of such basic decisions as finishing out the year less actively due to the holidays, or simply looking to start the new year fresh. While this may sound simplistic, volume clearly confirms a trend of decreasing activity. The market's history shows that professional participants, such as institutions, mutual funds, pension funds, hedge funds, banks, etc., determine trading patterns for the upcoming year in the last quarter of the prior year. Although the average investor is less important to seasonal trading patterns, active traders should consider seasonal periods one of the best times to trade.

One strategy is tax loss selling (TLS). Although seasonal trading opens the door for many strategies, TLS is among our favorites. First, here are some compelling statistics provided by the popular Yale Hirsch's *Stock Trader's Almanac*. We reference this often because the statistics it reveals are undeniable and objective. In fact, many trading strategies can be employed by simply playing the odds as revealed through statistical analysis. The *Stock Trader's Almanac* is a collection of such data and a great trading companion. Here is one simple example.

Year-end activity generated by institutions between November 1 and January 31 correlates with the market's greatest gains. This time period has dominated performance for the S&P 500 and the Dow Jones Industrials

F I G U R E   15.1

Note the average gains in the S&P 500 and the DJIA between November and January. The results and statistical significance are undeniable. TLS is a major reason for this phenomenon. (*Source: 2001 Stock Trader's Almanac.*)

MONTHLY % CHANGES (JANUARY 1950 – JUNE 2000)

	Standard & Poor's 500					Dow Jones Industrials			
Month	Total % Change	Avg.% Change	# Up	# Down	Month	Total % Change	Avg. % Change	# Up	# Down
Jan	80.0%	1.6%	33	18	Jan	80.7%	1.6%	35	16
Feb	8.1	0.2	28	23	Feb	11.5	0.2	29	22
Mar	60.7	1.2	34	17	Mar	56.5	1.1	33	18
Apr	65.9	1.3	35	16	Apr	93.0	1.8	32	19
May	10.6	0.2	28	23	May	− 2.6	− 0.1	26	25
Jun	16.8	0.3	28	23	Jun	3.2	0.1	26	25
Jul	59.1	1.2	28	22	Jul	60.6	1.2	30	20
Aug	− 1.1	0.0	26	24	Aug	− 5.3	− 0.1	28	22
Sep	− 13.4	− 0.3	22	28	Sep	− 27.5	− 0.6	19	31
Oct	33.1	0.7	29	21	Oct	10.1	0.2	28	22
Nov	85.2	1.7	33	17	Nov	78.4	1.6	34	16
Dec	93.4	1.9	38	12	Dec	89.6	1.8	36	14
% Rank					**% Rank**				
Dec	93.4%	1.9%	38	12	Apr	93.0%	1.8%	32	19
Nov	85.2	1.7	33	17	Dec	89.6	1.8	36	14
Jan	80.0	1.6	33	18	Jan	80.7	1.6	35	16
Apr	65.9	1.3	35	16	Nov	78.4	1.6	34	16
Mar	60.7	1.2	34	17	Jul	60.6	1.2	30	20
Jul	59.1	1.2	28	22	Mar	56.5	1.1	33	18
Oct	33.1	0.7	29	21	Feb	11.5	0.2	29	22
Jun	16.8	0.3	28	23	Oct	10.1	0.2	28	22
May	10.6	0.2	28	23	Jun	3.2	0.1	26	25
Feb	8.1	0.2	28	23	May	− 2.6	− 0.1	26	25
Aug	− 1.1	0.0	26	24	Aug	− 5.3	− 0.1	28	22
Sep	− 13.4	− 0.3	22	28	Sep	− 27.5	− 0.6	19	31
Total	**498.4%**	**10.0%**			**Total**	**448.2%**	**8.9%**		
Average		**0.83%**			**Average**		**0.74%**		

during each of the past 50 years, as well as the Nasdaq during the past 18 years. Therefore, if we as traders believe that historical data has predictive value, as well as believing in trading with the market trend ("the trend is your friend"), then we do not want to fade this very clear market statistic. The event is known as the "January effect." Statistics show that starting in mid-December each year, small-cap stocks begin to "coil" themselves into a position to dramatically outperform large-cap stocks early in the new year. Tax loss selling is the sole reason for this phenomenon. The data shows that traders do best to lean into small-cap positions starting in mid-December to take full advantage of the January effect. As Figure 15.1 reveals, for the past 50 years, November, December, and January have constituted each year's best three-month span.

TAX LOSS SELLING (TLS)

TLS is one of the greatest contributors to year-end strength. Even if you have never traded a TLS strategy, it must be considered because of its impact on the market, particularly to the extent that it increases volatility and decreases volume. Because fund managers are most active at year's end, we must explain their motives and how their activity has a spring-like effect on the market. We will explain in detail how you can watch the spring compress as the year comes to an end, torquing certain issues for a very bullish "pop" into the new year.

Let's begin with the participants who make this happen (see Figure 15.2). We like to think of them as accomplices, since they are effectively forced to help "load the spring."

F I G U R E   15.2

Examples of participants that load the spring.

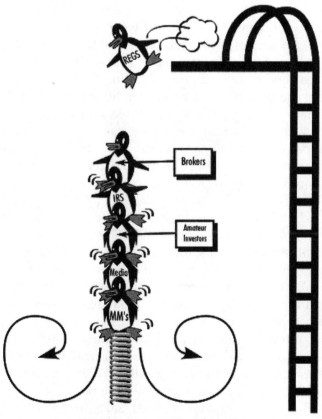

Our accomplices spring-load the market

ACCOMPLICES IN TAX LOSS SELLING

Our "accomplices," to name a few, are as follows:

Institutional money managers (mutual funds, pension funds, hedge funds, and banks)

The business and financial press (media)

Amateur investors

Spouses

The IRS and CPAs

Brokerage firms

Securities regulators

MONEY MANAGERS

Money managers must report their performance to the public. This forces them to show desirable holdings at critical times during the year. Because attention to their holdings is greatest when year-end position statements are issued, market activity will be commensurately high during this period. The natural desire of fund managers is to blow out the "dogs" of the portfolio at year's end in order to purge these laggards from the most widely monitored statement of the year, the year-end statement and portfolio. While the issues traded and held throughout the year are also posted on all quarterly statements, the fourth-quarter statement is the most monitored and watched by investors. Ratings services such as Morningstar, as well as executive committees of mutual fund companies, certainly take notice. Therefore, managers will tend to purge laggards from their portfolios as the fourth quarter closes.

There are additional motives beyond performance for purging underperformers. Barometers such as the S&P 500, the Nasdaq 100, the Russell 2000, and others are the benchmarks for these managers; therefore, the stocks within these indices are what allow them to index. When certain issues lag the index due to fundamentals and technicals, they can become candidates to be sold and even potentially removed from the major indices. Remember, it is not just the fundamentals that can hurt a company, but the perception that its stock could be purged from an index because it is lagging behind the group. Essentially, a good company may appear to be in the "slow reading group" relative to class, indicating weakness to indexers. Technical indicators will reflect this price action and exacerbate the sell-off as issues fall below key price levels and moving averages. Many issues, regardless of the profit performance and dividend yield, can stall because they become negatively perceived by participants such as fund managers. That said, as issues are dropped from major indices, less attention is paid to them as funds purge them from their radars. As a result, the forces of supply and demand will typically wreak punishment on such stocks in the form of falling prices and decreasing liquidity. While more could be said about why fund managers sell weak issues into year's end, the reasons listed above are sufficient motivators.

THE MEDIA AND THE AMATEUR

As negative price activity accelerates, media activity grows. Stocks gain media attention when they are dropped from an index or take a steep dive, as this is just the sort of thing the news media loves to report. It is also the kind of news that makes retail investors nervous and causes them to dump shares, though often belatedly. Suffice it to say that they are notorious for being the last in during bullish moves and the last out during bearish moves. Stockbrokers aid in the process of keeping investors in the losers too long. Investors usually hesitate to sell during the early stages of the sell-off, and brokers try to justify the stock, which in many cases was sold to the investor by the broker. Even worse, many investors average down by buying even more. Remember that brokers, given the chance to sell, will, and when investors call to complain, brokers are taught to turn tables and sell. This is why we could view brokers as wolves in sheep's clothing.

SPOUSES

The pummeling of investors—who are now underwater—is further accomplished by none other than their spouses. While spouses have no reason to exacerbate the situation, the emotional pressure brought after painful losses and margin calls is bound to cause a reaction. As the pain grows, so does the motivation to make it go away. The cure comes in the form of selling out of the position and putting it out of mind. Unfortunately, this painful catharsis invariably comes late for retail customers—often when prices are closer to support than to resistance. In fact, this is exactly why institutions tend to do very well during the end of the year and the first month of the New Year. They generally rid their portfolios of losers much earlier than the average retail investor, putting themselves in good position to buy back those issues at much lower prices, as we shall explain. For now, keep in mind that the pain obscuring retail investors' logic is also hiding the opportunity that professionals see (and that you too will see, as you master this strategy). The retail investors' pain is at a peak when forced to meet margin calls. As the pain becomes unbearable, the issue continues to plummet. The only sellers who remain are retail investors who have overstayed the trend. This leads to yet another potent pair of market depressants: the IRS and your accountant.

IRS/CPA

The IRS has seen to it that there is an escape hatch of sorts for these depressed issues, called Tax Loss Selling. The rule known as "date certain" states simply that if an individual wants to take the tax loss as a write-off, the trade must be executed by the last trading day of the year. This additional sense of urgency forces investors to take their lumps, but because most amateurs, ever hopeful, wait until the last minute to do so, they will almost invariably wind up selling at the worst possible time. Professionals know this, and they therefore tend to exit a position at the first sign of weakness. Because professionals include institutions, they have the most to sell and will do it the soonest, putting the amateur who hesitates at the end of the line. The tax rules, as well as the emotional factors that we have touched on, contribute not only to the pummeling of stocks at year's end but also to the large number of retail investors whose portfolios get decimated around that time. The Certified Public Accountant (CPA) is the messenger who explains this end-of-year exit hatch, and most people don't understand taxes and therefore act on the advice.

BROKERAGE FIRMS AND REGULATORS

The last group contributing to the year-end selling spree comprises brokerage firms and those who regulate them. Rules of the exchange prohibit certain activities, such as soliciting "penny stocks." Stocks that trade at $5 or less fall into this category, and once they get there, they usually fall off the radar of brokerage firms. When this happens, brokers will not solicit them and analysts will drop coverage, causing liquidity to dry up and the issue to fall further. Moreover, once stocks fall below $5, they are usually no longer marginable; investors still holding such issues must meet margin calls to bring the position to cash equivalent. This in turn further exacerbates the selling of the issue, pushing it even deeper underwater.

ADDITIONAL FACTORS

All of these negatives can cause issues to trade below their fundamental value. The steel industry is a classic example. The market capitalization of many issues discounts any objective reckoning of their revenues or cash position. When issues begin to trade near book value, they are often oversold. Certainly there is the fear that many of these issues will never recover, and that they will throw in the towel by filing for bankruptcy. However, many that are oversold will also rebound sharply, as we shall explore. These are the issues that create opportunities for the astute trader, and we are about to explore ways in which you can spot them. We should note first, however, that the final blow to many of these issues is a Chapter 11 reorganization bankruptcy. This typically sends issues to their ultimate lows, allowing a good buying opportunity for reboundable stocks. While these issues don't need to go Chapter 11, the mere perception they could is enough to depress them. United Airlines comes to mind. In many cases the bankrupt entities or candidates are artificially beaten down while reorganization takes place. Fundamentally such companies may be viable, but because of the external factors we spoke of earlier, they have been forced into Chapter 11 or near it.

Certainly, many factors play into the retracement of stocks into year's end, but the likelihood of issues getting "beat up" even more is greater when the issue has suffered a dramatic retracement from recent highs. This is because institutions that have owned these issues at higher levels will be strongly motivated to get them off the books as year's end approaches. The next step is to find these "loaded springs," companies beaten down at the end of the year and ready to bid higher as the new trading year commences.

SEARCH CRITERIA FOR TRADING CANDIDATES

The following are criteria and strategies for selecting and trading tax loss selling issues:

1. The issues must have traded over $10 during the year.
2. The issues must now be below $5 and within 10 percent of their 52-week lows. This means these issues are off by at least 50 percent, so most investors are already losers and the stock is prone to being oversold.
3. The market capitalization (market cap) must exceed $25 million.

STEP 1

Visit sites such as www.Marketwise.com or Reuters-Multexinvestor at www.Multexinvestor.com and research companies based on the criteria that suggest strong companies that have been oversold. There are many possible parameters, such as current price, market capitalization, earnings per share, and 52-week highs and lows. By limiting the parameters, an investor can generate a list of equities that fits a description and may be of interest. Once this list is obtained, finding good stocks to trade is much easier. Remember, there are no concrete criteria, but the ideas here will help you narrow your search. The parameters you set can be either very simple, such as one criteria (e.g. equities with an EPS above $5), or they can be very complex. For example, you could generate a list of stocks currently trading at or below $5 that have traded at or above $10 at some point during the past 52 weeks with market capitalizations exceeding $25 million. Such stocks could be good buy opportunities. Certainly these stocks may also be on their way out, but the list is easily manageable and researched, and you at least know that every stock on the list meets the criteria.

There are many sources for stock screening, such as Nasdaq.com or Multexinvestor.com. They make available all the data an investor needs to create stock-screening criteria with numerous parameters (over 80 of them on Multexinvestor.com). Nasdaq.com's screening is simpler, but with fewer available parameters. While this means that Nasdaq has a more user-friendly interface than Multexinvestor.com, it also means that the latter will allow you to screen with greater detail. We prefer Multexinvestor.com.

F I G U R E   15.3

A simple scan for stocks with 1) a price of under $5, 2) a 52-week high of over $10, and 3) a market cap of over $25 million.

Example

Using Multexinvestor.com's stock-screening application, the first criterion to be entered would be "Price<=5"; the second would be "PriceH>=10"; and the last would be "MktCap>=25." The result is a list of companies that meets all the criteria at each level. See Figure 15.3.

In the screening, there were 4831 stocks trading with a current price of $5 or less, 380 stocks with a current price of $5 or less *and* with a 52-week high price of above $10, and 292 stocks that met all three criteria. The list of companies that meets the set of all three criteria can be accessed by clicking on "292" in the "Results" column of the final criteria. The list can be saved as a spreadsheet or printed out. The Nasdaq.com screener does not allow for the easy downloading or printing of the list of stocks. With the stock screener, it is possible to write a very detailed list of criteria. More than one set of parameters can be set on each line with the use of "and/or" commands, as seen in Figure 15.4.

Multexinvestor.com also enables the user to input mathematical equations in the screening process. For example, to further limit the list of stocks, one can specify that the current price of the stock be within 10 percent of the 52-week low. This is added with the notation "Price<=(1.1*PriceL)" where

F I G U R E   15.4

Multiple rules are available to further narrow the scan.

Data Set Date: Friday, November 22, 2002	9170 Active Companies
Criteria	Results
1 {Price}<=5.AND.{PriceH}>=10.AND.{MktCap}>=25	292
2	
3	
4	
5	
6	

Add | Delete | Edit | Insert   User Defined Variables

Help

FIGURE   15.5

In addition to our basic criteria, we filtered the results further to find stocks that have prices within 10 percent of their 52-week lows.

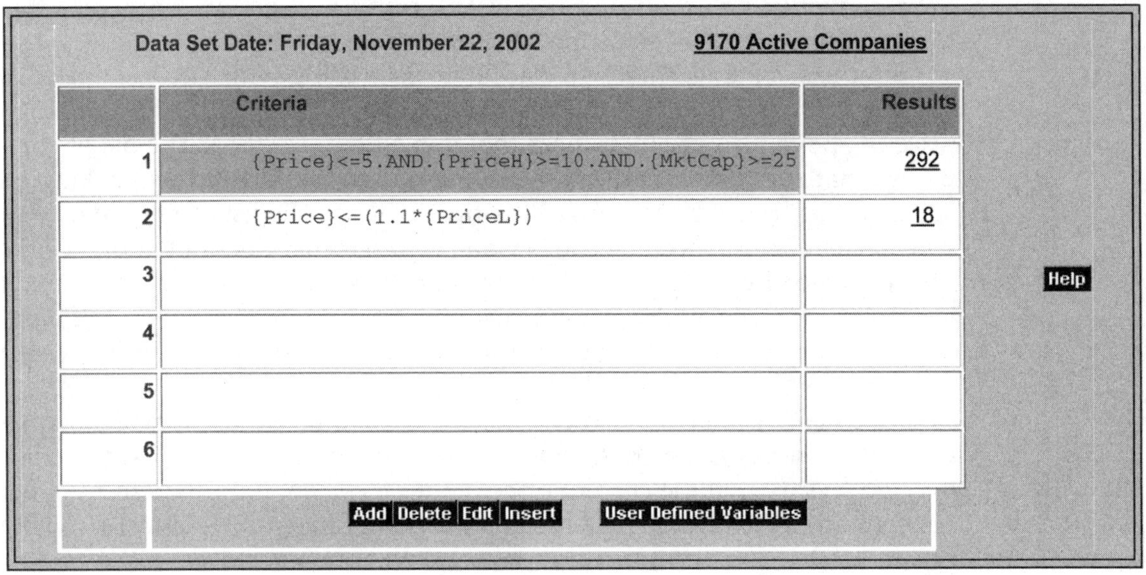

	Data Set Date: Friday, November 22, 2002	9170 Active Companies
	Criteria	Results
1	{Price}<=5.AND.{PriceH}>=10.AND.{MktCap}>=25	292
2	{Price}<=(1.1*{PriceL})	18
3		
4		
5		
6		

Add Delete Edit Insert   User Defined Variables

Help

"PriceL" is the 52-week low price. This will further limit the screening, thus providing a list of 122 stocks that meet all three criteria. See Figure 15.5.

Stock screening is a very powerful and useful trading tool for finding stocks to trade. A good time to use the screening is at year's end, when tax selling may result in bargains that can be found by using the correct stock-screening criteria.

Once your screening is done, you will have a list of candidates that can be watched for the first signs of strength.

Consider the bursting bubble of the Internet stocks. A number of stocks that were well above $100 per share now trade near or below $5. Given this dramatic decline, the last few years have created tremendous opportunities for tax loss selling. While such opportunities come and go over time, this strategy can work well every year. Some names that meet our criteria: Cutter & Buck Inc. (CBUK), Parker Drilling Company (PKD), and Mechanical Technology (MKTY).

BENEFITING FROM TAX LOSS SELLING

The circumstances that create forced liquidations include tax loss write-offs, margin rules, regulatory pressure, institutional selling, market psychology, the media, and indices. Opportunities in these situations are characterized by tremendous upside potential and limited risk. This creates a good risk/reward ratio, allowing you to trade size while committing very little capital. Because of these factors, the spring is loaded metal-to-metal, coiled and waiting to explode to the upside. These issues don't even need big news to move them dramatically, just an uptick in demand. Any buying whatsoever will cause these issues to surge. Many institutions and professionals will take advantage of the oversold condition, leaping back in with huge positions shortly after December 31 and moving the issues sharply higher in a very short period of time. The amateurs who sold the issues at year's end will once again be Johnny-come-latelies because of the wash sale rule, which prohibits investors from repurchasing for 30 days any issue for which they have taken a tax loss. They will miss out as these plays continue to gain strength after January 31.

With tax pressures gone and the wash sale rule in effect, investors who wanted out of the trade are out and will remain so for the 30-day period. Once this period ends, many participants will reenter the market to buy the same issues they lost money on. In fact, studies have shown that amateurs and money managers alike will often reenter the market in the same issues they lost money on to vindicate themselves. As ridiculous as it sounds, this phenomenon is real. Once the wash sale period expires, participants can repurchase the issue, strengthening rather than weakening it. Perhaps time spent understanding the company prompts investors to return. Any upside bias in the issue sends a signal to investors that they were initially correct in their analysis and therefore justified in reentering the position. This foolish mentality gives the participants another chance to be right, hence the vindication mentality.

Institutions follow a similarly weak logic in the sense that many funds will window-dress their portfolios at the end of each quarter to show quality holdings while trading riskier, illiquid issues in the early weeks and first month of the quarter. In this way they pursue a disproportionately strong January effect move to help them achieve the goal of meeting or beating the S&P 500 or other benchmarks of the fund. As they blow out the laggards into year's end, these institutions will often buy back the same issues at undervalued prices (perceived or real) in January. This buying activity provides instant support and strength for issues that were much oversold just days or weeks earlier. Because the liquidity of these issues often suffers for the reason stated earlier, they can experience explosive upside with modest demand and buying, resulting in V-bottom moves. The charts for two stocks, Cutter and Buck (Figure 15.6) and Parker Drilling Company (Figure 15.7), show the January effect in spades: V-shaped bottoms made in the first 30 days of the new year.

As we know, stocks move the most on the least volume, causing them to run hard with high velocity. This is another market phenomenon, whereby a

FIGURE 15.6

Daily chart of Cutter and Buck, Inc.

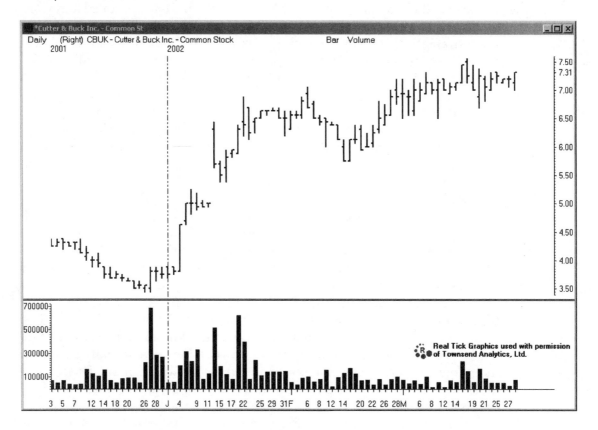

perceived sign of strength causes the greedy herd to converge on the buy side of a particular issue. This causes prices to spread out, rising quickly as sellers fail to meet demand within a narrow price range. Sellers are able to command higher prices as demand brings opportunity. As January comes to an end, institutions will capitalize on this supply/demand imbalance, accomplishing two important goals. First, they will blow out the trades for short-term profits. Second, they will exit low-sentiment issues to window-dress their portfolios. The window-dressing produces more desirable stocks that investors will likely want to own over time in portfolios. In this way the fund managers increase performance with these more volatile issues while creating the perception that they hold quality stocks by unloading the issues ahead of statements. While this may sound manipulative, it is plain reality— and that is why we don't own a single share of stock in any portfolio. We rent stocks, we don't own them!

F I G U R E   15.7

Daily chart of Parker Drilling Company.

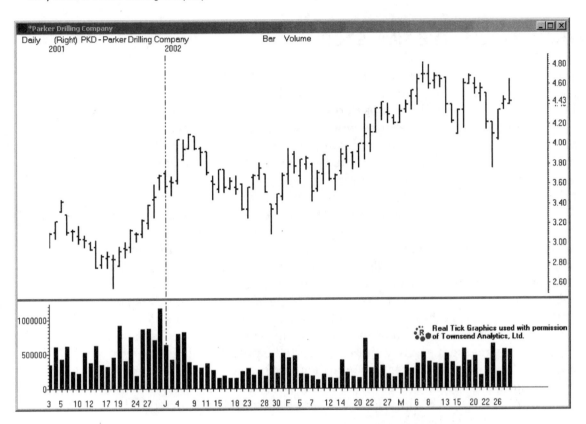

The uncoiling of the spring is remarkably similar to the process of coil-ing, since as the issue gains media and investor attention because of bullish movement, prices often recover back above $5 and become marginable again, as well as optionable. This added leverage brings in more speculators and al-lows for heavier trading activity. The same issues that depressed prices at year's end are now improving them in the first 8 to 10 weeks of the new year. Think of it as a New Year's resolution, except this market's "diet" is based on greed, optimism, and euphoria. As the issues rally back, most retail investors will once again be last in during the rally, just as they were the last out dur-ing the retracement. To make matters worse, many investors think about trading decisions in neat little blocks of time, such as a year. This sometimes causes them to hold late-rally purchases far too long while hoping for a price recovery. The same investors who sold the bottom after holding for a year are the ones who are most apt to show up again 12 months later. Dumb money keeps buying the same mistakes.

WHEN TO SELL: THE TIME STOP

When using the TLS strategy, the question arises as to when to sell. The answer can be found in the "time certain" motivation that forces amateurs out of the market because of IRS-imposed rules. I suggest creating a time-certain discipline for yourself to determine when to sell. This simply means having an exit strategy in place prior to employing the tax loss selling approach. The rule is simple: By the first month of the following year, the strategy will either have worked or not. Consider this a time stop. Either way, you are out of these trades. Personally, we trade candidates for tax loss by selling heavily and don't need a big move to motivate us to sell early. Because these issues are underpriced by the time we buy them at year's end (usually within two weeks of the time certain date), we can buy them heavily. Additionally, we feel that when a spring uncoils in certain issues, it will happen very fast or not at all. Therefore, if we don't see a notable change within the first 15 to 30 days, these issues are excised, usually with little or no loss. Regardless, using this strategy has nothing to do with fundamentals or technicals as a rule, and there is therefore never a reason to keep them. The strategy seeks to take advantage of a market tendency, but in the end, the positions are exited with or without a profit. Remember, we buy them at the worst possible time in terms of market perceptions, but at the best possible time in terms of the risk/reward spectrum. We buy weakness after all conceivable external factors have beaten the issues down.

An important consideration is that we not bet the farm. We suggest committing no more than 15 percent of your trading capital to this strategy. We have committed as much as 25 percent when the conditions were right, such as at the end of 2000 and 2001, and have seen as much as a 25 percent return before the end of January. The idea is to buy a basket of stocks that we feel are quality issues but have fallen from grace for reasons noted. We are simply looking for oversold situations in companies that have been around for a while and that show a strong tendency to get hit at year's end. Many companies met these criteria for 2000 through 2002 in particular.

This strategy follows the laws of physics in the sense that, as issues are oversold, they need to move up after all the downward pressure is removed. Tax loss selling pressure is gone, institutional selling is gone, individual selling is gone, margin pressure is gone, regulatory pressure is gone, media attention that highlighted negatives retreats, and index pruning is over with. Once these pressures have abated, issues will uncoil as soon as buying comes in—assuming the issues have survived. While this strategy can be employed in varying degrees, we choose to trade the low-price spectrum. The same strategies can be employed for larger-cap issues as well. The principles and psychology don't change, but the search criteria will. This is something you will need to experiment with, as there are no literal formulas to follow. The examples given are good examples, but remember that they are relative to the market and the dynamics of the prior tax year.

In conclusion, institutions typically show a strong first quarter based on this strategy alone. Because the performance improvement in the first quarter looks like a market turn to many, these same institutions use that sentiment to pull in more investor capital, which they will then put to work in index-based companies. In closing our brief explanation of the herd mentality that persists in the market, we should emphasize that this mentality persists precisely because human nature rarely changes. While the mechanics of the markets may have changed greatly due to new technology, they have changed very little psychologically. We have presented a simple overview of this psychology as it relates to tax loss selling, but it should be noted that many other dynamics affect the arena called the stock market. The TLS strategy is an excellent approach during year's end, but every professional trader understands that there is a line between the conviction that an idea will work and the discipline to know when it will not. As market events unfold, risk management must be kept at the forefront. Never fall in love with an idea to the point that you ignore clear signs that a trade is not working. This strategy describes events that recur annually, but the task of picking stocks to take advantage of this effect lies with the trader. We hope the strategies presented here help you in that search as you anticipate the year's end.

16 CHAPTER

RISK MANAGEMENT STRATEGIES

Many strategies exist when it comes to risk management; in fact, the topic itself is so subjective that many participants never truly adopt a consistent method of dealing with risk. Many systems talk exclusively about dealing with losses, but dealing with losses before dealing with risk is putting the cart before the horse. They are not the same thing, in spite of what many would believe.

Dealing with a losing trade before dealing with risk is analogous to reacting to price before recognizing the imbalance of supply and demand. Seasoned traders know that supply and demand imbalances act as leading indicators to price, in the same way that determining potential risk aids in determining potential loss. As a first step in risk management, traders need to evaluate criteria outside the market before evaluating the inherent risks of the market itself. These criteria include:

- Capital Risk
- Leverage Risk
- Confidence Risk

Capital Risk How much you can, and are willing to lose, relative to your account; additionally, how much you are willing to lose in any given trade. The latter has more to do with technical and position size risk, which we will address shortly. Traders must know their own threshold for pain, based on capital size and commitment. Some traders may choose to risk 100 percent of their trading capital, while others may never define how much they are willing to lose until their threshold is reached. Obviously, answering the question itself is the first step to defining risk. If a screaming fastball is heading for you, you don't need to wait until it hits you before reacting. Trading away 100 percent of your capital is the equivalent of taking one in the ear. Although you may fund an account with 100 percent risk capital, the signs of a functional (or nonfunctional) system are not invisible and they should be paid attention to before you face the total exhaustion of your capital. While we believe a trading account should only be funded with risk capital (that is, capital you are willing to lose), it is nonetheless necessary to define the breakpoints where analysis is required before risk capital is gone.

Leverage Risk   Too many participants look at leverage only in terms of the return on investment (ROI), but a trader needs to factor in capital risk as it applies to leverage as well. If you are willing to risk $100,000 in risk capital while using four to one leverage with equities (or more with futures), this leverage affects each trade in terms of position size. While simple to understand, most new participants forget to apply the effects of leverage to a consistent sizing model for trading. For example, you may decide to never risk more than 2 percent of risk capital in any one trade as a rule. This rule, if adopted, should not be flexible. It is there for your protection and cannot be adjusted—ever! Appling this rule means that losses in intrinsic terms are not linear. If you lose your first trade using the 2 percent rule, you lose $2000 (assuming a $100,000 account). If then you lose the second trade (assuming you take the full 2 percent loss), you lose $1960, etc. Therefore, the number of consecutive losing trades would be calculated as $y = 100,000 \, (0.98)^x$:

$\quad$ 10 = $81,707
$\quad$ 100 = $13,262
$\quad$ 120 = $8853
$\quad$ 200 = $1758
$\quad$ 300 = $233
$\quad$ 400 = $31

While having this many consecutive losing trades is unlikely, traders must consider how much they are willing to lose on any given trade, what the breakpoints are in order to evaluate when additional training is required, and what the impact of leverage will be on any trade.

Confidence Risk   Confidence risk is impossible to quantify, but it is very real nonetheless. The erosion of confidence is due not just to intrinsic loss of capital, but also because knowledge of why you are losing (and how to correct the loss) is elusive. How you deal with this is individual, but always know the market itself is the most expensive classroom. Perhaps a break from trading is required and professional education in learning new systems is called for at some point . . . at some breakpoint. Traders must know when they need help; it must be defined.

The risk management criteria that must then be addressed are risks inherent to the market. These factors can be broadly defined as follows:

- Systematic Risk
- Technical Risk
- Position Risk

Systematic Risk   News pending and news dissemination broadly define systematic risk. Economic, political, and market news all account for risk that cannot be controlled or anticipated with any high degree of accuracy. Therefore, the best safeguard against systematic risk is to use time as a hedge. The less time exposure to the market, the better. Good setups that can achieve rewards within limited time horizons are best.

Technical Risk and Position Risk   These risks are so closely aligned that we will explain them in tandem. Technical patterns and signals used to trade determine this risk. The risk/reward relationship of the setup measures the price levels, while the risk capital remaining in the account defines trade size. The Amgen (AMGN) trade shown in Figure 16.1 is an example.

In this example, we shorted AMGN just below the 50 percent Fibonacci level from the morning drop. The short entry was $51.43. Our technical stop was set at or near the 61.8 percent Fibonacci level at $51.65. The technical risk for the trade was set three ways

1. Technical risk was defined as a rally above the 61.8 percent Fibonacci level, which is the $51.65 price level. Any rally above this level would trigger the protective stop on a technical basis. Good traders will cover here regardless of financial risk tolerance. In this case the

F I G U R E   16.1

An intraday chart of Amgen Inc. (AMGN) that shows technically defined risk and potential.

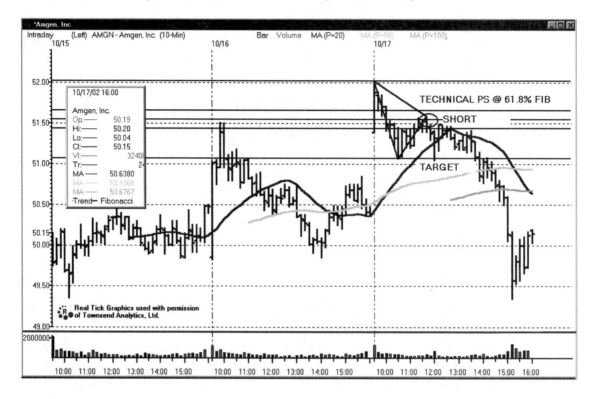

analogy of a screaming fastball applies, in that we can see it coming *before* it blindsides us because the setup is so good in terms of low risk and high reward. In this case, just because you are willing to lose 2 percent of risk capital doesn't mean you should. If a technical stop is met, get out—period.

2. Capital risk requires that we trade and risk no more than 2 percent of our risk capital, which allows for a $2000 loss ($100,000 × 0.02). If the technical protective stop is ignored, traders must also have a capital risk stop as a backup plan. This is determined by their position or size risk due to leverage.

3. Position and size risk decrees that when we are trading with the $100,000 account in this example, we can trade 1944 shares using no leverage, 3888 shares using a two to one margin, and 7777 shares using a four to one margin (entry price $51.43). In this case, the size dictates the protective stop level and overrides the technical protective

stop level when using margin as follows. (*Note:* Shorting requires a margin account, but that does not mean you must use all your buying power.)

No Margin = 1944 shares ($100,000 / 51.43)
Max Negative Move = $1.03 ($2000 / 1944)
Max Financial Risk = $2002

Two to One Margin = 3888 shares
Max Negative Move = $.51 ($2000 / 3888)
Max Financial Risk = $1982

Four to One Margin = 7777 shares
Max Negative Move = $.25 ($2000 / 7777)
Max Financial Risk = $1944

Given how risk is determined, these strategies provide for redundant safeguards even if discipline fails on a technical level. Additionally, always keep in mind that since successive losses are nonlinear, risk capital diminishes on an exponential scale, and therefore intrinsic loss tolerances do as well. The best practice is to adhere to good technical risk stops, provided that these also meet financial risk stops. Traders who follow this succession of risk management are far more likely to succeed in the market. We hope this lesson in risk management reinforces the concept that traders must survive before they thrive, because the market is the ultimate educator. Certainly there are many forms of risk management, and most are prone to subjective input and personal risk tolerances; therefore, the final lesson here is to adopt rules and tolerances for yourself based on your own unique situation and appetite for risk. Risk capital, trading methodologies, financial conditions, time constraints, and even spousal support will all play a large part in this process. Make sure you take time with this valuable step before engaging the market, because as we said before, the market is a most expensive classroom to learn in, yet paradoxically the ultimate educator.

TIME STOPS

One important factor that traders must consider is the use of a time stop. A time stop simply states that if the desired move does not occur within a designated time, the trade should be exited, regardless of the outcome. In Chapter 15 we talk about this in more detail regarding seasonal trading tactics. The concept here is based on a time-certain condition. If a stock does not rally within a measurable time frame, for example, the trade has a weaker chance for success. Because stocks fall on their own weight without buying support, traders should not expect a rally if the moment in time in which the rally should have occurred has passed. Earnings are one such example. If Intel, Inc. (INTC) reports better than expected earnings but the issue remains stable, exit! The chance for upside is very small. The chance for downside is great.

ACKNOWLEDGE UNCERTAINTY

While the techniques outlined all make good sense and will serve you well, without implementation they mean nothing. The first step to implementation is to "confess." We close this important chapter on this point. In the movie *Speed*, starring Keanu Reeves, when faced with a dire circumstance (ticking bomb), the main character repeats the question, "What do you do? What do you do?" To me, that question has to be answered with certainty and consistency every time, helping to determine your ability to manage oncoming risk with a predetermined action. There is no doubt that the market is perverse. There is no doubt that the market changes direction without reason, changes its trend and fails you at the precise times that you have the greatest level of confidence in it. Without a clear set of rules and, more importantly, the discipline to follow them, you are simply dead. The most important lesson to learn in dealing with the inevitable risk is to expect it to be put upon you virtually every day in the market. Confess that you don't know.

Accept that you, at that moment, are on the wrong side of the trade. You buy a stock at $45; it rallies to $47 and then trades down to $46.75. At that moment, even though you are profitable, you are on the wrong side of the trade. What do you do? Do you scale out half the position? Tighten the stop? The answer is up to you, but you must have a predetermined plan. Trading is simple if you can confess that you are incorrect at the precise moment that the market turns against your analysis. Profitability in this example has no more to do with the trade than losses do. At the precise moment that the market retraces and indicates signs of weakness, you are wrong. You can be wrong and still be a winner, or you can be stubborn and push on for irrational profit goals such as $48, based on your original target. It might sound funny and hard to believe, but people act out this stubbornness even in the face of profitability. If you think that is irrational, wait to see what losses do to them!

The mind has an uncanny way of becoming irrational. When the trade is held and the market is under the high of $47, the mind remembers that $47 level and wants it back. But when it was at $47, the mind wanted $48. When it retraces to $46, it wants $46.50 back, and so the story goes until the winner is a loser. The emotional attachment to targets has quite a strong gravitational pull. Without a stop and a predetermined plan, traders may never be able to rationally break out of this metaphoric black hole of thinking and cutting trades. When we see traders take winners and turn them into losers, we consider that unforgivable. Those traders are emotionally attached to their goals and are unwilling to confess or surrender that at that moment the market is going against them.

When learning to fly, the first thing you are taught is that when you get yourself into a situation that could threaten your life or others, confess. If you are in bad weather and can't get out, you confess to the controller and he will vector you out. If you are in a position you know you shouldn't be in, confess, and act on your plan. In trading, there is no air traffic controller looking out for you. It's just you and the market. You are your own support system, and therefore the discipline to follow these rules is an even greater responsibility. Learn to confess and surrender when the market tells you to, because the market, as we know, is always right.

MARKET MYTHS

The myths in the market are many. Many participants have contributed to these myths, including gurus, fund managers, and brokers. These myths principally revolve around prophets who claim they see the market's future. The true skill of trading, however, rides on an edge, a very small edge of uncertainty that we think of as the edge of indifference. To truly come to terms with this ever-changing animal called the stock market, traders must learn how to ride it with their hands firmly on the reins, while at the same time mastering the ability to roll with it, flow with it, become part of it, and never fight it. Its rhythms and cadences change from a lope to a sprint or a trot, and at other times it appears to be at rest. While this may sound chaotic, the order within the market is an internal phenomenon—not external. Individuals who can learn to accept seemingly chaotic conditions will find order in the market by flowing gracefully with it. If a trader's memories are filled with unpleasant experiences from the last ride, those memories serve as a hindrance instead of a learning experience. That trader becomes scared money. Scared money never wins in the market. The riders who get on the animal with a different outlook, who learn to use quantitative and qualitative analysis as an aid, not a crutch, are the ones that make money. Your attitude is the determining factor, not the indicator. Traders should strive to ride the animal, moving with it rhythmically and participating in its uncertainty. Good traders see the animal for what it is and ultimately win by riding with it, not by trying to defeat it.

The following are widely held market myths that are contributed to by the investment community. They have no more to do with trading than does trying to predict the distant future.

PRICES ARE FUNDAMENTALLY OVERBOUGHT OR OVERSOLD

The activity of trading involves acting on what the market is telling you; it is not a function of anything else. When we are short we would sell a stock right down to the bottom if we could. We don't decide how low we think a stock should go. We don't decide how high a stock should go either. Look at the dot-com era—we had no problem paying $300 for Yahoo. We had no problem paying the very highest prices for Amazon.com (AMZN). As long as we had data to point to a higher trend, we had no problem buying them. Price isn't relative to what is expensive or cheap. What does it really mean to say something is expensive or cheap? Relative to what? Fundamentals? We all know now that those things are just really distractions to reading the market objectively. The symmetry and reflectivity of the market tell us everything we need to know, so why be distracted by anything else? "Overbought" and "oversold" make no sense when used in a fundamental context, otherwise how could P/E ratios trade with such variance? These terms make sense only in a technical context.

RISK/REWARD

Would you risk a dollar to make a dollar? As an *experienced* trader, absolutely. This notion that a trade must produce a three to one reward/risk scenario to be worth it, or a two to one ratio, is overstated. Certainly, the three to one reward/risk ratio is a good opportunity, but the reward/risk evaluation is not purely objective. Let's put it into perspective. Have you ever gone to Las Vegas or Atlantic City to play cards or any other game of chance? When you do that, do you really believe that you have a statistical edge? Perhaps you do, perhaps you don't, but you do believe that your ability to play a game of chance gives you an opportunity to win. Ultimately you make the bet, say in a game of blackjack, and you slap down $10 a hand. What is your risk/reward scenario? At best, if the game is evenly played, it will be one to one. You risk $10 to make $10 (most don't play the hand anticipating getting blackjack). The point is, you risked $10 make $10 in a game that generally has a small edge (assuming you can count cards). You have to sum up the activity as either pure enjoyment or gambling. Most people that we know play cards to make money. Certainly it is also fun, but the same can be said about trading. Would you risk a dollar to make a dollar? Our answer is yes, because we believe good traders have the edge and are right more than they are wrong.

While we endorse a good risk/reward scenario in terms of risk management (and protective stops in proportion to your reward target), we believe short-term trading allows experienced traders to take many one to one scenarios, relying on a high win rate. New traders who have yet to master discipline are an exception, but if this is no longer an issue for you, we say go for it. Tools such as the Terra Nova Trade Evaluator will objectively determine if taking lower more balanced ratios make sense.

TRADE SIZE

Trading size or concentrated positions is overly risky. Risk is defined by time as well as size. When you pass your hand through a flame quickly enough to avoid getting burned, you are mitigating risk. Time is the true risk in the market, not position size.

DIVERSIFY

We completely disagree with diversification while trading. We believe that as a trader you need to keep your complete focus on the issues at hand. If you are trading with size and moving money in and out of the market quickly, diffusing yourself by diversifying into other positions is a mistake. Holding positions in the market has an emotional impact on your trading. For example, if you have $100,000 in an index fund, and another $100,000 that you are trading every day, waking up to a dramatic market downturn tends to impact your trading that day. You think about the impact the market condition is having on your index fund. Make a decision. Decide if you are going to be an investor or trader and don't try to do both.

INITIATE YOUR PROTECTIVE STOPS WHEN MET

While it would be a good practice to initiate your protective stops when they are met, most protective stops are actually initiated before the stop is achieved in active trading. You have to read the velocity and the angle of attack that the market is taking toward your stop. Just as the fastball can be perceived before it reaches you, so can the price action toward stops be perceived when associated with dramatic volatility and velocity. Getting out of the way before your protected stop is met is a good idea.

DOLLAR/COST AVERAGE

Consistently putting money into the market at regular intervals of time may be a fair investment strategy but a poor trading approach. Traders reverse the dollar/cost average. We don't put money into the market every day—just the opposite. We take money out of the market every day!

REALIZED VERSUS UNREALIZED MEANS SOMETHING

We have never understood the concept of realized losses and gains versus unrealized losses and gains. It doesn't make any sense. People (such as brokers) love to rationalize losses, stating "Well, it's an unrealized loss." How is that? It is realized the moment the trade works against the position, since the firm you trade with marks to market the debit, meaning they mark the price of the stock you hold at the close and debit (or credit) your account accordingly. If the debit forces a margin call, how is it that the loss isn't real? Just because you haven't sold it yet doesn't mean the money is not lost, otherwise why not waive the margin call? An unrealized loss and a realized loss are exactly the same thing. It may be a better way to emotionally detach yourself from the reality, but we think this is a term that has been put out there by the investment community that has little to do with the reality of markets. Certainly there are tax relationships to the phrase, but too many interpret the meaning for purposes of rationalization, and this is bad thinking for traders.

YOUR TRADING BUSINESS

There are many reasons to trade, but the only one we subscribe to is to make money. Sure it can be fun, but that's what hobbies are for, and hobbies cost money as a rule. Many people believe that making money in the market has to do with finding one winning trade after the next, but this means that success hinges on only good methods. The fact is, building wealth through trading hinges more on money management. Good athletes in professional sports seem to master methods through confirmation. They become masters because they made the all-star team. But does that mean they accumulate wealth? Many all-star athletes die broke! Methods are vital, no question, and in fact without strong methods, money management is of little value. But once methods produce results, money management is critical.

Remember your first paycheck? Many of us were shocked at the net result. Most of us had not planned for shrinkage through taxes. Shrinkage in trading works the same way. If you start with a $100,000 account and lose 10 percent from the start, you need to plan on making 11.1% back to be even. If draw down 20 percent, you need to make 25 percent to come back even ($100,000/$80,000). Not only do you need to stop the beating you are taking by losing money, you also need to swing back with better punches than you are being hit with. How do you deal with this? You have a plan—a plan that acts first to defend you from poor methods (losing money) and then strikes back with sound methods (making money). How you approach this is important. As a first step, your plan must determine breakpoints, thresholds of loss that stop the action and send you back to your corner. Staying in the ring and fighting a losing battle will not only exacerbate the problem, the fight back will become nearly impossible. To facilitate this process, we suggest viewing the market one day or round at a time. You must start each day by looking at several conditions and criteria that dictate your method for the market that day, and then have a plan to deal with winners and, more importantly, losers. Using this approach, which is something of a business model approach (treating trading like a business), you immediately separate yourself from the amateur way of thinking.

GAINING EXPERTISE IN YOUR TRADING BUSINESS

You will need to be active in the market for at least six months to a year, making a minimum of a thousand trades, to even begin to understand the market. If you are looking for quick answers, the stock market is not the place for you. If you are looking for quick money, you are not going to find that either. The only fast thing about the market is how quickly you can lose. If you are looking for a trading school or book that is going to perfectly define techniques that you can apply and make money from, again, they don't exist.

Ultimately, the only true teacher is the market itself. All we can do is forewarn you of the dangers, help define some risk parameters, and help create some level of understanding that puts you ahead of the tsunami of opportunities and risks the market provides. You need to position yourself mentally ahead of the amateur crowd, who either through negligence doesn't think about risk, or through apathy doesn't know it exists. Take the time to plan and treat this like the business it is.

THE JERRY MAGUIRE REPORT OF WALL STREET

The world is finally starting to understand Wall Street. It has been America's best-kept secret for years. We don't consider ourselves members of the community on Wall Street because much of the Street caters to the "sell side." The "sell side" is simply the services side of the market. It includes the brokerage firms, underwriters of initial public offerings (IPOs), research firms, analysts, and so on. These individuals and institutions sell services to those that need them: the "buy side." The "buy side" is made up of traders. These are the hedge funds, mutual funds, and speculators. Fortunately, some quality sell-side firms are starting to be viewed separately from the traditional retail firms that have hurt the investing community. Quality firms like Charles Schwab, Terra Nova, and other technology-driven firms support the average trader and investor.

Many traditional brokerage firms with traditional commission models, analysts, underwriters, and other services seemingly created to help the investing community have dropped the ball and dropped it badly, but this isn't new. Traditional firms have only recently been called to account by the media, but the history of the traditional sell-side firms has negatively affected traders for many years. VIP-status clients have enjoyed the good old boys' network with its valuable IPO allocation, research, and secondary offerings, while average traders have relied on sound methods of analysis, mastery of personal psychology, and rigid risk management principles. All these things are within the control of the trader. It's no wonder that traders avoid analyst ratings and research. We simply don't trust them. Firms that deliver real-time data and support produce a fair opportunity to trade the market with open access. In this environment, traders control the risk and are not subject to excessive market manipulation.

Frankly, we're angry. We are angry that insiders could get an inside track on ImClone when we as traders needed to grind it out honestly. We have no issue with the risk of trading; we have an issue with the members of the market who cheat to win.

Analysts are no better. There are certainly some honest analysts, but the majority work for traditional firms that pay them to support weak stock that the firms want to do secondary offerings on in order to raise capital for other endeavors that serve the needs of the firms. These analysts are driven to support these companies based on criminal direction from executives who don't care about the average trader or investor. As long as firms are motivated to support companies that are publicly traded through analysts' ratings, or those of brokers or IPOs, we will never trust the Street. Analysts who put price targets on stocks far above reasonable values, only to suck in unsuspecting investors who get to watch the same issues lose 95 percent of their value, should be put in jail.

Investors are also at fault for not being sophisticated. You don't buy anything without research, and you certainly don't ride it to the bottom before you figure out something is wrong. But the analysts do know better. They know what they know. Those of us who have been trading for a long time have always believed that the analyst community and insiders of Wall Street are to be taken with a grain of salt. We know because we have talked to the brokers and the analysts, we have listened to the earnings conference calls, we received the research reports, and we have learned to run away or fade it. It's the business, it's the game, it's intrinsic to the market. The traditional brokerage community has one primary objective: commission revenue. This goal is reinforced by management and most members of the firm. It is maintained through the clothes they wear, the cars they drive, the houses they live in, and the production reports that they are measured with—whatever it takes to maintain that way of life. But as traders, can we trust this information? Can we believe these research reports? Can we trust the fundamentals when Enron, WorldCom, Tyco, and their so-called objective accounting firms lie? How can we expect our fund managers to sift through all of this and render a good decision?

What we do know is that we can't expect anyone to take better care of our money than we do. We know that technical analysis and market elasticity account for all frauds, discoveries, victories, and uncertainties in the market through price and volume. We know that the market leaves clues, and we know that personal psychology dictates how well we pay attention to and respond to those clues. We know trading is the only answer if we are going to play the game of Wall Street! We also know it is a game we can win, because thanks to exchanges like Archipelago, it is also played on Main Street, U.S.A., where everything is out in the open.

The problem as we see it is that the game on Wall Street itself is sometimes crooked. At some point you wake up and you realize that the game is rigged, the business itself is wrong, and the unfortunate participants are the playing field on which it is played. Many good brokers are running from their traditional firms for these reasons, and they are aiding the transition from Wall Street to Main Street. We now hear about crooked CEOs, crooked analysts, crooked brokerage firms, crooked research and underwriting departments, and crooked allocations of IPO shares. Yes, I'll say it. It's a crooked game played on the hearts, souls, fears, and beliefs of the amateur investing public, magnified many times over by mutual funds and 401K plans that most people misunderstand. But today, we can play on a level, open platform thanks to pioneers like TerraNova, RealTick, Archipelago, MarketWise, and many other great firms.

One of our favorite books is *Pit Bull* by Marty "Buzzy" Schwartz. Buzzy Schwartz was an analyst. An analyst who wanted to be a trader. Someone who should have been able to make an easy transition. But in fact, he will admit that he was a net loser when he was trying to trade the markets as an analyst. And if an analyst can't make money, who can? The brokerage firms can—in commissions. He traded all that in on the belief that he could make his way on the floor of the AMEX, and he did. Having the honesty to walk away, buy a seat on the AMEX, and trade it out on the floor every day says that your love for the market isn't gone. The roles that we've mentioned, those of the analysts, underwriters, brokers, or some other variation of any of those, don't represent the love most of us ever really had. Those roles are not true market participation; in our opinion they are sell-side functions with a flawed business model.

True market participants are traders. Traders on the floor don't have fundamental analysis or technical analysis or any other kind of analysis except human analysis to work with. They can look into the eyes of the crowd, feel the momentum, feel the imbalance of supply and demand, and see human reaction in real time and react with real-time execution. That's the value of an exchange. That's why traders are there. That's truly trading. They recognize that they can't see the future. They know that they can only speculate about the very near future—minutes or hours at the most—based on the very short-term events that are occurring in the now, the present. That's what a trader does. That's what we do now, but with tools, analytics, and virtual exchanges. On the trading floor, the events that occur in the minutes prior are going to have the greatest impact on what happens in the minutes that follow. It's as simple as that—common sense. That's what you trade. That's what you know, and ultimately it is your responsibility not to put yourself in a position to be taken advantage of. The same is true for us virtual traders—we need to protect our capital. You may not think that individuals are taking money out of your pocket, but they are—CEOs, analysts, research reports, and subscription services that claim they can predict the market, or brokers who claim that they have this insight based on their analysts and their research. Ultimately, it is your responsibility to recognize that this is not reality. It is no more real than the magic diet pill on late-night TV that promises to give you the body of Arnold Schwarzenegger or Pamela Anderson. Falling for this lunacy, as hard as it is for me to say, is every individual's own fault. Stop looking for easy money; don't be driven by greed. We all know the path that leads to easy money is a dead end.

CONCLUSION

We have no money in the stock market and haven't for a long time. Not a dime. We don't own stocks—we rent them. Traders rent stocks. They are in, they are out, and they are in cash at the end of most days. In conclusion, use common sense, be smart about your money, and always remember that it if it sounds too good to be true (like some stock tip subscription that promises 600 percent returns), it isn't true. Mastering your own universe is about mastering your own mind—and that is what is asked of the trader! Trade wise!

INTERVIEWS

INTERVIEW WITH MARRGWEN TOWNSEND

Co-founder, Townsend Analytics, Ltd.

Our industry considers Townsend Analytics and its RealTick platform as the founding technology for electronic trading. MarrGwen Townsend's contribution at the business level has allowed the technology to flourish to what it is today, paving the way for an entirely new genre of trading. Traditionally, fundamentals and technicals have been the competing methods of traders, but with the work of the Townsends a new methodology has developed that incorporates the talents of floor traders as well. Today, floor traders are migrating to the electronic environment utilizing their acquired skills on the floor to help shape a new landscape of trading. This could not have been possible without the invention of real-time electronic quote dissemination and execution, arguably originating with MarrGwen and Stuart Townsend.

Q: Most people only see the application (RealTick), but could you explain some of what is behind the application, essentially the ticker plant that runs the data?

A: This is a question we like to answer since the backbone of the network is invisible to the user, yet the foundation of RealTick and Archipelago. The data comes from the various exchanges—the stock exchanges, the futures exchanges—it comes through dedicated lines like phone lines, but they are just bigger. It is delivered to our office in Chicago and basically gets processed by software that reads that data and translates it into a format that is common to our product. So, the New York Stock Exchange may send its data in one format and Nasdaq in another, and we translate it all into a proprietary format that our applications can read. Some of that data gets data-based, so you have tick data for time and sales, historical charts, etc. This data accumulates rapidly and therefore the data storage itself is a huge process, not to mention the processing of the data. The integrity of our system is directly correlated to the quality of our quote storage and processing. This has been one of our hallmarks; we pride ourselves for our very strong backbone behind the application as well as the application itself.

Q: One of the questions I probably get more than any other is: Why are some systems more robust than others? Personally, I have traded on many systems and I have noticed that RealTick is much more stable and "on time" than other systems. Is it the bandwidth or is it more than that?

A: One of the things that I have always said over the 17 years we have been in business is that "you're never done." This is because, first, there weren't many software firms when we started and there wasn't anybody doing what we were to learn from. We had to figure out our own way. We knew right away that we would never be finished. Once you accept this reality and build it into your business culture, it helps you make the right decisions. This kind of technology is different than a static application, such as a word processing program. If you left it on the same PC forever, you would never have to change it. Unless you tried to install some other driver, that PC could still be running WordStar today. Our environment is not like that.

The exchanges are sending more data all the time. They are sending different data, different formats, and you have to be continually committed to dealing with it. You can either see that as a problem or an opportunity. Once you decide you are never finished, since this is what the business is about, you continue to support and embrace changes in the environment; it's just part of what you do. I've seen some of these companies that kind of grew up behind us, so to speak, and they thought they could hire a bunch of developers, develop this stuff and let the developers go. They didn't get it. Customers need to learn that, too. I have had customers tell me, "I expect this to run on the same hardware forever."

And I tell them, "Well, you are going to be disappointed, because we can't control the environment." Right now, we are dealing with, don't quote me exactly, but I think that volumes have basically quadrupled in the past 12 months due to decimalization and other changes. Trading volume has not increased as much as this dramatic increase in quote volume.

The quote volumes are just going through the roof, and this is a big cost of doing business. You have to have more capacity, you have to have more bandwidth, you have to have more servers, you have to have more electricity, you have to have more air-conditioning, and yet, revenues don't always stay in step to offset these demands. While we could see this as a negative, we instead see it as opportunity since we believe this gives us the opportunity to show our customers how robust our network is and how committed we are. This is what drives speed.

Q: Seventeen years. That's a long time. What was the business motivation then, given the obstacles of the exchanges and the rules associated with them?

A: The personal computer was new in the early 80s. There were so many exciting opportunities to use computers to help traders. It was enough to cause us to take a chance and start a business. RealTick was really quite revolutionary at its inception (and still continues to be). For example, in the 80s RealTick was probably one of the first, if not the first program, that collected tick data on a PC. That's why it's called RealTick. Since PCs had not been around that long in 1985, the operating systems and the capacity were a real challenge. So saving tick data then was truly revolutionary. Our motivation was to use historical data to help traders make better decisions.

Q: What did your customer base do with this historical information given its revolutionary nature?

A: Just like today, the more information they have the better they do. Information is a good thing for making decisions. Before programs like RealTick, most people didn't have this information or data. Market data then was sold to larger institutions as a rule through terminals that were provided by some of the big market data vendors such as Reuters, Telerate, or Commodity Quote Graphics, all of which were just getting started in this field as well. Those were the choices and they were not PC-based. You got what you got. You got a display of data, but you didn't get data that you could manipulate and look at differently. Traders wanted different ways of looking at data, and this contributed to more advanced technical studies for individuals.

One example in gaining control and power over that data, and the first technical study we coded was developed and offered through the Board of Trade, was called the Market Profile. This profile showed the time of the trade in a letter bracket, which historically structured trades with time. For example, 8:00 to 8:30 was designated with the letter "A." As trades occurred during this time period, "A" was printed on a chart. At 8:30 it would switch to "B" and continue until 9:00 and then it switched to "C," and so on. As these charts developed, traders on the floor recorded this price/time action on cards they carried around on the floor, measuring all for these 30-minute brackets of price and time. We developed a better method. We had programmed RealTick to receive this data through a broadcast and we were able to save the data on a PC. Since we didn't have a strong opinion on how one might look at this data, we decided to make it configurable. Traders would then manipulate the data into a method of reading it that would help them detect support and resistance levels. This was hugely successful for the traders at the time. It was more information, and a different way of looking at it. It gave them just a little bit of advanced warning over what was going to happen. An "edge" as you have written about in your book.

Q: So these were early patterns, like charts that represented themselves as "A-B-C" for CBOT traders.

A: Right. It looks like a statistical bell curve on a normal day. There is actual literature on how to read them, but it basically relies on statistical theory standard deviation and regression of mean. If the data moved outside of, say, the 67th percentile, it's unusual and the likely reaction was to return within the curve. Other times you had breakout days and things like that.

Q: This is more a statement than a question. When you mentioned "you are never done," you could really draw that same conclusion from a trader's mindset too, in terms of the knowledge that they have to acquire over the years. You mentioned that if you go into software development with a mindset that you will never be done, you form the right perspective. Trading is the same, "you are never done."

A: I think you are right and I think that kind of humbleness is a good thing. I am sure you feel the same as I do. You probably have never been through a day in your life when you didn't learn something. The market forces you to relearn things if you are to be successful. That's a good thing. And, in fact, that's part of what's fun about the markets. You find something that works for a while, but as things change, you have to change with it.

Q: Graphical user interfaces (GUIs) have grown quite a bit since then;
     what are your thoughts on future decision support tools within
     RealTick?

A: It's definitely the traders and customers that drive functionality.
     People are more disciplined today, and many of our customers re-
     quest features to help them manage the many aspects of trading.
     They treat it as a business. The features in RealTick simply reflect
     the many points of view from many different traders and methods.
     While I feel that all the features are useful in RealTick, no single
     trader uses all the features. Therefore, the product has broad appeal
     from the institutional level to the retail level. Both segments are
     very important to us and both market segments have an important
     voice.

Q: Obviously the product wasn't created to be used in its entirety by
     any one person. So how would you suggest a person decide which
     features to monitor and implement?

A: I wouldn't think that it would be wise to try and use all the features.
     I think you develop a style that works for you and as you change,
     the features you need to change will exist in RealTick. I think one of
     the things that is especially good about RealTick is the flexibility of
     the product. We believe the trader and customer should be able to
     adapt the product to their individual (or institutional) needs. As I
     was saying about the Market Profile, just because it was originally
     designed to measure 30-minute brackets of time, we couldn't see
     any reason why that was a rule written in stone. Making it flexible
     meant it would work differently for different customers and it
     would work for the same customer differently over time. As the
     markets change, the product has the flexibility to evolve with the
     customer. I've been in places where the way somebody sets up
     RealTick on one screen versus another is almost impossible to rec-
     ognize. I mean, there are little things you recognize, but there are
     such different trading styles that people use that their layouts
     vary as much as the people using it. The biggest problem, I think,
     that we struggle with is making it simple enough that a new user
     doesn't get intimated. So, we have some things like Favorites and
     fixed pages that can get them set up. Some of the brokers that we deal
     with do some of that themselves. The best thing is education. Learn
     how to use it and continually experiment as experience grows.

Q: What primarily drives development?

A: Customers. No doubt about it. We have customers and they have
     business problems. I think what we've been able to bring to this
     market, and I've got to tell you this is Stuart's strength, is the abil-
     ity to look at a problem with a fresh perspective, with knowledge

of technology, and solve the business problem. I'll give you an example. RealTick was originally designed for futures. The profile displayed prices and everybody told us that futures could only take one tick at a time, and therefore it would only change one tick at a time. So, if it was the S&P, the price would only change by a nickel. But we couldn't find any reason that was the case, so we didn't restrict the software to work that way. A lot of software stopped working in the crash of '87 because the systems that were in place assumed that October 19th couldn't be happening, and it was just all bad data. As we know, it wasn't bad data.

Another example, we had risk management issues on the active trading market. The brokers were having trouble because people would get into bad positions and the brokers needed to notify them. They wanted to take the business, but they also needed to protect the firm. Everybody was used to thinking of risk management as an end of day thing. That's a business problem for a customer, right? So what we put in was real-time risk management, real-time margining, real-time signals for the brokers so they could see when an account was getting in trouble. It's customer-driven innovation. Another example, we did some of the original networking software to address business needs. Needs for common databases of historical data go back to the late 80s and originally we were running the quote feed into RealTick on a single PC. And as the market activity expands, it's harder and harder on a PC, which is a business problem for the customer. So, we separated out the server from the client and created an early network solution.

Q: It sounds like a Microsoft model, in the sense that some customer business problems are attempted to be solved through development. Is there a correlation?

A: RealTick has been in Windows since the first product was released in 1987. I think it was developed first for Windows 1.03. Somebody told me at one point we had more developers working on Windows programs than Microsoft did. We went to Windows to solve another business problem. RealTick was dependent on tick data. It ran on an individual's PC that was used for other purposes. They would shut down the program to do something like write a letter, copy a file, etc. They would then come back and restart RealTick and they would be missing data. They'd say "what's that about?" If you were not running the program, it was not collecting data. So, we started looking for some kind of task switching product and multitasking function. While it was pretty primitive, Windows was the option back then. It was solving a business problem for the customers. We went into Windows and it was tough at first because the memory issues were difficult. There were challenges until Windows 3.0 really solved the memory problems. By the time Windows 3.0 came out and it was widely accepted, we had a huge code base and probably more expertise in writing Windows programs than anybody in the world.

Q: We're on a kind of a timeline here and one of the other things that comes to mind is the explosion of active trading and some of the rule changes in '96 and '97. We obviously, as an industry, saw things explode and grow very rapidly, but you also had another innovation called Archipelago. Can you talk about that and when it started?

A: Archipelago was formed with the Order Handling Rules that came into effect in January of 1997. Archipelago was one of the ECNs originally given a "no action letters" by the SEC, which allowed for its existence. What was really revolutionary about Archipelago, again looking at things without any preconceptions of how they ought to be, was to create an open market. The other three ECNs that got started in January 1997 were all based on the idea of a closed market, meaning you would send an order to only that particular ECN. It would either match the order (buyer and seller) or it would remain unexecuted in its limit order file. What was and is really innovative about Archipelago, especially if you combined it with the anonymity it provides, was that Archipelago really and truly sought best execution among the entire market, as opposed to closed models that only sought liquidity within their own book. What Archipelago said and what we said to the SEC when we were trying to persuade them to authorize us, was that because we would route to other liquidity sources, we would not need critical mass of liquidity as closed ECNs would. We said, all we need is one customer and our commitment will be to get that customer to the best price. If Archipelago didn't have the other side of that trade at the best price, it would go out and find it. Hence, the name Archipelago. It connects islands of liquidity. The customer would always be able to get the best price, the true best execution model, while maintaining anonymity for the customer so that other dealers could not "shoot against the order." It was always about getting the best price. That was and still is revolutionary for the stock market.

Q: Archipelago is now an exchange; that too is revolutionary. Can you explain how it accomplished this?

A: Archipelago actually teamed up with the Pacific Stock Exchange and presented a new set of rules to the SEC to govern the Archipelago stock exchange. It really was very interesting, merging the old stock exchange model to the newest. Archipelago is also unique in that it trades listed and OTC issues.

Q: Will Archipelago look for listings?

A: Yes, Archipelago is looking for listings. That's definitely one of the exciting parts of being able to be an exchange.

Q: So, you have a pretty rich history starting back in 1985. Now we come to the year 2002 with RealTick and Archipelago as huge successes. What are you looking forward to? A lot of what I heard from the interview is that you approach things without preconceived ideas about what things should be. Do you see regulatory issues driving the next five years? Do you see it coming from more people trading or a proliferation of miniature hedge funds as a means of decentralization from mutual funds? What's the next quantum leap?

A: I don't know exactly, but I do feel it will be different. While I think there are always going to be traders, I also believe they will be looking at different markets. We're seeing that from our traders now. They are looking at foreign markets more. They are looking at futures markets more. We are doing exciting things in bonds and fixed income markets. Obviously, the U.S. stock market is still dominant, but investors are becoming more sophisticated. We are doing a lot of things that let people control how they enter the trade, order entry scripting, basket trading, and things that are more sophisticated that tie to markets all over the world. We will remain on the edge!

Q: What changes are in store for traditional Wall Street firms? Obviously, the news and scandals have not helped them much. How do you think these things, as well as technology, will impact traditional Wall Street?

A: I think the traditional players in the stock market, the ones that are going to survive, are the ones that evolve with it. The "buy" side was slower to evolve, but is now evolving rapidly, motivating traditional firms to have more interest in what we call direct access; people who want more control of their trade. There is a whole new generation of people. This downturn and the challenges in the stock market have resulted in a lot of people being laid off, and many have gravitated to trading for a living. New hedge funds are willing to embrace a new technology. They are going to compete against the ones that don't evolve. That's kind of the nature of competition and, all in all, is a good thing for the market. Traditional firms will need to embrace it to survive.

INTERVIEW WITH STUART TOWNSEND

Co-founder, Townsend Analytics, Ltd.

Stuart Townsend is considered to be the true pioneer of electronic trading. Industry leaders and competitors to RealTick alike credit the work of Stuart and Townsend Analytics as being the first to market; paving the way for an entirely new industry. The RealTick platform has become the standard for electronic traders and serves as the medium for the newest and first fully electronic stock exchange that supports both Nasdaq and listed securities—Archipelago. Archipelago was created and developed also by Townsend Analytics, and is rapidly changing the way traders (institutional and retail alike) access and trade the markets.

Q: Could you tell us a little bit about the history of Townsend Analytics, when it started and what it primarily was in business to do at the very inception?

A: Townsend Analytics started as a software development company, writing software for the Lotus Signal data feed. This was back in 1985. We were using the Signal FM receiver and wrote a DOS program that fed data to the well known "Market Profile" system, which was offered to traders on the floor of the Chicago Board of Trade (CBOT) by its creator Peter Steidlmayer. We developed this product as our first program on the PC, and it was quite popular.

Q: Stuart, can you describe what your role is today on a day-to-day basis? Are you still developing or overseeing the development?

A: I am very much involved with the development. I haven't written code in many years, but I am very involved in the design of products and bringing those products to market. Most of the time that I spend here is with my lead developers talking with them about things that we are going to do and helping them solve problems, and getting things through Q&A and into production.

Q: One of the questions that I get the most from traders is how to deal with the inevitable losses. Of course, my answer is always to make the decision before entering the trade where your threshold for pain is by placing a protective stop, but you've written a tool called the trailing stop, which I believe was the first of its kind. Can you talk a little bit about how that trailing stop works and the impact it is having on the users of RealTick?

A: The stops are often put in as a risk-control measure. If for example, you purchase stock and the price falls to a certain amount, you want an automatic order to cover the position. Many people think that's a way to guarantee you are not going to lose money, but this is simply not the case. You actually limit your risk, while leaving upside. If you ride a stock up for example, the trailing stop ensures you will not ride it all the way back down. What you would really like to do is have some way of selling that stock somewhere near the top and that's what a trailing stop does. Basically, you put a stop on at a certain level, perhaps a risk-control stop below where you've entered a trade, and then a trailing stop above the price that is traded, and then if the price moves up, it drags that stop along with it so that, when the stock eventually reverses and starts back down, the stop order has been executed at that point rather than waiting until the stock goes all the way back down to below the purchase price. That's the essence of it. So this stop we created is not so much a risk-control feature as something to try to maximize profit to avoid riding a stock all the way back down to below where you paid for it.

Q: It's one of my favorite features because, as we run toward major or minor resistance levels, we can have discretion whether we want to widen our trailing stop or narrow it. It really does speak to the age-old cliché, cut your losses short, let your profits run. The trailing stop does that all by itself, if you use it right. For example, if the market is rallying up to a 200-period moving average, you can bet I'm going to tighten up my trailing stop, expecting some resistance. Whereas, if I'm running up against a 50-period moving average, I might keep the stop a little wider to give it a chance to get through it. It really works great in a trading application. If a trader had a concept of putting in a bump feature to automatically widen or narrow a trailing stop, how would one go about presenting an idea like that or other ideas that are maybe completely unrelated to the stop? Is there a format so that a person could offer up ideas?

A: We are wide open to e-mail and we have customer support that we offer for people to discuss ideas. We encourage customers to talk about these sorts of things. In the latest versions of RealTick, some of this is also available through our order entry scripting and other interfaces where users with some technical knowledge can actually implement some of these ideas on their own.

Q: Does that mean that an individual would be able to write in their own scripting and develop their own systems within the RealTick system?

A: Yes. There is currently an order entry scripting interface that's available, as well as the ability to write your own studies and things like this that interact with RealTick studies and charts. That's a feature that is there. We write some of our own studies using that interface and we have written some order management tools as well, specifically some slicers and things like that for trade desks and order management.

Q: So a person or a small hedge fund, for example, could really trade a systems approach using the RealTick. Would that be a fair statement?

A: They certainly can. It requires some sophistication in the programming, but these applications could be written in Visual Basic and shortly you will be able to do it in C Sharp, the new programming language coming from Microsoft.

Q: Townsend Analytics obviously developed RealTick and Archipelago, but you do a lot more than that in terms of data dissemination and other forms of technology related to the financial markets. Could you talk a little bit about some of the other functions that Townsend Analytics provides?

A: Aside from the equities world, we have a very active futures and commodities product. RealTick is used by a lot of traders at CME and CBOT, as well as exchanges around the world. We have a major customer base in the energy field, petroleum natural gas. It is the basis for the Platte's terminal, which is distributed by the Platte's service, which is a McGraw-Hill Company. This is just one example. Most people think about us as being in the equities business, but we are very strong in the petroleum and natural gas industries as well. We also have a large European presence. We do route orders and disseminate prices with European stock exchanges that have primarily European customers. The largest customer base there is in Italy, and about 10 percent of the trades in the Milan Stock Exchange actually go through RealTick. We are also very active in Frankfurt and growing. We recently opened a data center in Frankfurt.

Q: Townsend Analytics is in obviously a lot of different markets. What about single stock futures?

A: We are actively working with One Chicago to both disseminate prices and have order entry capabilities. We've seen single stock futures before. We had business in Australia years ago where they had single stocks futures. It was not a very big part of the business there. It think it remains to be seen how big it will be here. Obviously, the hedging opportunities with single stock futures can be replicated, perhaps even cheaper, with options. The difference is it is a little easier to understand single stock futures, so you may see more interest in them. The margins are going to be similar, so it's not going to be markedly cheaper than trading in stocks. The SEC is not interested in replacing the Stock Exchange with a single stock futures exchange. I'm not in the camp that thinks it will be an overwhelming success. I think it will just be another product. I don't think it will have earth-shaking implications.

Q: Can you talk a little bit about the technology going forward?

A: I think that the ability to do highly quantitative trading is going to become more prevalent. More people can do that now since the technology is much cheaper. Our own data feed has, with the European and options markets, probably some 500,000 to 600,000 instruments on it. Basically, anyone with an Internet connection can access that data feed. They have to have appropriate bandwidth, depending on what you are trying to get, but tools that allow individuals to build portfolios are already here and this should contribute greatly to more people controlling their financial decisions.

Q: Self-managed type products.

A: Self-managed mutual funds basically. More people are starting to understand that the market is a legitimate way to make money and build wealth. It still remains one of the best investments in the long run, outperforming other investments. On the other hand, many have been burned as well, and people also now have a healthy understanding that it's not all up, up, up and new IPOs every month. So we expect a period of slow, but steady, growth. I expect new products that will help people manage, in a more controlled way, their wealth.

Q: What are your views on technical analysis versus fundamental analysis?

A: RealTick offers both forms of analysis tools. A variety of things such as risk analysis, basket trading, and Excel interfaces that allow you to build portfolios and then execute them through our basket trader, etc. There is a wealth of things for people to use and learn how to use. Different things appeal to different people. As you said, it is a very rich application. Very few people use very much of it, but across the board it is all used.

Q: Exactly, but as you said, there are a lot of ways to get to the market and different methodologies call for different features in the technology. On that vein, John Merriweather, the famous quantitative analysis trader of Long Term Capital, was hugely successful for a long period of time in terms of stock market timing; given that, he still suffered devastating losses with the Asian flu and the Russian ruble crisis. What is your opinion of more of the black-box type systems and technical approaches to the market?

A: Long Term Capital management is an interesting case, because that was much more than trying to look at a single instrument and do technical analysis. I think the majority of people in the market would say that technical analysis on individual stocks is valuable but works even better on the broader market. Technical analysis on a single stock is very personal, whereas quantitative analysis is generally broader. Now, what they were looking at was the relationships among different exchanges for mispricing in the market. I think the key here is the historical relationships, because they had done a tremendous amount of analysis with regard to prices in the United States versus Europe and Japan and had an elaborate system to take advantage of the mispricing.

Q: You are talking about empirical studies?

A: Yes. They are all empirical studies over a long period of time. Very advanced analysis and brilliant people worked on it. In other words, they were inferring some statistical rules based on the history that they had seen, and presumably that history has generated based on a set of market forces that operated within certain boundaries over a period of time, and generated this complex history, which they then analyzed and determined mispricing during a certain period of time. How they lost money was that the fundamental structure of the market changed. It was a massive change because it affected the pricing relationships among countries, specifically bond prices between Japan and the United States. It was a catastrophe for them that history had no data for. Therefore their analysis was ultimately wrong.

The same thing happens to people who are looking at a single stock over a short period of time, a few years even, in trying to predict the price of that stock based on history. It's fine if the stock is just moving through a small range, nothing is happening to the company, or the economy in which it operates; however, when the fundamental structure of the stock changes, the results will be the same in the absence of strong risk management. When prices go up, they will come back down to their normal level. Then when an accounting scandal is announced the next day, fundamental rules have changed, the process that is generating that activity, that history, is changed forever. This is an example of structural change. It could be something as hard to discern as the arrival of a new competitor or as obvious as the last example. Given both scenarios, as the perception of new news becomes known in the marketplace, prices change to reflect it. The events in this example have nothing to do with historical data, yet still influence current pricing. So this helps to explain the dynamics of the market and quantitative analysis such as the case with Long Term Capital.

Q: That's a great answer and that opens the door to individual psychology and how an individual deals with a dynamic set of rules.

How can we apply these principles to the individual trader and user of RealTick?

A: Being a trader, which involves stock trading behind the screen, is much about your feel for the rhythm of the marketplace. But, it's really no different than horse trading in the country corral. You have some idea of how bad that other guy wants the horse, which influences price. Obviously, having a little inside information that the Army is really buying horses this month always helps, but this information is rare or illegal to come by, which is obviously unacceptable. This is different than technical analysis, which relies on statistical analysis. Technical Analysis deals with the psychology of trading that determines where the market is heading. In that sense of trading, this is what traders must develop with proper training and experience. I think that is what MarketWise teaches, and this is the more enduring method of trading.

Q: It is interesting to hear that coming from you, given that you are considered a technology guru, which I mean in very favorable terms. If I could paraphrase what I think I heard, it sounds to me like you also very much recognize the psychological skills required to trade as well as the value of technology. Would that be a fair assessment?

A: Yes. In fact, the analytics are very useful in trying to analyze the psychology of the market if the trader chooses to embrace the technology this way. This is different than what LongTerm Capital tried to do.

Q: Do you have any thoughts of where technology could help reinforce these psychological aspects and skills of trading to help hone them beyond just the literal interpretation of an application or a system?

A: Some of the trade evaluation tools offered through firms such as TerraNova and Innerworth, for instance, has value by analyzing things such as how you felt while putting on a trade. What was your idea? What was the outcome, and what patterns are forming in your trading habits that suggest improvement or confirm good activity? So, it can help illustrate these things as a teaching device. Trailing stops conditional orders, and other tools that hedge against emotions can provide objectivity when it is most needed. These tools in RealTick help to eliminate the luxury of changing your mind in midstream. I believe this will contribute greatly to developing successful traders by minimizing the inevitable losses.

BIBLIOGRAPHY

Appel, Gerald. *Winning Market Systems: 83 Ways to Beat the Market.* New York: Traders Press, 1991.

Bass, Thomas A. *The Predictors.* New York: Henry Holt and Company, 1999.

Bernstein, Peter L. *Against the Gods: The Remarkable Story of Risk.* New York: John Wiley & Sons, 1998.

Cohen, Bernice. *The Edge of Chaos.* New York: John Wiley & Sons, 1997.

Colby, Robert W. *The Encyclopedia of Technical Market Indicators.* New York: McGraw-Hill, 1988.

Cramer, James J. *Confessions of a Street Addict.* New York: Simon and Schuster, 2002.

Douglas, Mark. *The Disciplined Trader.* New York: New York Institute of Finance, 1990.

Edwards, Robert D., and John Magee. *Technical Analysis of Stock Trends.* 7th ed. New York: St. Lucie Press, 1998.

Elder, Alexander. *Trading for a Living.* New York: John Wiley & Sons, 1993.

Elder, Alexander. *Come into My Trading Room.* New York: John Wiley & Sons, 2002.

Gleick, J. *Chaos.* New York: Penguin Books, 1987.

Hirsch, Yale, and Jeffery A. Hirsch, eds. *Stock Trader's Almanac 2002.* 35th ed. Old Tappan, N.J.: The Hirsch Organization Inc., 2001.

Kiev, Ari. *Trading to Win.* New York: John Wiley & Sons, 1998.

LeFevre, Edwin. *Reminiscences of a Stock Operator.* New York: George H. Doran Company, 1923.

Lerman, David. *Exchange Traded Funds and E-Mini Stock Index Futures.* New York: John Wiley & Sons, 2001.

Lukeman, Josh. *The Market Maker's Edge.* New York: McGraw-Hill, 2000.

Lynch, Peter. *One Up on Wall Street.* New York: Simon and Schuster, 1989.

Mackay, C. *Extraordinary Popular Delusions and the Madness of Crowds.* New York: Harmony Books, 1980.

Malkiel, B. G. *A Random Walk Down Wall Street.* New York: W. W. Norton & Co, 1973.

McMillan, Lawrence G. *Options as a Strategic Investment.* 4th. ed. New York: New York Institute of Finance, 2002.

Murphy, John J. *Technical Analysis of the Financial Markets.* Englewood Cliffs, N.J.: Prentice-Hall, 1999.

Nassar, David S. *How to Get Started in Electronic Day Trading.* New York: McGraw-Hill, 1998.

Nassar, David S. *How to Get Started in Electronic Day Trading Home Study Course.* New York: McGraw-Hill, 2000.

Nassar, David S. *Rules of the Trade.* New York: McGraw-Hill, 2001.

Nassar, David S. *Electronic Direct Access Trading Course*. Broomfield, Colo.: MarketWise Trading School, 2002.

Nison, Steve. *Japanese Candlestick Techniques*. New York: New York Institute of Finance, 1991.

Peters, Edgar E. *Chaos and Order in the Capital Markets*. New York: John Wiley & Sons, 1991.

Prechter, Robert R., Jr. *Conquer the Crash*, New York: John Wiley & Sons, 2002.

Prechter, Robert R., Jr., and A. J. Frost. *Elliott Wave Principle*. 6th ed. New York: New Classics Library, 1990.

Schumpeter, J. A. *Business Cycles*. New York: McGraw-Hill, 1939.

Schwager, Jack D. *Market Wizards*. New York: HarperBusiness, 1990.

Schwager, Jack D. *The New Market Wizards*. New York: HarperBusiness, 1992.

Schwartz, Martin S. *Pit Bull: Lessons from Wall Street's Champion Trader*. New York: HarperCollins Publishers, 1999.

Shannon, Brian. *The Technical Analysis Course*. Broomfield, CO: MarketWise Trading School, 2002.

Vaga, T. *Profiting from Chaos*. New York: McGraw-Hill, 1994.

White, E. N. *Crashes and Panics: The Lessons from History*. Illinois: Business One–Irwin, 1990.

Wilder, J. Welles, Jr. *The Adam Theory of Markets or What Matters Is Profit*. McLeansville, N.C.: Cavida Ltd., 1987.

Wilder, J. Welles, Jr. *New Concepts in Technical Trading Systems*. Greensboro, S.C.: Trend Research, 1978.

INDEX